Homographesis

Homographesis

essays

in gay

literary

and

cultural

theory

Lee Edelman

Routledge • New York & London

Published in 1994 by

Routledge
29 West 35th Street
New York, NY 10001

Published in Great Britain by

Routledge
11 New Fetter Lane
London EC4P 4EE

Printed in the United States of America on acid-free paper.

Library of Congress Cataloging-in-Publication Data

Edelman, Lee.
Homographesis : essays in gay literary and cultural theory / Lee Edelman.
p. cm.
Includes bibliographical references and index.
ISBN 0-415-90258-4 : ISBN 0-415-90259-2 (pbk.) :
1. Gays' writings, American—History and criticism—Theory, etc. 2. Gays' writings, English—History and criticism—Theory, etc. 3. Homosexuality and literature. 4. Gay men in literature. 5. Culture. I. Title.
PS153.G38E34 1993
810.9'920664—dc20 93-5862
CIP

British Library Cataloguing-in-Publication Data also available.

For Joseph Litvak
with every human love,
and in memory of my mother,
Shirley Frances Kandel Edelman,
who will always be love's face

Contents

Acknowledgments

ANY WORK PRODUCED in the field of gay critical and theoretical analysis owes a debt to the enabling performances of others whose courage—whether personal, intellectual, or emotional—offered a vision of what it might mean to engage the various discourses of sexuality in and as the work of one's life. Writing this book has been for me, in consequence, an experience of community—even if the fantasy that such a term must name has been instructively ruptured on many occasions during the production of these essays by reminders of, and encounters with, the fractiousness and divisions among the various constituencies that the word "community," when used to describe the relations among those whose self-definition is non-heterosexual, would all too seamlessly join. If the purpose of a book's acknowledgments, however, is to register the author's gratitude to those who have allowed the work to be imagined, completed, and released into the world, I want to begin by acknowledging the defiant tenacity and unyielding conviction of every gay man, every lesbian, bisexual, or "queer," who has refused to disavow desire or to cede to anyone else the right to define its "proper" object, expression, or form.

A number of individuals deserve particular mention for their assistance in helping me to produce this book. Whether they provided the opportunity for me to deliver as talks the ideas that would later take shape as chapters, offered their time and intelligence to help me develop those ideas more effectively, published in various collections earlier versions of essays included here, or engaged me in the ongoing conversations about theory, culture, and sexuality without which the pages of this book would still be blank, these people, sometimes in ways of which they were not aware, contributed centrally to this project and have earned my heartfelt thanks: Joanne Feit Diehl, D. A. Miller, David Halperin, Diana Fuss, Wayne Koestenbaum, Ralph Hexter, Barbara Johnson, Richard Mohr, Eve Kosofsky Sedgwick, Timothy Murphy, Suzanne Poirier, Joseph Allen Boone, Michael Cadden, Michael Moon, Jonathan Goldberg, John Clum, Ronald Butters, Robert K. Martin, Andrew Parker, Patricia Yaeger, Mary Russo, Doris Sommer, Marjorie Garber,

Rebecca Walkowitz, Jann Matlock, Paul Morrison, Philip Brian Harper, Jonathan Weinberg, Richard Meyer, and Wendy Goldberg.

It is a pleasure to be able to acknowledge the intellectual support of my colleagues in the English Department at Tufts University; I am happy, as well, to acknowledge the importance to my thinking here of the contributions made by the many students who have participated in my classes on literature, literary theory, and gay studies at Tufts. Among them I would like to mention in particular Marcos Becquer, Bonnie Burns, Kathi Inman, and Valerie Rohy, all of whom have been reminders to me of why the work of the academy matters. Bonnie and Val also deserve special thanks for their superb work as research assistants. This book is much the better for their contributions. Diane Tang's patience and generosity helped enormously in countless ways and I am delighted to express my appreciation.

I would like to thank Tufts University for the sabbatical leave during which this project was begun. The Stills Department of the Museum of Modern Art graciously assisted me in finding illustrations for Chapter 11; I am particularly grateful for the kind assistance of Terry Geesken.

At Routledge Bill Germano supported this project even, I am tempted to say, *before* it was begun. His deep commitment to literary and cultural scholarship, and his dedication to publishing important work in the field of lesbian and gay studies, cannot be acknowledged enough. More personally, I am grateful for the patience and good humor he displayed as numerous "deadlines" passed and he continued to wait for this manuscript, at last, to be completed. Stewart Cauley, Liz Tracy, Diane Gibbons, and Mary Neal Meador did outstanding jobs in the production of this book, and I want to thank them for all their assistance.

My mother, who died unexpectedly as the last essay to be written for this volume was being finished, offered a lifetime of love and encouragement, and weekly expressions of her interest in my progress on this book; I wish she were here to read it, or at least to show it to her friends. The thought of the pride and the pleasure she would have taken in that display will have to suffice for me now, just as the dedication that, could she have read it, could I have said it then, would doubtless have moistened her eyes, can now only moisten mine. I want to mention with thanks the loving support of the rest of my family: my father, Edwyn Edelman; my brothers, Mark and Alan; my sister-in-law, Erica; Joni and Larry Litvak; and my niece and nephews: Leah Edelman, Avi Edelman, Sam Edelman, Greg Litvak, and Doug Litvak.

Above all I want to thank Joe Litvak, my partner in everything, to whom the dedication of this book is offered as the smallest expression of a love that can never be adequately or too often expressed. He knows how thoroughly I rely on his brilliance, his generosity, and his inspiration. What is best in these pages is always and only a reflection of what he makes possible; everything else merely indicates how much I still have to learn.

Acknowledgments

Many of the essays collected here have appeared elsewhere in other forms. I am grateful to those who gave me permission to reprint them in this volume.

"Homographesis," in a shorter and somewhat different version, appeared in *The Yale Journal of Criticism*, 3:1, Fall 1989.

"Redeeming the Phallus: Wallace Stevens, Frank Lentricchia, and the Politics of (Hetero)Sexuality" is slightly altered from the text that was published in *Engendering Men: The Question of Male Feminist Criticism*, ed. Joseph Allen Boone and Michael Cadden (New York: Routledge, 1990).

"The Plague of Discourse: Politics, Literary Theory, and 'AIDS'" is revised from the text that appeared in *SAQ*, 88:1, Winter 1989.

"The Mirror and the Tank: 'AIDS,' Subjectivity, and the Rhetoric of Activism" was included in *Writing AIDS: Gay Literature, Language, and Analysis*, ed. Timothy Murphy and Suzanne Poirier (New York: Columbia University Press, 1992). Reprinted with the permission of the publisher.

"Tearooms and Sympathy; or, The Epistemology of the Water Closet" appeared in a shortened form in *Nationalisms and Sexualities*, ed. Andrew Parker, Mary Russo, Doris Sommer, and Patricia Yaeger (New York: Routledge, 1991). A longer, revised version, from which the version in this volume has been revised, appears in *The Lesbian and Gay Studies Reader*, ed. Henry Abelove, Michèle Barale, and David Halperin (New York: Routledge, 1993).

"Seeing Things: Representation, the Scene of Surveillance, and the Spectacle of Gay Male Sex" was published, in substantially similar form, in *Inside/Out: Lesbian Theories, Gay Theories*, ed. Diana Fuss (New York: Routledge, 1991).

Preface

Now, at the end of this project that has occupied my attention for the past few years, as I write the words that will serve as its preface, providing it with a "face" in advance for the reader standing at its threshold, I find that the enterprise of "face"-giving, of producing the fiction of a coherent identity, is so much the ideological operation called into question throughout this volume that it is only with some misgivings that I try to preface it here at all. In order to hold these misgivings in check, I will undertake to situate, rather than to specify, what *Homographesis* intends; I will try, that is, to touch on some of the contexts from which, in their different ways and with differing degrees of emphasis and engagement, the essays collected in this volume emerge. But the energies of this preface are not identical to those put into play by the essays themselves; as writings already possessing particular shapes and particular histories, writings that already, in several cases, have encountered a readership and a critical response, these essays seem to impel me toward acts of defense or disavowal in trying to write about them now. They induce me, as I seek to gather beneath some common rubric the logics they variously mobilize or confront, to claim for them the singularity of an identity that they neither seek nor attain. To the contrary, they might better be seen as possessing, to invoke a word that has historical resonance as a pre-Stonewall code for gay "identity," a sort of "musical" relation—a relation in which a leitmotif that swells into prominence in any given place may be sounded elsewhere in a different key or subordinated to another theme that claims, at least for that moment, dominance. What brings this volume together, then, is neither the linearity with which it unfolds the tenets of a continuous argument about the complexities and contradictions inherent in the notion of gay "identity," nor the insistence with which it specifies some definitive practice of gay literary criticism, but rather the determination, and, I hope, the rigor, with which it attempts to explore, through reference to a variety of cultural phenomena and literary texts, some aspects of the social environment within which gay identities in the West have been shaped, and some consequences of their having been shaped through particular rhetorical operations.

Conceived from the outset as pieces that would fit together, however resistantly, within the framework of this book, these chapters focus on the process by which Western culture, for purposes of social discipline and political control, has undertaken the project of bringing gay men, as embodiments of what is made to seem a determinate category of sexual identity, into the realm of representation—if only in order to represent that which cannot be *permitted* representation, or that which must be represented as occasioning a crisis in and for the logic of representation itself. While in this regard the intellectual debt implicit throughout this volume is to the work of Michel Foucault, the volume as a whole more explicitly examines social regulation and ideological power in terms derived from the linguistically-oriented psychoanalysis of Jacques Lacan and the rhetorically-based textual practices of Jacques Derrida and Paul de Man, especially as their deconstructive readings have been recast by the specifically political engagements of post-structural feminist critics in general, and of such exemplary individual readers as Barbara Johnson in particular. *Homographesis* thus attempts to show how gay theory can be conceived in relation to current work in literary and cultural analysis by unpacking representations of gay male sexuality in terms of the anxieties condensed therein about the logic of representation as such. The underlying assumption in each of these essays is that sexuality is constituted through operations as much rhetorical as psychological—or, to put it otherwise, that psychological and sociological interpretations of sexuality are necessarily determined by the rhetorical structures and the figural logics through which "sexuality" and the discourse around it are culturally produced. I argue in this collection that "homosexuality" is constructed to bear the cultural burden of the rhetoricity inherent in "sexuality" itself; the consequence, as this volume suggests, is that a distinctive literariness or textuality, an allegorical relation to the possibility—and, indeed, to the mechanics—of representation, operates within the very concept of "homosexuality." Each of these essays endeavors, therefore, to specify some of the ways in which the effects of that textuality can be traced in particular aesthetic products or cultural episodes from the modern West. These essays, in other words, endeavor to read the literary, cultural, and political implications of the tropologies of sexuality that are put into play once the field of sexuality becomes charged by the widespread availability of a "homosexual" identity, and they explore the determining relation between "homosexuality" and "identity" as both have been constructed in modern Euro-American societies.

The chapters of this volume return repeatedly, therefore, to the jointure of identity and representation. In doing so they attempt to read the relation between those terms through the lens of a post-structural criticism reappropriated for the explicitly (if paradoxically) gay-identified purpose of challenging the reification of identities, not excluding gay identities, while insisting nonetheless on the political importance of conducting this challenge under the ensign of a criticism that would define itself as gay. That the interrogation of identity proceeds in the name of the identity it sets out to interrogate testifies, as I see it, to the importance, on the one hand, of resisting the temptation to set aside any pre-defined space for a fantasmatically coherent and recognizable, because totalized and prematurely closed off, "gay" identity, while continuing, on the other hand, to affirm the energies—always potentially *resistant* energies—that can be mobilized by acts of gay self-nomination that maintain their disruptive capacity by refusing to offer any determinate truth about the nature or management of "gay" sexuality. Indeed, as I would inflect it, the signifier "gay" comes to name the unknowability of sexuality as such, the unknowability that *is* sexuality as such: its always displaced and displacing relations to categories that include, but also exceed, those of sex, gender, class, nationality, ethnicity, and race. As the figure for the textuality, the rhetoricity, of the sexual, "gay" designates the gap or incoherence that every discourse of "sexuality" or "sexual identity" would master. It constitutes the fissure *in* sexuality out of which sexuality emerges and against which any "sexual identity" would attempt to define itself. In order to disavow this unknowability, to deny or seal up the fissure that inheres in (and even *as*) sexuality, modern Western culture insists on both the psychic and visual determinacy of "homosexuality," and thus on its availability to (phobic) representation (often expressed dialectically through the claim of its non-availability) as a category of being that serves to contain, in both senses of the word, the unknowability of the sexual, the mechanistic displacement of desire through the unthreadable labyrinth of unstable signifiers that both produces and disappoints it. The legibility of gay sexuality as the site at which the unrepresentable finds representation as a resistance to the *logic* of representation thus effectively, if counter-intuitively, *secures* the order of representation and renders gay sexuality central to any enterprise of legibility, of identity-determination, that occurs within it. By attending to the construction of "homosexuality" as the reified figure of the unknowable within the field of "sexuality," this book will explore how "gay sexuality" functions in the modern West as the very agency of sexual meaningfulness, the construct without which sexual meaning, and therefore, in a larger sense, meaning itself, becomes virtually unthinkable. It will examine some of the ways in which the representations of gay male sexuality have nonetheless been construed as a threat to the logic of heterosexual, patriarchal representation precisely insofar as they expose as unnatural, which is to say, as arbitrary, the representations that pass for its "logic." In this sense gay male sexuality will be seen to occupy a position much like that of "writing" in the Western philosophical tradition—a tradition that enshrines, as Derrida has argued, a metaphysics of presence bespeaking its phonocentric orientation.

Like writing, gay male sexuality comes to occupy the place of the material prop, the excessive element, of representation: the superfluous and arbitrary thing that must be ignored, repressed, or violently disavowed in order to represent representation itself as natural and unmediated.

If this book, however, resists reading "gay identity" as a predetermined category of human experience, it explicitly claims and assumes its own cultural identity as a work of *gay* theory. By retaining the signifier of a specific sexuality within the hetero/homo binarism (a binarism more effectively reinforced than disrupted by the "third term" of bisexuality) even as it challenges the ideology of that categorical dispensation, this enterprise intends to mark its avowal of the multiple sexualities, the various modes of interaction and relation, that the hierarchizing imperative of the hetero/homo binarism attempts to discredit; it intends, that is, to affirm the numerous communal understandings and cultural practices that have arisen in various gay social contexts as ways of exploring and inventing a multitude of sexualities and "sexual" discourses both within and against the dualistic terms of the dominant order's self-misrecognition. This volume embraces its "gay" identity not to affirm the cognitive stability of "gay identity" as a category, but to endorse the deployment of "gay identity" as a signifier of resistance to the often violent, or violently exclusionary, *logic* of "identity" that nonetheless makes possible, at given moments for different constituencies, an "identity" of resistance.

To the extent that this volume aligns itself with such energies of resistance, some readers might want or expect it to deploy what has been called, in a trope that has yet to receive the analysis it demands, the "language of the street." They might expect it to refuse, if not denounce, the language of the academy. Such readers will be dismayed, infuriated, or bored by much of what follows. Just as I argue that sexuality is informed by, and even constructed through, the operations of rhetoric, so I believe that rhetoric carries with it a charged relation to sexuality for each of us. Language, syntax, the appurtenances of "style," *perform* more truly than they *register* an erotic cathexis, a condensation or dilation of pleasure, a circuit of fantasmatic identifications that articulate desire; and as it is always one's prerogative to be bored by what someone else may find desirable (though boredom itself is never innocent or exempt from a relationship to eros), so it is always one's prerogative to find someone else's relation to language too simple or too complex, too alien or too familiar to provide a recognizably satisfactory aesthetic/erotic pleasure.

While the language in which this book is written, then, defines a particular erotics of performance and style, it also responds to the historical context within which its argument is being made. There may come a time when books specifically written for a popular, "mainstream" audience will be able to make their own versions of the arguments that I make in this book now;

but for that to occur it will have been necessary for these ideas to have been argued, challenged, refined, and dispersed among the more "specialized" audiences toward which this volume is largely, though by no means exclusively, aimed: students and scholars of gay and gender studies, literary critics and cultural theorists, intellectuals, and people interested in a work that enters into the dialogue of contemporary criticism without the defensive need to pretend that it is possible, or desirable, to rehearse the whole of that dialogue before it can be engaged. Those who demand such rehearsals, after all, generally have a stake in preventing that dialogue from moving forward—a stake, that is, in keeping the humanities the neglected margin of the social order into which we siphon our sentimentalizing guilt about the inhumanity that we allow ourselves to practice, and even institutionalize, everywhere else.

The demand, for instance, that critical writing be purged of "jargon" and specialized language acquires its "humanistic" or "commonsensical" appeal only insofar as we are willing to ignore how the demonized term here, "jargon," serves as the very thing it denounces: a jargonistic code, like "family values" as used at the Republican National Convention in 1992, that assumes, disingenuously and with oppressive effects, the availability of a common ground of shared assumptions and understandings, of universally acknowledged truths and expressions, all of which are adequate to the expression of any concept worth our consideration. If "jargon" names, by contrast, merely the vocabulary of a particular discipline, the following pages do not pretend, or even desire, to be free of it. Metaphor, synecdoche, metalepsis, catachresis: such terms are the "jargon" of a rhetorical criticism that reaches back to Quintilian; cathexis, libido, narcissism, Nachträglichkeit: these loom large in the jargon—which is to say, the language—of psychoanalysis. The fiction of a common language that can speak a universally available truth, or even a universally available logic, is the fantasy on which the structures of dominance anatomized throughout this volume rest.

It is all the more disturbing, then, when voices on the left, especially voices of lesbian, gay, and bisexual journalists, "activists," or academics, join forces with conservative institutions of power to police the language of intellectual analysis by construing the ("left-leaning") academy, and ("left-leaning") academic theory, in terms of the nonproductive self-enclosure that a phobic regime has already attributed to the cultural category of the "faggot." It is not, I think, insignificant, for instance, that on the very day the *New York Times* reported Vice President Quayle's attack on the so-called "cultural elite" alleged to have installed itself, among other places, in "faculty lounges across America," the *New York Native*, a paper produced by and for the gay community, included an item that the Vice President himself might readily have endorsed: "Neither trusting nor taking seriously the pronouncements of academics has always been one of the bases of a sound mind and a healthy lifestyle, but the current crop of gay and lesbian 'queer theorists' puts both their ivory-towered forebears and contemporaries to shame when it comes to sheer, ignorant, gobbeldygook [*sic*]."[1] The coincidental timing of these attacks on the value (and values) of academic discourse suggests that the tendentious framing of what gets stigmatized in each case as the language of an "elite" operates to support the naturalization of a "lifestyle" that would define its "health" against an aberrance associated with the academy; and "health," for the gay journalist in the *New York Native* no less than for the former Vice President, is predicated upon the self-evidence of a language conceived as the transparent instrument, the unproblematic tool, through which dominant cultural logic displays its presence to itself. The assumption that "health" and mental soundness must be correlated with simplicity, ease of access, or the appeal to so-called "common sense" reinforces the hypostatization of the "natural" upon which homophobia relies and thus partakes of an ideological labor complicit with heterosexual supremacy. This is not to label the writer for the *New York Native* as "homophobic" or to say that complaints about "jargon" and linguistic difficulty serve "merely" to enforce the discipline of a heterosexual order; but it *is* to say that the unexamined values informing our judgments on matters that seem remote from the realm of sexuality may nonetheless be decisively inflected by the ideologies that produce or sustain the oppressive hetero/homo sexual opposition and that reinforce its iniquitous distribution of social rights and privileges.

The essays in this volume share the project of examining such ideological determinations as they manifest themselves in widely diverse literary, cinematic, and social "texts." By placing artifacts of "high" literary culture (poems, novels, critical theory) next to more "popular" cultural productions (broadsides, political slogans, films, journalistic accounts of historical events), the chapters that follow address themselves to the pervasive literariness or rhetoricity that structures our experience—even those experiences that seem to be wholly unmediated by the "literary." In the process, they articulate that structuring "literariness" in relation to the place held by "homosexuality" as a central figure for the "literariness" that materializes the modern representational economy and that thus constitutes the very threshold of sexual and social legibility. Indeed, these essays argue—sometimes explicitly, always implicitly—that "homosexuality" names the central problematic of sameness and difference to which legibility, and thus the production of identity, must respond. Although the very prefix of "homosexuality" calls attention to the putative "sameness"—"sameness," that is to say, of "sex"—that distinguishes homosexual object choice from the "difference" alleged to characterize heterosexual relations, this volume observes how "homo" and "hetero," same and different, switch places not only to the extent that a phobic culture marks homosexuality as the sign of difference from a heterosexual norm, but also insofar as homosexuality marks the otherness, the difference internal to "sexuality" and sexual discourse itself. The order of heterosexuality seeks to stabilize that difference through the articulation of sexual identities to which it can ascribe a fictive coherence, thereby betraying its own insistence on, and its own investment in, the logic of identity, the logic of the same. Joining "homo," the overdetermined signifier of this self-contradictory sameness, with "graphesis," a signifier pointing to the inscription of inscription itself as difference, *Homographesis* seeks to situate the critical discourse of sameness and difference within the context of the sexually freighted logic that underlies and informs it, and to offer, in so doing, an interpretive purchase on the questions of identity and otherness that loom so large in contemporary theory and in the politics of gay cultural analysis.

“. . . and in the homosexual phase which would follow Eurydice’s death . . . Orpheus sings no more, he writes.”

—*Jacques Derrida*

Part I

Literature/Theory/Gay Theory

1

HOMOGRAPHESIS

In the fall of 1987, when I was invited to participate in the conference that inaugurated the Center for Lesbian and Gay Studies at Yale, the organizers asked me to join other gay scholars in a panel whose title insistently posed for us the question of identity: "What's Gay about Gay Literature? What's Lesbian about Lesbian Literature?" Although the rubric for our session was substantially different by the time the conference program appeared, the mode of its title remained pointedly—and almost aggressively—interrogative; now, however, the question it raised was more trenchant and more skeptical: "Can There Be a Gay Criticism?" All of these questions implicitly presupposed that our interest and energy as gay literary critics is, or at any rate should be, focused on determining the specificity of a gay or lesbian critical methodology. They seemed to call upon those of us working from lesbian, gay, bisexual, "queer," non-heterosexual, or antihomophobic perspectives not only to confront the inscriptions of sexuality within the texts about which we write, but also to make legible within our own criticism some distinctively gay theoretical enterprise. The questions, in short, demanded of us a willingness to assert and affirm a singular, recognizable, and therefore reproducible critical identity: to commodify lesbian and gay criticism by packaging it as a distinctive flavor of literary theory that might find its appropriate market share in the upscale economy of literary production. In the process these questions directed us to locate "homosexual difference" as a determinate entity rather than as an unstable differential relation, and they invited us to provide our auditors with some guidelines by which to define "the homosexual" or "homosexuality" itself. How, they seemed to ask, can literary criticism see or recognize "the homosexual" in order to bring "homosexuality" into theoretical view? How, that is, can "homosexuality" find its place in the discourse of contemporary criticism so that it will no longer be unmarked or invisible or perceptible only when tricked out in the most blatant thematic or referential drag?

This imperative to produce "homosexual difference" as an object of cognitive and perceptual scrutiny remains central, of course, to a liberationist politics committed to the social necessity of opening, or even removing, the closet door. It partakes of the desire to bring into focus the historical, political, and representational differences that are inscribed in our culture's various readings of sexual variation and it impels us to recognize sexual difference where it manages to pass unobserved. But at just this point the liberationist project can easily echo, though in a different key, the homophobic insistence upon the social importance of codifying and registering sexual identities. Though pursuing radically different agendas, the gay advocate and the enforcer of homophobic norms both inflect the issue of gay legibility with a sense of painful urgency—an urgency that bespeaks, at least in part, their differing anxieties and differing stakes in the culture's reading of homosexuality and in its ability to read *as* homosexual any given individual. Practices such as "outing," or publicly revealing the sexual orientation of closeted lesbians or gay men—especially those who use their access to cultural authority to perpetuate the stigmatization of homosexuality—arise, of course, in response to the fact that homosexuality remains, for most, illegible in the persons of the gay men and lesbians they encounter at work, in their families, in their governments, on television, or in film. Just as outing works to make visible a dimension of social reality effectively occluded by the assumptions of a heterosexist ideology, so that ideology, throughout the twentieth century, has insisted on the necessity of "reading" the body as a signifier of sexual orientation. Heterosexuality has thus been able to reinforce the status of its own authority as "natural" (i.e., unmarked, authentic, and non-representational) by defining the straight body against the "threat" of an "unnatural" homosexuality—a "threat" the more effectively mobilized by generating concern about homosexuality's unnerving (and strategically manipulable) capacity to "pass," to remain invisible, in order to call into being a variety of disciplinary "knowledges" through which homosexuality might be recognized, exposed, and ultimately rendered, more ominously, invisible once more.

That such readings, or even the possibility of such readings, of a legible homosexuality should occasion so powerful a social anxiety and such widespread psychic aggression points to the critical, indeed, the *diacritical* significance that our culture has come to place on the identification of "the homosexual"; and it underscores, in the process, the historical relationship that has produced gay sexuality within a discourse that associates it with figures of nomination or inscription. As recently as 1986, for example, Chief Justice Burger, in a concurring opinion filed in the case of *Bowers v. Hard-*

wick, went out of his way to remind the court that "Blackstone described 'the infamous crime against nature' as an offense of 'deeper malignity' than rape, an heinous act 'the very mention of which is a disgrace to human nature.'"[1] So conscious was Blackstone of the impropriety considered to inhere in "the very mention" of this offense that he went on, in a passage not cited by Burger, to acknowledge the prohibitive relation to naming that came to name this offense itself: "it will be more eligible to imitate in this respect the delicacy of our English law, which treats it, in its very indictments, as a crime not fit to be named: '*peccatum illud horribile, inter christianos non nominandum*.'"[2] In his history of British criminal law, Sir Leon Radzinowicz suggests that a similar concern about the subversive relationship of homosexual practice to linguistic propriety may have influenced the report of the Criminal Law Commissioners when they undertook in 1836 to recommend reform in the legislative designation of capital offenses: "Sodomy, which they referred to as 'a nameless offense of great enormity,' they excluded for the time being from consideration, perhaps with the same feelings that influenced Edward Livingston when he omitted it altogether from the penal code for the state of Louisiana, lest its very definition should 'inflict a lasting wound on the morals of the people.'"[3]

If homosexual practices have been placed in so powerful, and so powerfully proscriptive, a relation to language, homosexuals themselves have been seen as producing—and, by some medical "experts," as being produced by—bodies that bore a distinct, and therefore legible, anatomical code. As early as 1750 it was possible for John Cleland, in his *Memoirs of a Woman of Pleasure*, to have Mrs. Cole affirm to Fanny Hill, with regard to male-male sexual desire, that "whatever effect this infamous passion had in other ages, and other countries, it seem'd a peculiar blessing on our air and climate, that there was a plague-spot visibly imprinted on all that are tainted with it, in this nation at least."[4] In the next century both Cesare Lombroso and A. Tardieu, applying a not wholly dissimilar logic, would claim to have developed physiological profiles that made it possible to identify "sexual deviants," thus allowing the nineteenth century's medicalization of sexual discourse to serve more efficiently the purposes of criminology and the law. As a result, John Addington Symonds would be able to invoke the received idea of the homosexual as a man with "lusts written on his face";[5] and the narrator of *Teleny* (1893), offering a strikingly similar pronouncement, could express his very real concern that his outlawed sexuality might be marked upon his flesh: "Like Cain," he says, "it seemed as if I carried my crime written upon my brow."[6] By the second decade of the twentieth century, such notions were less readily acceptable as scientific fact, but they were still available for appropriation as metaphors that could effectively reinforce the ideological construction of homosexual difference. Thus Lord Sumner could assert in 1918 that sodomites bore "the hallmark of a specialised and extraordinary class as much as if they had carried on their bodies some physical peculiarities."[7] Homosexuals, in other words, were not only conceptualized in terms of a radically potent, if negatively charged, relation to signifying practices, but also subjected to a cultural imperative that viewed them as inherently textual—as bodies that might well bear a "hallmark" that could, and must, be read. Indeed, in one of the most explicit representations of this perception of the gay body as text, Proust observed the way in which "upon the smooth surface of an individual indistinguishable from everyone else, there suddenly appears, traced in an ink hitherto invisible, the characters that compose the word dear to the ancient Greeks."[8] That this topos still effectively expresses a need to construe the gay body as legible (a need that continues to be deployed to significant disciplinary effect) is evidenced by its rearticulation some forty years later in James Baldwin's *Another Country*: "How could Eric have known that his fantasies, however unreadable they were for him, were inscribed in every one of his gestures, were betrayed in every inflection of his voice, and lived in his eyes with all the brilliance and beauty and terror of desire?"[9]

The textual significance thus attributed to homosexuality is massively overdetermined. Although homosexuality was designated as a crime not fit to be named among Christians, and although it was long understood, and represented, as "the love that dare not speak its name," Judeo-Christian culture has been eager to read a vast array of signifiers as evidence of what we now define as "homosexual" desire. Alan Bray has written valuably about the historical transition in Britain from the "socially diffused homosexuality of the early seventeenth century," a homosexuality whose signifying potential lay in its mythic association with sorcerers and heretics, werewolves and basilisks, to the emergence in the following century of a "continuing culture . . . in which homosexuality could be expressed and therefore recognized; clothes, gestures, language, particular buildings and particular public places—all could be identified as having specifically homosexual connotations."[10] With this transition we enter an era in which homosexuality becomes socially constituted in ways that not only make it available to signification, but also cede to it the power to signify the instability of the signifying function *per se*, the arbitrary and tenuous nature of the relationship between any signifier and signified. It comes to figure, and to be figured in terms of, subversion of the theological order through heresy, of the legitimate political order through treason, and of the social order through the disturbance of codified gender roles and stereotypes. As soon as homosexuality is localized, and consequently can be read within the social landscape, it becomes subject to a metonymic dispersal that allows it to be read *into* almost anything. The field of sexuality—which is always, under patriarchy, implicated in, and productive of, though by no means identical with, the field of power relations—is not, then, merely bifurcated by the awareness of homosexual possibilities; it is not simply divided into the separate but unequal arenas of hetero- and homosexual relations. Instead, homosexuality comes to signify the potential permeability of every sexual signifier—and by extension, of every signifier as such—by an "alien" signification. Once sexuality may be read and interpreted in light of homosexuality, all sexuality is subject to a hermeneutics of suspicion.

Yet while the cultural enterprise of reading homosexuality must affirm that the homosexual is distinctively and *legibly* marked, it must also recognize that those markings have been, can be, or can pass as, unremarked and unremarkable. One historically specific ramification of this potentially destabilizing awareness is the interimplication of homophobia and paranoia as brilliantly mapped by Eve Kosofsky Sedgwick, who observes that "it is the paranoid insistence with which the definitional barriers between 'the homosexual' (minority) and 'the heterosexual' (majority) are charged up, in this century, by nonhomosexuals, and especially by men against men, that most saps one's ability to believe in 'the homosexual' as an unproblematically discrete category of persons."[11] As Sedgwick notes elsewhere, these "definitional barriers" are the defensively erected sites of a brutally anxious will to power over the interpretation of selfhood (paradigmatically male in a patriarchally organized social regime)—a will to power that "acts out the structure of a much more specific erotic/erotophobic project as well: the project of paranoia. In the ultimate phrase of knowingness, 'It takes one to know one.'" Interpretive access to the code that renders homosexuality legible may thus carry with it the stigma of too intimate a relation to the code and the machinery of its production, potentially situating the too savvy reader of homosexual signs in the context, as Sedgwick puts it, "of fearful, projective mirroring recognition."[12] Though it can become, therefore, as dangerous to read as to fail to read homosexuality, homosexuality retains in either case its determining relationship to textuality and the legibility of signs.

Underwriting all of these versions of the graphic inscriptions of homosexuality, and making possible the culture of paranoia that Sedgwick so deftly anatomizes, is, as Michel Foucault asserts in his *History of Sexuality*, a transformation in the discursive practices governing the modern articulation of sexuality itself. Noting that sodomy was a category of "forbidden acts" in the "ancient civil or canonical codes," Foucault argues that in the nineteenth century the "homosexual became a personage, a past, a case history, and a childhood, in addition to being a type of life, a life form, and a morphology, with an indiscreet anatomy and possibly a mysterious physiology. Nothing that went into his total composition was unaffected by his sexuality. It was everywhere present in him: at the root of all his actions because it was their insidious and indefinitely active principle; written immodestly on his face and body because it was a secret that always gave itself away. It was consubstantial with him, less as a habitual sin than as a singular nature."[13] Homosexuality becomes visible as that which is "written immodestly" on the "indiscreet anatomy" of a specifically homosexual body only when it ceases to be viewed in terms of a universally available set of actions or behaviors, none of which has a privileged relation to the "sexual" identity of the subject, and becomes instead, in Foucault's words, "the root of all . . . actions" and thus a defining characteristic of the actor, the subject, with whom it now is seen as "consubstantial."

One way of reformulating this discursive shift is to see it as a transformation in the rhetorical or tropological framework through which the concept of "sexuality" itself is produced: a transformation from a reading of the subject's relation to sexuality as contingent or metonymic to a reading in which sexuality is reinterpreted as essential or metaphoric. When homosexuality is no longer understood as a discrete set of acts but as an "indiscreet anatomy," we are in the presence of a powerful tropological imperative that needs to produce a visible emblem or metaphor for the "singular nature" that now defines or identifies a specifically homosexual type of person. That legible marking or emblem, however, must be recognized as a figure for the now metaphorical conceptualization of sexuality itself—a figure for the privileged relationship to identity with which the sexual henceforth will be charged. In keeping, therefore, with the ethnographic imperative of nineteenth-century social science, "the homosexual" could emerge into cultural view through the attribution of essential meaning—which is to say, the attribution of metaphorical significance—to various contingencies of anatomy that were, to the trained observer, as indiscreet in revealing the "truth" of a person's "sexual identity" as dreams or somatic symptoms would be in revealing the "truth" of the unconscious to the emergent field of psychoanalysis.

Thus sexuality, as we use the word to designate a systematic organization and orientation of desire, comes into existence when desire—which Lacan, unfolding the implications of Freud's earlier pronouncements, explicitly defines as a metonymy—is misrecognized or tropologically misinterpreted as a metaphor.[14] Yet if we view this misrecognition as an "error," it is an error that is inseparable from sexuality as we know it, for sexuality cannot be identified with the metonymic without acknowledging that the very act of identification through which it is constituted *as* sexuality is already a positing of its meaning in terms of a metaphoric coherence and necessity—without acknowledging, in other words, that metonymy itself can only generate "meaning" in the context of a logocentric tradition that privileges metaphor as the name for the relationship of essence, the paradigmatic relationship, that invests language with "meaning" through reference to a signified imagined as somewhere present to itself. As Lacan writes in a different context, "metonymy is there from the beginning and is what makes metaphor possible";[15] but it is only within the logic of metaphor that metonymy as such can be "identified" and retroactively recognized as having "been" there from the start. Metaphor, that is, binds the arbitrary slippages characteristic of metonymy into units of "meaning" that register as identities or representational presences. Thus the historical investiture of sexuality with a metaphoric rather than a metonymic significance made it possible to search for signifiers that would testify to the presence of this newly posited sexual identity or "essence." And so, reinforcing Foucault's assertion, and pointing once more to the convergence of medical and juridical interest upon the question of sexual taxonomy in the nineteenth century, Arno Karlen notes that the "two most widely quoted writers" on homosexuality "after the mid-century were the leading medico-legal experts in Germany and France, the doctors Casper and Tardieu. Both were chiefly concerned with whether the disgusting breed of pederasts could be physically identified for courts."[16]

In citing this material I want to call attention to the formation of a category of homosexual person whose very condition of possibility is his relation to writing or textuality, his articulation, in particular, of a "sexual" difference internal to male identity that generates the necessity of reading certain bodies as *visibly* homosexual. This inscription of "the homosexual" within a tropology that produces him in a determining relation to inscription itself is the first of the things that I intend the term "homographesis" to denote.[17] This neologism, with which I hope to name a nexus of concerns at the core of any theoretical discussion of homosexuality in relation to, and as a product of, writing or textuality, literally incorporates within its structure—and figuratively incorporates by referring back to the body—the notion of "graphesis," which was broached in an issue of *Yale French Studies* edited by Marie-Rose Logan. In her introduction to that issue, Logan defines "graphesis" as "the nodal point of the articulation of a text" that "de-limits the locus where the question of writing is raised" and "de-scribes the action of writing as it actualizes itself in the text independently of the notion of intentionality."[18] Following, that is, from Derrida's post-Saussurean characterization of writing as a system of "différance" that operates without positive terms and endlessly defers the achievement of identity as self-presence, the "graphesis," the entry into writing, that "homographesis" would hope to specify is not only one in which "homosexual identity" is differentially conceptualized by a heterosexual culture as something legibly written on the body, but also one in which the meaning of "homosexual identity" itself is determined through its assimilation to the position of writing within the tradition of Western metaphysics. The "writing," in other words, as which homosexuality historically is construed, names, I will argue, the reduction of "différance" to a question of determinate difference; from the vantage point of dominant culture it names homosexuality as a secondary, sterile, and parasitic form of social representation that stands in the same relation to heterosexual identity that writing, in the phonocentric metaphysics that Derrida traces throughout Western philosophy from Plato to Freud (and beyond), occupies in relation to speech or voice. Yet as the very principle of differential articulation, "writing," especially when taken as a gerund that approximates the meaning of "graphesis," functions to articulate identity only in relation to signs that are structured, as Derrida puts it, by their "non-self-identity."[19] Writing, therefore, though it marks or describes those differences upon which the specification of identity depends, works simultaneously, as Logan puts it, to "de-scribe," efface, or undo identity by framing difference as the misrecognition of a "différance" whose negativity, whose purely relational articulation, calls into question the possibility of any positive presence or discrete identity. Like writing, then, homographesis would name a double operation: one serving the ideological purposes of a conservative social order intent on codifying identities in its labor of disciplinary inscription, and the other resistant to that categorization, intent on *de*-scribing the identities that order has so oppressively *in*scribed. That these two operations, pointing as they do in opposite directions, should inhabit a single signifier, must make for a degree of confusion, but the confusion that results when difference collapses into identity and identity unfolds into différance is, as I will suggest in what follows, central to the problematic of homographesis. For if, to anticipate myself for a moment, the cultural production of homosexual identity in terms of an "indiscreet anatomy" exercises control over the subject (whether straight or gay) by subjecting his bodily self-representation to analytic scrutiny, the arbitrariness of the indices that can identify "sexuality"—which is to say, *homo*sexuality—testifies to the cultural imperative to *produce*, for purposes of ideological regulation, a putative difference within that group of male bodies that would otherwise count as "the same" if "sexual identity" were not now interpreted as an essence installed in the unstable space between "sex" and the newly articulated category of "sexuality" or "sexual orientation."

In order to make as clear as possible what homographesis would entail, let me spell out the ways in which it names, on the one hand, a normalizing practice of cultural discrimination (generating, as a response, the self-nomination that eventuates in the affirmative politics of a minoritized gay community), and on the other, a strategic resistance to that reification of sexual difference. In the first sense, homographesis would refer to the cultural mechanism by which writing is brought into relation to the question of sexual difference in order to conceive the gay body as text, thereby effecting a far-reaching intervention in the policial regulation of social identities. The process that constructs homosexuality as a subject of discourse, as a cultural category about which one can think or speak or write, coincides, in this logic of homographesis, with the process whereby the homosexual subject is represented as being, even more than as inhabiting, a body that always demands to be read, a body on which his "sexuality" is always already inscribed.

Just as the superimposition of an allegedly stable metaphoric significance upon the metonymic category of desire *makes possible* conventional figurations of the legibility of a distinctive homosexual "morphology," so it produces the *need* to construe such an emblem of homosexual difference that will securely situate that difference within the register of visibility. This reference to a visible analogue of difference draws, of course, upon cultural associations that joined sodomy with effeminacy in the European mind long before the "invention" of the homosexual.[20] As Randolph Trumbach has noted, between the twelfth and the eighteenth centuries men engaging in sodomy with other men were already likely to be characterized as effeminate, but since sexual relations between men were not viewed as expressions of sexual "orientation," those associations with effeminacy were largely metonymic, focusing on aspects of behavior that were defined as affectation or mimicry.[21] Trumbach goes on to suggest that it is "very likely that in early seventeenth-century London there was a sodomitical network or subculture that perhaps, because it was not as large as it later became, because policing was not as effective as the Societies for the Reformation of Manners later made it, and, most of all, because sodomy with men was not yet conceived of as excluding sex with women, was not attacked in the early seventeenth century in the way it occasionally was in the eighteenth."[22]

In the discursive transformation toward which Foucault's work gestures, these contingent connections between sodomy and effeminacy undergo translation into essential or metaphorical equivalences as soon as sexuality itself undergoes a metaphorizing totalization into a category of essence, into a fixed and exclusive identity. "In this culture," Trumbach writes, "the sodomite became an individual interested exclusively in his own gender and inveterately effeminate and passive. A man interested in women never risked becoming effeminate as he had once done, since there was never a chance that he might passively submit to another male. In this world it was no slander to say that a man was debauched or a whoremonger—it was a proof of his masculinity—and such cases disappeared from the courts, but adult men could not tolerate a charge that they were sodomites."[23] Once sexuality becomes so closely bound up with a strict ideology of gender binarism, and once male sexuality in particular becomes susceptible to (mis)reading in relation to radically discontinuous heterosexual and homosexual identities, it becomes both possible and necessary to posit the marker of "homosexual difference" in terms of visual representation—in precisely those terms that psychoanalysis defines as central to the process whereby anatomical distinctions register and so become meaningful in the symbolic order of sexuality. Unlike gender difference, however, which many feminist and psychoanalytic critics construe as grounding the notion of difference itself, "homosexual difference" produces the imperative to recognize and expose it precisely to the extent that it threatens to remain unmarked and undetected, and thereby

to disturb the stability of the paradigms through which sexual difference can be interpreted and gender difference can be enforced.

Thus while homographesis refers to the act whereby homosexuality is put into writing under the aegis of writing itself, it also suggests the putting into writing—and therefore the putting into the realm of *différance*—of the sameness, the similitude, or the essentializing metaphors of identity (and specifically of male heterosexual identity as the exemplary figure for the autonomy and coherence of the subject as present to himself) that homographesis, in its first sense, is intended to secure. The graphesis, the cultural inscription, of homosexual possibilities, by deconstructing the binary logic of sexual difference on which symbolic identity is based, effectively disrupts the cognitive stability that the visual perception of "sameness" and "difference" would otherwise serve to anchor. Insisting on a second order of visually registered sexual difference, homographesis both responds to and redoubles an anxiety about the coherence of those identities for the solidification of which it is initially called forth. For the recurrent tropology of the inscribed gay body indicates, by its defensive assertion of a visible marker of sexual otherness, a fear that the categorical institutionalization of "homosexual difference" might challenge the integrity and reliability of anatomical sameness as the guarantor of sexual identity: that the elaboration of difference among and within the proliferating categories of sex, gender, and sexuality might vitiate the certainty by which one's own self-identity could be known. To put it simply, the historical positing of the category of "the homosexual" textualizes male identity as such, subjecting it to the alienating requirement that it be "read," and threatening, in consequence, to strip "masculinity" of its privileged status as the self-authenticating paradigm of the natural or the self-evident itself. Now it must *perform* its self-evidence, must represent its own difference from the derivative and artificial "masculinity" of the gay man. The homosexual, in such a social context, is made to bear the stigma of writing or textuality *as his identity*, as the very expression of his anatomy, by a masculinist culture eager to preserve the authority of its own self-identity through the institution of a homographesis whose logic of legibility, of graphic difference, would deny the common "masculinity," the common signifying relation to maleness, of gay men and straight men alike.

To frame this in another way, the disciplinary labor of homographesis (in its first, identity-producing sense) can be unpacked as a compulsory marking or cultural articulation of homosexual legibility that proceeds from a concern that the homosexual might be inscribed, as I would put it, in the purview of the homograph. As an explicitly graphemic structure, the homograph provides a useful point of reference for the consideration of a gay graphesis. A homograph, after all, refers to a "word of the same written form as another but of different origin and meaning"; it posits, therefore, the necessity of reading difference within graphemes that appear to be the same. The *Oxford English Dictionary*, for instance, cites a definition from 1873 that describes homographs as "identical to the eye," and another that refers to "groups of words identical in spelling, but perhaps really consisting of several distinct parts of speech, or even of words having no connexion." "Bear," for instance, as the signifier that designates a particular thick-furred quadruped is etymologically distinct from "bear" as a signifier for the action of carrying or supporting; by the same token, it is only the metonymic accident of linguistic transformation that produces, from different origins, "last" as the name for a shoemaker's instrument and "last" as an adjective used to describe the thing that comes after all others. Homographs insist upon the multiple histories informing graphic "identities," insist upon their implications in various chains of contingent mutations, that lead (and "lead" itself is a homograph) to situations in which the quality of sameness, once subjected to the "graphesis" that signifies writing as de-scription or as designation through differentiation, reveals the impossibility of any "identity" that could be present in itself. While the regulatory delineation of identities that homographesis reinforces seeks to affirm a difference in "meaning," a difference in "etymology," between heterosexual and homosexual personhood, it seeks to deny its implication in the signifying ambiguity of the homograph by asserting the presence, inscribed on the gay body, of a legible analogue of difference that makes it a heterographic structure, corresponding, metaphorically, to the asserted heterogeneity, the *essential* difference, of hetero- and homo-sexuality.

It is only in its second sense, therefore, as a mode of strategic or analytic resistance to the logic of regulatory identity, that homographesis acknowledges, even speculates on, its relation to the homograph, emphasizing the extent to which the homograph exemplifies something central to the writing or graphesis with which homosexuality is linked by the institutionalization of homographesis as a discipline of social control. The homograph itself, after all, permits the specification of its various and unrelated meanings only through its deployment within a particular grammatical structure or syntagmatic chain. Bearing no singular identity, the homograph (elaborating, in this, a property of writing—and therefore of language—in general) precipitates into meaning by virtue of its linear, its metonymic, relation to a context that seems to validate, which is to say, "naturalize," one denotation over another. Invoking, in this way, the aleatory collocations of metonymy to call into question metaphor's claim for the correspondence of essences or positive qualities present in themselves, homographesis (as it articulates the logic of the homograph) works to deconstruct homographesis (as it designates the marking of a distinct and legible homosexual identity). By exposing the noncoincidence of what appears to be the same, the homograph, like writing, confounds the security of the distinction between sameness and difference, gesturing in the process toward the fictional status of logic's foundational gesture. In fact, while homosexuality derives both its name and its cultural identity from the ostensible sameness extending between the subject and the object of desire, homographesis would suggest an inevitable exchange of meanings in the prefixes "homo" and "hetero." The imperative to differentiate categorically between hetero- and homo-sexualities serves the dominant "heterosexual" principle of an essential (and oppositional) identity while homosexuality would introduce difference or heterogeneity into what passes for the same. Where heterosexuality, in other words, seeks to assure the sameness or purity internal to the categorical "opposites" of anatomical "sex" by insisting that relations of desire must testify to a difference only imaginable outside, and thus "between," those two "natural," "self-evident" categories, homosexuality would multiply the differences that desire can apprehend in ways that menace the internal coherence of the sexed identities that the order of heterosexuality demands. Homosexuality is constituted as a category, then, to name a condition that must be represented as determinate, as legibly identifiable, precisely insofar as it threatens to undo the determinacy of identity itself; it must be metaphorized as an essential condition, a sexual orientation, in order to contain the disturbance it effects as a force of dis-orientation. Recalling in this context metaphor's appeal to the idea of essence or totalizable identity,[24] we can say that homographesis, in its second or deconstructive sense, exposes the metonymic slippage, the difference internal to the "same" signifier, that metaphor would undertake to stabilize or disavow. It articulates a difference, that is, from the binary differentiation of sameness and difference, presence and absence: those couples wedded to each other in order to determine identity as sameness or presence to oneself. In this sense homographesis, in a gesture that conserves what it contests, defines as central to "homosexuality" a refusal of the specifications of identity (including sexual identity) performed by the cultural practice of a regulatory homographesis that marks out the very space within which to think "homosexuality" itself. Like writing, that is, it de-scribes itself in the very moment of its inscription.

Now the usefulness of this homographic implication to the concept of homographesis may become clearer if we return to the original question of defining "homosexual difference." For the literature in which homosexuality enters the Western field of vision characteristically arrives at what passes for a moment of sexual revelation or recognition; but that moment, on closer inspection, can be seen as the point at which what is "recognized" is also constituted and produced, the point at which an act of retroactive interpretation finds expression as an act of visual or perceptual "clarification." Let me focus my consideration of this process on two brief examples chosen from canonical works that engage, in very different ways, a graphesis of homosexuality.

The first instance that I wish to adduce is a moment of recognition from *The Picture of Dorian Gray*—or, rather, it is the temporal juxtaposition of two separate but apparently analogous moments in the text. In the earlier of these moments Dorian is listening to Lord Henry Wotton's diatribe against belatedness and influence, his call for the courageous realization of one's intrinsic identity or nature:

> But the bravest man amongst us is afraid of himself. The mutilation of the savage has its tragic survival in the self-denial that mars our lives. . . . The only way to get rid of a temptation is to yield to it. Resist it, and your soul grows sick with longing for the things it has forbidden itself, with desire for what its monstrous laws have made monstrous and unlawful.
>
> . . . You, Mr. Gray, you yourself, with your rose-red youth and your rose-white boyhood, you have had passions that have made you afraid, thoughts that have filled you with terror, day-dreams and sleeping dreams whose mere memory might stain your cheek with shame—[25]

Though Dorian interrupts Lord Henry here, the sinuous and insinuating logic of these words produces an epiphany that dazzles him: "Yes, there had been things in his boyhood that he had not understood. He understood them now. Life suddenly had become fiery-coloured to him. It seemed to him that he had been walking in fire. Why had he not known it?" (19).

If Dorian's life blazes out with fiery colors just when he seems to realize that he "had been walking in fire" all along, it is because his perception has been influenced by the tropological construction, the rhetorical coloring, so effectively deployed in Lord Henry's speech. And since that rhetoric insists upon the need to "realize one's nature perfectly" (17), it is inscribed within the ideology of identity and essence that characterizes metaphor. The effect of Lord Henry's seductive oration opposing subjection to another's influence —which, as he argues, makes one merely "an actor of a part that has not been written for him" (17)—shows itself as Dorian becomes "dimly conscious that entirely fresh influences were at work within him. Yet they seemed to him to have come really from himself" (18).

In a moment fraught with irony, the discourse denouncing influence itself *becomes* a potent influence and the ideology of metaphoric totalization or essence implicit in Lord Henry's speech—the ideology that insists upon the necessity of "realiz[ing] one's nature perfectly"—produces the very "nature" or self that it seems only to reveal. Dorian appears to recognize as much when he muses upon Lord Henry's eloquence just prior to his moment of sudden illumination: "Words! Mere words! How terrible they were! How clear, and vivid, and cruel. One could not escape from them. And yet what a subtle magic there was in them! They seemed to be able to give a plastic form to formless things, and to have a music of their own . . . Was there anything so real as words?" (19). It is, of course, to Dorian himself that Lord Henry's words have given "plastic form" by making possible this revelation of the meaning of his experience; indeed, their informing power is not least to be observed in the way they make possible Dorian's retroactive understanding of his earlier state as one of "formless" or uncomprehending boyhood.

Ed Cohen, in a noteworthy essay on *The Picture of Dorian Gray*, points to the process by which, as he puts it, "Lord Henry's language creates a new reality for Dorian" so that "the young man's concept of his own material being is transformed—he is 'revealed to himself.'"[26] Where Cohen's focus falls primarily upon the constitution of Dorian's "material being," or what he calls elsewhere the "representations of his identity,"[27] I am more interested in the way in which identity turns out to be a trope of representation—specifically a trope of metaphoric correspondence that asserts its dominance over the metonymic contingency that it seizes upon and vivifies with meaning.

Cohen quite rightly juxtaposes the effect produced on Dorian by Lord Henry's speech with the effect produced on the younger man by Basil Hallward's painting: "Dorian made no answer, but passed listlessly in front of his picture and turned towards it. When he saw it he drew back, and his cheeks flushed for a moment with pleasure. A look of joy came into his eyes, as if he had recognized himself for the first time" (24). Implicitly bringing into play Lacan's theorization of the mirror stage, Cohen writes of Dorian's response: "The image organizes the disparate perceptions of his body into an apparently self-contained whole and reorients Dorian in relation both to his own identity and his social context. . . . Dorian's identification with the painted image constitutes a misrecognition as much as a recognition, leading him to confuse an overdetermined set of representations with the 'truth' of his experience."[28] One might reposition this Lacanian interpretation of Dorian's moment of self-interpretation by conceiving of Dorian as occupying a homographic relation to his painted image—a relation, that is, of apparent identity in which signifiers are perceived to be the same as, or to mirror, one another even though this metaphoric privileging of the image misrecognizes the contingency, the "accident," that produced it. After all, as Basil explains to Lord Henry, "every portrait that is painted with feeling is a portrait of the artist, not of the sitter. The sitter is merely the accident, the occasion. It is not he who is revealed by the painter; it is rather the painter who, on the coloured canvas, reveals himself" (5). Tellingly, when Dorian finds himself affected so deeply by Lord Henry's words that they "seemed to him to have come really from himself," the words that produce this effect of self-discovery—and that allow Basil at the same time to finish his painting by catching "just the effect [he] want[s]—the half-parted lips, and the bright look in the eyes" (19)—are explicitly located in the register of chance: "The few words that Basil's friend had said to him—words spoken by chance, no doubt, and with willful paradox in them—had touched some secret chord that had never been touched before, but that he felt was now vibrating and throbbing to curious pulses" (18). The accident of Lord Henry's speech, with its arbitrarily selected subject matter, effects the constitution of Dorian's subjectivity through a metaphoric identification with, and an appropriation of, a particular image—whether literalized in Basil's painting or figured in the "plastic form" his experience acquires when he hears Lord Henry's words—to which his relation is more accurately defined as one of metonymic contiguity. Just as Dorian will interpret as a scene of recognition the moment in which he actually *produces* (what he [mis]takes for) his own identity by viewing the painting to which his relationship, as Basil puts it, is only one of "accident" or "occasion," so too he configures his life into the coherence of a narrative shaped by an internal necessity in response to Lord Henry's words, which the novel qualifies as "spoken by chance." Thus while Lord Henry, in his call for "self-development," castigated those who submitted to being influenced, declaring them no better than "an echo of some one else's music" (17), Dorian can only acquire his "identity" through the influence of those words against influence, since the "secret chord" that he misrecognizes as the realization of his nature vibrates with an energy not its own, an energy borrowed from the "touch," the random contact, that characterizes metonymy.[29]

Ironically, after this crystallization of his identity through the misrecognition of his homograph (figured in the painted image and the verbal portrait of an autonomous self), after, that is, his own metaphoric naturalization of the contiguous, Dorian goes on to repudiate the very register of metaphoric identity through which that self-(mis)recognition has been produced. For the identity that he comes to fix as his own is one that refuses the concept of fixed identity—as Wilde observes of him later in the text: "He used to wonder at the shallow psychology of those who conceive the Ego in man as a thing simple, permanent, reliable, and of one essence" (143). Dorian, as a consequence of his metaphoric constitution of his identity *through* the homograph, thus arrives at a homographic reading of identity—a reading of essence and "Ego" in terms of differences and divisions brought together only by metonymic contact. But the very denial of fixed identity is an effect of Dorian's necessarily unstable identification with the picture of himself—an identification posited through and across the differences the picture opens up within the notion of "identity" as such.

Prominent among those differences, of course, is the question of sexual difference—a question that led to an intriguing line of questioning during the Marquess of Queensberry's trial for libel. Cross-examining Wilde, Edward Carson, the counsel for the defendant, read into the record a passage from *Dorian Gray* in which Basil warns Dorian of the "dreadful things" that are being said about him in London:

> You don't want people to talk of you as something vile and degraded. Of course you have your position, and your wealth, and all that kind of thing. But position and wealth are not everything. Mind you, I don't believe these rumours at all. At least, I can't believe them when I see you. Sin is a thing that writes itself across a man's face. It cannot be concealed. People talk of secret vices. There are no such things as secret vices. If a wretched man has a vice, it shows itself in the lines of his mouth, the droop of his eyelids, the moulding of his hands even.[30]

Cutting through what seemed to him an elaborate series of figural evasions, Carson followed the citation of this passage by bluntly and literal-mindedly (though not, for all of that, erroneously) inquiring: "Does not this passage suggest a charge of unnatural vice?"[31] Though Wilde avoided a direct answer to the question, his deployment of the trope of legibility in the passage cited by Carson calls attention to a feature of his novel that may well have contributed to the disturbing effect it had on its contemporary readers: Dorian's clear implication in a world of "unnatural vice" fails to produce the "appropriate" inscription of difference upon his body; that inscription, instead, is displaced onto the picture to which he stood at first in a relation misrecognized as one of self-evident similarity or metaphoric identity. That sameness or identity is both reinforced and subverted as the painting alone, that "most magical of mirrors" (106), is written over with the markings of difference generated by Dorian's illicit actions, making it "the visible emblem of conscience" (91–2) and the "visible symbol of the degradation of sin" (95). As the picture's initial similitude concealed its homographic otherness, so Dorian himself—like the novel in which he figures—threatens, as an embodiment of undifferentiated sexual difference, to confound the security with which the sameness of (heterosexual) identity can be known. Even the moralizing conclusion of the novel, in which the "proper" attributes of portrait and person are reassuringly restored and Hallward's certainty that "sin . . . writes itself across a man's face" is justified by the image of Dorian's corpse lying "withered, wrinkled, and loathsome of visage" (224), even this cannot compensate fully for the unsettling possibility raised by the text: the possibility that the sameness on which identity is predicated can prove to be merely a homograph that masks a difference as bafflingly unreadable, and as disruptive to the order of social logic, as that between Dorian Gray and the picture that represents his self-(mis)recognition.

I want briefly to recontextualize the issues of recognition and inscription addressed in *The Picture of Dorian Gray* by adducing as my second example of homographic misrecognition a passage from the overture to Proust's *Cities of the Plain*, a text that focuses much of its energy upon the visualization of the homosexual, literalizing that purpose in the narrator's observation of a flirtatious encounter between M. Jupien and the Baron de Charlus. In language that recalls the moment of Dorian's access to understanding, the narrator, after watching the ritual of desire enacted by these two men, declares: "From the beginning of this scene my eyes had been opened by a transformation in M. de Charlus as complete and immediate as if he had been touched by a magician's wand. Until then, because I had not understood, I had not seen."[32] At this moment it is Charlus who is said to undergo a transformation, but that claim displaces the transformation experienced by the narrator himself as he discovers, in the course of observing this scene, the two-fold imperative of reading homographically—as he learns, in other words, not only that the appearance of similitude can conceal a disorienting difference (of "meaning," as it were) internal to each of the sexed identities through which the symbolic articulates subjects, but also that a disciplined attention can recover the ideological coherence of identity precisely through the vigilance with which it seeks out and "reads" that category of person projectively constructed to embody, to signify by assuming as its characterizing identity, this destabilizing rupture in identity itself. It is significant in this regard that the passage reverses the normal sense-making process through which Western epistemology represents its rationality or logic as self-evident. Seeing no longer precedes in order to produce, as by "nature," understanding; understanding, instead, becomes the prerequisite for a subsequent act of seeing, conjured as by "a magician's wand," that figures the transformative agency of ideological perception. Consonant, in other words, with the disciplinary mandate of homographesis, the conceptual elaboration of a binary hetero/homo sexual difference generates as its analogue a post-facto inscription of sexual "identity" in the realm of the visual.

As was the case when Dorian heard Lord Henry speak, or when he first saw Basil's painting, this moment of recognition retroactively produces the various "meanings" that it appears, instead, to reveal. Thus the "truth" of Charlus's sexuality, when read as the metaphor or essence of his identity, invests with meaningfulness those actions that were hitherto understood as merely contingent; but this reading of Charlus as homograph—as a signifier whose apparent self-identity misrepresents a difference that may go unrecognized but is not unrecognizable—dismantles the integrity of Charlus's identity only to refigure the difference, the internal contradiction, that deconstructs it as the graphesis of his *categorical* identity as a homosexual. And in the passage with which I want to conclude these glancing remarks on Proust, the narrator expresses that homographesis in terms that place the issue of gay visibility in explicit relation to issues of writing or graphesis:

> Although in the person of M. de Charlus another creature was coupled, as the horse in the centaur, which made him different from other men, although this creature was one with the Baron, I had never perceived it. Now the abstraction had become materialized, the creature at last discerned had lost its power of remaining invisible, and the transformation of M. de Charlus into a

> new person was so complete that not only the contrasts of his face and of his voice, but, in retrospect, the very ups and downs of his relations with myself, everything that hitherto had seemed to my mind incoherent, became intelligible, appeared self-evident, just as a sentence which presents no meaning so long as it remains broken up in letters arranged at random expresses, if those letters be rearranged in the proper order, a thought that one can never afterwards forget.[33]

Here we have the unfolding of a homographesis fully cognizant of the retrospective act of interpretation that produces meaning from phenomena understood initially to be arbitrary and inconsequential. The model for this homographesis comes, explicitly, from the legibility of writing itself—from the "proper" ordering ("*l'ordre qu'il faut*") that allows us to make sense of what otherwise presents itself unintelligibly as so many "letters arranged at random." The ascription of propriety and necessity to this ordering, its perspectival unveiling of "meaning," invokes the governing logic of metaphor as the figure for the presence of "meaning" as such, but the "meaning" that becomes "self-evident" through the proper arrangement of these random letters remains rooted in the metonymic contiguity of the graphemes through which the sentence they form takes shape. Thus this metaphor for the legibility of Charlus as homosexual, this metaphor for the graphesis of homosexuality itself, gestures toward the meaningfulness of a proper—which is to say, a *metaphoric*—identity that can only be produced through the syntagmatic relation characteristic of metonymy.

How, one might ask, can such rhetorical analyses of the figurations of homosexual legibility offer us any purchase on the original question of an emergent gay critical practice? To what interventions in the politics of sexuality can the concept of homographesis lead? In the first place, I would answer, a recognition of the cultural inscription of the gay body as writing or text suggests that a necessary project for gay critics and for the expanding field of gay theory must be the study of the historically variable rhetorics, the discursive strategies and tropological formations, in which sexuality is embedded and conceived; it suggests that the differing psychologies of figuration in different places and at different times bear crucially on the textual articulations and cultural constructions of sexuality; and it suggests that the sphere of gay criticism need not be restricted to the examination of texts that either thematize homosexual relations or dramatize the vicissitudes of homosexual/homosocial desire. By focusing on the historical emergence of homosexuality in an entrenched relation to questions of social power and the constitution of identity, the project of homographesis would locate the critical force of homosexuality at the very point of discrimination between sameness and difference as cognitive landmarks governing the discursive field of social symbolic relations. Not only the logic of sexual identity, but the logic informing the tropology

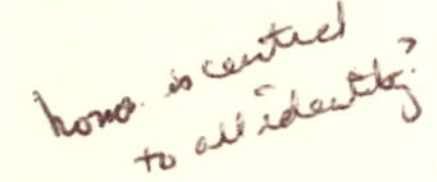

through which identity and difference themselves are constructed, registered, and enforced by the naturalized operation of the Law thereby becomes susceptible to gay critical analysis.

But no sooner do I make this claim than I am mindful of a criticism the preceding paragraph may provoke: for to make the relation between rhetoric and tropology and the psychic mechanisms of identity and desire central to the concerns of gay theory risks the charge of seeming to advocate or condone an apolitical formalism. It is, however, precisely the inescapable politics of any formalism, the insistence of ideology in any and every graphesis of (gay) sexuality (insofar as it seeks to articulate and reify form itself, morphology, as a meaningful structure of identity) that the study of homographesis takes as its very point of departure. To do otherwise, to remain enchanted by the phantom of a political engagement outside and above an engagement with issues of rhetoric, figuration, and fantasy is to ignore the historical conceptualization of homosexuality in a distinctive relation to language and to endorse an understanding of interpretation that is, as Paul de Man writes in another context, "the elective breeding ground of false models and metaphors; it accounts for the metaphorical model of literature as a kind of box that separates an inside from an outside, and the reader or critic as the person who opens the lid in order to release in the open what was secreted but inaccessible inside."[34]

As this language implies, the metaphysical privileging of metaphor and its essentializing logic can be seen as the "breeding ground" in which a heterosexual order (re)produces the ideology of identity by prescriptively articulating a hierarchical relation between categories defined as polar opposites. The heterosexual valence of metaphor is particularly evocative in the passage cited above because this "breeding ground of false models and metaphors" generates a paradigm of reading or interpretation as the opening of a box to reveal a truth that was "secreted but inaccessible inside." If it is difficult, in the context of the present essay, not to read the box that contains a secret as a version of the closet (especially since de Man sheds light on his remark by referring to a passage from Proust's *Swann's Way* in which the narrator's grandmother urges him to abandon the "unhealthy inwardness of his closeted reading," in de Man's suggestive gloss), it is also difficult not to see it as a figure for the gay body as homograph, anxiously imagined as containing a "difference" that threatens to remain "secreted but inaccessible inside." The cultural discipline of homographesis as a practice intending the "release" or disclosure of the "truth" that is identity through a "metaphorical model" of reading, responds defensively to that threat, and in the process suggests the implicitly heterosexual structure informing the belief that interpretive privilege inheres in the deployment of "the inside/outside metaphor."[35]

But this inside/outside metaphor governs both the homophobic and the antihomophobic insistence upon the distinction between straight and gay. Such an institutionalization of difference, I have argued, serves to reconfirm the logic of identity, the sameness of the self; by asserting the legibility of sexual difference, social subjects, whether straight or gay, gain access to a powerful instrument through which to constitute and mobilize "communal" energies. But straight and gay readers have different stakes in their insistence upon the reading (which is also the inscribing) of sexual difference. Rather than re-engage in our critical practice this heterosexually inflected inside/outside, either/or model of sexual discriminations, lesbian and gay critics might do well to consider Barbara Johnson's description of a deconstructive criticism that would aim "to elaborate a discourse that says *neither* 'either/or,' *nor* 'both/and' nor even 'neither/nor,' while at the same time not totally abandoning these logics either."[36] For however enabling the metaphoric conceptualizations of sexuality have been for particular groups or on particular occasions, and however tempting the metonymic disruption of "sexual identities" may seem, we must bear in mind, as Jane Gallop writes with reference to the reading of gender, that "any polar opposition between metaphor and metonymy (vertical versus horizontal, masculine versus feminine) is trapped in the imaginary order, subject to the play of identification and rivalry"[37]—in other words, that it reproduces the essentializing binarism subtending the logic of identity and informing the "metaphorical model" of reading. The misrecognitions through which the hetero/homo antithesis shapes our world require the rigors of a rhetorically sophisticated, psychoanalytically inflected analysis precisely in order to imagine a politics capable of reflecting the complexities of a subject who can only speak from within the coils of those ideological misrecognitions.

The rhetorical analysis called for in the strategic practice of homographic de-scription refuses to recognize itself, therefore, as distinct from the politically engaged; it refuses, that is, to deny the rhetorical organization of "politics" itself.[38] The historical siting of homosexuality at the ambiguous intersection of the metaphoric and the metonymic may help to account for such current phenomena as the brutal insistence on a specific and legible homosexual identity that underlies the escalating frequency and violence of assaults upon gays and it can illuminate the persistent counterfactual belief in the metonymically contagious dissemination of "AIDS." Merely accounting for such phenomena will not, to be sure, put an end to them, but it can allow us to formulate strategies through which to confront the imperatives of our moment more effectively, and it can help us to see how some acts of resistance may themselves be implicated in the underlying logics, and thus reproduce the very structures, that result in our oppression.

If the project of a deconstructive homographesis can never successfully disentangle itself from the regulatory homographesis against which it would gain some leverage, this only bespeaks the emergence of gay theory from within the symbolic discourse that demands the reification of identities. To write about the cultural discipline of articulating homosexuality with reference to writing is to produce another moment in that same discursive field; but the enterprise of a strategic, oppositional homographesis would hope to make a critical difference by attending to the ideological implications of the marking of sexual difference. For to escape both the constrictions of a sexuality that is silenced and the dangers of a sexuality inscribed as essential, we must construct retroactively out of the various accidents that constitute "our" history a difference from the heterosexual logic of identity—propped up as it is by the notion of a disavowed and projected sexual difference—in order to deconstruct the repressive ideology of similitude or identity itself.

2

REDEEMING THE PHALLUS

Wallace Stevens, Frank Lentricchia, and the Politics of (Hetero)Sexuality

The critical literature written about Wallace Stevens for over half a century now offers little that could be understood as providing a "gay reading" of the poet or his work—this despite the fact that it is remarkably easy to view Stevens in a purple light; easy, that is, at the very least, to see him in terms of a *fin-de-siècle* aestheticism evocative of a culturally identified "decadence" inseparable from associations with sexual irregularity. As early as 1924, after all, Stevens's poetry could be described in the highly charged language of self-conscious perversity and artifice displayed in the following passage from a review of *Harmonium*:

> Just as in the 'nineties, golden quill in hand, Aubrey Beardsley, seated under a crucifix, traced with degenerate wax-white finger pictures that revealed a new world, a world exact, precise, and convincing, squeezed out, so to speak, between the attenuated crevices of a hypersensitive imagination, so in his poetry Wallace Stevens chips apertures in the commonplace and deftly constructs on the other side of the ramparts of the world, tier upon tier, pinnacle upon pinnacle, his own supersophisticated township of the mind.[1]

Eight years later another reviewer, foregoing such gorgeously elaborated syntax, would propose a similar reading of Stevens by describing him more concisely as "a very Proust of poets";[2] in 1935 Ronald Lane Latimer would suggest a relationship between Stevens's poetry and the work of Ronald Firbank, leading Stevens to acknowledge that he had read Firbank's novels although he insisted that he had "long since sent the lot of them to the attic";[3]

and as late as 1953, only two years before the poet's death, William Empson would raise once more the question of Stevens's literary and intellectual brotherhood when he proposed that "Mr. Wallace Stevens, very well-to-do it appears, and growing up in the hey-day of Oscar Wilde, was perhaps more influenced by him than by Whitman."[4]

I cite these comments, on the one hand, to evoke the way in which Stevens, virtually from the outset of his public poetic career, was defined in relation to a literary culture already associated—more or less explicitly—with homosexuality; but I cite them, on the other hand, to indicate by synecdoche the sort of analysis that this essay will not endeavor to produce. Instead of engaging the question of a "gay style" or a "gay aesthetic," I want to consider in the following pages some ways in which a gay reading practice that attends to the social inscriptions of ideology can make visible certain definitive stresses inhabiting our culture's texts—stresses that might seem to have little relation to what our critical institutions continue to define as the narrowly specialized (i.e., insignificant) concerns of gay men and lesbians. I plan to proceed with that consideration by focusing on some strategies by which literary criticism in particular attempts to evade, contain, or dismiss what it tendentiously—and defensively—construes as "the homosexual"; I will refer to Stevens's poetry, therefore, not, primarily, as a body of texts through which to trace the workings of a deeply embedded (hetero)sexual ideology, but more obliquely, as an instrument of analytic leverage that can help to articulate a critique of those gestures whereby criticism refuses or denies its own positioning within a framework that a gay theory might enable us to read.

I. Let me start by quoting from an interview with Frank Lentricchia that was conducted by Imre Salusinszky. Near the beginning of the conversation, Lentricchia assails American literary feminists for their alleged inability to distinguish between a "woman of privilege" and a "working woman," between, as Lentricchia puts it, "Nancy Reagan and [his] mother." He explains that he cannot be wholly sympathetic with the American feminist project until, as he phrases it later in the interview, feminists attend to "the contextualization of sexuality within economic realities." His withholding of total sympathy produces the following exchange:

> IS [Salusinszky]: One finds the same tensions between the radical left and, for example, the Gay Rights Movement, which is, even more than feminism, primarily a bourgeois oppositional group.
>
> FL [Lentricchia]: I've said to very close gay friends of mine that they're very radical on one issue, and they're with Reagan on most of the other issues. They don't much disagree.
>
> IS: But the "one issue" of feminism is an all-embracing one, in a way that the gay rights issue is not.

FL: Well, the one issue of feminism *may* be an all-embracing one, if it doesn't conceive of female sexual identity and the socialization of females as some sort of isolatable territory for Elaine Showalter and Sandra Gilbert to examine.[5]

It may be worth mentioning that the possibility of a gay theory of reading, a gay literary practice that might serve as a more appropriate analogue to American literary feminism, is not conceivable within the context of this interview recorded in March of 1986; but what I want to focus on more carefully here is the implicitly validated—because unrefuted—assertion that the "gay rights issue is not" an "all-embracing one." Within this dialogue the token of the limited scope of gay rights as an issue is its isolated status in the political agenda of Lentricchia's "very close gay friends." In the midst of an argument with American feminism grounded in his resistance to what he sees as its tendency to universalize women's experiences, to naturalize gender difference while ignoring the significance of other social determinants such as ethnicity, class, and race, Lentricchia nonetheless unself-consciously adopts a familiar and insidiously totalizing perspective that allows his "very close gay friends" to stand in rhetorically for gay people as a whole. The effect of this substitution—independent of any question of motivation or intentionality on Lentricchia's part—is to reinforce an always potent strand of American homophobic ideology whereby the left in particular envisions its antithesis in the image of the narcissistically self-absorbed gay man: politically reactionary, indeed, Reaganesque, except in defense of the right to pursue the gratification of his own desires. Implicit in the mobilization of this broadly accessible post-Wildean construction of male homosexuality is the assimilation of gay men to a repudiated realm variously defined as that of aristocratic privilege or of self-aggrandizing bourgeois ambition to embody an elitist high cultural ideal.[6] Although the invocation of this particular construction of male homosexuality could lead us back to the images cited earlier of Wallace Stevens as dandy or rarefied aesthete, I want to take a route back to Stevens that is simultaneously more circuitous and more direct: more direct because Lentricchia follows up on his remarks by using Stevens to exemplify the interdependence of "sexual and economic self-consciousness"; more circuitous because I want to approach Lentricchia's ideas by looking at two of his essays in which the reading of Stevens briefly sketched in the interview finds fuller articulation.

Both of the essays I have in mind appeared initially in *Critical Inquiry*. The first, "Patriarchy Against Itself—The Young Manhood of Wallace Stevens," was published in the summer of 1987 and reprinted as part of the final chapter of Lentricchia's *Ariel and the Police*; the second, "Andiamo!," appeared in the winter of 1988, and it constitutes Lentricchia's response to two published responses to his earlier piece: one written by Donald Pease, the other jointly authored by Sandra Gilbert and Susan Gubar. The argument propounded in "Patriarchy Against Itself" repudiates what Lentricchia describes as the essentializing tendency of American literary feminists; the essay asserts that by failing to recognize the self-contradictory structure of patriarchal ideology—an ideology in which gender difference is naturalized as the determining ground of identity at the expense not only of women but also of men or "patriarchs" themselves[7]—these feminists, represented in Lentricchia's essay by Showalter and Gilbert and Gubar, unwittingly wind up espousing the system of values "that patriarchy invents" (777). To escape yet another repetition of that "manichean sexual allegory" (775), Lentricchia explores the construction of the modernist literary tradition in terms of its anxious positioning between an economic sphere construed by the bourgeoisie as the definitive arena of masculine self-fashioning and a cultural sphere construed as the province of a genteel, ineffectual, and marginalized femininity.

By examining Stevens in such a context Lentricchia, as Donald Pease appreciatively writes, "makes audible a previously unheard cultural voice, a voice calling from the feminist unconscious of the male patriarchate."[8] Summarizing Lentricchia's argument (in a way that Lentricchia largely endorses in his response), Pease explains how such a voice arises:

> Before the patriarch can dominate others he is divided from within into two figures, the dominant or "masculinized" and the submissive or "feminized" male. In the patriarchal unconscious, the figure who demands conformity to certain imposed standards of masculinity is in a necessary relation to another figure who must conform to those standards. Whether this figure conforms or not does not matter. As the figure who should do the conforming, he is what Lentricchia describes as the feminized male cohabiting the identity of the masculine patriarch. In submitting (or more pointedly in failing to submit) to the patriarchal demand to be masculine, this male experiences "becoming masculine" as cultural feminization.[9]

Lentricchia phrases this notion succinctly; in his view "the basic ideological point has to do with social engenderment, and it means, among other things, if you're male, that you must police yourself for traces of femininity" (743). This necessity arises because "the ancient social process called 'patriarchy' consists also in the oppression of patriarchs; the 'interest' of patriarchy lies also in the confusion of men, in teaching men who will not conform how to alienate and despise themselves, and even men who do conform" (774–775).

One might, at this point, be struck by the sense of having heard this all before—of having heard it in a variety of different contexts and in the service of differing political agendas; indeed, it may be hard *not* to hear it most resonantly as a repetition of the "manichean sexual allegory" that Lentricchia himself has dismissed. That allegory, however, now returns with a difference:

internalized within the space of the male psyche (seen here as doubly victimized insofar as it suffers both its "masculinized" and its "feminized" aspects as oppressions) this revisionary manichean scheme assures that the historical experiences of women within modern patriarchal social structures can now be read as ancillary to a larger and male-centered project of ideological deconstruction by which "patriarchy against itself dismantles itself from within" (775). Without disputing that patriarchy operates coercively on men as well as on women (though from the benches of governments to the bleachers of ballparks, the world is filled with vast numbers of men who "conform" to the "'interest' of patriarchy"—and thus gain access to social power—without, unfortunately, seeming to "despise" themselves in the least) one can nonetheless become suspicious when Lentricchia goes on to declare: "Patriarchy does not and cannot understand the self-subverting consequences of what it conceives (to use [Toril] Moi's word) as its 'interest.' If we can speak of a social process as having intention, then we have to follow through and say that it also has an unconscious" (775). What troubles here is not the notion that patriarchy "has an unconscious," but that its unconscious is one more *thing* that patriarchy can *have.* The "deconstruction" of patriarchy that Lentricchia would perceive when "patriarchy against itself dismantles itself from within" serves not to dismantle but to reinforce the coherence of patriarchal identity by insisting that patriarchy and its unconscious share the same name, the same patronymic: that the unconscious is not something fundamentally other but the other as appropriated or domesticated by the same.

Feminism, in other words, can only become an "all-embracing issue" when it ceases to be an "isolatable territory for Elaine Showalter and Sandra Gilbert to examine" and becomes instead a province susceptible to colonization by oppressed patriarchs claiming access to the unconscious of patriarchy itself—an unconscious that may be viewed as "feminized" but must not be construed as female. The absolutes of gender binarism have not been dismantled here but merely displaced; read not as fixed biological determinants but as culturally specific psychic positions, the masculine and the feminine—even when their operations are situated "within" the male psyche—still derive their efficacy from the ways in which they function as social and historical tropes. They necessarily participate, that is to say, in the process whereby biological differences come to ground ideologies of gender. Lentricchia's internalization of those binary positions, therefore, does not evade, but merely relocates, the manichean schematization that informs the social consequences of gender as it is ideologically construed.

To some extent the manichean conflict that is thus repositioned in Lentricchia's essay must always get reproduced so long as the argument is framed in terms of gender alone. Indeed, what is striking about Lentricchia's reading of authority in the literary culture of modernism is his failure to consider the numerous ways in which the awareness of homosexual possibilities and the insistence of homophobia as a mode of social control both complicate and reorient "social engenderment" in Western cultures—and in particular, the ways they effect the "social engenderment" of what he chooses to identify simply as the "feminized male."[10] In fact, one reason for the familiar sound of Lentricchia's evocation of the patriarchal insistence that men "police [themselves] for traces of femininity" is that it echoes, but in a less satisfying way, observations made earlier and more cannily by Eve Kosofsky Sedgwick concerning the emergence of those terroristic regulatory mechanisms that have reshaped since the eighteenth century the interpretive contours of all relationships between men: "Not only must homosexual men be unable to ascertain whether they are to be the objects of 'random' homophobic violence, but no man must be able to ascertain that he is not (that his bonds are not) homosexual. In this way, a relatively small exertion of physical or legal compulsion potentially rules great reaches of behavior and filiation."[11] My purpose in citing this passage is not merely to place Lentricchia's categories beside Sedgwick's so as to find the former wanting; instead, I would view Lentricchia's argument as a representative cultural instance of the way in which some of the most sophisticated, politically engaged, and ideologically self-conscious literary criticism of our moment founders in its efforts to interpret the social and literary inscriptions of gender by refusing to recognize that for modernist culture lesbian and gay issues may also be "all-embracing" and require a theoretical articulation that would illuminate not only our literary texts but also the various maneuvers that make possible the gestures whereby literary criticism refuses and resists that recognition. And that refusal is all the more noteworthy in this case because Lentricchia himself addresses the question of homosexuality in his essay on Stevens.

Lentricchia argues that Stevens, in his anxious response to a society that "masculinized the economic while it feminized the literary" (766), felt the need to "recover poetic self-respect, whose name was necessarily phallic" (757). He sees the enactment of this imperative in the seventh section of "Sunday Morning" where the poet imagines "a ring of men," "supple and turbulent," who "chant in orgy on a summer morn." The production of this vision, in Lentricchia's reading, serves to distance Stevens from the effeminacy that Keats and such poets as Stedman, Stoddard, and Taylor seemed to represent. If Keats became "a word signifying sexual otherness to the econo-machismo of Stevens's culture" (761), Stevens, according to this logic, had to produce a poetry that would repudiate Keats—and thus the feminization that Keats had come to signify—in the name of a phallic masculinity that, as Lentricchia argues, finds its most compelling American literary embodiment in Whitman.

What seems particularly interesting, and particularly suspicious, about this account of the patriarchal insistence upon an oppressively phallic masculinity is that this vision of phallic insistence is identified by Lentricchia with homosexuality. When he first evokes Stevens's vision in section seven of "Sunday Morning," a vision he will later characterize as the "absurd no woman's land" (775) of patriarchal fantasy, Lentricchia describes it as the imagination of a community that is "homogeneously male and in some sense homosexual" (757). The casual imprecision with which he deploys the category of the "homosexual" here allows him to inflect its significance shortly afterwards by referring to an American tradition of "homoerotic pleasure"—a tradition that acquires both its distinctive tone and its political resonance in Lentricchia's essay from the way in which it echoes, of all things, the earlier work of Leslie Fiedler.[12] Thus Lentricchia sees Stevens as joining himself with

> mainline American visions of male utopias: certain raft passages in *Huckleberry Finn*, the "Squeeze of the Hand" chapter in *Moby-Dick*, Rip Van Winkle's fantasy in the Catskills of men at play, many, many things in Whitman and, more recently, the Brooks Range conclusion of Norman Mailer's *Why Are We in Vietnam?* What Stevens imagines for the social future is a place without women; men who work, but whose work cannot be distinguished from the homoerotic pleasure of sexual indulgence. . . . The contradictions of Stevens's early life and poetry—work, poetry, and nature itself, the conventional realm of female authority—all are reclaimed for a masculine totality, fused in an image of masculine power: Father Nature. (759)

As this passage suggests, what is designated in Lentricchia's reading as "in some sense homosexual" not only becomes complicitous with, but provides the very pattern for, the patriarchal imperative to stigmatize and discredit all that is feminine, including, significantly, the feminized male himself. In the totalitarian resonance of the "power" informing this "masculine totality" Lentricchia evokes the dark obverse of what he describes as its "language of fraternity . . . and equality" (759). For this "homosexual" community embodies the social energies that perform the exclusionary operations of patriarchy; and though "seductive" even to Lentricchia, the representation of communal "orgy" in this "astounding" poetic vision merely recuperates the privilege of the phallus and, thereby, given the logic of his reading, implicitly defines as "homosexual" the libidinal energy that underlies the oppressive mechanisms of "social engenderment."

This reading of the relationship between homosexuality and the socioeconomic structures of patriarchy may recall, ironically, a similar analysis offered by Luce Irigaray. Echoing Lentricchia's vision of a "homosexual" masculine totality, Irigaray asserts, in "Women on the Market":

> The work force is thus always assumed to be masculine, and "products" are objects to be used, objects of transaction among men alone.

> Which means that the possibility of our social life, of our culture, depends upon a hom(m)o-sexual monopoly? The law that orders our society is the exclusive valorization of men's needs/desires, of exchanges among men.[13]

Irigaray proceeds to unpack the logic of this position as she declares: "Reigning everywhere, although prohibited in practice, hom(m)o-sexuality is played out through the bodies of women, matter, or sign, and heterosexuality has been up to now just an alibi for the smooth working of man's relation with himself, of relations among men."[14] In his reading of "Sunday Morning," Lentricchia, like Irigaray, unmasks the "power" of patriarchy—and of patriarchy's oppressively exclusionary fantasies—as a force working toward the production of utopian communities whose relationships nakedly emerge at last as "in some sense homosexual." One could productively apply to Lentricchia, therefore, the analysis that Henry Louis Gates, Jr. so persuasively offers of Irigaray: "Plainly, this 'revelation' is intended to confirm the corruption of the patriarchal order. Plainly, too, Irigaray's redemonization of an already demonized category is not just an unhappy coincidence."[15] For Lentricchia this implicit "redemonization" of homosexuality participates in an effort to redeem the straight male from complicity with the mechanisms of patriarchal oppression; he is seen, therefore, not as the *agent* of patriarchal power but as its *victim*, and, in prospect, as the means of its undoing. The covert invocation of Fiedler in Lentricchia's interpretation of "Sunday Morning" figures in this exculpatory strategy by appealing to Fiedler's ideological construction of male homosexuality as an anxiously misogynistic evasion of mature heterosexual relationships; Lentricchia draws upon this prejudicial analysis of "American visions of male utopias" in order to label as "homosexual" the libidinal economy subtending the operations of patriarchal authority. Where homosexuality was regressive psychologically for Fiedler, it is regressive politically for Lentricchia; like the latter's "very close gay friends," homosexuality itself in this analysis is allied with Reagan on every issue except for the right to experience the "homoerotic pleasure of sexual indulgence."

II.

To frame within the context of a gay reading Lentricchia's own framing of homosexuality, I must make rather quickly a number of preliminary observations. To begin, Lentricchia studies Stevens's resistance to the bourgeois feminization of literary culture in the context of his own attack on American literary feminism—an attack focused largely on feminism's failure to engage the specificity of economic determinants in the construction of social history. But Lentricchia's repudiation of literary feminism for tending towards an "aristocratic social model" (782) and for privileging a "formalism of gender" (775) to justify a critical practice that "leap[s] to the literary" (781) at the expense of the economic, reenacts the same "capitalist" (761) logic of "econo-machismo" that he analyzes in Stevens: a logic that led

Stevens to "phallicize" his poetry as a defense against the socially disengaged—or "feminized"—formalism practiced by the aesthetic aristocracy of his day.[16] It is all the more interesting, therefore, that Lentricchia, himself a male at work in a culturally "feminized" profession,[17] should claim the ability to articulate the "self-subverting consequences" (775) of patriarchal organization while arguing that feminism, like that which he defines as "in some sense homosexual," actually serves the patriarchal interest by "insist[ing] on the values of the phallus" (777).

Lentricchia returns to this last assertion in "Andiamo!," where he replies to Gilbert and Gubar's response to "Patriarchy Against Itself," by referring to their essay's epigraph from Stevens—an epigraph in which, with Lentricchia in mind, they cite the following lines from "The Bird with the Coppery, Keen Claws": "He munches a dry shell while he exerts/ His will, yet never ceases, perfect cock,/ To flare, in the sun-pallor of his rock." Lentricchia counters that Gilbert and Gubar misread not only his own representations of gender, but Stevens's as well, and they do so, he says, because they "take the 'perfect cock' even more seriously than some of us boys do. Certainly more seriously than Stevens does in the poem from which they quote the phrase."[18] The logic of his earlier essay implies that it is inevitable that feminists and homosexuals would take the "perfect cock" too seriously since they are the ones who complicitously enact the "values of the phallus." But "some . . . boys" (should we read, some *heterosexual* boys?), who gain cognitive authority by their positioning outside the fetishistic realm of phallic fixation, are capable of articulating the self-subversion implicit in the patriarchal ideology of the phallus. Lentricchia thus seeks to absolve his enterprise from the taint of patriarchal cooptation even while that enterprise attempts to appropriate the power of radical subversiveness for the implicitly heterosexual and implicitly male (or male-identified) critic who has been able to master the hurly-burly world of economic realities.

But the phallus will out, and the discursive contexts in which Lentricchia gestures toward the exposure of his own may tell us something about what is at stake in his attempt to reconfigure the politics of gender. Had I space I would consider a telling moment from Salusinszky's interview with Lentricchia in which he reveals the extent of the phallic investment at issue in his work by responding as follows to critics who challenged his view of de Manian deconstruction: "If I'm wrong about de Man: well, show me. I've shown you mine, now you show me yours" (205). But a similar, and more significant, moment is inscribed at the outset of "Andiamo!" Before addressing Gilbert and Gubar, Lentricchia comments briefly on the analysis of his essay offered by Donald Pease. In the process he alludes to a quotation from Kenneth Burke cited by Gilbert and Gubar as another epigraph to their response: "The picture of Frank Lentricchia on the jacket of his *Criticism and Social Change* is enough to make an author feel relieved on learning that Lentricchia is largely on his side."[19] Taking issue with a particular aspect of Pease's reading, Lentricchia writes: "Those of you who know Don will appreciate why the mere thought of disagreeing with him makes me go limp. Consequently, it comes as a great relief to me (and to my wife) to learn that he is largely on my side."[20]

Surely Lentricchia would say of this what he said of "the infamous photograph"[21] referred to by Burke: that it should be understood in "a tradition of self-mocking send-ups of macho stances" and that it offers "not a defense of stereotypical masculinity but its comic subversion."[22] With such assertions Lentricchia claims access to subversive energies that in some as yet unspecified way dismantle patriarchy from within; but he fails to see that "sending up" may be synonymous with erection. Indeed, Lentricchia's "relief" on discovering that Pease is "largely on [his] side," and able therefore to reinforce his potency rather than making him "go limp," must be read in relation to the parenthetical, because logically obtrusive, insistence on the heterosexual uses toward which Lentricchia's potency is put: the relief, he assures us, is experienced not only by himself but by his wife as well. We can only imagine what sort of relief is provided by such a gratuitous invocation of his wife as the guarantor of his virility.

Through all of this, of course, Lentricchia is not taking the "'perfect cock' too seriously"; he's having fun displaying the phallus and "subverting" it at once. What could be more delightful or further from the dour and essentially *patriarchal* seriousness that marks the feminist or "homosexual" investment in the phallic? But might it not be useful, even at the risk of seeming to take Lentricchia's self-representations too seriously, to inquire just what, if anything, is getting subverted here or to ask how the miming of heterosexual male privilege by a heterosexual male differs from the persistently oppressive enactment of that privilege in the culture at large? After all, isn't one of the hallmarks of that privilege the right to claim that it's all in fun—since, as Lentricchia himself might suggest, "some of us boys" will, in fact, *be* boys? Let me be clear about what I am suggesting: Lentricchia has not only stated but demonstrated his sensitivity to gay rights as a matter of social policy. Indeed, at the end of "Andiamo!" he insists that he "can think of one sexual difference in Reagan's America, which threatens to override all differences: gay men, regardless of class and race, may face criminalization and indefinite detention on the sole basis of their sexual orientation."[23] Yet he fails, nonetheless, to recognize that the scope of this "sexual difference" extends beyond questions of social policy alone, that like the question of feminism, to which it may never be entirely assimilable but from which it is never wholly separable either, homosexuality is indeed an "all-embracing issue" whose decisive effects in the shaping of modern ideologies of gender and sexuality can be traced in the strategic blindness at work in his own cultural critique.

III. Rather than examine in detail how that blindness inscribes itself in Lentricchia's reading of Stevens, I want to suggest how Lentricchia reproduces the sexual ideology that his essay anatomizes by glancing at a provocative, though rarely examined, work from the middle of Stevens's career, a work that Stevens decided to exclude when he compiled his *Collected Poems.* The poem is "Life on a Battleship," and the battleship to which the title refers is quite pointedly identified as *The Masculine.*[24] The poem presents a series of meditations on the "rules of the world" (30) as drafted by the captain of the ship, who speculates, as does the poem itself, about the possible relations between the parts and the whole in the organization of society. Describing the captain as an "apprentice of/ Descartes" (31–32), "Life on a Battleship" explores the ideological import of efforts to codify the "grand simplifications" (32) of life as dogma, as the "*Regulae Mundi*" (31) by which to determine the governance of human interactions, and it does so in a context that reinforces the relation between questions of social power and questions of masculinity.

Like the photographic representations of Lentricchia and their relation to the iconography of phallic empowerment, however, "Life on a Battleship" has occasioned disputes about its meaning that center, significantly, on questions of tone. Harold Bloom, for instance, declares that the poem is "almost wholly a mockery"[25] while Joseph Riddel emphasizes its "belligerantly [*sic*] rhetorical posture" and defines both the poem and its hero as "self-mocking and yet serious."[26] Thus the instability that governs the relationshipof send-ups to seriousness and subversion is already inscribed in the various critical interpretations of this particular text, and that instability, importantly, emanates from a work that self-consciously reads gender, sexuality, and class in terms of a social organization centered on phallic authority.

"Life on a Battleship" repudiates a Marxist-inspired ideal of collective society in favor of an Emersonian celebration of individual autonomy, and it does so by analyzing this ideological conflict as itself an enactment of differing ways of constructing masculinity. Thus the collectivist vision (as the poem represents it) fetishizes a phallocentric notion of unity and imagines transforming *The Masculine*, as battleship, into "the largest/ Possible machine, a divinity of steel" (12–13) that would become "the center of the world" (15). As "both law and evidence in one" (37), *The Masculine*, in this ideological framework, appears to be simultaneously self-evident and self-authorizing: "a divinity/ Like any other, rex by right of the crown,/ The jewels in his beard, the mystic wand" (41–43).

Such rhetoric makes clear that the collectivist ideal, at least from the poet's perspective, reproduces the hierarchy of aristocratic privilege against which it defines itself; as the captain of *The Masculine* observes: "The war of the classes is/ A preliminary, provincial phase,/ Of the war between individuals"

(3–5). Class struggle must give way to the conflict of individuals and the collectivist ideal of a worker's paradise must produce instead a "paradise of assassins" (7)—a world of collective antipathy in which the desire for individual distinction and privilege necessarily reasserts its appeal.[27] For Stevens as for Lentricchia this return of the aristocratic is inscribed within a realm that takes its ideological tint from its contiguity with that which can be viewed as being "in some sense homosexual," its contiguity, that is, with the erotics of power in a domain that is, definitionally here, portrayed entirely as *The Masculine.* For the privilege of authority aboard this embodiment of *The Masculine* finds expression in the captain's ability to make the men on the battleship bend to his word—a word whose authority is reinforced by the might of "ten thousand guns" (22). As Stevens notes in a passage that pinpoints the phallic imperative whose logic governs this reductively unitary world: "On *The Masculine* one asserts and fires the guns" (75). Imagining a future in which he has seized this phallic authority so completely that he "would only have to ring and ft!/ It would be done" (19–20), the Captain delights to envision a world in which all men "did/ As [he] wished" (25–26): "fell backward when [his] breath/ Blew against them or bowed from the hips, when [he] turned/ [His] head" (26–28). In this fantasy the bodies of the other men respond to his every desire; they must obey the most whimsical or sadistic command that he voices "to please [him]self" (20).

The sort of intimacy implied by the physiological specificity of this language locates this exercise of power in the realm of sexual authority; and the rapacious interchangeability in the poem of sexual and political authority is precisely what is at issue in the text's revitalization of the socio-economic metaphor that governs its opening lines: "The rape of the bourgeoisie accomplished, the men/ Returned on board *The Masculine*" (1–2). Class conflict or the conflict of economic ideologies achieves its representational force here through the image of sexual violation. The bourgeoisie, already feminine in the French from which the term is borrowed, is envisioned as having been violently overpowered by the champions of the working class who dwell aboard *The Masculine.* But since Stevens, as Stevens himself knew well, was nothing if not, in his public life, the embodiment of a bourgeois ideal, it is possible to see this "rape" as the expression of his anxious positioning in relation not only to questions of "social engenderment," as Lentricchia would have it, but also to the unarticulated questions of sexuality that intersect with, inflect, and complicate the historically specific interpretations of gender.

Interestingly, while both Stevens and Lentricchia conduct arguments against particular ways of construing the economic—Stevens attacking the phallic insistence of a socialism that masks an older dream of aristocratic privilege and luxury while Lentricchia attacks the phallic insistence of a bourgeois ideology he defines as "econo-machismo"—the discredited positions are located in each instance in relation to sexual interactions between men: interactions that are culturally articulable in terms of "homosexuality." Such a maneuver, for Stevens as for Lentricchia, allows these interactions to embody an ideology that each can "expose," though in different ways, as fundamentally conservative in its enshrinement of authority and privilege. And this appears to be structurally necessary so that each can reappropriate, in the name of an ideology allegedly more open to difference, the very phallic authority that he claims to subvert by sending-up.

Thus in Stevens's poem the quasi-Emersonianism with which the poet refutes the collectivist vision does not disavow the dominance of the masculine, but seeks to redefine masculinity as always already containing within itself the subversion of phallic bravado:

> . . . if
> It is the absolute why must it be
> This immemorial grandiose, why not
> A cockle-shell, a trivial emblem great
> With its final force, a thing invincible
> In more than phrase? There's the true masculine,
> The spirit's ring and seal, the naked heart. (46–52)

This "true masculine," with its capacity to see through the "grandiose" posturings of anxious phallicism (and to acknowledge its own vulnerability by defining itself as the "naked heart") finds its parallel in Lentricchia's effort to define a position from which the male might escape the symptomatic "phallic gestures" enforced upon him by "patriarchy in its capitalist situation" (413). But even when dressed as a "cockle-shell" in modest self-effacement, the "perfect cock" of "the true masculine" neither conceals nor subverts itself: rather, it seeks to become still more perfect, "invincible/ In more than phrase," by appropriating even the power of subversion as its own.

My purpose, however, is not to argue for some more "authentically" subversive position, but to show through what agencies, and at whose expense, the alleged subversion effected by this ideological framing of the issue is produced. And toward that end it is important to note that the phallus—which, as "mystic wand" (43), presided over the tendentious fantasy of authority that colored the captain's reduction of law to a unity not wholly distinguishable from *The Masculine* itself—returns at the end of "Life on a Battleship" to empower the poet's own belated Emersonian assertions. "The good, the strength, the sceptre moves/ From constable to god" (88–89) he writes, tracing, as he did in "Sunday Morning," the process by which the law, like other mechanisms of human authority, finds justification through a projective displacement that misreads it as a transcendent structure of meaning, a divine and thus absolute mandate that enforces a univocal truth. The disciplinary entitlement of the "constable," the ability to act as the representative of the law, springs from a relation to the "sceptre" whose "circle" (90) or sphere of influence grows larger as it moves toward the hand of the deity imagined to underwrite its authority. But here, as in "Sunday Morning," Stevens suggests the imaginative poverty inherent in this fictive projection of divinity; the authority assumed to originate from the divine hand holding the "sceptre" travels in the opposite direction instead, "from constable to god, from earth to air" (89). And as a weak mythological misrecognition of the imagination's own strength, as a phantom constructed by men unwilling to assume the burden of their creative potency and visionary centrality, the divine hand inevitably "fails to seize" (92) the phallic "wand" that would represent, in such a world view, the source of all authority, the self-presence that grounds the metaphoric totalizations of essence in a patriarchy structured through analogy to the logic of a paternal deity. With that failure Stevens signals his rejection of any trajectory of power that depends upon the originating fiat of a divine father whose presence, as in these lines from "The Auroras of Autumn," can seem to anchor not only the poetic imagination but also the onto-theological system within which that imagination operates:

> Master O master seated by the fire
> And yet in space and motionless and yet
> Of motion the ever-brightening origin,
>
> Profound, and yet the king and yet the crown. (IV, 19–22)

Repudiating so central—and so centrally masculine and imperial—a locus of authority, the poem concludes with the poet foreseeing a future in which the phallic sceptre "returns to earth" (80) to underwrite a version of Emersonian self-reliance. Liberated from subjection to a transcendental masculinity embodied in a master envisioned as the "immemorial grandiose," every man is now empowered—but also, and more problematically, *required*—to become the king in his own castle. Such a notion, as Eve Kosofsky Sedgwick lucidly explains while discussing a passage by Juliet Mitchell, carries with it a powerful charge as a representative instance of bourgeois ideology at work:

> The phrase "A man's home is his castle" offers a nicely condensed example of ideological construction in this sense. It reaches *back* to an emptied-out image of mastery and integration under feudalism in order to propel the male wage-worker *forward* to further feats of alienated labor, in the service of a now atomized and embattled, but all the more intensively idealized home. The man who has this home is a different person from the lord who has a castle; and the forms of property implied in the two possessives (his [mortgaged] home/ his [inherited] castle) are not only different but, as Mitchell points out, mutually

> contradictory. The contradiction is assuaged and filled in by transferring the lord's political and economic control over the *environs* of his castle to an image of the father's personal control over the *inmates* of his house.[28]

The return of the sceptre, therefore, cannot be read outside the historical context of middle-class male self-definition. Indeed, its critical significance, for Stevens, derives from its relation to a discourse of autonomy that intersects with, and makes possible, a discourse of visionary self-articulation. For when the sceptre returns to earth after the banishment of the gods:

> It will be all we have. Our fate is our own:
> Our good, from this the rhapsodic strophes flow,
> Through prophets and succeeding prophets, whose prophecies
> Grow large and larger. Our fate is our own. The hand,
> It must be the hand of one, it must be the hand
> Of a man, that seizes our strength, will seize it to be
> Merely the center of a circle, spread
> to the final full, an end without rhetoric. (102–109)

As an American prophet who would have his "strophes" succeed the rhapsodies of Emerson, Stevens here draws a larger circle—a circle "spread to the final full"—around that earlier traced by the Emerson of "Circles." He enacts, that is, a self-allegorizing version of the Oedipal relations that organize, as Harold Bloom has so forcefully argued, the dominant masculine literary tradition of the West.

The language with which this circle is "spread," however, demands attention; for the spreading of the circle—and thus the act of empowerment through which the poet becomes autonomous, becomes, himself, a man—requires in the first place, as Stevens puts it, that "our strength" be "seize[d]" by the "hand of a man," requires, in other words, the intervention of a power that is explicitly gendered and implicitly eroticized. "Seize," the verb that articulates the violent force of that intervention, is the same verb that named the activity by which the Captain envisioned his appropriation of *The Masculine*: "Suppose I seize/ The ship, make it my own and, bit by bit,/ Seize yards and docks, machinery and men" (7–9). Such acts of seizure cannot evade coloration by the initial reference to "rape" and it might not be far-fetched to suggest that the language with which "Life on a Battleship" concludes leaves itself open to the sort of analysis that would read a textual re-inscription of that rape in the activity whereby "the hand/ of a man . . . seizes our strength . . . to be/ Merely the center of a circle, spread/ To the final full." Such a reading would define the final image as "an end without rhetoric" indeed.

Pace Lentricchia, this does not make the scene of phallic empowerment "in some sense homosexual"—nor will it do to resolve the issue by calling it "homosocial" instead.[29] For what distinguishes this enabling seizure or rape of one male by another is its determining *hetero*sexuality—its participation, that is, in a psychic economy that defines itself *against* the historically available category of the "homosexual." The poem represents this scene in which, as it were, a man is made, as one of a necessary and productive violence; the issue is not one of same-sex desire but rather of submission to phallic Law so as to earn the privilege of inhabiting the "center of a circle, spread/ To the final full." Thus desire in this scene attaches only to the affirmation of the poet's centrality and "strength"; and the act of seizure only signifies to the extent that it makes possible a socially sanctioned introjection of masculine authority. What may at first glance appear to figure a scene of "homosexual" rape, then, should be viewed instead as a curious sort of apotropaic fantasy that phobically reflects the anxiety of the heterosexual male about the meaning of his desire for the phallus *as signifier* of autonomy and social entitlement[30]—an anxiety made all the more urgent by the necessity that his own phallic power only represent or reenact a social authority identified with the phallic pre-eminence of the father(s). Thus the focus at the conclusion of "Life on a Battleship" falls on the poet's achievement of a position from which to declare the self-dependence, the autonomy, that distinguishes those who are able to wield the "sceptre": "Our fate is our own," he twice proclaims, marking the "strength" of his own imagination in contrast to the impotence of those who receive their intellectual insemination from others. But this affirmation of autonomy is colored by the poem's indication that the centrality of the free-standing subject comes only to men whose "strength" has been "seize[d]" by "the hand/ Of a man" that can move them to ejaculations in which "the rhapsodic strophes flow."

The intersection of the literary and the economic in the credo, "Our fate is our own," becomes more apparent when the phrase is juxtaposed against a passage that Lentricchia quotes from Stevens's journal of 1900, a passage in which Stevens discusses Philip Henry Savage, a poet who had died the previous year: "Savage was like every other able-bodied man—he wanted to stand alone. Self-dependence is the greatest thing in the world for a young man & Savage knew it."[31] This fiscal Emersonianism surely participates, as Lentricchia argues, in a broad nexus of class and gender issues; but as the last lines of "Life on a Battleship" imply, it is also informed by an ideology of sexuality bound up with those questions of gender and class. It bespeaks, that is, a deep-rooted concern on the part of bourgeois heterosexual males about the possible meanings of dependence (emotional or economic) on other males —a dependence whose danger lies not in the threat of a "feminization" that would destabilize or question *gender*, but in the threat of a "feminization" that would challenge one's (hetero)sexual identity.[32] In this way the bourgeois ideology of male economic "self-dependence" effects its self-definition, at least in part, against a "homosexuality" construed in terms of the indolence and wealth of an economically unproductive aristocracy.

Neither homosexual nor homoerotic, the conclusion of "Life on a Battleship" disavows all dependence on other men even as it unfolds a narrative of submission to the power of the phallus as the necessary *precondition* to the achievement of phallic autonomy. This narrative defines the scene of submission not as the fulfillment of a "homosexual" desire at the core of patriarchal phallicism, but as the product of an embattled male heterosexuality that expresses therein its disquieting—and dangerous—confusion about how to respond to its culturally mandated investment in the phallus.[33] The trajectory of the poetic narrative, in consequence, is toward the rehabilitation of the phallus, its affectionate re-erection in a place of privilege and respect, through the repression of its status as the "immemorial grandiose," as the signifier of the Law and as the violent agent of "rape," and through the representation of it instead as "a trivial emblem great/ With its final force, a thing invincible/ in more than phrase," in short, as "the true masculine,/ The spirit's ring and seal, the naked heart." Lentricchia similarly manifests a desire to effect such an act of redemption when he observes with unmistakable sympathy and perhaps no small amount of wistfulness: "In the literary culture that Stevens would create, the 'phallic' would not have been the curse word of some recent feminist criticism but the name of a limited, because male, respect for literature" (767).

In this way, for Lentricchia, as for Stevens, the larger project is one that undertakes the redemption of the phallus, that seeks to transform its image, to make it, as it were, more likeable. No longer the emblem of repression and rigidity that humorless feminists and homosexuals fetishize, the new phallus, we are meant to believe, has gotten in touch with its emotions and dares to let it all hang out. As I began by looking at an interview with Lentricchia, so I will conclude by referring to another interview in which he figures prominently. I have in mind a fictive interview that Lentricchia includes in "Andiamo!," an interview in which he literalizes the scene of patriarchal indoctrination by imagining a particular moment of sexual instruction by his father. Having been accused by Gilbert and Gubar of suffering from male hysteria, or, as they call it, "testeria," Lentricchia asks:

FL: Dad, what's testeria?
Dad: *Figlio*! What happened to your Italian? It's TestaREEa! *Capisce*?
FL: Yes.
Dad: Tell me.
FL: A store where they sell that stuff.
Dad: In big jars!
FL: Let's go there![34]

This fantasy of male empowerment takes shape as a revisionary anecdote of the jars, an anecdote sufficiently significant to Lentricchia that he titles his essay by rendering its punchline, "Let's go there," in his father's Italian, "Andiamo!" Such a return to the language of the patriarch seems very much to the point, for here, as throughout Lentricchia's argument, the phallus returns to the father. Thus what Lentricchia writes with regard to Stevens's "Anecdote of the Jar" seems applicable here as well: "Jars . . . seem to have designs upon power."[35] Indeed, the ambiguous "stuff" of desire dispensed from the jars of this "TestaREEa" constitutes the very essence of phallogocentric power insofar as it conflates associations of heads (the Italian "testa") and texts (the Italian "testo") with sperm (the "stuff" of testicles) and testosterone (the "stuff" of maleness).

This fantasy, of course, expresses itself rhetorically as a joke; but here as elsewhere Lentricchia's humor reinforces an ideological investment that he otherwise denies. It reinforces, that is, the alleged ability of heterosexual men to occupy positions more authoritative (because derived from the sexual authority of their fathers) than those available to the feminists, lesbians, or gay men who find themselves excluded from both Lentricchia's humor and the invitation that his title, "Andiamo!," would extend. After all, it is as a response to the challenge embodied by feminists, lesbians, and gay men that the fantasmatic "TestaREEa" is imagined in the first place—imagined as a zone of traditional security, familiarity, and empowerment: as a haven in which heterosexual men accused of suffering from "testeria" can find shelter from attack and safely indulge in their celebration of male (hetero)sexual potency while continuing to deny that they take too seriously the prerogatives of the phallus.[36] Lentricchia's scene of paternal instruction may offer us phallicism with a baby face, but it celebrates the same old phallus of Western patriarchal power.

The "subversive" effect of Lentricchia's intervention in the politics of gender, then, is undermined by his inability to recognize its relation to the sexual ideologies of modernism, ideologies that require interpretation not only in terms of gender binarism, but also in terms of the cultural analysis that a gay reading can provide. In the absence of such an analysis, the redemption of "the phallic" from its status as the "curse word of some recent feminist criticism" will only signal the patriarchal redemonization of feminism and homosexuality; and Lentricchia, like the critical institutions for which he serves here as a representative, will continue to misrecognize his investment in the enterprise of the "TestaREEa": an investment that makes him not merely a consumer, but a profit-making shareholder in the ideology it purveys.

3

THE PART FOR THE (W)HOLE

Baldwin, Homophobia, and the Fantasmatics of "Race"

My mind was filled with the image of a black man, younger than I, perhaps, or my own age, hanging from a tree, while white men watched him and cut his sex from him with a knife.

—*James Baldwin*[1]

On the field of battle, its four corners marked by the scores of Negroes hanged by their testicles, a monument is slowly being built that promises to be majestic.

And, at the top of the monument, I can already see a white man and a black man *hand in hand.*

—*Frantz Fanon*[2]

The discourse of black resistance has almost always equated freedom with manhood, the economic and material domination of black men with castration, emasculation. Accepting these sexual metaphors forged a bond between oppressed black men and their white male oppressors. They shared the patriarchal belief that revolutionary struggle was really about the erect phallus. . . .

—*bell hooks*[3]

I. It is no secret that during his lifetime, and after, there were those who referred to James Baldwin, unflatteringly, as "Martin Luther Queen."[4] The pleasure of nomination, the prestige of "knowing" responsible for that nickname's circulation, attests to a fantasy of scopic candor, a fantasy of seeing and naming, as does the child in the tale of "The Emperor's New Clothes," what D. A. Miller has identified as the "open secret," the "secret that everybody already knows."[5] During the Birmingham desegregation struggle of 1963, after all, *Time* magazine, reporting on American "race" relations in a story that earned Baldwin a place on its cover, supplemented its visual image of the author with a coyly titillating verbal portrait;[6] in the essay immediately following its account of the incendiary violence in Bull Connor's domain—an account that included a critical assessment of the strategic interventions of Dr. Martin Luther King, Jr. ("the Negroes' inspirational but sometimes inept leader"[7])—*Time* described Baldwin (who was not, it claimed, "by any stretch of the imagination, a Negro leader") in the following barely coded terms: "He is a nervous, slight, almost fragile figure, filled with frets and fears. He is effeminate in manner, drinks considerably, smokes cigarettes in chains, and he often loses his audience with overblown arguments" (26). Such a passage, of course, in its own fretful way, signifies neither more nor less than "Martin Luther Queen."

That nickname, however, like the article from *Time*, engages in a labor of signification that repays the sort of careful analysis its "wit" undertakes to ward off. As a trope for "James Baldwin" that demonstrates access to the fetishized knowledge the commerce in which defines the worldliness of those "in the know," "Martin Luther Queen" takes part in the enforcement of a normalizing sexual taxonomy, generating, for those positioned to exploit it, a surplus value of cultural authority through the policial recognition and identification of the gay man whose sexuality must be represented as legible precisely because it "threatens" to pass unremarked.[8] The reading of the gay body performed by this nickname converges, however, with an insistence on that body's ostensibly more "obvious" inscription as "racial." Martin Luther King, by the early sixties one of the most widely recognizable living Americans of African descent, serves in this figure to represent by synecdoche the African-American population in general, and, in particular, those African-Americans engaged in the avulsive, and often fatal, struggle to claim their civil rights. Where the allusion to Martin Luther King, however, invokes a representative part for the whole, suggesting thereby the interchangeability of blacks in the racial imaginary of white America, the tropological translation of "King" into "Queen" substitutes, in the misogynistic parlance that regularly gets turned against gay men as well, a "hole" for the signally representative "part" of any "King" or patriarch.[9]

Now "queen," of course, as the designation—in many cases the self-designation—of a certain type of gay man, does not insist on its conceptual grounding in the genital difference that underlies a binary categorization of male and female; but in the context of this figure its capacity to mean rests precisely on its displacement of, and thus on its differential relation to, the anticipated signifier, "King." It bespeaks, that is, the *absence* of "King" and thus functions here as a *signifier of absence* by declaring the absence of what Lacan has called the transcendental signifier. Playing upon the metonymic coincidence of King's name with a signifier of social power, this trope enacts a symbolic castration with unmistakable parallels to the brutal literalism with which whites historically have inscribed their racism on the bodies of black men who claimed, or who could be taken, through the synecdochic logic of racism, as appropriately representative of others who claimed, equal access to the privileged signifier of cultural authority under patriarchy.[10] The nickname thus cuts, as it were, two ways; its "humor" interimplicates racism and homophobia to invoke against Baldwin what Marlon Riggs has described as the "Negro faggot identity," the representation of black gay men as ineffectual "comic eunuchs"[11]; and at the same time it turns against Martin Luther King, and by extension against the movement in which he participated, not only the razor of symbolic castration, but also the force of the objectifying gaze that reduces black male identity to the part that stands, in the racist imagination, for the whole.

Synecdoche, as this description suggests, can be read as the master trope of racism that gets deployed in a variety of different ways to reinforce the totalizing logic of identity.[12] In America, for example, the figure of "blood," with its pseudo-biological provenance, has historically governed the discrimination of "race" through the classificatory calculus that yields such "types" as the "mulatto," "quadroon," and "octoroon." This mathematic of "blood" emerges, however, from a single racist theorem: wherever an admixture of "black blood" is at issue, one part determines the whole. In *Tell Me How Long the Train's Been Gone*, Baldwin refers to this phobic logic through the voice of Leo Proudhammer's brother: "'Our mama is *almost* white,' Caleb said, 'but that don't make her white. You got to be *all* white to be white.'"[13] And just as *any* proportion of "black blood," in the murderous binarism of white supremacy, signifies, ultimately, an "essence" that is "black," so any representation of a black woman or man can stand tropologically, from the racist perspective, for the "essential character" of "the race" as a whole. Isn't this, after all, what motivates, on the one hand, the dominant cultural characterization—once common and explicit, now, for the most part, only implied—of any successful African-American—successful, that is, as defined by the terms of the dominant culture itself—as "a credit to the race," even as it explains, on the other hand, the fervor so readily aroused throughout white America by the tendentious and exploitative representations of a Willie Horton or a Tawana Brawley? Isn't this what prompted Ishmael Reed to remark, with regard to Steven Spielberg's cinematic adaptation of *The Color Purple*, "though defenders of Walker's book, upon which the movie was based, argue that these creations were merely one woman's story, critics in the media have used both the book and the movie as excuses to indict all black men"?[14]

As synecdoche informs, at every level, the discourse through which "race" finds articulation within the white-dominated structures of social control, so it governs as well the visual logic to which the fiction of "race" itself refers: the logic that specifies personhood through reference to a skin whose "color" must submit to interpretation as, for example, black or white, though each of those labels is itself a crude and patently untenable synecdoche of pigmentation. Thus Malcolm El-Hajj Malik El-Shabazz observes in *The Autobiography of Malcolm X*, "We're all black to the white man, but we're a thousand and one different colors," and Baldwin concurs in *No Name in the Street*: "the children are as vari-colored—tea, coffee, chocolate, mocha, honey, eggplant coated with red pepper, red pepper dipped in eggplant—as it is possible for a people to be; black people, here, are no more uniformly black than white people are physically white."[15] In the service of the visual economy wherein "color" and "skin" stand in for identity, the "racialized" body, whose "meaning" depends on the synecdoche of pigmented flesh, comes to figure, moreover, in the racist imaginary, the insistence of the flesh or the body itself; it can always be fragmented, anatomized, as it were, to locate yet another part that can be appropriated and made to testify to the fictitious but inescapable "truth" of the whole. Meditating on the vexed epistemology of "race," Diana Fuss cites a noteworthy example of such an effort at categorical determination as narrated by Booker T. Washington in his autobiography, *Up From Slavery*. Describing the uncertainty of a train conductor trying to discover, without the embarrassment of having to ask, the "race" of a traveler seated in the "part of the train set aside for the coloured passengers," Washington recalls: "The official looked him over carefully, examining his hair, eyes, nose, and hands, but still seemed puzzled. Finally, to solve the difficulty, he stooped over and peeped at the man's feet. When I saw the conductor examining the feet of the man in question, I said to myself, 'That will settle it'; and so it did, for the trainman promptly decided that the passenger was a Negro, and let him remain where he was. I congratulated myself that my race was fortunate in not losing one of its members."[16]

If the conductor here enacts a popular version of the "scientific" ethnography, the quasi-anthropological "rationalism" we might choose to associate with Schoolteacher—the white man in Toni Morrison's *Beloved* who, as Mae G. Henderson writes, "is concerned with sizes, densities, details, appearances, externalities, and visible properties"—his evaluative study of the indeterminate passenger carries with it implicitly the potential violence that Henderson incisively notes in Schoolteacher's imperialistic investigations: "The dismemberment of Schoolteacher's method is the discursive analog to the dismemberment of slavery."[17] Indeed, the specific historical force that inheres in the notion of "dismemberment" seems to echo in Washington's "congratulat[ing] [him]self" that his "race" has been able to avoid, in this instance, "losing one of its members." It would be possible, of course, to invoke at this point the metonymic relation of feet to genitalia that Freud would consider a fetishistic displacement of the "member" most tellingly "stooped over and peeped at" as the privileged token of sexual identity and *therefore*, as I want to go on to suggest, as the most heavily invested and insistently mythologized portion of the "racialized" male anatomy (in Baldwin's *Just Above My Head*, Crunch bitterly complains "I'm tired . . . of being treated like something hanging on the other edge of a prick"[18]); but even without appealing to so specific a tropology, we can recognize, in the fetishization of the visual as adequate to discern the hypostatized difference that the "racialized" body must inevitably reveal, a borrowing from—and a repositioning of—the scopic logic on which the prior assertion of sexual difference depends. "Racial" discrimination, in both senses of the word, like the project I have defined as "homographesis," is propped up on, or, as Freud might put it, occupies an anaclitic relation to, the privileging of the scopic drive in the psychic structuring of sexual difference. The interpretive energies directed toward the reading of "race" and sexuality both, therefore, give rise to a massive epistemological machinery, a vastly overdetermined analytic methodology, whose delusory "rationality" involves and intends, in Henderson's word, a "dismemberment," the oscillation of which between the literal and the figurative (an oscillation distinctive of fetishism as a mode of defense against castration) effectively returns the question of difference to the allegedly stable, because allegedly "natural," difference between the sexes.

Thus when Frantz Fanon, in *Black Skin, White Masks*, rejecting an ontology of "race" so as to focus on the psychic structures of imperialism that call "racial" discourse into being, writes "not only must the black man be black; he must be black in relation to the white man," he implicitly identifies the narcissism invested in the mythology of "racial" supremacy as reenacting the logic of phallic masculinity under compulsory heterosexuality—a logic of visual difference that necessitates the display of the "other" in the position of "lack" in order to reassure the dominant subject, by contrast, of his (phallic) "possession" (110). This fantasy of "possession" comes to signify, in turn, with the facility of a metonymic slippage, possession of the (fetishized) gaze that objectifies and commodifies the other-as-(b)lack, thereby effecting, in the historical context of colonization and enslavement, the racist interpretation of the black body as material supplement, as that which is to-be-possessed. Fanon describes, from his own experience, the conscription of the "racialized" body into the signifying structures of a Euro-centric patriarchy that fetishizes the scopic drive: "And then the occasion arose when I had to meet the white man's eyes. An unfamiliar weight burdened me. The real world challenged my claims. In the white world the man of color encounters difficulties in the development of his bodily schema. Consciousness of the body is solely a negating activity" (110).

Burdened with the substance, the "weight" of a physicality that produces a distinctly "negating" effect, Fanon's body enters the white economy of meaning—with its logocentric privileging of a signified linked to the pulmonary lightness of spirit—in the place of material representation, the place, that is, of the signifier. Thus consigned to represent representation in the gaze of "the white man's eyes," he finds himself possessed by the scopic logic that denies him possession of himself: "On that day, completely dislocated, unable to be abroad with the other, the white man, who unmercifully imprisoned me, I took myself far off from my own presence, far indeed, and made myself an object. What else could it be for me but an amputation, an excision, a hemorrhage that splattered my whole body with black blood?" (112). Internalizing the colonial script that requires, as Homi Bhabha perceptively elaborates it, "the production of differentiations, individuations, identity effects through which discriminatory practices can map out subject populations that are tarred with the visible and transparent mark of power,"[19] Fanon suffers the "dismemberment," or, as he puts it, the "amputation," that registers for him the experience of "dislocat[ion] . . . from [his] own presence." Thus appropriated by a discourse in which he signifies as "(b)lack," Fanon here can only see himself through a gaze he no longer possesses: a gaze that, instead, possesses him, construing him as "an object" that differentially confirms the subject-defining status of the imperialistic gaze itself.[20]

Just as the gaze needs the object, however, so phallic "possession" depends upon "lack"; for Lacan, therefore, inquiry into the ontology of the subject is as misguided as, from Fanon's perspective, is inquiry into the ontology of "race." Indeed, to the extent that the scopophilia on which the fantasy of "racial" differentiation relies harks back to the process through which the psychic construction of sexual difference takes place, the black body, as material supplement or signifier, as that which must be possessed in order to validate the dominant subject's putative possession of the phallus, must endure a symbolic inscription corresponding to that of the female body. It must represent, that is, or "be" the "phallus" so the dominant subject can "have" it. Judith Butler offers a canny gloss on this dialectic of "being" and "having":

> To "be" the Phallus is to be the "signifier" of the desire of the Other and *to appear* as this signifier. In other words, it is to be the object, the Other of a (heterosexualized) masculine desire, but also to represent or reflect that desire. This is an Other that constitutes, not the limit of masculinity in a feminine alterity, but the site of masculine self-elaboration. For women to "be" the Phallus means, then, to reflect the power of the Phallus, to supply the site to which it penetrates, and to signify the Phallus through "being" its Other, its absence, its lack, the dialectical confirmation of its identity. By claiming that the Other

> who lacks the Phallus is the one who *is* the Phallus, Lacan clearly suggests that power is wielded by this feminine position of not-having, that the masculine subject who "has" the Phallus requires this Other to confirm and, hence, be the Phallus in its "extended" sense.[21]

The applicability of this structure to a notion of "race" that relies on the psychically resonant fiction of a *visible*, because anatomically specified, difference seems, from the perspective of a Western history that joins "racial" alterity to physical bondage, implicit in Butler's own text: "The interdependency of these positions recalls the Hegelian structure of failed reciprocity between master and slave, in particular, the unexpected dependency of the master on the slave in order to establish his own identity through reflection" (44). Rather than use this model to unpack the relation of "racial" to sexual difference as one of metaphor or analogy, however, I want to explore the specific confusions that attend the volatile positioning of that relation somewhere between the figurative and the literal in the representation of black men. I want, that is, to consider the violent indeterminacy that prevents castration, in the specific context of American "racial" history, from signifying only as trope, and to think, in consequence, about some of the ways in which, as bell hooks bluntly puts it, "racism and sexism are interlocking systems of domination"[22]—systems that generate a "racial" discourse suffused with homophobia insofar as it plays out the incoherences of a heterosexual masculinity that cannot afford to acknowledge, as it cannot afford to deny, the centrality of its narcissistic investment in, and hence the intensity of its desire for, the culturally institutionalized authority of the phallus that never fully distinguishes itself from the anatomical penis. In what follows, then, I hope to articulate a few of the complex relations among a) the specular logic that connects the insistence on racial differentiation with the project I have identified as homographesis; b) the rhetorical operations whereby identity is constituted out of a process—both psychic and cognitive—in which the designations of "sameness" and "difference" are always necessarily tropological; and c) the heterosexual misrecognitions of the penis that have had such fatally determining effects in the histories of race and sexuality both.

II. Noting that "slavery does away with fathers," Frederick Douglass called attention to the logic through which white "ownership" of Africans and African-Americans undertook to deny slaves access to the symbolic order of sexual meaning under patriarchy: as he put it with reference to the slave's exclusion from the social prerogatives of family, "the order of civilization is reversed here."[23] One need not, of course, view patriarchy as itself a desideratum in order to recognize the destructiveness of a system that enshrined the paternal privilege (simultaneously figured and given a visceral literality by the specifically sexual privileges taken by "the master") while at the same time disavowing the meaningfulness of the paternal relation for the slave. Douglass himself identifies a number of those effects and gestures toward their participation in a psycho-sexual economy: "the fact remains, in all its glaring odiousness, that, by the laws of slavery, children, in all cases, are reduced to the condition of their mothers" (58). Here, as Henry Louis Gates, Jr. writes, "the patrilineal succession of the planter has been forcibly replaced by a matrilineal succession for the slave"[24]—a process that not only excludes the slave from a relation to the Name-of-the-Father, but also (and thereby) articulates the logic that mandates that slaves, regardless of gender, figure in mimetic relation not to their "mothers" but to the "condition of their mothers": to the radical condition, that is, of "woman" in a patriarchal dispensation that, to quote Teresa de Lauretis, "produces the human as man and everything else as, not even 'woman,' but non-man."[25]

In her influential essay, "Mama's Baby, Papa's Maybe: An American Grammar Book," Hortense Spillers incisively marks the repercussions of this system on "the African-American woman," who, as she argues, "becomes the powerful and shadowy evocation of a cultural synthesis long evaporated—the law of the Mother—only and precisely because legal enslavement removed the African-American male not so much from sight as from *mimetic* view as a partner in the prevailing social fiction of the Father's name, the Father's law."[26] Though African-American men, however, may have been kept from "*mimetic* view" as participants in, and thus as beneficiaries of, that patriarchal social fiction, the fiction itself (and the real authority that accrued to those men it legitimated) remained on prominent display for African-American women and men alike, coming, indeed, to instantiate, as it sought to do all along, the very economy of power into which emancipation would lead. If it established, in other words, the context within which Spillers can make the important, and potentially empowering, assertion that "the black American male embodies the *only* American community of males which has had the specific occasion to learn *who* the female is within itself" (80), it also established the context within which the necessity of that knowledge can seem disabling rather than empowering: can seem the enduring, and alienating, legacy of a history that made "race," like sexual difference, into an object of the scopic drive and thus, "in all its glaring odiousness," to cite Douglass once again, assigned all children of slavery—male and female—to the "condition of their mothers."

That sense of alienation, reflected in Fanon's experience of himself as "an object" and elaborated in his discussion of those mechanisms of acculturation through which "the young Negro subjectively adopts a white man's attitude" (147), finds a certain canonical expression in W .E. B. Du Bois's description of "this double-consciousness, this sense of always looking at one's self through the eyes of others, of measuring one's soul by the tape of a world that looks on in amused contempt and pity. One ever feels his twoness, —an American, a Negro; two souls, two thoughts, two unreconciled strivings; two warring ideals in one dark body, whose dogged strength alone keeps it from being torn asunder."[27] The self-division that results, in this passage, from the fetishization of a gaze that remains the prerogative of "others" (in particular, of the white male, who, as Fanon makes clear, "is not only the Other but also the master, whether real or imaginary" [138])—a gaze that is linked, if "only" metaphorically, to the differentiating logic of measurement that Schoolteacher deploys and represents—can be healed, Du Bois argues, only by resolving the specific history it bespeaks: "The history of the American Negro is the history of this strife—this longing to attain self-conscious manhood, to merge his double self into a better and truer self" (5). Such a translation of conflict into harmony, of self-division into "truer" selfhood, in the hope of escaping the duplicity, the double positioning imposed by the necessity of "always looking at one's self through the eyes of others," replicates the governing logic that shapes the patriarchal subject and thus properly describes the cultural ambition "to attain self-conscious manhood." It recapitulates, that is, the structuring belief in the coherence of identity, the unity of drives, that informs the fiction of "manhood" and allows it to serve, within a patriarchal dispensation, as the referent of subjectivity and selfhood.

But is the "self" in the term "self-conscious" any "truer," any more one's "own" self (and any less, therefore, one's "owned" self) than the self that is always "looking at one's self through the eyes of others"? A "manhood" qualified as "self-conscious," to formulate this notion another way, is surely an unreliable anodyne for a state of division defined as "double-consciousness"; indeed, the problem and the solution are barely distinguishable from one another. "Self-consciousness," after all, denotes not only the reassuring awareness of one's identity as a subject, but also, and antithetically, an uncertainty of selfhood that springs from the uneasy apprehension of one's appropriability as an object, or, as the *Oxford English Dictionary* explains, a condition of being "so far self-centered as to suppose one is the object *of observation by others*" (my emphasis). Though Du Bois explicitly maintains that he "wishes neither of the older selves to be lost," that he "simply wishes to make it possible for a man to be both a Negro and an American" (5), the self-consciousness of the "manhood" he envisions as the fulfillment of that wish suggests that such a "manhood" must be the *enactment* of a masculinity whose distinguishing characteristic is its power, as he puts it, to "look on" others with "contempt and pity," to occupy the place of the non-"racialized" (because non-specularizable) master of the gaze. If the fantasy of masculinity (and I would want that genitive to be read with the full force of its double meaning) is the fantasy of a non-self-conscious selfhood endowed with absolute control of a gaze whose directionality is irreversible, the enacted—or "self-conscious"—"manhood," to which the passage by Du Bois refers, is itself a performance *for the gaze of the Other*, as the *OED* makes clear; it is destined therefore to be always the paradoxical *display* of a masculinity that defines itself through its capacity to put *others* on display while resisting the bodily captation involved in being put on display itself. This paradox, which represents the internal distanciation of (heterosexual) "masculinity" as such, acquires a vicious performative charge in the context of a "racial" history in which self-consciousness and narcissism are entangled in the enduring chiasmus of male desire—first and foremost *heterosexual* male desire—for possession of a phallus culturally envisioned as always somehow more authentically situated on the *other* side of the "racial" divide, no matter which "side" one inhabits.

I will return to a fuller consideration of this fantasmatic chiasmus, but first I want briefly to examine another passage in which self-consciousness and narcissism are brought into relation in the context of "racial" difference. Houston A. Baker, Jr., in an analysis of Richard Wright's essay, "The Literature of the American Negro," contrasts what Wright describes, on the one hand, as the "Forms of Things Unknown," the popular cultural productions generated within (and for primary consumption by) the African-American community, with, on the other hand, the "high" cultural manifestations that occur on what Wright calls the "Narcissistic Level," a phrase that Baker glosses as "the self-consciously literate level."[28] The works in which African-American authors exhibit this "self-consciously literate" engagement with dominant white cultural institutions, however, are precisely those products (as Baker evokes them: "'protest' poems and novels") that endeavor to demonstrate, for the judgmental gaze of those dominant institutions, the equivalence (what Wright calls the relationship of "entity") that would allow them to stand on an equal footing with the aesthetic products of white America. This level of cultural labor, then, earns its designation as "Narcissistic" only by identifying itself with the judgmental gaze that would measure or evaluate it. It thus mirrors what Homi Bhabha describes as "the familiar exercise of *dependent* colonial relations through narcissistic identification so that, as Fanon has observed, the black man stops being an actional person for only the white man can represent his self-esteem."[29]

To that extent the products of the "Narcissistic Level" reproduce the self-compromising structure that Baldwin, in "Everybody's Protest Novel," discovers at work in the logic of Wright's *Native Son.* Contending that Bigger Thomas's tragedy lies in the fact "that he has accepted a theology that denies him life, that he admits the possibility of his being sub-human and feels constrained, therefore, to battle for his humanity according to those brutal criteria bequeathed him at his birth," Baldwin emphasizes the devastating violence of such a "narcissistic" internalization whereby the self-worth of those viewed as "inferior" depends upon their valorization of the angle of vision that judges them "inferior" in the first place—a valorization that accepts the "brutal criteria" laid down by the dominant culture while taking issue with the judgment to which those criteria have led.[30] "We find ourselves bound," he says, "first without, then within, by the nature of our categorization" (32). Conceived in relation to these centripetal forces, narcissism names, in what constitutes only an *apparent* contradiction, the masochistic engine of an alienation that derives from the subjection of the self to an endless discipline of internal scrutiny *as if* from the perspective of the Other;[31] thus the "self-conscious manhood" that Du Bois presents as the resolution of the culturally enforced anxiety of African-American male self-worth, evokes, instead, a manhood in question, constantly under surveillance, and subject to measurement "by the tape of a world that looks on in amused contempt and pity."

That such a characterization could define the status of "manhood" per se in the symbolic order of (heterosexual) masculinity does not reduce the force of its entanglement in a specifically "racialized" social context that generates for men, both black and white, though not for black men and white men *alike*, a pervasive paranoia. To formulate this more clearly, let me recall Freud's remark that, "Paranoia is a disorder in which a sexual aetiology is by no means obvious; on the contrary, the strikingly prominent features in the causation of paranoia, especially among males, are social humiliations and slights."[32] Consider, in this regard, the following passage, originally published in 1902, in which Butler Harrison Peterson, an African-American educator, implies the sexual aetiology of a specific type of "social humiliation" experienced by African-American men:

> In proportion as the feeling of self respect and self dependence is taken away, and a man is taught to look upon himself as merely the tool in the hands of another, the instrument of another's will and pleasure, without responsibility of his own, just in that proportion the foundation of moral character is undermined. Nothing can be more demoralizing in its effect upon the character. Strip a man of all that constitutes manhood; of all self reliance and self respect; of all the rights which nature has conferred upon him, and all the faculties with which God has endowed him; take away from him all control and disposal of himself, all ownership of himself, and all that can stimulate to activity, and incite to noble attainment and excellence, is gone at once. He sinks down to the level of a brute.[33]

Here again an insistence on the gaze and on the particularities of its social construction (how "a man is taught to look upon himself") effect what Fanon called an "amputation" and Henderson a "dismemberment." Within the heterosexual regime of patriarchal domination, for a man to be made to see himself "*as* . . . [a] tool" (my emphasis) is to lose his claim to "have" a "tool"; it is to be "strip[ped] . . . of all that constitutes manhood" precisely because he is "the instrument of another's will and pleasure": the instrument, to be more specific, of another *man's* "will and pleasure."[34] Thus as viewed through the racist gaze of a culture that privileges straight white men, the African-American male, to return to the literally reductive phrasing I used earlier, must *be* the "part," (i.e., the "tool") that stands for the "hole" (the stripping away, the absence, of "all that constitutes manhood") in order that the white male subject, through his fetishistic deployment of the gaze, can "have" the "part" that the black man, in racist fantasy, both *is* and *lacks*.[35]

To invoke the discourse of "paranoia," however, in order to characterize the disfiguring effects of this insistent discipline of specularization should not be construed as a means of pathologizing the African-American male who is subjected to the violence of the racist gaze: it should alert us, instead, to what Ishmael Reed calls the "justifiable paranoia" of African-American men in a culture that obsessively portrays and produces them, in Peterson's words, as "tool[s] in the hands of another, the instrument[s] of another's will and pleasure." Evoking the disciplinary force of the televisual medium that effectively keeps watch on those who think they are watching it, Reed observes in passing that "on television, black men are typically shown naked from the waist up, handcuffed, and leaning over a police car" (157). The semiotics of this posture, which constitutes, within the sign-system of patriarchal ideology, the humiliating "position" the subordinated are commanded to "assume," resonates with unmistakable socio-sexual significance: a significance, that is, in which what Freud called "social humiliations" allow us to catch a glimpse of their motivating "sexual aetiology." The unrelenting depiction of black men as criminals by a white-controlled journalistic establishment empowered to determine what counts as "news" inflects those handcuffs with the force of the more archaic signifier, "manacles," even as the bent-over posture conjures the enforced passivity (with its erotic connotations) of the subordinated man reduced to the materiality of a body ("naked from the waist up") that is put, quite literally, "in the hands of another," and thus made "the instrument of another's will and pleasure."

Surely it is not irrelevant in this context that African-American literature, on numerous occasions, should figure the oppressive force of the official institutions that embody white authority over African-Americans—and over African-American men in particular—in terms of white males demanding that black males submit to their sexual domination. In *Beloved*, for instance, Toni Morrison describes how Paul D begins to retch as the group of black prisoners to whom he is chained is required to kneel in the morning mist while they await with trepidation the unrefusable demand that they satisfy

> the whim of a guard, or two, or three. Or maybe all of them wanted it. Wanted it from one prisoner in particular or none—or all.
>
> "Breakfast? Want some breakfast, nigger?"

> "Yes, sir."
> "Hungry, nigger?"
> "Yes, sir."
> "Here you go."
> Occasionally a kneeling man chose gunshot in his head as the price, maybe, of taking a bit of foreskin with him to Jesus.[36]

Similarly, in *Tell Me How Long the Train's Been Gone* Baldwin portrays the brutality inherent in the racist social order through the psychic mutilation suffered by Caleb Proudhammer while incarcerated for a crime he did not commit: an experience emblematically condensed in the menace posed by Martin Howell, a guard, who torments his prisoner by demanding, "Nigger, if my balls was on your chin, where would my prick be?"[37] That the white guards in both of these cases enact the conjuncture of racism and homophobia rather than any determinate index of their sexual orientation, that they violate the bodily integrity of their prisoners in order to reinscribe the social humiliation and abasement of the black male, does not prevent them from occupying the site at which what Reed called the "justifiable paranoia" of African-American men unfolds in a culturally enforced relation to "homosexuality."

Though these passages, in other words, portray neither guard nor prisoner, neither white man nor black, as "being" homosexual, homosexuality itself, in the heterosexual world view compulsively intent on totalizing it, comes to "mean" in both instances the violent disappropriation of masculine authority that underlies the paranoid relation of black and white in our modern, "racially" polarized, patriarchal social formation. For homosexuality, in the dominant optic that registers its presence in these passages (and that optic registers any act of male-male sex as "homosexuality"), comes into focus only as the conflictual undoing of one man's authority by another; it signifies, that is, only as a failed, debased, or inadequate masculinity—a masculinity severed from the ground of its meaning in a phallic "possession" betokening one's legitimate status as a subject. Insofar as male-male sexual activity "means," in these passages, enforced passivity (and *therefore* emasculation for a social order that identifies passivity or penetrability with the emptying-out or abjection of independent will and autonomous selfhood), "means," in other words, the humiliation of one man by another, it is telling that in each of these cases such activity is condensed in the image of an African-American man compelled, through violence or the threat of violence, to figure in an act of fellatio as the person who, as one says, "goes down." This image, produced as an epitome of white supremacist domination and brutalization of blacks, correlates the reduction in size, the diminution in stature or relative height of the black man constrained to "go down" on the white (who, in consequence, towers over him physically) with the denial of the black man's agency through his transformation into a material receptacle, the malleable object of the white man's "will and pleasure."

In this way the terrorizing force of white racism—a racism historically expressed, as Fanon makes clear, through the specific violence of castration—acquires visibility through the demonization of male-male sexual relations: relations popularly construed as themselves effecting, though for the most part "only" by metaphor, a similar sort of castration or violent alienation from the cultural authority for which the phallus serves as signifier.[38] Made to articulate the "racial" dynamic of a masculinist culture, homophobia allows a certain figural logic to the pseudo-algebraic "proof" that asserts: where it is "given" that white racism equals castration and "given" that homosexuality equals castration, then it is proper to conclude that white racism equals (or expresses through displacement) homosexuality and, by the same token, in a reversal of devastating import for lesbians and gay men of color, homosexuality equals white racism.

Fanon, for instance, affirms the identity of white racism with homosexuality by asserting bluntly and unproblematically that "the Negrophobic man is a repressed homosexual" (156) and he subsequently interprets "homosexuality" as practiced by black natives of Martinique as a mere effect or byproduct of colonial relations:

> Let me observe at once that I had no opportunity to establish the overt presence of homosexuality in Martinique. This must be viewed as the result of the absence of the Oedipus complex in the Antilles. The schema of homosexuality is well enough known. We should not overlook, however, the existence of what are called there "men dressed like women" or "godmothers." Generally they wear shirts and skirts. But I am convinced that they lead normal sex lives. They can take a punch like any "he-man" and they are not impervious to the allures of women—fish and vegetable merchants. In Europe, on the other hand, I have known several Martinicans who became homosexuals, always passive. But this was by no means a neurotic homosexuality: For them it was a means of livelihood, as pimping is for others. (180, n. 44)

I quote this statement in its entirety because its specification of the invariably "passive" position assumed by those Martinican men who "became homosexuals" in Europe both resonates with the position of the one who "goes down," the position occupied by the African-American men in the passages cited earlier, and speaks to a crucial contradiction in the ideology that interimplicates "homosexuality" with the practices of "racial" domination. If, for instance, as I suggested above, a homophobic logic can conclude that "white racism" equals "homosexuality" insofar as each of those terms individually can be represented as equal to "castration," the uninterrogated term here—

the term that must be, but is not, equal to itself for such an argument to make sense—is "equals." And the inequality inhabiting "equals," the signifier that designates identity, lies precisely in the indeterminacy of its relation to the active/passive distinction, and thus in the way that distinction complicates identity itself. To put it somewhat differently, the same word, "equals," substitutes for antithetical predicates when mediating between the act of castration and the collective subjects figured by the abstractions "white racism" and "homosexuality": the primary meaning of these equations, after all, is that white racists (literally) *castrate others* while homosexuals (figuratively) *are castrated themselves.* Though both, in a given cultural calculation, may be "equal" to castration, and therefore "equal" to each other as well, "white racism" and "homosexuality" stand opposed to one another when the copular that specifies their status vis-à-vis castration is articulated in the grammatical terms of an active/passive binarism.[39]

The scenes of forcible fellatio conceived by Morrison and Baldwin, however, implicitly acknowledge what the citation from Fanon can help to make explicit: an irreducible contradiction in the ideology of homophobia that allows it to stigmatize homosexuality as too passive and too active at once. Insofar as male homosexuality connotes, to the straight imagination, a submission, inherently emasculating, to the desire either *for* or *of* another man, its prime conceptual referent remains the opening or availability of the male body to an act of penetration. The phobic belief in the subject-annihilating force of such an act motivates the white guards to torment their black prisoners with the threat of coerced involvement in that abjectifying denial of their "masculinity."[40] Seen from this angle of vision, the guards homophobically terrorize their prisoners with the prospect of compulsory inscription in the position of the "homosexual," or more precisely, the position of the "faggot."[41] While such a perspective—the perspective associated with the guards within the imagined literary scenes—situates "homosexuality," conventionally, as a condition of passivity and penetrability, the scenes themselves, in context, encourage the reader to locate "homosexuality" as properly characteristic of the "active" participants, of the guards instead of the prisoners. Like those Martinicans whom Fanon describes as "always passive" in their "homosexual" transactions with European men, the African-American prisoners made to adopt the postures of passivity are exempted from any diagnosis of "neurotic homosexuality" since their passivity, more than a "means of livelihood," is depicted as a means of staying alive. Their tormentors, however, like the Europeans who trade money for sex with the "passive" Martinican men, are framed so that their very "activity," their willful agency in these encounters, appears as the token of a desire that defines their behavior as expressing a "true," if otherwise repressed, "homosexual" identity.

If active and passive thus seem to trade places, if the logic of these passages demands that the brutalizing agent of homophobic discipline be perceived through the lens of an equally homophobic suspicion, this does not mean that homosexuality as such has escaped its psychic representation in the Western imaginary in terms of the receptive male body subjected to penetration; for the ostensibly "active" participants in these fictional scenes of male-male sex are interpreted as "active" only in disseminating the intolerable passivity as which "homosexuality" continues to signify for a masculinist heterosexual regime. The "nature" of these "active" or insertive men is emblematized, therefore, not by their behavioral embodiment of penetrative male sexuality, but rather by their "active"—one might even say "infectious"—(re)production and multiplication of the penetrated male body. Understood as doing unto others what has been done, if not physically then psychologically, unto them, the guards, in their "neurotic homosexuality" can be read as enacting the "emasculation" (properly—that is, homophobically—interpreted as their own) of those who, from the vantage point of both an outraged heterosexuality *and* the guards themselves as imagined from within that outraged heterosexuality, represent the "authentic" manhood enshrined in the straight male fantasy of that mythic being—the "real man"—whom the fantasy itself exposes as oxymoronic. The violence of the assault corresponds, then, to the putative "essence" of homosexuality itself; for homosexuality registers as a castration that destabilizes the foundational distinction between active and passive, generating the intolerable image of a male body that passively submits to penetration. In so doing it fantasmatically effects, by "allowing" for the cultural *representation* of that submission, a generalized and uncontrollable *reproduction* of that submission (a reproduction, it is important to note, that the phobic imagination always literalizes) insofar as the penetrated body is construed as acting contagiously to penetrate and thereby delegitimate the male body as such. The claim that white racism equals homosexuality rests, then, on the assertion, only apparently paradoxical, that activity can equal passivity, or, more precisely, that certain forms of activity can operate as a psychic defense against the disturbance produced by an unsettling identification with, an unacknowledged desire for, or an unacceptable temptation by, the "passive" or "homosexual" position.

The complexities generated by these figures in which the racist persecution of African-American men is imaged through the violence of male-male sexual (which is construed as male *homo*sexual) aggression, prevent the passages by Morrison and Baldwin from being dismissed as simple demonstrations of an authorial inclination to draw upon the homophobia that seems to be America's one endlessly renewable, though by no means "natural," resource. The figures themselves, after all, *as* figures produce a confusion of trope and referent that has everything to do with the confounding and dismantling of the active/passive distinction. While it is clear, in other words, that these textual moments put the fear and hatred of homosexuality strategically into play, only the particularity of a reading can determine if the passages are to be interpreted as homophobic themselves or, conversely, as subjecting homophobia to a much-needed critical analysis. The obvious answer, that these alternatives need not be conceptualized as mutually exclusive, suggests that in addressing homophobia, these figures both draw upon and speak to it at once, that they allow an analysis of its centrality in shaping our modern "racial" discourse only at the risk of deploying, or even actively soliciting, it. Confirming thereby the self-implicating tendency of any representation produced within so contradictory and overdetermined a set of cultural assumptions as those that govern our ways of thinking about sexuality and "race," these figures gesture at the same time toward something more specific here at stake. For the homophobia that projectively interprets—and, in light of the destabilization of active and passive effected by these figures, *reversibly* interprets—either the guards or the prisoners in these textual instances as subject to "homosexualization," names, in fact, the common denominator linking both the guards and the prisoners across the chasm of the "racial" divide, the common denominator shared not only by those fictional antagonists, but also by the readers of these narratives who, regardless of "race," engage these passages as testifying to the truth of an underlying relation that articulates "racial" oppression with homosexuality instead of with homophobia. As a result, the *misrecognized* homophobia that, once filtered through the lens of "race," determines the specific form of our racist fantasmatics, generates a *recognizable and self-conscious* homophobia that no longer serves simply to separate paranoiacally but also, and at the same time, to integrate ideologically, across their various historical differences, the dominant white and dominant African-American cultural communities.

Now it may be the case, as bell hooks has argued, that as African-Americans "have been more integrated into White society, [they] have actually adopted certain constructs of homophobia that were, in fact, inimical to early forms of Black cultural life,"[42] but it is also true, as she notes in a passage I use as one of this chapter's epigraphs, that a black resistance associating "freedom with manhood, the economic and material domination of black men with castration, emasculation," has entangled itself in the anxious specularity that allies it with its "white male oppressors" in the belief that "racial" opposition and struggle is "really about the erect phallus." This privileging of, and competition for, possession of the phallus testifies, of course, to the structuring sexism of patriarchal organization; but no modern contestation of "manhood" can be divorced from the homophobic energies that give it meaning, and in the context of "race" these energies assure that "castration" and "emasculation" will resonate as the defining characteristics of those whom Amiri Baraka referred to as "faggots till the end of the earth."[43] If such a context makes it all but inevitable that the discourse of black resistance, among some in the African-American community, will be informed by a homophobia as virulent as that pervading the white culture around them, it also renders more intelligible the claim made by certain black nationalist leaders in the sixties (Eldridge Cleaver, for example) and certain Afrocentrist theorists today (Molefi Keke Asante, for example) that homosexuality is a form of white decadence introduced to black women and men from without.[44]

This claim has been movingly and persuasively contested by Ron Simmons in "Some Thoughts on the Challenges Facing Black Gay Intellectuals"; but in the course of that essay Simmons declares, in language like that used by bell hooks above, that "we should also include homophobia as another attitude that black males have adopted largely from the white culture" (221), an assertion whose structural logic uncannily parallels that of the claim it refutes. Both pronouncements, that is, identify something external in its essence, whether homosexuality or homophobia, as imposing itself on an alarmingly receptive African-American community so that in each case the issue to be engaged is the perceived vulnerability of the (communal) black body to (ideological) penetration by whites. The metaphorics of colonization give voice to a paranoia—however justifiable—characteristically marked by the anxious-making confusion of inside and outside, self and other. Where those black nationalists and Afrocentrists who denounce homosexuality among African-Americans read it as a passive internalization of the oppressor's alien practices, and thus as a potentially genocidal subversion of a "natural" black masculinity, their gay-affirmative counterparts interpret such homophobic attitudes as themselves betraying the internalization of a "foreign" practice that undermines the specificity of black cultural experience. Can the coupling of "race" and sexuality be thought outside the specularity of such a chiasmus in which "homophobia" and "homosexuality" can so easily change places with each other while "internalization," the demonized pivotal term, continues to name the anxiety of lost identity, of passive receptivity, phobically instantiated in the representations of coercive male-male sex? Can identity itself be renegotiated in the force field where "race" and sexuality are each inflected by the other's gravitational pull? Can it open itself to self-difference without being figured either as "hole" or "whole"? To broach these questions I would like to turn briefly to some passages from a text that reexamines the connections among racism, castration, and homosexuality, a text that attempts to bring into focus the contradictions inhabiting an "identity" burdened by its unsettlingly specular relation to a history that implicitly identifies identity (including its own identity as explanatory narrative) as a part (mis)taken for the whole.

III. In *Just Above My Head*, James Baldwin's last novel, the narrator, Hall Montana, struggles to come to terms with the death of his brother, Arthur, by reconstructing and intertwining the stories of four decades of their lives as they unfolded against the landscape of American "racial" strife. In one of the novel's many meditations on the difficulty of such narrative (re)constructions and the unreliability of historical understanding—meditations that self-consciously interrogate the authority of any voice claiming to know the meaning of its relation to the tale it tells—Baldwin's narrator observes:

> Memory is a strange vehicle. Or perhaps, *we* are the vehicle which carries the increasingly burdensome and mercurial passenger called memory. *I looked over Jordan.* Oh, yes, but the event, the moment, engraved in me, which *is* me more surely than my given name is me: escapes my memory. Memory is mercurial and selective, but passion welds life and death together, riding outside and making no judgment. *You* are, yourself, the judgment. (149)

The confusion to which this passage speaks is the confusion inherent in the effort to situate the subject who is speaking: the confusion, that is, of inside and outside exemplified here by the inability to determine whether memory is a vehicle in which we ought to imagine ourselves as being carried or if we, instead, are the vehicles that ought to be imagined as carrying it. As my phrasing suggests, this chiasmus associates the permeability of the boundary separating inside from outside with the undoing of the absolute distinction between the passive and the active voice. These acts of disarticulation, moreover, follow in the text from two attempts to assert identity through metaphoric definition ("memory is a strange vehicle"; "*we* are the vehicle"). If metaphor, however, is the vehicle, so to speak, in which this figural meditation on identity is conveyed, the tenor of the passage would seem to insist that such metaphoric knowledge, responding to a totalizing imperative, can only emerge through the perspectival distortions characteristic of synecdoche: that the definitions produced by metaphoric equations contain, that is, as an irreducible excess, the figurative mode within which they themselves already are contained. Like memory and the subject who remembers, then, metaphoric knowledge—the "truth" assertions or "identities" that metaphor produces—and the mediating figuration that is metaphor as such shift back and forth undecidably between container and thing contained, elaborating, thereby, the cognitive problematic not of metaphor but of synecdoche.[45] Indeed, the figural logic of this passage, more than the thematized topic of "memory," deserves to be acknowledged as what is most emphatically elusive or "mercurial" here; what slips away, what evades our grasp, is the fixed center, the regulating principle, that could make sense of the unstable spatial relations among memory, subjectivity, historical "event," and what the passage refers to as "passion."

Though the question of identity and essence inhabits the center of this meditation—as evidenced by the focus on that "which *is* me more surely than my given name is me"—the "event" that is constitutively "engraved in" us as the very origin of identity is not, in fact, this passage claims, to be found in memory at all. That "event," that determinant of identity inaccessible to the memory that identity is alternatively said to shape or be shaped by, gets defined, instead, through the difficult reference to "passion," which "welds life and death together, riding outside and making no judgment." Resisting the specular exchange in which memory and subjectivity continuously engage, "passion" here names the externality of desire: its historicity, its contingency. "Passion," in other words, designates the vast and incoherent complex of social forces that implants desire *in* us so that we misrecognize it *as* us; its salient attributes, therefore, are, first, its status as that which is always "outside"—even outside the symbolic binarism of life and death, which it "welds . . . together"—and, second, its refusal to pass judgment, to evaluate the historical effects of the various drives it encompasses and puts into play. We, upon whom the historical specificities of "the event, the moment" are engraved, *we* are those judgments, as this passage makes clear, both insofar as what we "are" is a judgment on the forces, the cultural histories and the libidinal rhetorics, whose operations produce us and insofar as the histories we produce in turn are the judgments we pass on the forces, the drives, that we projectively locate outside us; but the judgments that we "are" are never, as a consequence, our "own." Indeed, when Baldwin, in a typically chiastic phrasing from *Just Above My Head*, writes that people are "not only what their history has made of them, they are also what they make of their history" (483), he is not so much establishing a dichotomy of active and passive that preserves a space in which to celebrate autonomous subjectivity as he is implying that active agency itself is produced within, and determined by, the particularity of a history. As effects or fragmentary crystallizations of passions that always exceed us, we are "judgment[s]," then, insofar as our identities are totalizing readings that try to contain the passions within which they, and we, are already necessarily contained. Noting that "written history is, and must be, merely the vocabulary of power" (480), Baldwin points out that "the paradox, here, is that power, rooted in history, is also, the mockery and repudiation of history. The power to define the other seals one's definition of oneself—who, then, in such a fearful mathematic . . . is trapped?" (481). Whose power "trap[s]" or contains the other in the inescapable misrecognitions through which a particular history gives access to "definition" or identity?

By raising the question of judgment in relation to the social and psychic imperatives that compel us to internalize culturally elaborated identities as our own—that is, to internalize them as *ourselves*—Baldwin's discussion of memory and subjectivity harks back to the account of internalized judgment, of the self-mutilation attendant upon "always looking at oneself through the eyes of others," produced by W. E. B. Du Bois in his analysis of the African-American's struggle to embrace an identity that could reconcile the "warring ideals" that "American" and "Negro" denote. Baldwin, much later in *Just Above My Head,* makes explicit his novel's reliance on the account of identity and self-division formulated by Du Bois when he pointedly echoes the earlier writer's evocation of the "double-consciousness" that so pervasively shapes the African-American experience that, as Du Bois famously puts it, "The history of the American Negro is the history of this strife—this longing to attain self-conscious manhood." Baldwin's allusion to Du Bois, however, complicates the question of self-consciousness and manhood since its narrative motivation is Arthur's affair, while in Paris, with a white Frenchman named Guy: "And, indeed, for the very first time, and almost certainly because he is sitting in this unknown avenue, he puts the two words together *black American* and hears, at once, the very crescendo of contradiction and the unanswering and unanswerable thunder and truth of history—which is nothing more and nothing less than the beating of his own heart, his song" (473).

For Arthur, portrayed as gay throughout the novel, this interlude with Guy, occurring between the two most important erotic and emotional commitments of his life—those involving Crunch and Jimmy, both African-American men—brings him to an understanding of history (and thus of "racial" history) that draws upon the work of Du Bois but does so only to revise it. Where Du Bois offers hope that history will allow for a reconciliation of the divisive "double-consciousness" tormenting the black psyche and make possible the achievement of the coherent identity he defines as "self-conscious manhood," the passage from Baldwin reads history itself as the source of contradictions so profound and inescapable that we ourselves exist as their expression, as their effect, and the "unanswerable thunder" of history resounds as the "beating of [our] own heart[s], [our] song." Yet the contradiction that constitutes history for Baldwin recuperates or unpacks a contradiction already latent in the passage from Du Bois: the contradiction, discussed in detail above, that allows him to figure a resolution to the African-American condition of "double-consciousness" by reference to an idealized "manhood" itself depicted as "self-conscious." For Baldwin's novel appropriates from Du Bois his awareness of the painful division and alienation of a self-consciousness always already "doubled" as the mark of its penetration—indeed, its constitution—by the other: a doubling or division assuring that the judgments we "are" come always from somewhere else. It is not by mere accident, therefore, that Baldwin reiterates this idea in an essay first published as "Freaks and the American Ideal of Manhood" (later reprinted as "Here Be Dragons") or that in doing so he returns to the particular figure by which he describes the internalization of history in *Just Above My*

Head: "The object of one's hatred," he writes, "is never, alas, conveniently outside but is seated in one's lap, stirring in one's bowels and dictating the beating of one's heart."[46]

The tropological anatomy associating the "heart" with an otherness "seated in one's lap" or "stirring in one's bowels," or, as in the passage from the novel, with the "song" that emerges from one's mouth, suggests an eroticization of those specific body parts representing thresholds or zones of exchange between an inside and an outside, boundaries at which the narcissistic cathexis upon which identity depends is effected and threatened at once. Like a skin that might always *not* testify to the "racial" identity imagined precisely as its automatic, involuntary admission, these parts in which inside and outside commingle problematize the distinction between self and other that their intensified cathexis attempts to reinforce.[47] As the parts upon whose integrity the integrity of the whole synecdochically depends, they define the unity of identity, what Du Bois would affirm as "self-conscious manhood," as inseparable from the fetishization of those parts in which the "outside" already inheres.

The anxiety of an identity whose integrity is violated by the inescapable presence of the other within it, even though that otherness is needed for the constitution of identity itself, recalls Lacan's description of the mirror stage, which, as he puts it, eventuates in the "assumption of the armour of an alienating identity."[48] It should recall, as well, Fanon's suggestion that "it would indeed be interesting, on the basis of Lacan's theory of the *mirror period*, to investigate the extent to which the *imago* of his fellow built up in the young white at the usual age would undergo an imaginary aggression with the appearance of the Negro" (161). Now the psychoanalytic narrative according to which the visual observation of an organ (like the observation of the skin, the organ made to carry the ostensible mark of "racial" difference) produces, at a decisive moment, an experience of "aggression" against the *imago*, is not, of course, Lacan's mirror stage, but Freud's account of the castration complex. Interestingly, however, Fanon's text at this point refuses to specify whether the "aggression" against the imago experienced by the "young white" upon the "appearance of the Negro" assigns to the white man or the black man the psychic position ascribed to the "female" in the drama of castration. He does not tell us, that is, whether the black man enters the white man's field of vision as the image of bodily coherence that differentially interprets the white body as lacking, or as the image of that lack against which the white body must narcissistically defend. Insofar as Fanon goes on to insist that "for the white man The Other is perceived on the level of the body image, absolutely as the not-self—that is, the unidentifiable, the unassimilable" (161), he would seem to suggest that the "appearance of the Negro" impinges upon the white psyche and bodily ego much as the "recognition" of woman's "castration" impinges upon the psyche of the male: that the black body itself, in other words, becomes a repository for the "young white's" disavowed relation to embodiment as lack. But immediately before he proposes this reading, Fanon depicts the same relationship in antithetical terms. "At the extreme," he writes, "I would argue that the Negro, because of his body, impedes the closing of the postural schema of the white man—at the point, naturally, at which the black man makes his entry into the phenomenal world of the white man" (160). He expands upon this notion obliquely by offering a parenthetical analogy for the "influence exerted on the body by the appearance of another body. (Let us assume, for example, that four fifteen-year-old boys, all more or less athletic, are doing the high jump. One of them wins by jumping four feet ten inches. Then a fifth boy arrives and tops the mark by a half-inch. The four other bodies experience a destructuration)" (160–61). In this version it is clearly the "young white" who experiences a "destructuration" that draws its affective force from its allusion to the Freudian narrative of the female castration complex: in particular, from the moment in which the young girl, through her visual perception of the penis, comes to see herself as "castrated" and suffers, thereby, a narcissistic wound that reenacts the rupture, split, or "wound" inherent in the primal narcissism through which identity as "armour," as unfractured skin, is effected for Lacan.[49] If African-American "manhood," for Du Bois, is imperiled by the "double-consciousness" that responds to the self-alienating presence of the other—and the other's disapproving judgment—within, the assurance of white male identity that depends upon the impenetrability, the psychic and bodily coherence, of an external "armour" or skin finds itself similarly at risk, similarly self-alienated by an internalized act of judgment, or even, indeed, of measurement, when confronted, Fanon argues, like the young girl, by the visual image of "The Other's" body: in this case, that of "the Negro [who], because of his body, impedes the closing of the postural schema of the white man."

The figure of impeded closure here speaks to the persistence of an opening, a hole, in the protective "armour" of white male identity—a hole through which the integrity of the white man's body, which was secured by its difference from the black man construed as "the unidentifiable, the unassimilable," is now represented as subject to a violation, a destructuration, precipitating fears of psychic dismemberment. For that hole, that impeded closure, bespeaks the negation of the penis, the fetishized part in which the wholeness and coherence of the subject's identity is invested. Moreover, since the black man, according to Fanon, "is viewed as a penis symbol" (159), his threat to the white male "postural schema" cannot be dissociated from the homophobic anxiety provoked in the straight male psyche by the prospect of consignment to the passive position (or "posture") with which "castration" fantasmatically coincides. Thus the visual perception of the black man's "blackness" within a racist culture, like the mere representation of gay men or gay male sexuality in a homophobic regime, signifies for the dominant order as an act of aggression, an assault that sodomitically unmans the very body through which that dominant order represents itself;[50] for the eye compelled to "take in" such a vision paradigmatically experiences the involuntary penetration that the subject fears to suffer elsewhere.[51] The predictable psychic defense, therefore, requires a violent chiastic reversal of the passive and active positions, requires that the eye preemptively seek out what it fears to be made to take in and that the dominant order "castrate" those whom it fears to be castrated by.

The deformations, both psychic and physical, that such a defense must occasion, however, invariably stage what they seek to ward off: so thorough a determination or penetration of one's identity by the identity of the other that the "homosexualization" homophobically repudiated can seem, from an equally homophobic perspective, to be affirmed beyond dispute. Consider, for instance, how Baldwin frames, in *Just Above My Head*, his narrator's imagined but unvoiced response to those white Americans whose racism allows him no respite from uncertainty about his own safety or the safety of those he loves:

> Maybe the difference between us is that I've never been afraid of the prick you, like all men, carry between their legs and I never arranged picnics so that I could cut it off of you before large, cheering crowds. By the way, what did you do with my prick once you'd cut the black thing off and held it in your hands? You couldn't have bleached it—could you? You couldn't have cut yours off and sewn mine on? Is it standing on your mantelpiece now, in a glass jar, or did you nail it to the wall? Or did you eat it? How did it taste? Was it nourishing? (398)

In the reading of white racism offered here, Baldwin concurs with Fanon in construing it as betraying, in Fanon's words, "a feeling of impotence or sexual inferiority" (159); but Baldwin calls attention more emphatically to the complex exchange of inside and outside, self and other, that inheres in castration as the historic form in which white "racial" hatred found its grotesquely distinctive expression. The violent appropriation of the phallic part in an effort to make oneself "whole" participates, as the questions at the end of the passage cited above make clear, in a logic of internalization, of making oneself the "hole" through which it then becomes possible to take on or take in the part. Imagined as having incorporated or "eat[en]" the culturally fetishized black "prick," the representatives of white racism change places here with those African-American prisoners described in *Beloved* and *Tell Me How Long the Train's Been Gone* as subject to the threat of having to take in orally the "pricks" of their oppressive white guards. This passage, like the passages from the other two novels, could be read, therefore, as interpreting white racism in terms that link it conceptually, for the normative straight-identified reader, with an image most frequently employed to figure "homosexuality," terms that reinforce, in the process, Fanon's categorical, and categorically homophobic, generalization that "the Negrophobic man is a repressed homosexual." Yet if we pause for a moment to allow for a closer analysis of Fanon's text, it may be possible not only to call into question the ground on which he bases his assertion but also to bring into sharper focus Baldwin's distance from that assertion in *Just Above My Head.*

Discussing the definition of "phobia" in order to explicate his statement that for the dominant subject in a racist culture "the Negro is phobogenic" (154), Fanon explains that the phobic object is one that arouses "both fear and revulsion" (154). Proceeding to describe the fear of the black man experienced by racists, both male and female, as "a terror mixed with sexual revulsion" (155), he contends that this revulsion must "in no case be taken literally" (156), that whenever the phobic object becomes the occasion for such powerful emotions we are "observing a complete inversion" (156) of affect that represents the ego's self-defense through the mechanism of denial. From within this logic he is able to conclude that "the Negrophobic woman is in fact nothing but a putative sexual partner—just as the Negrophobic man is a repressed homosexual." How, then, should the reader interpret Fanon's own subsequent remark, offered in response to Michel Salomon's avowal that black men give off an "aura of sensuality"? "I have a confession to make to you," Fanon declares in an apostrophe to Salomon, "I have never been able, without revulsion, to hear a *man* say of another man: 'He is so sensual!'" (201). Must we read *this* "revulsion" from the phobic object (the "homosexual" man) as the sign of a "complete inversion" of affect that subjects Fanon himself to characterization as "a repressed homosexual," or can we acknowledge that to do so would merely perpetuate the identification, itself homophobic, of homophobia with homosexuality (however qualified as "repressed") in order to construct it as alien to an authentically heterosexual orientation? The agonistic relation to the penis, after all, as expressed by the conflation of violence and desire that marks the scene of castration, reflects, as Baldwin and Fanon allow us in different ways to recognize, the constitutive incoherence that marks heterosexual masculinity itself.

Fanon, for instance, may argue that, for the "Negrophobic" man, "the Negro is the incarnation of a genital potency beyond all moralities and prohibitions" (177)—which means, to put it more simply, that the black man "is turned into a penis" (170); but he also acknowledges that black men, self-alienated by their acculturation within a racist society, may internalize a fantasmatic white identity that signifies, as he puts it, the desire "to be a man" (216). White men and black men, in other words, in ways that are crucial for relations between the "races," anxiously identify "maleness" as an attribute associated, though associated differently for each, with the condition of the other. The essentializing white fantasy of the black male's intensified biological potency and virility, which makes possible the racist reduction of black men to the status of genital part, finds its chiastic inversion in the black recognition of the arbitrary arrangement of political power that grants white men, as part of the social body, the authority to stand for the whole. A desire, on the one hand, for the imaginary biological or material potency of the penis is thus matched by a desire, on the other hand, for the symbolic privilege of the phallus. And this homophobically elaborated chiasmus of desire that pivots upon the confusion of synecdoche and metaphor in the misrecognition (at root catachrestic) of penis as phallus, of organ as Law, does not in either case testify to the truth of a repressed homosexual identity, but defines, instead, the characteristic structure of straight male subjectivity. It responds, in other words, to the organizing imperative of heterosexual masculinity, decisively shaped as it is by the terroristic logic of castration, to distinguish between antithetical conditions of either having or being the phallus: a distinction that finds its corollary in the heterosexual imperative to erect a protective barrier between what is imagined to be the straight male *identification with* and what is imagined to be the gay male *desire for* the penis/phallus.[52] Fanon's homophobic interjection, however, like the homophobia through which "race" relations are commonly articulated by white men and black men both, demonstrates that this is a barrier more honored in its breach than in its observance; for the difference between identification and desire, especially for a culture that persistently bullies all men into desiring the "appropriate" masculine identification, can never be secure enough to escape the need for the relentless disciplinary reinforcement that bespeaks its conceptual fragility. The chiastic crossing of penile/phallic identification and desire thus returns us to the self-deconstructing notion of a "manhood" that could be "self-conscious" and internally coherent or unfractured at once, which is, as Baldwin writes with reference to "whiteness" as a racial identity, "not a conceivable condition, but a terrifying fantasy, a moral choice" that can signify only as a mode of phobic exclusion; for one can say of straight sexuality in relation to homosexual possibilities exactly what Baldwin says of whiteness in its diacritical relation to the construct of "blackness": "nobody has . . . ever *wanted* to be white, unless they were afraid of being black" (515).

Returning, then, to Baldwin's reflections on castration in *Just Above My Head*, while it may appear, given his suggestion that the mutilation of black men arises from the racist's desire to "eat," to incorporate orally, their "pricks," that he is merely aligning white racism, once again, with homosexuality—an appearance that would find some additional support in the novel's explicit association of Birmingham and Sodom (183)—Baldwin counters the homophobic implications of such an alignment by juxtaposing against it the depiction of gay male relations that enact a logic at odds with the synecdochic essentialism of castration.[53] One need only consider, in this regard, how Baldwin, as if to provide a contrast with the brutally self-ignorant (hetero)sexual relation of white men to black men—and to the black man's penis—as played out in the scene of castration, describes Arthur Montana as he first performs oral sex on another man:

> Arthur's tongue descended Crunch's long black self, down to the raging penis. He licked the underside of the penis, feeling it leap, and he licked the balls. He was setting Crunch free—he was giving Crunch what he, somehow, knew that Crunch longed and feared to give him. He took the penis into his mouth, it moved, with the ease of satin past his lips, into his throat. For a moment, he was terrified: what now? (208)

The prospect that terrifies liberates too—liberates (though only, in this case, temporarily) from the terrorism of a culturally mandated homophobia that penetrates male subjectivity, producing modern "masculinity" as such, in order to demonize thereafter the very possibility of being penetrated. For Arthur and Crunch, then, to be set free—the language, of course, must resonate in the context of African-American history—means to experience their manhood as something more than "an embattled, a bloodstained thing" (342), to experience it not as perpetually contested in their relations with other men (and therefore, necessarily, as the narcissistic "stake" in any erotic relations with women), but as something another man can enter into, can actually enable them to realize, if he can overcome the "self-conscious[ness]" of his manhood and thus overcome the homophobic anxiety that Baldwin, recalling Du Bois once again, describes as "the double weight of the judgment without and the judgment within" (244).

Yet as black men already burdened by the "double-consciousness" that reflects their historical determination by the demand that they *be* the part, the "tool," that white men alone can *have*, Arthur and Crunch, at the moment of their erotic and emotional involvement with one another, risk psychic annihilation through the double dismemberment of synecdochic logic; violently reduced by the racist synecdoche that takes genital part for the whole, they are subject as well to the distinctly homophobic rewriting of synecdoche that polices "masculinity" by decreeing that the (male) "part" can *only* properly "stand" for the (female) "hole." Given its ominous doubling of the "double-consciousness" that splits black identity, it is appropriate that this moment of sexual discovery—mixing as it does both terror and liberation—should take place while Arthur and Crunch are performing in a gospel quartet on a tour of the South. This juxtaposition of a repressive political geography against "the vast and unmapped geography of himself" (301) that Arthur first dares to negotiate in his sexual relation with Crunch reinforces the novel's analysis of racism as congruent with homophobia rather than with homosexuality, and it links the "racial" paranoia instilled in the gospel quartet by their consciousness in the South of "the eyes which endlessly watch them" (186) with the homographic anxiety that Arthur will feel when, after his intimacy with Crunch, he starts to wonder "if his change was visible" (226).[54] Crunch will go mad and Arthur die young as a consequence of internalizing the abjectifying judgments, both racist and homophobic, of the culture around them: internalized judgments that condemn them for engaging in other acts of "internalization"—acts in which their bodies open up to take in the phallic signifier to which they will thereby be viewed as having ceded any legitimate claim.

Before being crushed by the weight of those judgments, though, Arthur and Crunch will know moments of freedom, moments that Arthur, years later, will rediscover with Jimmy and with Guy, in which they affirm the possibility of a "manhood" predicated on their shedding the deforming self-consciousness of a "masculinity" enacted through a performative display of homophobia:

> [Arthur] had never done this before. In the same way that he knew how Crunch feared to be despised—by him—he knew, too, that he, now, feared to be despised by Crunch. *Cocksucker.*
>
> Well. It was Crunch's cock, so he sucked it; with all the love that was in him, and a moment came when he felt that love being trusted, and returned. A moment came when he felt Crunch pass from a kind of terrified bewilderment into joy. A friendly, a joyful movement, began. *So high, you can't get over him.* (208)

Appropriating the language of a gospel hymn, Arthur testifies to the salvational potential he locates in this access to a "manhood" whose meaning is decisively rewritten in this transformative "moment"; but the healing of the divided psyche that such a salvation could effect requires a trust, indeed, a faith, sufficient to withstand the world's reprobation. Not so much troping on the gospel songs that give voice to the emotional strength of the black church as discovering within them a different meaning, adequate to the expression of a different experience, Baldwin does more than merely acknowledge the eros inhabiting the language of religious surrender and redemption—an acknowledgment upon which he predicated the ambiguous resolution of *Go Tell It On the Mountain.* He suggests, beyond this, that the "new" identity into which Arthur and Crunch can be born again is one mutually determining and relational, effected not through a fortification of boundaries but through a willingness to allow the boundaries of their identities to be penetrated:

> Crunch lay on his belly for Arthur and pulled Arthur into him, and Arthur lay on his belly for Crunch, and Crunch entered Arthur—it was incredible that it hurt so much, and yet, hurt so little, that so profound an anguish, thrusting so hard, so deep, accomplished such a transformation, *I looked at my hands and they looked new, I looked at my feet and they did, too!* But that is how they sang, really, something like fifteen minutes later, out of the joy of their surrender and deliverance, out of their secret knowledge that each contained the other. (213)

When Baldwin's narrator, in a passage discussed earlier, sought a figure through which to characterize the logical connection between memory and subjectivity in the representation of identity, he could only imagine as incompatible alternatives either one or the other as the vehicle in which its counterpart was contained. Here, however, the synecdochic logic that permits the substitution of part for whole, or container for thing contained, opens onto a figure that refutes the positional stability of inside and outside upon which synecdoche, however it tropes upon it, nonetheless relies. The assertion that "each contained the other," though subject to literalistic interpretation as referring to the way in which each now carries in his body the other's sperm or seed, proposes, in fact, the possibility of a male identity no longer dependent for its self-constitution on phobic exclusions—a possibility almost as unimaginable within the terms of our cultural logic as is the geometry of two non-identical objects each of which contains the other while being contained, at the same time, within it.[55] Sameness and difference, from such a perspective, lose their difference without becoming the same.[56] Inhabiting one another, these terms come to designate, when used to elaborate a particular relation, the contingency or historicity of any reading, of any act that confers identity; they bespeak the emergence of meaningful, recognizable shape or definition as the fractionalizing articulation of a context that, because it resists being totalized, always exceeds its representation. They name, in other words, the terms of a necessarily synecdochic misrecognition whereby the self-sameness of identity, the always *fantasmatic* totalization of its coherence, signifies only *through* and *as* the fetishization of its parts. Expressing, in every sense of the term, the *partiality* of the interpretations of "identity" constituted through the relations they define, sameness and difference draw the line between inside and outside, self and other, with all the arbitrariness of the shifting borders that determine, for example, the national authority to which a given population, at any moment, owes its taxes, if not its allegiance.

To the extent, then, that Arthur and Crunch reinterpret "manhood," and thus, in Western terms, subjectivity in its paradigmatic form, as the ability to incorporate what is "foreign" without experiencing a loss of integrity, and without being constrained by the (hetero)sexist either/or logic of active and passive, they point to the partial understanding of "manhood" that passes in dominant culture for the whole, and they disarticulate the coercive "wholeness" of an identity based on fantasmatic identification with a part. They thus make visible to the novel's reader the invisible operation of *différance* that destabilizes every signifier, offering a glimpse of the process through which a signifier like "manhood" can communicate the singularity of a fixed identity only where a community of "readers" has learned how *not* to see the differences within that identity and its signifier both. "Perhaps history," as Baldwin suggests, "is not to be found in our mirrors, but in our repudiations: perhaps the other is ourselves"; and as if generalizing from the mutual containment of Arthur in Crunch and Crunch in Arthur, Baldwin expands on this supposition by declaring: "Our history is each other. That is our only guide. One thing is absolutely certain: one can repudiate, or despise, no one's history without repudiating and despising one's own. Perhaps that is what the gospel singer is singing" (481).

Fittingly, in light of this last remark, Arthur and Crunch confirm their new understanding of "identity" by performing gospel songs and hymns identical to those they sang before they began their erotic involvement. Now, however, what is patently the same is also, and at the same time, different; as Arthur and Crunch contain each other, so, too, do the various "meanings" of their apparently identical songs. Like the homographic sameness of two signifiers, visually indistinguishable from one another—signifiers that are actually products of different histories and etymologies—the "same" text now exhibits discontinuous, potentially contradictory, meanings that reflect its determination through contiguity to different parts of the context that contains it.[57] Thus the spiritual devotion implicit in "*So high, you can't get over him*" cohabits with the homoerotic specificity of the song's performance by Arthur and Crunch. And just as Arthur, contemplating the aftertaste of Crunch's ejaculation into his mouth, is "frightened, but triumphant" and wants, as Baldwin declares, "to sing" (209), so the experience of singing in the novel comes to figure the erotic exchange of inside and outside, the taking in and giving back of a language seen as the prototype of the "foreign" substance that penetrates, and constitutes, identity.

As the very machinery of difference, however, language, for Lacan, differentiates the symbolic from an imaginary associated with a fantasmatic relation of closeness or sameness. But what, exactly, *is* the difference between symbolic difference and imaginary sameness when the latter can only be understood or known through the differentiating language of the symbolic, and the former can only be cathected by appropriating the affect of the imaginary? Indeed, while language may be a privileged symbol of the symbolic order itself—the counterpart to the phallus through which symbolic identity is articulated—it operates, nonetheless, through the investment of contiguity, the differential arbitrariness of the signifier, with the paradigmatic force of imaginary sameness and presence. In this way the metonymy that is language acquires the capacity to generate the metaphoric meaningfulness that constitutes identity only through the mediation of a synecdoche that allows us to internalize language as part of ourselves, thus enabling us to represent it as something we contain, not something containing us. The synecdoche that makes language a part of us may thus make us a part of the symbolic, but only by predicating every act of relationality that language will permit not on the production of those differences through which language as a system operates, but on the imaginary misrecognition of particular aspects of "difference" as conceptually the "same" through the displacement of narcissistic libido onto certain aspects of social "otherness"—perhaps most notably, onto language itself as the very medium of our subjectivity.

Yet as the history of colonial relations shows, the alienation that can attend culturally specific recognitions that one's language is not one's own—that it is, instead, the mark of one's status as subordinate, or even as "owned"—can generate a fatal sense of oneself as possessed, and thus as a possession. Henry Louis Gates, Jr. recounts a striking example in the death of Edmond Laforest, "a prominent member of the Haitian literary movement called La Ronde," who, "with an inimitable, if fatal, flair for the grand gesture, stood upon a bridge, calmly tied a Larousse dictionary around his neck, then leapt to his death. While other black writers, before and after Laforest, have been drowned artistically by the weight of various modern languages, Laforest chose to make his death an emblem of this relation of overwhelming indenture."[58] For Laforest, as for those historically subjected to colonial rule more generally, the symbolic order into which their internalization of a colonizing language admits them, is one in which they are given identities that cast them as representatives of a discredited imaginary whose attributes, as viewed by the symbolic, include irrationality, sensual immediacy, and an immature or narcissistic eros inadequately mediated by cultural law. But if the Lacanian symbolic coincides with the disruption of the imaginary's "immature" dyadic relations through the intervention of a third term, the phallus that enshrines the Name-of-the-Father—the term that governs, thereafter, language as systematic articulation—the fracturing of what was whole (a fracturing that is at the "origin" of the symbolic) can be seen as that against which the symbolic constitutively defends by establishing itself as a network for the mastery of loss through substitution; what is repudiated in (and as) the imaginary is precisely, in other words, the coherence or sameness to which the symbolic order itself aspires through its totalizing system of differentiations. What, after all, is signified by the phobic exclusions that characterize the armored identity conferred by the symbolic if not a desire for a wholeness or integrity that can only be effected by means of a purifying act of separation and division?[59]

To enter into language is always, therefore, to be sundered into identity and to be imbued with a need to defend that identity as a bulwark against the negativity, the endless differentiation, of the language (in which) one has become. While this is no less true for dominant subjects than for those subjects colonized by their internalization of the language, ideology, or social relations of a culture that projectively devalues them, the effects of this recognition, as Houston A. Baker, Jr., points out, are quite different:

> If one claims, following a post-structuralist line, that to possess the "gift" of language is to be possessed, then one immediately situates him- or herself in a domain familiar to the diaspora. *Possession* operates both in the spirit work of voodoo and in the dread slave and voodoo economics perpetuated by the West. What is involved in possession, in either case, is supplementarity—the immediately mediating appearance, as specter or shadow, of a second and secondary "self." In specifically diasporic terms, "being possessed" (as slave, but also as a BEING POSSESSED) is more than a necessary doubling or inscribed "Otherness" of the *con-scripted* (those who come, as necessity, *with* writing). For in the diaspora, the possessed are governed not simply by *script* but also by productive conditions that render their entire play a *tripling*.[60]

Baker uses the concept of "tripling" to describe the condition of the colonized subject who, like Caliban in *The Tempest* when he curses those others who taught him the language through which he comes to curse himself *as* other, "is aware of a cursed 'self' cursing a notion of 'self'" that renders any resistant identity, any *other* self, "alienating and fearful" (393). Rather than represent this situation as the incapacitating double-bind of what Du Bois calls "double-consciousness," Baker proposes the act of tripling to break the deadlock of "a discourse radically overdetermined by the dualism of self-and-other" (382). "Supraliteracy," however, the name that Baker proposes for this "liberating" (382) third term, does not so much undo the self/other dyad as give another turn to the screw of their relation in which stigma continues to attach to the "passive" position of *getting* screwed. Denoting, after all, as Baker puts it, "the committed scholar's 'vernacular' invasion and transcendence of fields of colonizing discourse in order to destroy whitemale hegemony" (382), "supraliteracy" continues to figure internalization or invasion by the "other" as an act of appropriation that "destroy[s]."[61] This is not to suggest, by any means, that "supraliteracy," especially in its privileging of a vernacular idiom consisting of "sounds which have been taken for crude hooting, but which are, in reality, racial poetry" (394), is not a critically valuable strategy of resistance and empowerment; it is to argue, rather, that "supraliteracy" recurs to the logic by which identity signifies a coherence linked to the unviolated integrity of the borders defining an autonomous self.

Baldwin's novel offers no imitable social vision of how the phobic resistance to penetration through which the identity of the subject is constructed can be displaced by a receptivity, a non-exclusivity, that would *not* be destructive in its undoing of identity as we know it. For Baldwin as for Baker "invasion" must "destroy" the "hegemony" of constituted identities in a repetitive enactment of the dominant logic that predicates social reality on the ego's aggressively paranoid insistence on its coherence and autonomy. Baldwin's narrative, therefore, depicts Arthur and Crunch succumbing to the self-alienating force of the internalized homophobia that tears them apart as soon as Crunch feels the need for "some unassailable corroboration of his manhood"—a manhood that Arthur, from Crunch's perspective, can, by that time, "only . . . menace" (447). For his part, to the very moment of his death, Arthur, despite almost fourteen years of intimacy with Jimmy, realizes that he "will never be released from the judgment, or the terror, in his own eyes" (555). If neither Crunch nor Arthur can survive his openness to penetration by the other, if that openness leaves both of them vulnerable to the internal divisions that attend their penetration by homophobic ideologies, the novel, and Baldwin, remain committed nonetheless to the hope of dismantling the armored identities that keep self and other, inside and outside, resolutely, if arbitrarily, distinct. *Just Above My Head* insists on the necessary permeability of such identities, even in the face of its candid acknowledgment of the risks such permeability can entail; and it offers, near the end, a paradigm for that receptive openness to what is "foreign" when its narrator, Hall Montana, who presents the novel as his attempt to make sense of his relation to his brother and his brother's life, does, as he says, "what [he] ha[s] most feared to do: surrender[s] [his] brother to Jimmy, give[s] Jimmy's piano the ultimate solo" (550). He allows his narrative authority to give way to that of his brother's lover, whose voice penetrates the text to assume, for a few pages, the authorial "I." Opening to incorporate Jimmy, ceding, or merging, its subjectivity with his, Hall's text accepts its internal difference, embraces an identity as that which is not identical to itself, and affirms thereby, the concluding words of Baldwin's essay, "Here Be Dragons"—the concluding words, as well, of his collected non-fiction, *The Price of the Ticket*: "each of us, helplessly and forever, contains the other—male in female, female in male, white in black and black in white. We are a part of each other. Many of my countrymen appear to find this fact exceedingly inconvenient and even unfair, and so, very often do I. But none of us can do anything about it."[62] Baldwin's articulation of "race" in terms of homosexuality may suggest, in this context, that insofar as each of us, like Arthur and Crunch, invariably "contains the other," we are none of us ever properly to be viewed as part, or "hole," or whole. For to "contain each other" and to be "part of each other" name conditions that, while they are not the same, are not wholly different either—though just where difference gives way to sameness and sameness turns into difference neither can, nor should, be defined. Identity—including racial and sexual identity—depends upon the fracture or refraction of unarticulated sameness into the language of difference that would compensate for, and disavow, its partiality; it depends, that is, on the totalization that misrecognizes part for whole in order to create the fiction of the ego, and the subject, as fixed and real. But "shades cannot be fixed," as Baldwin notes in *Just Above My Head*, "color is, eternally, at the mercy of the light" (483).

Part II

Equations, Identities, and "AIDS"

4

THE PLAGUE OF DISCOURSE

Politics, Literary Theory, and "AIDS"

I. In "The Metaphor of AIDS," an article published for a popular audience in the Sunday magazine of the *Boston Globe*, Lee Grove, an instructor of creative writing and American literature at the University of Massachusetts, reflects on the ways in which the "AIDS" epidemic has altered his understanding of literary texts and his relation to the teaching of literature. Referring specifically to the Renaissance pun that brought together, at least linguistically, the experiences of orgasm and death, Grove writes:

> 'To die,' 'to have sex'—that coupling has always been figurative, metaphorical, sophisticated wordplay, a literary conceit, one of those outrageous paradoxes dear to the heart of a racy divine like John Donne.
>
> Outrageous no longer. The coupling isn't figurative anymore. It's literal.[1]

My purpose in the pages that follow is to consider the highly charged exchange between the literal and the figural as it informs the discussion of "AIDS" in America and to explore the political uses to which the ideological framing of the relationship between the two has been put. Toward that end my subtitle locates "literary theory" between the categories of "politics" and "AIDS" to indicate my belief that both of those categories produce, and are produced as, historical discourses susceptible to analysis by the critical methodologies associated with literary theory.

This is not to say that literary theory occupies some unproblematic or privileged position in the course of my discussion; to the contrary, I want to insist that literature, including that form of literature that is literary theory, is by no means distinct from political discourse, and thus from either the discourse on "AIDS," or the politics that governs the discourse on "AIDS." By the same token, politics and "AIDS" cannot be disentangled from their implication in the linguistic or the rhetorical. Indeed, one of the ideological oppositions that this essay would call into question is that whereby the biological, associated with the literal or the "real," is counterposed against the literary, associated with the figural or the fictive. That opposition is already deeply and unavoidably political, which is to say, it bespeaks an ideologically determined hierarchy of values in which power—the power to speak seriously, to speak with authority, and to influence policy—is very much at stake in the claim to speak literally, and thus to speak, as popular idiom would have it, the "literal truth."

To trace the direction of the remarks that follow, I will argue, in contrast to the position asserted in the quotation from Lee Grove's article, that the "AIDS" epidemic is not to be construed as a literal encounter with the defiguralization that characterizes the Lacanian real, but rather, and more dangerously, as a construction made to figure the annihilation as which the eruption of the real, at least as imagined from within the symbolic order of language and social relations, must always be experienced. It serves, therefore, as the breeding ground for any number of figural associations or projections whose virulence derives precisely from their naturalized presentation under the aspect of literality. Indeed, I will be suggesting that the most disturbing feature of the Western discourse on "AIDS" is the way in which the literal is recurrently and tendentiously produced as a figure whose figurality remains strategically occluded—and thus as a figure that can be used to effect the most repressive political ends.

What I will be arguing, to put it more bluntly, is that the unremittingly hysterical terms within which the Western discussion of "AIDS" has been conducted reflect an untenable, but politically manipulable, belief that we can separate biological science, and the social policy that draws on that science, from the instability and duplicity that literary theory locates in the operations of language. I want, therefore, to consider the discursive production of and reaction to the epidemic of "AIDS" in the West insofar as it makes visible the interrelation between the language of politics and the politics of language, to consider, in other words, how the terms of the discourse that properly *constitutes* "AIDS" are implicated in ideological operations that can work at cross-purposes to the explicit political agendas of those who attempt to deploy them against the dominant institutions of power. Toward that end I will be focusing primarily on the relations among three things: the metaphors through which the language of biology gives us access to the operations of the body; the culturally specific and phobically inflected identifications of homosexuality with illness and contagion; and the poststructural analysis of figurative language and its effects upon our understandings of literary and cultural texts.

II. Though my subject necessarily involves literature and "AIDS," my focus falls not on those literary works wherein the urgency of "AIDS" achieves thematic inscription, but rather on the inevitable inscriptions of the literary in the discourse on "AIDS" itself. The text that provides the occasion for my analysis, the text on which my remarks will turn or trope, is a relatively brief and familiar one: "Silence=Death." This slogan has achieved wide currency, particularly—though by no means exclusively—within the gay community, both as a challenge to the murderously postponed and cynically inadequate official responses to "AIDS" and as a rallying cry for those who have borne the burden of care-taking, suffering, and death, calling upon them to defend themselves against the dangerous discourse of mastery produced by medical or legislative authorities attempting to defend their *own* vested interests in the face of this epidemic. It is important to note, in this context, that issues of defense achieve an almost inevitable centrality in the discursive framing of "AIDS" in ways that differentiate the "meanings" of this epidemic from those of others. Because the syndrome itself attacks the body's mechanisms of defense; because once it does so science as yet can offer no defense against it; because in the West it has appeared primarily among groups already required to defend themselves against the toxic intolerance of the dominant order; because the scientific establishment and the national political institutions that fund the scientific establishment feel called upon to defend their professional prestige against the questioning of medical authority that has been occasioned by this disease; because individuals and groups have sought to defend themselves, often with appalling acts of violence, against any contact with "AIDS" or those they construe as embodiments of it; and because some politicians, in order to defend against political opposition, deploy the "AIDS" issue strategically to ensure their political survival; for all of these reasons the question of defense is inextricable from, and decisively informs, any consideration of "AIDS." And as this preliminary formulation of the issues suggests, my interest here is in the complex interactions among notions of discourse, defense, and disease—particularly as these notions intersect with the homophobic construction and deployment of homosexuality in the West to converge at the virulent site of discursive contention that is "AIDS."

These last words seem to define "AIDS" in a way that few in the medical profession would recognize, so let me offer at the outset a definition of "AIDS" that will seem more literal, or more "proper." According to current scientific understanding, and I hasten to add that it is not my intention necessarily to endorse that understanding, "AIDS" results from infection with some quantity of HIV or Human Immunodeficiency Virus, which attacks the cells of the immune system, particularly the T-helper or T-4 cells, and impairs the body's ability to defend itself against viral, fungal, and parasitic infections. Medical researchers would thus characterize "AIDS" as an infectious condition in which the stake is "literally" the possibility of defense, the possibility of maintaining the integrity of the organism's regulatory differentiation from what is not itself. As David Black puts it in *The Plague Years*, his anecdotal "chronicle" of "AIDS," "the immune system is the body's complex and still imperfectly understood defense mechanism. Its job is to tell the difference between Self and Not-Self."[2] I will come back to the Emersonian implications of this description of the immune response, but for now I want to examine the notion of defense and its importance not only in the bio-logic articulated within the organism by "AIDS" but also in the reactive or defensive discourse of "Silence=Death." For while that slogan urges those in the communities most immediately affected by "AIDS" to defend themselves, it does so by appealing to defensive properties that it implicitly locates in discourse itself. The slogan, most frequently depicted in a graphic configuration that positions its text, in white, beneath a pink triangle on a field of black, alludes, after all, to the active, officially organized Nazi campaign against homosexuals (identified in the concentration camps by the pink triangle they were required to wear) in order to propose a gay equivalent to the post-Holocaust motto popular among Jewish activists: "Never again." At the same time, "Silence=Death" can be read as a post-"AIDS" revision of a slogan widely used in the gay community some years ago—"Out of the closets and into the streets"—and as such it similarly implies that language, discourse, public manifestations, and the production of identity are necessary weapons of defense in a contemporary strategy of gay survival. For if we claim that "Silence=Death," then one corollary to this theorem in the geometry governing the relationship among discourse, defense, and disease is that language, articulation, the intervention of voice, can be salutary, vivifying: that discourse can defend against the death that must result from the continuation of our silence.

But to speak of mechanisms of defense, particularly in terms of linguistic operations, is necessarily to invoke the specter of Freud, who offered a taxonomy of psychic defenses in his studies of the unconscious and its operations. And here, as always, Freud calls into question the basis for any naive optimism about the success of our defensive maneuvers. I would like, therefore, to cite at this point a passage from H.D.'s memoir of her own psychoanalysis by Freud that speaks to the relation between discourse and defense in a particularly telling way. Only once, according to H.D., did Freud ever "lay down the law" and that was when he said "never—I mean, never at any time, in any circumstance, endeavor to defend me, if and when you hear abusive remarks made about me and my work." H.D. then goes on to recall, "He explained it carefully. He might have been giving a lesson in geometry or demonstrating the inevitable course of a disease once the virus has entered the system. At this point, he seemed to indicate (as if there were a chart of the fever patient, pinned on the wall before us), at the least suggestion that you may be about to begin a counter-argument in my defense, the anger or frustration of the assailant will be driven deeper. You will do no good to the detractor by mistakenly beginning a logical defense. You will drive the hatred or the fear or the prejudice in deeper."[3] Defense here is necessarily failed defense; far from being salubrious, it serves only to compromise further one's immunity and to stimulate greater virulence. Interestingly enough, this corresponds to the process through which, some medical researchers suggest, HIV moves from a state of latency within an infected cell to a state of active reproduction. The defensive "stimulation of an immune response" seems to be one of "the conditions that activates the production of new" HIV that can then go on to invade and infect other cells.[4] As this implies, defensive maneuvers may inadvertently disseminate or intensify infection.

Significantly, Freud's psychological argument in warning H.D. against engaging in defensive interventions on his behalf echoes the medical advice dispensed centuries earlier by Plato in the *Timaeus.* Writing specifically about the wisdom of pharmacological efforts to defend the body against disease, Plato sounds a cautionary note: "diseases unless they are very dangerous should not be irritated by medicines, since every form of disease is in a manner akin to the living being, whose complex frame has an appointed term of life. . . . And this holds also of the constitution of diseases; if anyone regardless of his appointed time tries to subdue them by medicine, he only aggravates and multiplies them."[5] The word here translated as "medicine" derives, as Jacques Derrida writes in "Plato's Pharmacy," from the Greek word *pharmakon*, signifying a drug or philter occupying an ambiguous position as remedy and poison at once (70). Commenting on this passage from Plato, Derrida observes: "Just as health is auto-nomous and auto-matic, 'normal' disease demonstrates its autarky by confronting the pharmaceutical aggression with *metastatic* reactions which displace the site of the disease, with the eventual result that the points of resistance are reinforced and multiplied."[6] Thus for Plato, as for Freud, gestures of defense can aggravate rather than alleviate one's condition. Freud, of course, is referring explicitly to language or discourse as a mechanism of defense against one's enemies or detractors; H.D. alludes to the "course of a disease once the virus has entered the system" only as a figural embellishment. Plato, on the other hand, is referring explicitly to medical defenses against disease. But as Derrida argues in "Plato's Pharmacy," considerations of discourse are decisively at issue in Plato's discussion as well. I would like, therefore, to digress for a moment in order to make clearer just what is at stake in Plato's notion of the *pharmakon* as read by Derrida.

In the long and complicated argument that he unfolds in "Plato's Pharmacy," Derrida shows how Plato identifies writing, in the *Phaedrus*, with the *pharmakon*, thus rendering it simultaneously a poison, a remedy, a magical philter, and a rational medical technology. If writing as *pharmakon* is already, at the beginning of Western culture, producing an entanglement of literary and medical discourse, its antithesis, the self-presence or self-identity of speech, is associated by Plato with the vital force as which he views *logos*. Derrida characterizes this aspect of Plato's thought in the following words:

> *Logos* is a *zoon*. An animal that is born, grows, belongs to the *phusis*. Linguistics, logic, dialectics, and zoology are all in the same camp.
>
> In describing *logos* as a *zoon*, Plato is following certain rhetors and sophists before him who, as a contrast to the cadaverous rigidity of writing, had held up the living spoken word.[7]

Derrida's strategy in deconstructing the opposition between speech and writing is to show how the living word of speech is itself already informed by a certain type of writing, by differential articulation, by an *archi-écriture*. But of particular importance for my purposes here is the way in which Derrida's reading of Plato insists upon the inextricability of the textual and the biological even as it uses rhetorical or literary analysis to call into question the logocentrism of the Western philosophical tradition.

To return from this digression, let me cite once again Derrida's gloss on Plato's wariness about the *pharmakon* in the *Timaeus*. "Just as health," Derrida writes, "is auto-nomous and auto-matic, 'normal' disease demonstrates its autarky by confronting the pharmaceutical aggression with *metastatic* reactions which displace the site of the disease, with the eventual result that the points of resistance are reinforced or multiplied." Now bearing in mind that Derrida's reading of the *pharmakon* explicitly attends to the critical conjunction of discourse and biology informing the Platonic opposition between writing as supplement and *logos* as *zoon*, or speech as living word, this suggests that defensive strategies deployed—in the realm of discourse or disease—to combat agencies of virulence may themselves be informed by the virulence they are seeking to efface, informed by it in ways that do not produce the immunizing effect of a vaccine, but that serve, instead, to reinforce and even multiply the dangerous sites of infection. In that case we might do well to return to "Silence=Death" in order to reexamine the ideology at work in its alignment of discourse and defense.

Before doing so, however, let me briefly reformulate what I hope to have suggested thus far, and let me do so by presenting a number of formulae that reproduce, like mutations, the rhetorical form of "Silence=Death." My first move was to trope upon or translate that text into its implicit corollary, Discourse=Defense, and trope, as I would pause here only long enough to note, is itself, as Harold Bloom reminds us in his interpretations of Freud, the very essence and meaning of defense. In response to this equation of discourse with defense, I adduced Freud's admonitory words to H.D., words that I would read here as serving, in effect, to suggest the possibility that Defense=Disease. Finally, I invoked Derrida's analysis of the *pharmakon* as that which occupies simultaneously the position of pathogen and remedy, even as it straddles the realms of the biological and the linguistic, and which therefore allows us to perceive an identity that I would translate as implying that Disease=Discourse, an identity already implicit in the argument of "Plato's Pharmacy," especially when Derrida remarks that "metaphoricity is the contamination of logic and the logic of contamination."[8] This last formulation, of course, makes clear that the rationalism of philosophical logic—a rationalism that provides the foundation for Western medical and scientific practice—is not untainted by the figurality that philosophy repudiates as literary, and, in consequence, as deceptive, inessential, and, because threatening to the "truth" of its literality, as expendable. Both logic and contamination, then, are very much at stake in the unfolding of these infectiously multiplying equations. Perhaps by returning to the germ of these remarks it will be possible to see how the logic of equations, which is to say, the logic of identities, distinctively contaminates the Western discourse on "AIDS."

Against my initial text, "Silence=Death," let me juxtapose a passage from an open letter written by Larry Kramer, "AIDS" activist and author of, among other works, *The Normal Heart*, a play about the difficulties of getting Americans—gay and straight alike—to pay attention to the "AIDS" epidemic. Outraged by dilatory and inadequate responses at the early stages of the medical crisis, Kramer is quoted as having addressed these words to the press and to the leaders of the gay rights movement: "That all of you . . . continue to refuse to transmit to the public the facts and figures of what is happening *daily* makes you, in my mind, equal to murderers";[9] I would place beside this a graffito that David Black describes as having been scrawled on a wall at New York University: "Gay Rights=AIDS";[10] and then I would like to adduce a somewhat less overtly homophobic but no less insidious version of this notion as offered by Frances FitzGerald in her analysis of the effects of "AIDS" on San Francisco's Castro Street community: "The gay carnival, with its leather masks and ball gowns, had thus been the twentieth-century equivalent of the Masque of the Red Death."[11] Finally, I would adduce a quotation from a "26-year-old-never-married woman" cited by Masters and Johnson in *Newsweek* magazine's excerpt from their controversial book on "AIDS": "No sex, no worries. No sex, no AIDS. It's really a very simple equation, isn't it?"[12] What we can begin to notice here is by no means a "simple equation" but rather a complex *pattern* of equations that may lead us to consider just what is involved in this effort to translate differences (such as silence/death; leaders/murderers; gay rights/"AIDS") into identities through a language patterned on the rhetorical form of mathematical or scientific inevitability (A=B), a language of equations that can be marshalled equally in the service of homophobic ("Gay Rights=AIDS") or antihomophobic discourse ("Silence=Death").

In thinking about this we must bear in mind that it is precisely the question of equality, the post-Stonewall insistence by gays on equal rights, that has put into motion in unprecedented ways both of these discursive fields. Indeed, the complex issue of "AIDS" is massively overdetermined by the fact that the homophobic response to the demands for gay social and political equality, long *before* the phenomenon of "AIDS," was predicated on the historic equation of homosexuality with the unnatural, the irrational, and the diseased. The logic of homophobia, it is important, therefore, to note, rests upon the very binarism that enables Plato in the *Phaedrus* to assert the hierarchical privilege of speech at the expense of a devalued, even demonized, writing—and lest this seem too frivolous or far-fetched an association on my part, let me cite another passage from Derrida's deconstructive analysis of Plato: "the conclusion of the *Phaedrus* is less a condemnation of writing in the name of present speech than a preference for one sort of writing over another, for the fertile trace over the sterile trace, for a seed that engenders because it is planted inside over a seed scattered wastefully outside: at the risk of *dissemination*."[13] Insofar as Derrida's deconstructive logic displaces the opposition between speech and writing by identifying speech as just another "sort of writing," he calls into question the logic of the Western philosophical tradition that claims to be able to identify and distinguish the true from the false, the natural from the unnatural. In so doing he enacts the law of transgression that he sees as operative in "both the writing *and* the pederasty of a young man named Plato," a "transgression . . . not thinkable within the terms of classical logic but only within the graphics of the supplement or of the *pharmakon*."[14] Deconstruction itself, as a disseminative project, can thus be subsumed beneath the rubric of the homosexual and one can read, by contrast, in the recurrent equations cited earlier as responses to the "AIDS" epidemic, an insistence on the possibility of recuperating truth, of knowing absolutely, even mathematically, some literal identity unmarked by the destabilizing logic of the supplement or the indeterminacy of the *pharmakon*. This leads to a situation in which homophobic and antihomophobic forces alike generate, as defensive reactions to the social and medical crisis of "AIDS," discourses that reify and absolutize identities, discourses that make clear the extent to which both view the "AIDS" epidemic as a threat to those structures through which they have been able to constitute their identities for themselves.

Of course the Western heterosexual symbolic order has long construed homosexuality as a threat to the security or integrity of its own defensively articulated identity. In our heterogeneous and often contradictory mythology of homosexuality, "the love that dare not speak its name" was frequently designated as the crime *inter Christianos non nominandum*, and it was so designated not only because it was conceived as something lurid, shameful, and repellent, but also because it was, and is, conceived simultaneously as something so attractive that even to name or represent it is to risk the possibility of tempting some innocent into a fate too horrible—or too seductive—to imagine. One corollary of this fear of seduction through nomination or representation is the still pervasive homophobic misreading of homosexuality as contagious—as something one can "catch" through contact with, for instance, a teacher or a parent who is lesbian or gay. Thus even before the historical accident of the outbreak of "AIDS" in the gay communities of the West, homosexuality was conceived as a contagion, and the homosexual as a parasite waiting to feed upon the straight body. One instance that may evoke synecdochically the insidious logic of homophobic ideology was produced in 1977 in a dissent written by William Rehnquist, now chief justice of the United States, in response to the Court's refusal to grant certiorari in the case of *Gay Lib. v. University of Missouri.* As an essay in the *Harvard Law Review* described the case, "the university had refused to recognize a gay students' organization on the ground that such recognition would encourage violation of Missouri's anti-sodomy statute. In support of the university's position, Justice Rehnquist argued that permitting the exercise of first amendment rights of speech and association in this instance would undercut a legitimate state interest, just as permitting people with the measles to associate freely with others would undercut the state's interest in imposing a quarantine."[15] Here, in 1977, the ideological configuration of both homosexuality and discourse in relation to disease, and the invocation, albeit in metaphor, of quarantine as an acceptable model for containment, is offered as an argument against the right to produce a nonhomophobic public discourse on homosexuality.

If such a context suggests the bitter urgency of the activists' assertion that "Silence=Death," it does not suffice as a reading of the slogan or of the slogan's relation to the historically determined logic that governs the interimplication here of discourse, defense, and disease. For what is striking about "Silence=Death" as the most widely publicized, gay-articulated language of response to the "AIDS" epidemic is its insistence upon the therapeutic property of discourse without specifying in any way what should or must be said. Indeed, as a text produced in response to a medical and political emergency, "Silence=Death" is a stunningly self-reflexive slogan. It takes the form of a rallying cry, but its call for resistance is no call to arms; rather, it calls for the production of discourse, the production, that is, of more text, as a mode of defense against the opportunism of mainstream medical and legislative responses to the continuing epidemic. But what can be said beyond the need to speak? What discourse can this call to discourse desire? Just what *is* the discourse of defense that could immunize the gay body politic against the opportunistic infections of demagogic rhetoric?

III. One activist's answer to this question can be glimpsed in the accusation leveled by Larry Kramer at gay leaders and the press: "That all of you . . . continue to refuse to transmit to the public the facts and figures of what is happening *daily* makes you, in my mind, equal to murderers." Kramer explicitly calls for the production of discourse in order to defend against the transmission of disease. In so doing he makes clear that the defensive discourse is a discourse of "facts and figures," a discourse that resists the demagogic rhetoric of homophobic ideologues by articulating a truth that it casts in the form of mathematical or scientific data beyond the ambiguity of rhetoric. In a similar fashion, the text of the slogan "Silence=Death" takes the form of a formula that implies for it the status of a mathematical axiom, a given, a literal truth not susceptible to figural evasion or rhetorical distortion. In this context, the pink triangle that appears above the slogan in its graphic representations functions not only as an emblem of resistance to homosexual oppression, but also, and crucially, as a geometrical shape—a triangle *tout court*—that produces a sort of cognitive rhyme with the equation mark inscribed in the text, reinforcing semiotically the scientific or geometric inevitability of its equation.

At the same time, however, the very formula of mathematical discourse (A=B) that appeals to the prestige of scientific fact evokes the paradigmatic formulation or figure of metaphoric substitution. A=B, after all, is a wholly conventional way of representing the process whereby metaphor improperly designates one thing by employing the name of another. Though "Silence=Death" is cast in the rhetorical form of a geometric equation, and though it invokes, through that form, the necessity of articulating a truth of "facts and figures," the fact remains that the equation itself necessarily takes shape as a figure insofar as it enacts a metaphorical redefinition of "silence" as "death." What this means is that the equations that undertake to pronounce a literal, scientifically verifiable, truth cannot be distinguished from the disavowed literariness of the figural language those equations attempt to repudiate or exclude. The "truth" of such equations can only seem literal so long as we ignore that the literal itself is produced here by figural sleight of hand.

The rhetorical form of "Silence=Death" thus translates the mathematical into the poetic, the literal into the figural, by framing the call to discourse in terms that evoke the distinctive signature of metaphoric exchange. It would be useful in this context to recall for a moment Harold Bloom's identification of trope and defense and to cite yet one more equation, this one actually a *series* of equations proposed by Bloom in his essay, "Freud and the Sublime": "Literal meaning equals anteriority equals an earlier state of meaning equals an earlier state of things equals death equals literal meaning."[16] "Silence=Death," read in light of this, would gesture metaphorically toward the process of linguistic exchange or tropological substitution that resists or defends against the literality that Bloom, following Freud, identifies with death and sees as producing the reductive absolutism that informs the reality principle. Indeed, "Silence=Death" would seem thereby to cast itself as that most heroic of all texts: a text whose metaphoric demand for greater textual production, a text whose defensive appeal to discourse, would have the power "literally" to counteract the very agencies of death by promoting a deconstructive analysis capable of exposing the duplicity inherent in the false equations that pass for truth and that make possible, as a result, such virulent formulations as "Gay Rights=AIDS." In this case, for trope to operate as defense would involve, in part, the repudiation of what passes for the "literal truth" of "AIDS" by attending to the ideological investments that inform the scientific and political discourse about it and by articulating the inevitable construction of the disease within a culturally overdetermined array of figural associations. "Silence=Death" might be interpreted, then, as a slogan that requires neither silent assent nor the mere reiteration that routinizes, and thereby silences, the slogan itself. It would demand, instead, its own mutation into the forms of critical reading and resistance that call into question *any* equation that represents "truth" as a literal fact and not as a figural frame.

Such a reading would insist, of course, that "Silence=Death" can claim no immunity against contamination by the figural—a contamination that is evident in its own defensive production of the figure of literality, the figure of mathematical precision. But the logocentric politics governing the postulation of identity in "Silence=Death" aligns that formula, despite its explicitly antihomophobic import, with the logic of natural self-identity implicit in Plato's binary distinction between speech and writing, the fertile and the sterile trace, a logic that provides the ideological support for the homophobic terrorism that Plato endorsed when he cited the need to defend the "law of restricting procreative intercourse to its natural function by abstention from congress with our own sex, with its deliberate murder of the race and its wasting of the seed of life on a stony and rocky soil, where it will never take root and bear its natural fruit."[17] Appealing, in other words, to the self-evidence of identity inscribed in its formulaic equation, "Silence=Death" configures the activity of life with the (re)production of discourse (however oppositional) and thus plays out the logic that privileges procreative intercourse over homosexual sex by aligning the former with active production and the latter with "murder of the race." To the extent that "Silence=Death," after all, those who are silent or refuse to accept that figures equal facts, become, as Larry Kramer put it bluntly, "equal to murderers."

The equations that mark the discourse on "AIDS," then, suggest that in the face of the epistemological ambiguity provoked by this epidemic, in the face of so powerful a representation of the force of what we do not know, the figure of certainty, the figure of literality, is itself ideologically constructed and deployed as a defense, if not as a remedy. (We might note one manifestation of this deployment of the figure of knowledge or certainty in the way that political debate about "AIDS" in America has been counterproductively fixated on proposals to divert millions of dollars from necessary research toward compulsory testing of various populations to determine the presence of HIV antibodies. Given the persistence of the American identification of "AIDS" with the gay male community, it is hard not to see this as informed fantasmatically by a desire to combat uncertainty not only about who has been infected with HIV, but also, and perhaps more deeply and irrationally, about how to differentiate between straight and gay.) Precisely because the defensive appeal to literality in a slogan like "Silence=Death" produces the literal *as a figure* of the need and desire for the shelter of certain knowledge, such a discourse is always necessarily a dangerously contaminated defense—contaminated by the Derridean logic of metaphor by which its efforts to achieve a natural or literal discourse untainted by rhetoric are destined to reproduce the ideology of reified identity as "truth" or presence that marks the reactionary medical and political discourse it seeks to counteract. The discursive logic of "Silence=Death" thus contributes to the ideologically motivated confusion of the literal and the figural, the proper and the improper, the inside and the outside. And in so doing, significantly, it parallels the operations of the human immunodeficiency virus as it attacks the mechanism whereby the body is able, in David Black's words, to distinguish between "Self and Not-Self."

HIV, scientists tell us, is a retrovirus that reproduces by a method that depends upon an enzyme called reverse transcriptase. This "allows the virus to copy its genetic information into a form that can be integrated into the host cell's own genetic code. Each time a host cell divides, viral copies are produced along with more host cells, each containing the viral code."[18] At issue in the disease itself, then, are questions of inscription and transcription, questions of reproduction and substitution. The virus endangers precisely because it produces a code, or speaks a language, that can usurp or substitute for the genetic discourse of certain cells in the human immune system. "AIDS" thus inscribes within the biology of the human organism the notion of parasitic transcription. And this metastatic or substitutive transcription of the cell is particularly difficult to counteract to the extent that HIV, like metaphor, operates to naturalize, or present as proper, that which is improper or alien or imported from without. Subsequent to the metonymy, the contiguous transmission, of infection, the virus establishes itself as part of the essential material of the invaded cell through a type of metaphoric substitution. It changes the meaning of the cellular code so that each reproduction or articulation of the cell disseminates further the altered genetic message. Moreover, one of the properties of HIV is that it can change the "genetic structure of [the] external proteins" that constitute the outer coat by which the immune system is able to recognize it; thus it can evade the agents of the immune system that work to defend the organism against what is alien or improper. Even worse, since HIV attacks the immune system itself, depleting the T-4 or T-helper cells, it prevents the immune system from being able to "recognize foreign substances (antigens) and . . . eliminate them from the body."[19] Thus even as it works its tropological wiles within the infected cells, HIV is subverting the capacity of the immune system to read the difference between what is proper to the body or "literally" its own, and what is figural or extrinsic.

But the metaphoric flights of fancy that are at work in the scientific discourse on "AIDS," just as they are necessarily at work in my own metaphorizing discourse, the flights of fancy in which the failures of discourse as defense are already inscribed within disease, have no literal warrant in "nature." Reverse transcriptase and immune defense systems are metaphoric designations that determine the way we understand the operations of the body; they are tropological readings that metastasize the metabolic by infecting it with a strain of metaphor that can appear so natural, so intrinsic to our way of thinking, that we mistake it for the literal truth of the body, as if our rhetorical immune system had ceased to operate properly, or as if the virus of metaphor had mutated so successfully as to evade the antibodies that would permit us to distinguish the inside from the outside, the proper from the improper. This brings to mind once again the Derridean analysis of writing's parasitic relation to *logos* in Western philosophy since Plato: "In order to cure the latter of the *pharmakon* and rid it of the parasite, it is thus necessary to put the outside back in its place. To keep the outside out. This is the inaugural gesture of 'logic' itself, of good 'sense' insofar as it accords with the self-identity of *that which is*: being is what it is, the outside is outside and the inside inside."[20] But since, as Derrida elsewhere notes, "metaphoricity is the logic of contamination and the contamination of logic," no discourse can ever successfully achieve the logic of self-identity, the logic of scientific equation, without a trace of the infection of metaphor that finds the enemy, the outside, the alien always already entrenched within. Emily Dickinson, anticipating Derrida's reading of the *pharmakon*, observed, "infection in the sentence breeds";[21] in the case of "AIDS," though, we might rather say that infection endlessly breeds sentences—sentences whose implication in a poisonous history of homophobic constructions assures that no matter what the explicit ideology they serve, they will carry within them the virulent germ of the dominant cultural discourse.

If my conclusion presents the somber circularity of Discourse=Defense=Disease=Discourse, I cannot conclude without trying to locate the zone of infection within these remarks. What I have been suggesting is that any discourse on "AIDS" must inscribe itself in a volatile and uncontrollable field of metaphoric contention in which its language will necessarily find itself at once appropriating "AIDS" for its own tendentious purposes and becoming subject to appropriation by the contradictory logic of homophobic ideology. This essay is not exempt from those necessities. As much as I would insist on the value and urgency of examining the figural inscriptions of "AIDS," I am sufficiently susceptible to the gravity of the literal to feel uneasy, as a gay man, about producing a discourse in which the horrors experienced by my own community, along with other communities in America and abroad, become the material for intellectual arabesques that inscribe those horrors within the neutralizing conventions of literary criticism. Yet as painfully as my own investment in the figure of literality evokes for me the profound inhumanity implicit in this figural discourse on "AIDS," I am also aware that *any* discourse on "AIDS" must inevitably reproduce that tendentious figurality. At the same time, I would argue that the appeal of the literal can be an equally dangerous seduction; it is, after all, the citation of the pressing literality of the epidemic with its allegedly "literal" identification of homosexuality and disease, that fuels the homophobic responses to "AIDS" and demands that we renounce what are blithely dismissed as figural embellishments upon the "real," material necessities of human survival—embellishments such as civil rights and equal protection under the law. We must be as wary, then, of the temptations of the literal as we are of the ideologies at work in the figural; for discourse, alas, is the only defense with which we can counteract discourse, and there is no available discourse on "AIDS" that is not itself diseased.

5

THE MIRROR AND THE TANK

"AIDS," Subjectivity, and the Rhetoric of Activism

" . . . analysis, while necessary, may also be an indefensible luxury."

—*Leo Bersani*[1]

I. Writing/ "AIDS"

If all writing demands a subject—both insofar as it engages an economy of reference and insofar as it posits a subject-position—it might be useful, in order to explore some aspects of the relations between writing and "AIDS," to consider the possibility that "AIDS" itself cannot unproblematically function as the subject of our writing since "AIDS" is ideologically constructed as a form of writing itself: as an inscription of difference whose "subject" is always the subject of ideology. "AIDS," in the first place, and on the most literal level, lacks a coherent medical referent, remaining a signifier in search of the determinate condition or conditions it would signify. A diagnostic term describing the state in which the immune system—compromised, it is currently thought, through HIV infection—can no longer ward off certain officially designated opportunistic diseases, "AIDS" constitutes so unstable a signifier even in the arena of medical discourse that on June 9, 1991 the *Boston Globe* reported:

> Officials of the Centers for Disease Control said Friday that they are considering changing the way they define AIDS, a move that could double the number of Americans officially classified as suffering from the disease.
>
> Because AIDS causes a general devastation of the immune system, it is marked not by one symptom, but by dozens of infections, cancers and other conditions. The proposed change, which comes at the suggestion of the Conference of State and Territorial Epidemiologists, would broaden the official classification of AIDS to encompass thousands of HIV-infected people who have none of the conditions included in the 14-page government definition.

To this acknowledgment that even a "14-page definition" cannot secure the referential adequacy of "AIDS" we must add the more widespread conflation, largely promulgated by journalists and politicians, of "AIDS" and HIV seropositivity—a conflation that rhetorically identifies the effect with the medical indicator of the putative cause as if such referential violence could, paradoxically, reinforce the coherence of "AIDS" by achieving its totalization and its ideological compaction. And if the imprecision with which cultural "authorities" thereby encourage the public to view "AIDS" serves the purposes of those intent on writing "AIDS" as a linear narrative progressing ineluctably from a determinate beginning to a predetermined end, that fact makes it all the less likely that "AIDS" "itself" could be our subject, since the signifier both connotes and denominates a dense and contradictory array of medical diagnoses, social experiences, projective fantasies, and "political" agendas.

"AIDS," then, resists our attempts to inscribe it as a manageable subject of writing—exceeding and eluding the medical, sociological, political, or literary discourses that variously attempt to confront or engage it—to the extent that as an historical phenomenon in the so-called Western democracies it has itself taken shape—has been given shape—as that which writes or articulates another subject altogether: a subject whose content is suggested but not exhausted by reference to "male homosexuality." The discursive field of "AIDS" thus unfolds as a landscape of displacements, and given those displacements and the slipperiness of the subject, every effort to resist ideological enforcement in one place carries with it the threat of resowing the seeds of ideological coercion in another. To take this threat seriously, or to suggest that we cannot afford *not* to take this threat seriously, does not mean that we should respond to the task of "writing AIDS" by writing it off from the outset or that we ought to domesticate the intolerable losses that "AIDS" must always denote by framing "AIDS," with the security that attends a certain sort of knowingness, as a recognizable instance of a now familiar postmodern problematic, as if "AIDS" could be defined as *merely*, in Paula Treichler's words, an "epidemic of signification," or as *nothing but*, in a phrase I myself used earlier, a "plague of discourse."[2]

And yet, as Jeffrey Weeks acknowledges by titling an essay "Post-Modern AIDS?," intellectual efforts to theorize the epidemic, its constructions and its representations, frequently invoke, toward differing ends and with varying degrees of insight and engagement, some notion of the postmodern.[3] Roberta McGrath, for instance, observes: "HIV—which is a simulacrum of DNA—is the first human retrovirus, perhaps the first post-modern disease."[4] Donna Haraway makes a similar point in "A Manifesto for Cyborgs," identifying "AIDS" with the forces of "simulation" (characteristic of what she calls the postmodern "informatics of domination") as opposed to the forces of "representation" (characteristic of the world order of industrial capitalism).[5] Remarking upon the temptation to respond to "AIDS" with global assertions that would read it as a figure for an historic shift in the cultural paradigm of "meaning," Robert Glück considers the claim that "AIDS is the disease of the Eighties. Why? Well, the destruction of the immune system is an allegory of the breakdown of 'basic structures' now experienced by our country and the West."[6] And Simon Watney affirms that the "challenge of AIDS reeducation exemplifies the insight of Ernesto Laclau and Chantal Mouffe that what is being exploded in the postmodern period, 'is the idea and the reality itself of a unique space of constitution of the political.'"[7]

Perhaps the importance of postmodernism as the framework within which these and other intellectuals have attempted to conceptualize or respond to "AIDS" can be seen most interestingly in *AIDS DemoGraphics*, a volume in which Douglas Crimp and Adam Ralston identify the program, politics, and principles characteristic of "AIDS activist art."[8] Describing the work produced by such collectives as Gran Fury, the Silence=Death Project, and various committees from within ACT UP, Crimp and Ralston find not only "techniques of postmodernist appropriation" (18) and a "sophisticated postmodern style" (19), but also a survival of the radicalism with which, before becoming institutionalized itself, "postmodernist art advanced a political critique of art institutions" (19). One essential aspect of this critique that "AIDS activist artists" are credited with perpetuating is a challenge to the ideology whereby modernism (and the museum or literary canon as cultural establishments that both mirrored and enshrined it) affirmed an order of meaning that could be shaped, transformed, and revolutionized by the genius of the individual artist. As Crimp and Ralston observe:

> Questions of identity, authorship, and audience—and the ways in which all three are constructed through representation—have been central to postmodernist art, theory, and criticism. The significance of so-called appropriation art, in which the artist forgoes the claim to original creation by appropriating already-existing images and objects, has been to show that the "unique individual" is a kind of fiction, that our very selves are socially and historically determined through preexisting images, discourses, and events.

> Young artists finding their place within the AIDS activist movement rather than the conventional art world have had reason to take these issues very seriously. (18)

All who are interested in writing and "AIDS"—interested, that is, in how those two terms interrogate, reflect, and displace one another in the discourses through which "AIDS" is constructed—have reason to take seriously this recurrent conjunction of "AIDS" and postmodernism, to read it as gesturing toward a cultural logic centrally at stake in the conflict being waged over "AIDS" and "representation."

In this context it is not insignificant, after all, that what Fredric Jameson discusses as a crucial component of postmodernism—one that can, as he sees it, help to "explain why classical modernism is a thing of the past and why postmodernism should have taken its place"—can also illuminate the intersection of postmodernism and "AIDS": "this new component," Jameson argues, "is what is generally called 'the death of the subject.'"[9] Now to claim that we can hear in the discourse on "AIDS" reverberations of this postmodern "death of the subject" is to approach the always unstable demarcation between, on the one hand, producing a *reading* of the allegories through which the political unconscious manifests itself in the social imagination and, on the other hand, simply producing such potentially dangerous allegories oneself. Yet insofar as "the death of the subject" enters popular discourse most directly through the various challenges posed to the identification of subjectivity as such with the particular subject-position associated with straight, white, middle-class men, "AIDS," which popular mythology continues to construe as largely exempting straight, white, middle-class men from its ravages, could not fail to inflect and to be inflected by the vicissitudes of "the subject" in contemporary Western culture. "AIDS," then, can be figured as a crisis in—and hence as an opportunity for—the social shaping or articulation of subjectivities because, in part, the historical context within which "AIDS" in the West achieved its "identity" allowed it to be positioned as a syndrome distinctively engaging identity as an issue. In fact, I would argue that whatever the direction from which we approach the subject of "AIDS" we are brought up against our own constitution as subjects of—and in—ideology and that the politics of "AIDS" as a subject of discourse is inseparable from the politics of "the subject" itself—inseparable, that is, from the ideological construction and the cultural fantasmatics of agency.[10]

Even within those marginalized communities in which a great deal of critical energy has been expended to analyze the official representations of "AIDS," much of that energy has been directed toward prescriptions of the "proper" constitution of the discursive subject in and through what Simon Watney has called "an AIDS activist cultural practice" or "an AIDS activist aesthetic."[11] Such a practice, as he argues in an important essay, "Representing AIDS," is predicated upon "a cultural politics that is sensitive to the complex processes that produce subjectivities, and hold them in place" (190). Addressing himself to the question of photography but in a way that bears extension across the spectrum of artistic modes, Watney insists that an "AIDS activist aesthetic" must counter those representational practices that depend upon a "familiar humanist pathos to stir reluctant sympathies" (179). In light of this canny observation, it may be worth considering the extent to which even the "AIDS activist aesthetic" interpellates a subject whose agency continues to be bound up problematically with the pathos of such a humanism, in that its subject continues to be caught within the falsely naturalized oppositions that give rise to our notions of sex and gender and sexuality—each of which stands in a critical relation to the conceptualization of subjectivity.[12]

My purpose, of course, is not to disable the indispensable work, including Watney's own, produced from within this activist aesthetic; rather, I would elaborate some of the difficulties encountered in the project of "writing AIDS" in order to hold open options for the inscription of narratives, and the interpellation of subjects, in ways that differ from those that govern so unyieldingly both the dominant discourse on "AIDS" and much of the contestatory counter-discourse that defines itself as "activist." In the process I by no means intend to suggest, as the syntax of the previous sentence may imply, any symmetry between the lethal cynicism of the government's manipulation, and even its deployment, of "AIDS," and the life-saving resistance by "AIDS activists" to the various forms that manipulation has taken. Instead, I want to examine some ways in which the overlapping crises that we experience as "AIDS" produce an oppositional political discourse that has the potential, in its necessary struggle against both the officially sanctioned representations of the epidemic and their intended constitution of a "normal" or "healthy" subjectivity, to naturalize and reposition certain aspects of the ideological structures that inform and produce those noxious representations and those oppressive subjectivities in the first place.

II. Genesis and Genocide

On June 3, 1991, as journalists began to comment on the tenth anniversary of America's first official reports of what is now considered "AIDS," an editorial in New Hampshire's *Manchester Union Leader* could still insist on the truth of the genealogical narrative that has lodged itself so firmly in the Western cultural imagination that it underlies, in many cases, even the most "sophisticated" responses to the epidemic: "homosexual intercourse is the genesis of every single case of AIDS in that every case is traceable—either directly or indirectly—to the practice. However the disease is transmitted, the sexual perversion that is anal intercourse by sodomites is the fundamental point of origin."[13]Tempting as it might be to dismiss such a statement as the ignorant, even risible, cant of a right-wing political extremist, the myth that it recirculates remains the most significant fiction our culture has produced in its efforts to understand "AIDS." Whether sublimated into the neutralizing discourse that warns of "AIDS" "spreading" from "high risk groups" to the "general population," so called, or moralized into the media's sensationalized renderings of those they insist on defining (against their always unspoken but implicit antitheses) as the epidemic's "innocent victims," the inescapability—indeed, the vitality—of a fiction that not only allows but actually *requires* the "general public" to imagine a scene—in fact, a primal scene—of anal sex between men bespeaks an imperative in the framing of "AIDS" that we ignore at our own risk.

Whatever the scientific or epidemiological "truth" about "AIDS" and HIV transmission, the logic within which "AIDS" has been made to signify in the West calls forth, as Leo Bersani observes in his provocative essay, "Is the Rectum a Grave?," the "seductive and intolerable image of a grown man, legs high in the air, unable to refuse the suicidal ecstasy of being a woman" (212). Bersani recognizes that this cultural fantasy defines gay men categorically in terms of a particular erotic practice—sometimes described as "receptive anal intercourse," more commonly known as "getting fucked"—and that this definition allows gay men to be inscribed in the role that "properly" is inhabited by (heterosexual) women. For a man to permit himself to be so inscribed can be understood as "suicidal," then, since it connotes a willing sacrifice of the subjectivity, the disciplined self-mastery, traditionally attributed only to those who perform the "active" or penetrative—and hence "masculine"—role in the active-passive binarism that organizes "our" cultural perspective on sexual behavior.

In a phrase that registers the persistence not merely of a sexual but also of an erotic politics in the fantasmatics of subjectivity, Bersani, commenting on the Athenian belief in "a legal and moral incompatibility between sexual passivity and civic authority," draws the inevitable conclusion: "*To be penetrated is to abdicate power*" (212). David Halperin, underscoring this point, relates it to "the cultural poetics of manhood"[14] through which the political subject was called into being in the "democratizing initiative in classical Athens" (102) so as "to promote a new collective image of the citizen body as masculine and assertive, as master of its pleasures, and as perpetually on the superordinate side of a series of hierarchical and roughly congruent distinctions in status: master vs. slave, free vs. unfree, dominant vs. submissive, active vs. passive, insertive vs. receptive, customer vs. prostitute, citizen vs. non-citizen, man vs. woman" (102–103). Within this conceptual paradigm, which is, regrettably, our enduring heritage, to allow oneself to be displaced from the "superordinate side" of masculine self-assertion to the subordinate position of feminine receptivity registers as "suicidal" precisely to the extent that it signifies, and not "merely" as a figure, what could be called the "death of the subject." For given the unthinkable coincidence of power and passivity, the act by which a subject assumes the posture of an "object" constitutes the one act that a subject, *as* a subject, lacks the freedom to perform. Far from being logically inarticulable, however, that impossible performance, that confounding of the foundational distinction between activity and passivity, bears so crucially on the ideological delimitation of subjectivity itself that it appears to *demand* articulation at those moments when, as in the "crisis" that is "AIDS," "the subject" is the subject in question.

Consider again, for example, the vile mythology rehearsed by the editorial in the *Manchester Union Leader*: "homosexual intercourse is the genesis of every single case of AIDS. . . . [T]he sexual perversion that is anal intercourse by sodomites is the fundamental point of origin." Not surprisingly, this rabid fundamentalism of the fundament produces its genealogy of "AIDS" in the allusive penumbra cast by Genesis, the text that constitutes our cultural Constitution far more than any legal document of state (as the U.S. Supreme Court all but officially announced in its decision in *Bowers v. Hardwick*). In contrast to the subject-formation related in, and effected by, the biblical narrative, however, the editorial's myth of the "genesis" of "AIDS" gestures toward the decomposition of the subject by proffering the act of anal intercourse—which is, in the homophobic imaginary of the West, to proffer the spectacle of gay men in the so-called "passive" or "receptive" position—as the negative counterpart of the theory that used to be packaged as "creation science." In this version of a now familiar quasi-Miltonic speculation on the origins of "AIDS," the gay male anus as the site of pleasure gives birth to "AIDS" as a figuration of death.

Significantly, this account of what gets interpreted as the definitional act of de-generation credits the anus, like the God of Genesis, with performing an act of creation *ex nihilo*, even if the nihilism of the anus thus threatens to annihilate all creation.[15] For if the creation of the universe recounted in Genesis provides a model for subjectivity through its image of absolute agency asserting its will by creating and shaping matter, the narrative that traces the origin of "AIDS" to the spontaneous emergence of a virus through an act of male-male anal sex parodically inverts that perfect congruence of self-present intention and creative act, reducing the "creator," in this case, to the condition of so much matter that finds itself subjected, in the end, to what it has "created." In the logic of this allegoresis, then, the act by which the subject renounces the autonomy that affirms his subjectivity leads directly to the "literal" realization of this symbolic gesture in the subject's death.

Moreover, just as the "passivity" identified with gay male anal intercourse results, according to this narrative, in the death of the *individual* subject, so a culture's passive acquiescence to or toleration of male-male anal sex—and thus of the category-disrupting act of passivity that male homosexuality connotes—serves as the "fundamental point of origin" for a more universal death of the subject, for the apocalyptic reversal of Genesis that radiates outward from those that Genesis, after all, enables the law to call "sodomites." As Eve Kosofsky Sedgwick importantly reminds us:

> From at least the biblical story of Sodom and Gomorrah, scenarios of same-sex desire have had a privileged, though by no means an exclusive, relation in Western culture to scenarios of both genocide and omnicide. . . . [O]ne of the few areas of agreement among modern Marxist, Nazi, and liberal capitalist ideologies is that there is a peculiarly close, though never precisely defined, affinity between same-sex desire and some historical condition of moribundity, called "decadence," to which not individuals or minorities but whole civilizations are subject.[16]

Thus at the present historical moment in which "kicking butt" is the formula of choice for asserting the value of autonomy and aggressive indominability in America, it is not merely by way of pun that gay male sexual desire, construed as annulling the subject in the pleasurable receptivity of the anus, gets fantasmatically rewritten as a fatal attraction to the end. Yet as our societal fascination with the "butt," however phobic its expression, makes clear, the violence of the assertion that "butt" must be "kicked" betrays a recognition of its demand on our attention, as if what needed to be "kicked" were not an object of scorn but a habit. Indeed, the threat of sodomitical apocalypse condensed in the *Manchester Union Leader*'s editorial invests the anus with the gravitational attraction of what, astronomically speaking, it is proper to describe as a "black hole," implying that if a man's anus—or metonymically, his "butt"—is allowed to exert an attractive force on any man at all, every man will eventually collapse before (if not into) the "self"-destroying force of the "virus" that *is*, and is not merely the product of, accession, which becomes addiction, to the anus's desire.[17]

I mean to suggest, then, that the currency achieved by the scenarios of "genocide and omnicide" in the public discourse that locates the origin of "AIDS" in gay male anal sex[18] responds, by displacement, to what Michelangelo Signorile, prophetically one hopes, has described as "The Last Gasp of the White Male Heterosexuals."[19] It testifies, in other words, to the anxiety of decline and impending doom that marks, in this case, not merely a *fin de siècle* or millennial malaise, but more profoundly, the deep-rooted recognition of the imminent end of an empire, the demise of the imperial subject secure in his centrality to, his identification with, history and civilization. Given that, as Craig Owens has noted, "the representational systems of the West admit only one vision—that of the constitutive male subject—or, rather, they posit the subject of representation as absolutely centered, unitary, masculine," postmodernism in its popular version can seem to intend the fall of the West insofar as it would effect the death of the subject by, as Owens puts it, "upset[ting] the reassuring stability of that mastering position."[20] Faced with this prospect of being toppled from the pedestal on which he has placed himself, the ideological subject as white male heterosexual elicits from "AIDS" a discourse of crisis through which to affirm his privileged standing; for the performative effect of these representations of the apocalyptic end of the subject is to define the subject coercively as he who repudiates his end. Subtended by the always excitable fantasy of threat to this subject's agency, the originary myth linking "AIDS" to the "addictive" passivity of the anus in intercourse is mobilized largely in order to reaffirm, and thereby to shore against his ruins, the white male heterosexual as uniquely autonomous in his moral agency, and thus as uniquely occupying the position of the subject who, like Adam in Milton's Protestant reworking of Genesis, is in himself sufficient to stand because also free to fall.

III. Narci-schism

This fantasy of the fall or death of the (white, male, heterosexual) subject can, of course, mean different things in different discursive contexts. Reading it from within a gay-inflected psychoanalytic framework, I have argued elsewhere that it can register as "a falling *away* from the always endangered 'integrity' of maleness as culturally construed, and thus as a falling *back* into that dreaded but seductive, maternally-identified preoedipal eros from which, on the one hand, heterosexual masculinity is imagined to have emerged, and against which, as an absolute alterity, it needs, on the other hand, to define itself."[21] Drawing upon Lacan's hypothesis of the mirror stage as both precipitate and prolepsis of the subject's self-constitution, this argument seeks to unfold the logic behind the derisive representation of gay men as narcissistically fixated and oriented toward the mother. It does so by considering the mirror stage and the castration crisis in relation to one another as the two determining moments in the formation of the heterosexual male subject that defensively *generate* the myth of that subject's unidirectional development (out of and away from identification with—and domination by—maternal power) precisely because each of those moments *refutes* such unidirectionality to the degree that its subject-shaping force depends upon its capacity to elicit *retroactively* the history out of which the subject thereafter will be said to have emerged. The fact that the subject emerges, however, not from that history (whether of the *corps morcelé* or of identification with the mother who already has been "castrated"), but rather from *the narrative that enables him to posit his emergence* from that history, means that the *expe-*

rience of such a history is never, properly speaking, the subject's property, and that the subject can never, *as* a subject, experience it, therefore, at all. To the contrary, from the perspective of the constituted subject, the possibility of experiencing what it can retroactively hypostatize as its "history" can only figure the *prospect* of the subject's dissolution. The critical moments of the mirror stage and the assumption of the castration complex, then, effect the identity of the self as (male) subject through the identification of subjectivity with autonomous control or self-mastery, the achievement of which is linked, in each case, to an assertion of distance—and difference—from the mother who had been, until then, an imaginary mirror for what can be said to have been the subject-to-be only *after* this "mirror" is disavowed.

Jane Gallop, in a compelling analysis of this process as played out in Lacan's essay on the mirror stage, appropriately compares it to the mythology of Genesis.

> The mirror stage is thus high tragedy: a brief moment of doomed glory, a paradise lost. The infant is "decisively projected" out of this joy into the anxious defensiveness of "history," much as Adam and Eve are expelled from paradise into the world. Just as man and woman are already created but do not enter the human condition until expelled from Eden, so the child, although already born, does not become a self until the mirror stage. Both cases are two-part birth processes: once born into "nature," the second time into "history." When Adam and Eve eat from the tree of knowledge, they anticipate mastery. But what they actually gain is a horrified recognition of their nakedness. This resembles the movement by which the infant, having assumed by anticipation a totalized, mastered body, then retroactively perceives his inadequacy (his "nakedness"). Lacan has written another version of the tragedy of Adam and Eve.[22]

Because the apocalyptic narratives of "AIDS" unfold in allusive relation to Genesis (as do such arguments against homosexuality as the platitudinous reminder that "God created Adam and Eve, not Adam and Steve"), the psychic stakes in the death of the (white, male, heterosexual) subject, and thus in the defensively mobilized anxiety that shapes the mythology of "AIDS," can be located not only in Lacan's psychoanalytic reinterpretation of the Fall, but also in such canonical rewritings of Genesis as the *Paradise Lost* toward which Gallop nods in the passage cited above. For Milton characterizes Adam as a free and rational moral agent, a paradigmatic subject, by framing the moment that Book VIII might allow us to interpret as Adam's mirror stage in a mirroring relation to the description, in Book IV, of Eve's fascination with her image as reflected in a lake.

Where Narcissus, in the Ovidian narrative from which Milton draws in this latter scene, pays for his specular fixation by "dying at life's prime,"[23] Eve escapes such a fate through the external mediation of the divine voice, a third term whose linguistic intervention both lays down and *is* the Law:

What there thou seest fair Creature is thyself,
With thee it came and goes: but follow me,
And I will bring thee where no shadow stays
Thy coming, and thy soft imbraces, hee
Whose image thou art, him thou shalt enjoy
Inseparably thine, to him shalt bear
Multitudes like thyself, and thence be call'd
Mother of human Race. (IV, 468–475)

Responding to this voice, Eve comes upon Adam and, judging him "less fair,/Less winning soft, less amiably mild,/Than that smooth wat'ry image" (IV, 478–480) of herself, turns back toward the lake before Adam persuades her that she must see herself in relation to him and not in the mirror of her own reflection. If Eve, however, thus fails at first to recognize in Adam the "sympathy and love" (IV, 465) that she saw and was drawn to at once in her own image, Adam, in Book VIII, recognizes himself immediately in Eve, or to be more exact, he immediately (mis)recognizes Eve *as himself* in a way that parallels but reverses Eve's (mis)recognition of her image *as someone else.* Describing to Raphael his first glimpse of Eve, Adam recalls the words he spoke: "I now see/Bone of my bone, Flesh of my Flesh, my Self/Before me" (VIII, 494–496). Raphael underscores the point that this is, in fact, a *mis*-recognition when he somberly warns Adam against such a narcissistic over-estimation of Eve, urging him against "attributing overmuch to things/Less excellent" (VIII, 565–566).

Thus Adam's true constitution as a human subject takes place when he discovers his *status* as a subject in differential relation to Eve—when he learns, in other words, as Raphael puts it, that Eve is "worthy well/Thy cherishing, thy honoring, and thy love,/Not thy subjection" (VIII, 468–470); yet as Raphael goes on to suggest, the dangerously misplaced narcissism that marks this overestimation of Eve can only be controlled by encouraging Adam's "proper" narcissistic estimation of himself *in his difference from her*: "weigh with her thyself;/Then value: Oft-times nothing profits more/Than self-esteem, grounded on just and right/Well managed" (VIII, 570–573). In effect, the text affirms Adam as subject by justifying his love for Eve not as his "Self," but as the "image" of himself, as, in this particular context, the *object* through which he can recognize (and thus attain) his rightful position as subject.[24]

Such a constitution of Adam as subject requires and exacts, however, Eve's anterior disavowal of attraction to the "wat'ry image" of *her* "Self"—requires, that is, that her narcissism be categorically separated from his. As Mary Nyquist argues, "It is not hard to see that Adam's own desire for an other self has a strong 'narcissistic' component. Yet Adam's retrospective narrative shows this narcissism being sparked, sanctioned, and then satisfied by his creator. By contrast, though in book 4 Eve recalls experiencing a desire for an other self, this desire is clearly and unambiguously constituted by illusion, both in the sense of specular illusion and in the sense of error."[25] But Eve's "error," of course, is error only by ideological fiat of the text; she cannot, after all, see herself in Adam as he can see himself in Eve, for while she is constructed as *his* image, he is not constructed as *hers*. Only in the watery mirror can she find an image of her own, and that image reflects her "accurately"—it allows her to recognize herself—because it gives back to her the image of her status *as* image or reflection.

One might say, therefore, that Eve's narcissism, justly so called since it alludes to Narcissus, must be sacrificed to legitimize, or at least to obscure, what the text seems to want us *not* to construe as *Adam's* narcissism. The latter gets honorifically represented, instead, as active engagement with otherness, as movement into and authority over a world located outside of, and defined as different from, the self. In this sense Milton's rewriting of Genesis reinforces an argument Michael Warner makes in his essay, "Homo-Narcissism; or, Heterosexuality." Meditating on the psychoanalytic pathologization of homosexuality as narcissistic (because interpreted as love of the "same"), Warner explores the logic behind the modern insistence on limiting what gets articulated as legitimate "difference" in erotic relations to the "difference" defined as gender. He contends that "the allegory of gender protects against a recognition of the role of the imaginary in the formation of the erotic. It provides reassurance that imaginary intersubjectivity has been transcended. To the extent that our culture relies on the allegorization of gender to disguise from itself its own ego erotics, it will recognize those ego erotics only in the person of the homosexual, apparently bereft of the master trope of difference."[26]

In the dominant culture's ideological definition of same and different, private and public, passive and active, personal and political, Eve's "ego erotics," which are assigned the position of interiority and self-involvement, are characterized pejoratively as antithetical to Adam's—much as gay sexuality is characterized, both in psychoanalytic discourse and in the Western imagination, as narcissistic and therefore as structurally distinct from heterosexual eros. Like Adam, then, heterosexual masculinity displaces the narcissism that marks the imaginary structuring of its own erotic relations in order to call itself into being (as the modern *institution* of heterosexual masculinity) in the posture of mastering subject. Activity, change, sociality, civilization, life itself, from within the logic of heterosexuality—which is to say, from within the governing logic of the subject—depend upon this *imaginary* emergence from, this *imaginary* transcendence of, "imaginary intersubjectivity."

Male homosexuality in general, though, and its synecdoche, gay male anal sex in particular, bear the stigma and retain the lure of such an "imaginary intersubjectivity" insofar as they seem to effect the subject's fall from master to matter: his fall *back*, in other words, from the fantasized achievement of coherence and autonomous agency to a state of mirror-like receptivity that appears, from the vantage point of the differentiated self, as inherently "self"-negating. Were we to think of gravity, for a moment, as expressing the narcissism of matter, we might consider, in this regard, that the place of the anus, as what I have called the "black hole" in the mythology of "AIDS," figures the *lethally disavowed narcissism* that heterosexual masculinity, to define itself as such, must misread instead as the *lethal narcissism* associated with gay men—"lethal" because it draws the male subject back into his imaginary "history," the non-being that is the experientially unapproachable condition of non-differentiation, by permitting the gay man to take himself, narcissistically, as an object, and allowing him, in consequence, as an object, to be "taken."

The popular homophobic discourse on "AIDS" that depends upon these apocalyptic conjunctions of narcissism, passivity, the anus, and death serves, then, to secure the ideological construction of the subject as heterosexual male in much the same way that Adam's identity as Adam is secured not only on the condition that Eve *not* be Adam but also that she not, as it were, be *Steve.* Such an ideological construction depends upon the ability to posit persuasively as a categorical difference what might, under a different discursive regime, be interpreted as "the same." The result, as D. A. Miller recognizes, is that "straight men unabashedly *need* gay men, whom they forcibly recruit (as the object of their blows or, in better circles, just their jokes) to enter into a polarization that exorcizes the 'woman' in man through assigning it to a class of man who may be considered no 'man' at all. Only between the woman and the homosexual together may the normal male subject imagine himself covered front and back."[27] Indeed, one might add, only *against* women and gay men may the "normal male subject" imagine himself *to be a subject* at all.

If the widespread homophobic mythology of "AIDS" constellates narcissism, passivity, and the anus as dangers against which to mobilize, and thereby reinforce, the heterosexual logic of the subject, it ought, perhaps, to be cause for concern when this same constellation is similarly demonized in the discourse designed to effect the constitution of an oppositional gay male subjectivity. Take, for example, a poem from Paul Monette's *Love Alone: Eighteen Elegies for Rog,* a powerful, emotionally gripping volume written in response to the "AIDS"-related death of Monette's lover, Roger Horwitz.[28] Aptly titled, "Manifesto" participates in the ongoing campaign to refashion the gay subject in terms of an "AIDS activist" identity that deploys, on occasion, as the mirror image against which it would call itself into being, a contemptuous depiction of non-"activist" gay men as narcissists addicted to pleasure, resistant to struggle, and therefore themselves responsible for the continuing devastations of "AIDS." As if invoking Genesis to effect the genesis of a communal gay identity as warriors or resistance fighters, "Manifesto," which immediately follows a poem in which the narrator discusses the difficulties of surviving a loved one with a character called "Eve," begins by condemning, and distancing itself from, the "self-love" of a character called "Adam":

> unsolicited Adam S diagnosed 9/85
> and lucky calls to say all sickness is self-
> induced and as I start to growl oozes self-
> beatification *taking a course in miracles*
> he says and I bark my way out of his wee
> kirk and savage his name from the Rolodex
> another triumph of self-love (1–7)

Though Monette goes on to particularize the form of this Adam's "self-love" as adherence to the "new age" anti-"AIDS" regimen with which Louise Hay is notoriously associated, these lines take aim at those responses to "AIDS" that appear to turn "inward" and toward the "self" instead of outward and toward "others"—responses that are construed as narcissistic, which is to say, as apolitical.

This familiar demonization of narcissism finds expression in familiarly phobic terms as Monette, in a bitter apostrophe, scorns this Adam's self-involvement: "deep-throat/your pale sore body lick your life like a dog's/ balls" (19–21). Is it a coincidence that this "political" repudiation of narcissism (in the name of responsible activism) relies on the putatively self-evident disgust with which the reader is expected to respond to the bestializing figure of auto-fellatio, of "deep-throating" one's own body so that it turns in upon itself, both physically and emblematically, to take itself as its own object? Or that the stigmatization of narcissism so easily swallows up the erotic practice whose popular association with gay men has been enshrined in the denigrating epithet, "cocksucker," wielded against all who fail to embody—or who fail to embody *adequately*—the active, penetrative relation of the (straight, male) subject to the world? Recapitulating the violent refusals undergirding that relation, the activist terms in which the "proper" gay subject is interpellated here position political engagement as the unselfish, socially conscious alternative to the self-centered and destructively hedonistic pleasures associated with a gay sexuality defined, as in the phobic discourse of the culture at large, by the mirror and the anus:

> no we need
> the living alive to bucket Ronnie's House
> with abattoirs of blood hand in hand lesions
> across America need to trainwreck the whole
> show till someone listens so no they may not
> coo in mirrors disbarring the fevered the choked

and wasting as losers who have not learned
like Adam the yoga with which to kiss their own
assholes (25–33)

The point, need I say, is neither to label these lines as homophobic nor to deny the importance of collective interventions to resist the political and economic profiteering that occurs at every level of the government's inadequate responses to "AIDS"; rather, it is to focus on the logics and implications of some of the terms through which an "AIDS activist" identity, here and elsewhere, is being formed—formed, to be sure, both for and by, but also, I think, in significant ways, *at the expense of*, gay men.

Far from signaling opposition to the various forms of "AIDS activism," however, such a focus—though certainly susceptible to representation as narcissistic, inwardly directed, and consequently outside the field of combat—should be interpreted, I believe, as one of the forms such "activism" might take: a form, indeed, in which "activism" ceases to constitute itself in tendentious opposition to a "narcissism" whose stigmatization (as "passivity") uncannily reenacts the defining moment of heterosexual male subject-formation. It is true, after all, to make this point clearer, that when Larry Kramer declares that Vito Russo (who died of "AIDS"-related causes on November 7, 1990) "was killed by 25 million gay men and lesbians who for ten long years of this plague have refused to get our act together. . . . We're killing each other. Can't you see that?," he means something very different from what Patrick Buchanan means when he alleges that "homosexuals, bisexuals [and] IV drug users" with "AIDS" "have killed themselves because they could not or would not control their suicidal appetites."[29] But the difference in what we can acknowledge these two assertions to *intend* should not obscure the similarity in the ideological structures on which they rely: structures that make it easy—indeed, that attempt to make it *natural*—to represent the gay community as murderous in its attachment to "narcissistic" gratification.

While recognizing the difference in meaning that differing subject-positions thus produce, we need to remember how complicated and fissured an oppositional subject-position must be—complicated by its construction within a dominant ideology whose contradictions it may attempt to exploit, but whose logic(s) it can never simply escape. The smoothness with which Kramer's and Buchanan's polemics come together in their depiction of gays as killers *may* signify their common need to resist what Leo Bersani has termed the "self-shattering and solipsistic *jouissance*" that is sexuality itself;[30] but it *certainly* bespeaks a political investment in a shared ideology of the subject—a subject fantasmatically brought into being through an act of self-cohesion (Kramer's "get[ting] our act together") that makes its foundational moment the primal scene of differentiation from what it reads as the torpor or passivity of its imaginary "history," the state of non-organization to which, as Freud argues in *Beyond the Pleasure Principle*, the death drive would have us return. Despite its merely metonymic relation to the psychoanalytic definition of the term, this is the state phobically constructed as "narcissistic" in the dominant elaboration of modern subjectivity; for narcissism, within this logic, connotes the very nondifferentiation from which the active, masculine subject, in what I would call his narci-schism, differentiates himself.

In Monette's "Manifesto," therefore, those who are excoriated for the self-absorption that is figured as eagerness to "kiss their own/asshole" are depicted as murderously indifferent, as people who, "even if they last forever/ will only love the one poor thing themself/and bury the rest of us" (41–43). By tossing bombs at FDA labs and pelting the limousines of bureaucrats, however, the "proper" gay subject as defined by the poem, the subject the narrator implies he has become, displays his command of the aggression needed to elbow his way into the "political" world—an aggression manifest in "Manifesto" primarily through the passion with which the narrator insists on his difference from the mirror-bound narcissists reviled for a passivity defined precisely as *not* knowing the difference between their ass and their elbow. But the activist identity conceived in this way reinscribes through displacement the "self"-love that Monette so movingly evokes in his relationship with Rog, when, for example, in "The Very Same," he recalls how his lover "used to say in [his] cranked up bed/playfully astonished *But we're the same person*" (32–33). In the aftermath of Roger's death, the survival through transference of the ego erotics invested by Monette in that shared identity prompts his rejection of "self"-regard in favor of the political activism of a newly constituted communal self: "I had a self myself/once but he died when do we leave the mirror/and lie down in front of the tanks" (69–71).

Here, as in the rhetoric of "AIDS" activism more generally, the pathos that lends such urgency to the call to resist injustice readily compels assent: not simply, or even primarily, the pathos of what the media self-righteously sell to the public as the "suffering victims of AIDS," but the pathos of the political subject confronting the bad faith and the deadly contradictions of those institutions that not only shape social policy but also, and more profoundly, call forth the subject within ideology. It is all the more painful, therefore, when the rhetoric of "activists," in its resistance to the dominant discourse, redeploys the ideology of that discourse in order, narcissistically, to reinforce an "activist" identity by stigmatizing as narcissistic the community, already so-stigmatized, from which they emerged.

Consider, in this light, the ramifications for a self-nominated "activist" community if one were to bracket the word "sexual" in the following sentence from *Policing Desire*, Simon Watney's indispensable study of "AIDS," representation, and the media: "It is easy to detect a variety of specific defences against what are understood as 'passive' sexual acts, on the part of men whose sense of self is constructed around notions of sexual 'activity.'"[31] Watney's keen insight into such self-definition predicated on the projective expulsion of a specifically *sexual* passivity, however, does not prevent him from reinscribing a version of that projective expulsion in his own work. Examining elsewhere the ideological labor of "an AIDS activist cultural practice," he writes, "this is not for one moment to defend passivity or a retreat from active political engagement."[32] Though Watney, of course, is by no means rejecting any form of erotic experience here—least of all any form of lesbian, gay, or bisexual experience—the presupposition that it goes without saying that passivity is "not for one moment" to be defended cannot escape ideological determination in a culture always predisposed to observe and condemn the proffered "ass" in "passive." "Passivity" lies beyond the pale of defense in the rhetoric of certain "AIDS activists" because for them, as for the dominant cultural subject, it enters a fantasmatic dialectic with "activity" to describe a form of "activity" that would drain "activity" of its "proper" meaning, thereby both threatening, and defining by antithesis, the subject-position they proclaim; as in the originary myth of "AIDS" rehearsed by the *Manchester Union Leader*, such "passivity" can be interpreted by some "AIDS activists" as lethal, even genocidal. "We are such passive people, we gay people," Larry Kramer laments; and addressing the Boston Lesbian and Gay Town Meeting in 1987, he declares, "I'm tired of you, by your own passivity, actively colluding in your genocide."[33]

Do I mean, then, to defend "passivity or a retreat from active political engagement"? Am I defending the "narcissism" of those gay men who refuse to "leave the mirror/and lie down in front of the tanks"? If a short answer to these questions is demanded mine must, obviously, be *yes*, with the proviso that to defend those ways of responding to the epidemics that converge as "AIDS" is neither to advocate nor to encourage them for the gay community as a whole, but to accept them as part of the complex and contradictory vision—at once social, political, and erotic—that vitalizes our community. With the luxury of a less condensed reply, I would suggest that it is never, in any event, a question of leaving the mirror. It is a question, rather, of which mirror we choose to reflect the image we will recognize as ours: whether, that is, on the one hand, in our defense of an already beleaguered gay identity, we want to emulate the widespread heterosexual contempt for the image of a gay sexuality represented as passive and narcissistic in order to embrace, as our new mirror image, the power of the tanks beneath which we would lie; or whether, on the other hand, we want to refuse the "choice" ideologically imposed by such a binarism—whether we want to deny the incompatibility of passivity and power, and thereby to undertake the construction of a gay subjectivity that need not define itself against its own subset of demonized "faggots." For those of us who are and who love gay people, it ought to be possible to affirm and participate in the work of "AIDS activism" without transforming that rubric into an identity whose exclusions uncannily mirror the exclusions of the culture at large. It ought, that is, to be possible to affirm the legitimacy and value of the innumerable ways in which lesbians, gay men, bisexuals, and their allies can participate in the continuing resistance to "AIDS" even while—indeed, even sometimes *by*—resisting the essential but, at moments, too narrowly conceptualized "politics" of "activism."

Isaac Julien has commented on the fact that "the basic hidden message of safe sex in many cases is no sex—an anti-sex message in a post-sex climate";[34] and the tendency toward a similar antipleasure agenda can too easily find its way into the self-constituting rhetoric that characterizes a certain "AIDS activism." Legitimately challenging the ideological complicities of the logics with which politicians, artists, and academics have approached the representations of "AIDS," challenging especially what they see in such work as a tendency to rely on and to reinforce the values and politics of bourgeois humanism, "AIDS activists" can seem at times to demand an ascesis as fully glamorized through its relationship to "power" (and as salvific in its purificatory refusal of passivity) as the bourgeois aesthetic they rightly condemn for fixating on and oppressively enforcing the ubiquity of its own image. Ascesis, of course, has an eros of its own, but its eros is bound to the rigor with which it renounces an eros of luxury. I have tried to suggest that such ascesis, expressed as narci-schism, is the erotic mode of the dominant subject: that the civic authority of subject status is purchased through the projective refusal of the luxurious "passivity," derided as "narcissism," that signifies the erotic indulgence of the self that always threatens to undo the "self." To gain the power of "political" intervention, even in the midst of an epidemic, by buying into the logic of ascesis that grounds the valorization of "politics" over, and in opposition to, the category of "pleasure," must prove a Faustian bargain for the gay community historically oppressed by the very operation of that logic.

The fiction of a "political activism" that would permit us to "leave the mirror," then, signals, ironically enough, the extent to which "AIDS" can be read as effecting the crisis—the marking of difference—that marks, if you will, a sort of mirror stage for the gay communities of the West. Critics of psychoanalysis in general, and of Lacanian psychoanalysis in particular, of course, have argued against the ahistorical tendency of psychoanalytic explanation: against the assumption, for instance, that the subject that emerges by way of the mirror stage must always and necessarily take shape as a subject through the sort of "narci-schism" I discussed above. In naming the overlapping "crises" called "AIDS" as the mirror stage for gay identity, I do not intend to imply that that structure compels us to generate, in an eternal return, the subject-position, the identity concept, that the dominant culture has taught us. But neither do we have the option of simply asserting *ex cathedra*, even *ex* St. Patrick's Cathedral, that our subject-position can be exempted from the ideological consequences—and the *historical* "returns" or repetitions—of its constitution within the dominant culture. To the extent that we are capable of identifying those junctures where the gay subjectivity we seek to produce recapitulates the oppressive logic of the culture that necessitated its emergence, we have the chance to displace that logic and begin to articulate the range of options for what might *become* a postmodern subject; we have the chance, in other words, to challenge, as Andreas Huyssen suggests postmodernism must, "the *ideology of the subject* (as male, white, and middle-class [and we must add, as he does not, heterosexual]) by developing alternative and different notions of subjectivity."[35]

Producing "different notions of subjectivity," however, is not the same thing as occupying a different position as a subject; though dialectically related, the latter is not simply produced by the activity of the former. Written into a discourse of power relations whose network enfolds our own discourse within it, making possible at once our resistances, our transformations, and our reproductions of it, we cannot act to reconstruct the social order without being ourselves the vectors through which the social order acts. Dressed in the garb of material politics, "AIDS activists" may propose, idealistically, that we can "let our discourse infect and recode the message in master discourses and knowledges (from fiction to sociology to deconstruction) rather than let this 'new' thing ["AIDS"] be treated through 'old' practices";[36] but that hope of a discourse that is "ours" and not "theirs," a hope mirrored by the binarism of "new" and "old," rests on the fantasy of a "political" subject not constituted from the outset through a subjection to language. As Diana Fuss puts it in her acute analysis of the relations among politics, identity, and subjectivity, "to see politics as a 'set of effects' rather than as the concealed motor which sets all social relations into motion would prevent us from reifying politics and mystifying its 'behind-the-scenes' operations."[37] Because the "message in master discourses and knowledges" is never a coherent "message" at all, because the "power" of those discourses unfolds within networks of tropology, rhetoric, and grammar that never resolve into a stable conceptual field—let alone a stable conceptual field outside of which we have a place to stand in order to "infect and recode" them like some "new" organism, some "new" virus, entering the system as if created *ex nihilo*—we must recognize that "our" "activist" discourse is only a *mutation* of "their" "master discourses" and that its effect on them, though certain, is also always unpredictable. However appealing the assertion of a "politics" capable *simply* of reclaiming or recoding the oppressive structures of dominant culture may be—however attractive the fiction of a clear-cut distinction between the subject and object positions in any such "reappropriation"—we always have reason to question the logic of agency in such a myth of the subject and reason, therefore, to wonder, as Aretha Franklin once sang, "who's zoomin' who?"

IV. A Queerer Mirror

One way to reframe these issues is to look, as Diana Fuss enables us to formulate it, at the politics of "politics" as it is deployed in the rhetoric of "activism." "Politics," Fuss argues, "represents the aporia in much of our current political theorizing; that which signifies activism is least actively interrogated" (105). This is true, of course, in no small part because "political activism" and the theoretical interrogation sometimes dismissed, from the "activist" perspective, as merely "academic" are situated, by the political framing of such a "politics," in an antithetical relation. "The indeterminacy and confusion surrounding the sign 'politics,'" as Fuss quite rightly observes, "does not typically prevent us from frequently summoning its rhetorical power to keep 'theory' in its place" (106). That it can do so, and do so effectively, bespeaks the extent to which "politics" designates the subject's "proper" sphere as agent and thus the extent to which the politics of "politics" coincides with the foundational differentiation of the subject through the exclusionary logic of active and passive, outside and inside, public and private. In the terms of Monette's "Manifesto" that I have been drawing on above, this could be phrased as the difference, itself constructed from the vantage point of "politics," between enthrallment before the mirror and movement outward to confront the tanks. If, however, both are ways of engaging and producing a mirror image for, and as, one's self—and if, therefore, they can be viewed as acts that, structurally, mirror one another—the difference that "politics" erects between them arises from the originary refusal of "politics" to allow that mirrors do not reflect the "sameness" of identity, but the instability of sameness and difference that "identity" holds in tension. For "politics," as the assertion of agency, loses the efficacy of intervention, and thereby ceases to be what it would recognize as "politics," insofar as it begins to reflect on the instability of the ground on which it rests. Such reflection, after all, is the province of the "theory" that such a "politics" works to "keep . . . in its place"; it is the hallmark, indeed, of the mirror that "politics" becomes "politics" only by leaving.

If "AIDS," though, is viewed as the mirror in which the gay subject is being rewritten, we may be able to displace the logic whereby "political activism" reaffirms the discourse of coherence (including the coherence of the self) and mastery (including the mastery of the self) in order to fantasize the coincidence of agency and intention. In doing so we might try to articulate what might be called a passive agency, an agency that acknowledges its inescapable participation in the production of social effects while acknowledging its inability to control the effects in whose production it thereby figures. Such a notion would require the recognition that powerfully "political" effects can be generated even by those who would seem, from an "activist" perspective, to be a- or anti-political.

We do well to remember, in this regard, that the Stonewall riots, however enabled by the political organizers and homophile societies that created a context for claiming gay rights, resulted from the resistance of people remote from the mainstream of gay political "activism": those young people, transvestites, and drag queens at the Stonewall who, as the *New York Mattachine Newsletter* observed in 1969, "[were] not welcome in, or [could] not afford, other places of homosexual social gathering."[38] The defiant luxury of their contempt for the police who conducted what should have been a routine raid on June 27, 1969, the narcissistic splendor of their campy posturing before the law's ascetic eye, moved the gathered crowd to action in defense of their right to be "narcissistic," their right to enact what the discursive authorities could define as homosexual "passivity." Nor, as we describe the material conditions that led to the rebellion at Stonewall, should we forget the significance of elements as aleatory and apparently counter-political as the "self-indulgent" gay sentimentality of mourning a Judy Garland, lost to an overdose of sleeping pills, whose burial earlier that afternoon evoked a powerful emotional response in many of the drag queens and transvestites whose very susceptibility to such identifications might well have been repudiated as regressive, even masochistic, by normalizing gay activists. Edmund White described what took place at the Stonewall Inn that Friday night in a letter written two weeks after the weekend's momentous events: "Someone shouted, 'Gay power,' others took up the cry—and then it dissolved into giggles. A few more prisoners—bartenders, hatcheck boys—a few more cheers, someone starts singing 'We Shall Overcome'—and then they start camping on it. A drag queen is shoved into the wagon; she hits the cop over the head with her purse. The cop clubs her. Angry stirrings in the crowd."[39] The drag queen striking the cop with her purse to defend the dignity of her narcissism before the punitive gaze of the law remains a potent image of the unexpected ways in which "activism" can find embodiment when the dominant notions of subjectivity are challenged rather than appropriated.

In fact, in the wake of "AIDS," some might say, such a mutation of the gay subject can already be seen in the process by which, in certain quarters, "gay" is being rewritten as "queer." Departing from the work of "AIDS activists"—as Alexander Chee explains, "people are tired of groups with egos, processes, personality cults, and politicking"[40]—"queer nationalism" would reinvent the politics of sexuality by insisting on the fluidity and shiftiness of differences without the need to affirm the difference of a cordoned-off "politics" or "activism." "Rather than a strategic politics that confronts powerful institutions directly or uses lobbying and electoral campaigns to bring about change," write Allan Bérubé and Jeffrey Escoffier, queer nationalism embraces "theatrical demonstrations, infiltrations of shopping malls and straight bars, kiss-ins and be-ins."[41] Though "queer" as the endlessly mutating token of non-assimilation (and hence as the utopian badge of a would-be "authentic" position of resistance) may reflect a certain bourgeois aspiration to be always *au courant*, its vigorous and unmethodical dislocations of "identity" create, at the risk, to be sure, of producing a version of identity politics as postmodern commodity fetishism, a zone of possibilities in which the embodiment of the subject might be experienced otherwise.

Such specific embodiments of gay subjectivity, and the pleasures that attend them, are topics I do not want to end this essay without addressing. For if the mirror has been a privileged trope for the privileging of the body and its gratifications in the history of Western gay men, it occupies a decisive place in the current narratives of "AIDS" as well. It is symptomatic that John Weir, in *The Irreversible Decline of Eddie Socket*, recounts as follows his eponymous hero's moment of recognition: "Eddie Socket got it. AIDS. 'America is dying slowly,' he said, sitting on the lid of a toilet seat and staring into a mirror, in the bathroom just outside the doctor's office where he was diagnosed."[42] As this suggests, the mirror is, in many ways, the distinctive site of the articulation of "AIDS." Reflecting the transformations the body must undergo, it also figures the discursive compulsion to reflect on the history that can seem to have led to this counternarcissistic confrontation with the body whose undoing the specular moment can seem at once to disclose and, causally, to explain. It readily figures, by seeming to mandate, the retroactive production of meaning that Alain Emmanuel Dreuilhe evokes in the first chapter of *Corps à corps: journal de SIDA*: "La maladie n'était prévisible que retrospectivement" ("Only in retrospect could the disease have been anticipated").[43] The mirror's rewriting of the body recurrently catalyzes, in the various discourses on "AIDS," the narrative impulse that generates "meaning" through a temporal logic of before and after that slides into a logic of cause and effect.[44] Across the spectrum of political perspectives, the "before," and thus the "cause," of "AIDS" is consistently represented as the narcissistic hedonism of gay men after Stonewall so that "AIDS" can be read as a mirror for what D. A. Miller, ventriloquizing the various homophobic dispositions of the dominant culture, unpacks as "the disease of gayness itself,"[45] the disease that exposes and abases the "irresponsibility" of gay liberation.

Commenting on this pervasive reconstruction of the past, Dreuilhe evokes the satisfactions this explanatory "history" affords the dominant subject: "D'après le cliché le plus répandu, même dans les milieux libéraux, les gays d'avant le SIDA ne pensaient qu'à faire l'amour et à danser, dépensant leur argent en futilités. Des cigales homosexuelles. La pitié de bien des hétérosexuels, aux États-Unis comme ailleurs, est mitigée par une vague et malsaine satisfaction qui chatouille secrètement leur envie" (50) ("According to the most widespread cliché, common even in liberal circles, gays before AIDS only thought about having sex, dancing, and spending their money on trivialities. Homosexual grasshoppers. The compassion of many heterosexuals, in the United States as elsewhere, is mitigated by a vague and unwholesome satisfaction that secretly titillates their desire"). In the mirror of "AIDS" the erotic abandon, the luxurious collapse into the "black hole" of desire, must give way, depending on the stripe of the narrative, to death, as a recognition of the wages of sin; to monogamy, as a recognition of the immaturity of "promiscuity"; or to "activism," as a recognition of the political folly of defining gay identity through sexuality alone. Bound by the logic of a developmental chronology that moves historically toward the disclosure of truth, these narratives, despite the significant differences in their attitudes toward sexuality, all celebrate a subject whose narci-schism eventuates in "political" authority.

But there are other ways of seeing the gay subject in the mirror that is "AIDS." In *The Motion of Light in Water*, for instance, Samuel Delaney lovingly recalls his erotic encounters with other gay men, individually and in groups, in apartments, in toilet stalls, and in trucks on New York's piers at night. In the midst of these potent memories he interrupts himself:

> What is the reason, anyone might ask, for writing such a book as this half a dozen years into the era of AIDS? Is it simply nostalgia for a medically unfeasible libertinism? Not at all. If I may indulge in my one piece of science fiction for this memoir, it is my firm suspicion, my conviction, and my hope that once the AIDS crisis is brought under control, the West will see a sexual revolution to make a laughing stock of any social movement that till now has borne the name.[46]

Delaney's memoir thus works to keep the knowledge of sexual pleasures in circulation, to counter the construction of a "politics" against, even if "only" *rhetorically* against, the body and its claims for indulgence.

Beside this "piece of science fiction," this act of imaginative activism, I would place a passage from a novel by Hervé Guibert, *A l'ami qui ne m'a pas sauvé la vie*, in which the narrator, a person with "AIDS," looks up as a medical technician draws a sample of his blood:

> Je me suis vu à cet instant par hasard dans une glace, et je me suis trouvé extraordinairement beau, alors que je n'y voyais plus qu'un squelette depuis des mois. Je venais de découvrir quelque chose: il aurait fallu que je m'habitue à ce visage décharné que le miroir chaque fois me renvoie comme ne m'appartenant plus mais déjà à mon cadavre, et il aurait fallu, comble ou interruption du narcissisme, que je réussisse à l'aimer.

> I accidentally saw myself at that moment in a mirror and I found myself extraordinarily beautiful, although I had not seen anything more there than a skeleton for several months. I had just discovered something: it would be necessary to accustom myself to this emaciated face that the mirror each time gave me back as if it no longer belonged to me but already to my corpse, and it would be necessary, either as the height of narcissism or as its interruption, that I succeed in loving it.[47]

In the face of "AIDS," which he will not allow to usurp his own face here, the narrator insists on the necessity of learning to embrace the body anew: on the need to love, not leave, the mirror, by rediscovering the luxury of narcissism from within an experience constructed on every side as a rupture in narcissism itself. This affirmation of a self-regard that would make every mirror a stage defines, like the poses of the drag queens at Stonewall, a strategic mode of resistance not to be slighted by the discourse of "politics" as our lives are rewritten by "AIDS," a mode of resistance alert to the dangers we encounter in allowing gay politics to become a "politics" as usual.

And since the question of address must itself be addressed in the always specular fantasy that propels the use of the first person plural, let me say that the "we" to whom I refer, and to whom these remarks are largely directed, includes those lesbians, gay men, and bisexuals who are responding to the emergency in which we live by producing a variety of strategies that allow us, as part of the resistance to everything that "AIDS" has come to signify, to reinvent ourselves and our social relations, insofar as that can be done, by trying to imagine new subjectivities whose pleasures and politics no longer require conceptualization through antithesis. To be sure, in our historical moment, it is easy to gain access to discursive authority by defining oneself, at least rhetorically, in opposition to narcissistic indulgences, by appropriating a resolutely aggressive, outwardly focused, and thus responsibly "political" position that claims to speak both from and for a populist perspective and against the perspective of intellectuals, academics, and other "special" interests. But the oppositional "activists" who deploy such a strategy within the gay community risk writing "AIDS" as another chapter in the politics of a "politics" constituted as such through the repudiation of that "homosexuality" against which the Western subject and his agency are defined.[48] In the process, such "activists" risk playing out within the ranks of the gay community a projective and only spuriously self-empowering "political" logic similar to the one Marlon Riggs has discerned in the African-American community's popular iconography of black gay men: "What strikes me as most insidious, and paradoxical, is the degree to which African American depictions of us as black gay men so keenly resonate American majority depictions of us, as black people."[49] Such internalizations of dominant logic, the pain of which Riggs knows all too well, can only result in the confirmation of dominant subjectivity.

"Activism" then? Of course "activism": the work of "AIDS activists" is saving our lives; but an "activism" that need not define itself against the "narcissism" and "passivity" that figure the place of gay male sexuality in the Western cultural imaginary. If, as Bersani persuasively puts it in the phrase that I took as my epigraph, "analysis, while necessary, may also be an indefensible luxury," we ought not to ignore the unstable relation between necessity and luxury that problematizes what can or cannot be defended in the midst of an epidemic that targets precisely our modes of defense. Indeed, at a moment when the "activist" interpellation of the oppositional subject invokes the logic of ascesis that underwrites the dominant subject's authority, such "luxuries" as analysis and narcissism, both figured by the mirror, may themselves prove necessary as instruments of defense that can disclose the possibility of a politics in whose name the mirror need not be cracked—a politics whose lineaments no mirror as yet has ever fully shown.

Part III

Body Language / Body Politics

6

THE SODOMITE'S TONGUE AND THE BOURGEOIS BODY IN EIGHTEENTH-CENTURY ENGLAND

The anonymous author of *Satan's Harvest Home* (1794), offering "Reasons for the Growth of Sodomy" in mid-eighteenth-century England, conjures a resolutely masculine vision of the glorious British past, describing the normative fashioning of the "Gentleman of former Days"[1] in an account that even contemporary readers must have recognized as needing the Augustan equivalent of a warning from the surgeon general: "Caution: retroactive bourgeois mythologizing may be dangerous to your health." More exactly, as I hope to suggest in this essay, to the extent that such mythologizing plays a central role in the normalization of homophobia not *in* but *as* male socialization in the course of the eighteenth century, this mythologizing imposes a standard of *health* that constitutes a significant danger in itself.[2] Indeed, it is the very discipline of health, tendentiously articulated as the health of discipline, that shapes the essentially middle-class trajectory of the gentleman's life that *Satan's Harvest Home* imagines unfolding in a fantasmatic England before the growth of sodomy.

"Subject to Order and Correction" (45), at least as the author of the pamphlet portrays him, the pre-modern gentleman in the making is depicted as having applied himself at school with equal diligence to study and the sort of wholesome athletic exercise that "sent him home with his Blood in a fine Circulation and his Stomach as sharp as a Plowman's" (45–46). His passions tempered, but not debilitated, by such an education, and with nothing of the "Valetudinarian in his Constitution" (46), he found himself, "in the Flower of his Health," "blest with an endearing Wife" (46) and with children who signified and embodied his interest in serving the ideological trinity consisting of "his King, his Country, and his Family" (46). Describing a representative of this now vanished breed as if he stood before him still, the author sums up his class-inflected vision of a capitalist sexual economy when he observes that "Application to Business keeps him from Debauch, and his Success spurs him on, that he soon sees a fine Provision made for himself and Family; and his (perhaps small) Patrimony, amply augmented" (47).

If this idealized discipline of familialism underwrites, all too familiarly, the primal socio-economic mandate that the middle class increase and multiply, the author of *Satan's Harvest Home* sees, by contrast, the lax moral climate of 1749 as producing, in the place of such industrious gentlemen, the mere "Figure of a Man" (49) whose effeminacy signals inevitable decline: "Thus, unfit to serve his King, his Country, or his Family, this Man of Clouts dwindles into nothing, and leaves a Race as effeminate as himself; who, unable to please the Women, chuse rather to run into unnatural Vices one with another, than to attempt what they are sensible they cannot perform" (50). This terrifying prospect of dwindling into nothing, the economic obverse of "application to Business," which results in "fine Provision" and a patrimony "amply augmented," finds its ultimate realization, according to the author, in sodomitical relations between men; and those relations, in turn, find their visible ensign in the "hateful, predominant, and pernicious" custom of "Mens Kissing each other" (51) and "Slavering every Time they meet," an "Unmanly, Unnatural Usage" that the author identifies as "the first Inlet to the detestable Sin of Sodomy" (52).

I would like to think through some aspects of the logic by which it was possible, in the eighteenth century, to link the fashioning of a proto-middle-class "gentleman" to a concern that male-male kissing provided a manifest "inlet" to sodomy, especially since the concept of sodomy itself—that "utterly confused category" as G. S. Rousseau, quoting Foucault, describes its provenance in Augustan England—mobilized anxieties about possible ruptures or "inlets" in the middle-class body then achieving its modern ideological formation.[3] Let me suggest at the outset that to whatever extent one man's kissing of another man came to be seen not only as a fashionable custom,[4] but also as a code or come-on for other acts of same-sex eros and intimacy, the particular exchange of bodily fluids derogatorily identified as "slavering" or "tonguing" by the author of *Satan's Harvest Home* constituted a topos that gained tropological significance in the century's discourse on sodomy. Captain Rigby, for instance, in 1698 is reported to have put his tongue into William Minton's mouth when he tried to seduce him on Guy Fawkes Day during a public display of fireworks,[5] and this image recurs throughout the criminal records of sodomy trials in the course of the eighteenth century. When Nicholas Leader accused George Duffus of a sodomitical assault in 1721, he testified that Duffus "began to hug me and kiss me, and call me his Dear. I asked him what he meant by it? He answer'd, *No*

Harm, nothing but Love, and presently got upon me, and thrust his Tongue into my Mouth";[6] similarly, Joseph Sellers, who participated in a plot to entrap mollies in 1726, testified that Thomas Wright "kiss'd me with open Mouth"[7] and that Martin Mackintosh "thrust his hand into my Breeches, and his Tongue into my Mouth."[8] In 1760 James Fassett, a student at God's Gift College in Dulwich, deposed that Richard Branson, assaulting him with intent to commit sodomy, first "kissed my Lips only" then "kiss'd me again, putting his Tongue into my Mouth; and sucking my Lips."[9]

The records of these trials give little information about the ways in which this topos might have figured in the social-symbolic order that shaped and was, in turn, shaped by the contemporary discourse on sodomy. I would suggest, however, that to some extent such information can be gleaned from a pamphlet that appeared in 1739 beneath the title, "A Faithful Narrative of the Proceedings in a late Affair between the Rev. Mr. John Swinton, and Mr. George Baker, both of Wadham College, Oxford."[10] This document was published by friends of George Baker to clarify the meaning of another document that had recently appeared in the London newspapers—a letter in which Baker recanted his claim that Rev. Swinton had engaged in sodomitical relations with a servant boy named Robert Trustin. In order to establish the appropriate context for interpreting Baker's letter, the pamphlet begins by recounting an episode that took place at the College earlier in the year when the Warden, Robert Thistlethwayte, allegedly attempted sodomy on the body of William French, "a young Gentleman of about two years standing" (2) at the College. When French, after a private interview with the Warden on February 3, 1739, returned to his friends morose and "disorder'd" (3), reviling Thistlethwayte as a villain and a scoundrel, and claiming it was in his power to have the Warden expelled, were he so inclined, George Baker, one of French's companions, became suspicious. Recalling previously circulated rumors that Thistlethwayte "did not love Women" (4), Baker got French to acknowledge that the Warden had made a sodomitical attempt upon his person and then successfully encouraged French to prosecute Thistlethwayte, as he put it, "for the good of the College" (6). It is at this point that Rev. Swinton became involved in the affair; a friend of the Warden's, he joined him in urging French to accept a handsome provision instead of pressing charges, and when French refused to do so, Swinton, though he had admitted that he could give testimony that would corroborate French's accusations, failed to show up on the day he was scheduled to present his evidence to the Vice Chancellor. Though Swinton returned thereafter to Wadham and did present testimony before the Grand Jury that helped to substantiate French's charge, Thistlethwayte absconded after the Grand Jury returned an indictment that charged him with attempted sodomy. With this the whole incident might have come to an end, had not Baker, in March, received a letter from a former student at the College suggesting that Rev. Swinton himself, during the letter-writer's period of residence at the College, had committed sodomy upon the body of a servant boy, Robert Trustin. Though Baker got Trustin to acknowledge before witnesses that Swinton had indeed taken him into his bed and engaged in sodomitical acts, when brought before the Vice Chancellor to confirm the accusations that Baker now leveled against Swinton, Trustin, whom the "Faithful Narrative" alleges to have been bribed in the interim by Swinton's Bedmaker, testified instead that he had been bribed by *Baker* to testify against *Swinton*. Questioned, subsequently, in the presence of witnesses who had heard his earlier story, the inaptly named Trustin proved himself a testator whose words one could put little trust in. Responding in the affirmative to questions at one moment and in the negative to the same questions when they were repeated in the next, Trustin rendered his testimony hopelessly self-contradictory; Baker's case against Swinton collapsed, and Swinton thereafter insisted that Baker sign a recantation of his charges. With much reluctance and serious misgivings Baker finally did so, unaware that the document would be published by Swinton and create the impression that Baker had maliciously fabricated his accusation. The "Faithful Narrative," by specifying the circumstances precipitating Baker's charges, sought, then, to repair the damage done to Baker's reputation.

Though the narrative, toward this end, insists that it confines itself "strictly to Fact" (19), I want, nonetheless, to attend to this narrative as if it were a literary *fiction* in order to elicit a few of the ways in which it frames the question of sodomy and to bring into focus some of the contexts within which it suggests that sodomy could signify in England near the middle of the century. To begin I would observe that one of the categories through which this text conceptualizes sodomy is as a crisis in, or a perversion of, the process of signification itself. Sodomy is articulated here, that is, both alongside and in terms of the problematization of social exchange and the inhibition, disturbance, or obstruction of meaningful speech. Thus when William French, after his meeting with the Warden, behaves so strangely before his friends that they beg him to tell them what is wrong, he responds, the pamphlet claims, as follows: "*The matter*, said he, *the Murther of one's Father, or whole Family is nothing to it; you can't conceive anything bad enough*: But he would not tell them what it was" (3). This refusal or inability to speak the truth of sodomy, or more precisely, to represent a gentleman's body in its vulnerability to sodomitical assault, is reenacted by the text of the pamphlet itself, which leaves every detail of this assault unspoken, arguing that "the Particulars are judged too gross and obscene to be repeated" (7).

Whatever we make of this ellipsis in the narrative—and I think it reflects, at least in part, the conceptualization of sodomy in relation to linguistic instability or disruption—we ought not to interpret the reticence it announces as squeamishness about the forthright discussion of same-sex sexual relations. For the pamphlet then proceeds to cite the testimony of Robert Langford, a butler, who describes how the Warden attempted "to kiss and tongue him, and to put his Hand into his Breeches" (16); it goes on to report the deposition of William Hodges, a barber, who claims that "the Warden said to him . . . How does thy Cock do, my dear Barber? Let me feel it; and then went to kiss him" (18); and more graphically still, it recounts the discussion between Baker and Trustin in which the boy describes the intimate details of his experiences with Swinton: "The Boy then affirmed . . . that he used to lie in Bed with Mr. Swinton; that Mr. Swinton used to tickle and play with him in the Morning; that he used to play with Mr. Swinton's Cock, which used to stand; that Mr. Swinton used to kiss him. Mr. Baker asked him, Whether Mr. Swinton used to put his Tongue in his Mouth? to which the Boy answered, No. And then being asked, whether Mr. Swinton did not use to get upon his Back, he answered, No; but said, that he used to get upon his Belly, between his Thighs, and that he used to put his Cock in his A___H___,[11] and that he felt something warm come from him, and that he sometimes made him wet between his Thighs" (22). In light of these vivid descriptions, the pamphlet's silence about the particulars of Thistlethwayte's attempt on French's virtue, the gap where the narrative refuses to represent what went on behind the Warden's locked door, suggests that what is "too gross and obscene to be repeated" is not so much the description of a sodomitical assault, as the representation of the violability, or, more exactly, the *penetrability*, of the ideologically articulated body of that liminal construct, the middle-class gentleman.[12] Bearing in mind that the Warden is alleged to have failed in his sodomitical assault upon French, and recalling, on the one hand, the butler's testimony that Thistlethwayte tried to "kiss and tongue him" and, on the other hand, Baker's question to the servant boy, "Whether Mr. Swinton used to put his Tongue in his Mouth," we may reasonably assume that the Warden's attack began with, and perhaps did not go much beyond, his kissing and tonguing the young gentleman named, almost too appropriately, French.

We return to this particular topos, then, with the possibility of seeing it as a switch point of sorts connecting the evolving discourse on sodomy with the uncertainty or danger that sodomy is construed as posing to the function of discourse itself. The topos thus moves toward the status of a trope so that the representation, however formulaic, of one man's tongue in another man's mouth can not only figure the penetration of one orifice as an inlet for, and an image of, the sodomitical penetration of another, it can also suggest the connotative overlay in sodomy's cultural construction of an anxiety about the authority and autonomy of one's own signifying practices. More specifically, and to insist once again on the class-inflected focus of this particular anxiety, sodomy, while readily articulable as a vice of the court[13] or a depravity of the lower classes, poses so significant a symbolic threat to the assertion of bourgeois subjectivity that it retains the force of its historical status as a sin "too gross and obscene" to be discussed only insofar as the integrity of a *gentleman's* body is at stake; but where the object of the sexual assault is, instead, a servant boy or a butler, his body is unproblematically available for spectacular representation in the pamphlet. The narrative gap in the text, then, would foreclose the possibility of *viewing* the gentleman's body as subject to penetration; that gap, one might say, both figures and seals the opening in the symbolically masculine body of the middle class itself, thus sealing its potential inlet to sodomy precisely because the notion of sodomy has come to include in its figural orbit a challenge to the bourgeois gentleman's most valuable and hence most anxiously defended property: the interiority that both signals and constitutes his autonomous subjectivity, and thus the authority whereby he controls the meaning of his signifying acts. Those signifying acts, after all, as Leo Braudy notes in a reading of *Clarissa*, came increasingly in the eighteenth century to be seen as threatened by a social economy that sought, as Braudy puts it, "to steal your self away, to penetrate your ideas, to prepossess your feelings, to bend your will to [its] own."[14]

In fact, on a variety of levels the "Faithful Narrative" displaces sodomy into, or allegorizes it as, the destabilization of discursive authority that is evoked by the topos of one man thrusting his tongue into another man's mouth. As the social-symbolic burden of this figure lies precisely in the question of who speaks through whom, who controls or manipulates the discourse (by penetrating the body) of the other, so the two crucial moments in the "Faithful Narrative"'s attempt to exonerate Baker both center on alienated speech acts, acts in which one person's tongue imposes itself on, and thereby usurps, another's. In the first of these moments, the servant boy's evidence is marred by a self-contradiction that the "Faithful Narrative" ascribes to the fact of his having been bribed by Rev. Swinton, who thereby figurally reproduces in the text the sodomitical topos of the invasive tongue speaking through the body of a male who is both commodified and denied authority over his own discourse as a result. More significantly, perhaps, in the second of these moments, Rev. Swinton, having escaped prosecution for sodomy by manipulating the servant boy's speech—effectively bending the boy, one more time, to his will—imposes his language on Baker himself by drafting and demanding that Baker put his name to a strongly worded recantation. The pamphlet makes much of Baker's resistance to endorsing such a text, even though his failure to do so might result in expulsion from the College or even legal prosecution, and it cites his conversation with the Vice Chancellor to clarify how he was finally persuaded to sign: "Baker continued, Mr. Vice Chancellor, You must be very sensible that every Thing contained in this Recantation, is directly the reverse of my real Sentiments; and that it is expressed in such Terms, as will admit of no other Construction, but that I have designedly, and without any Grounds whatsoever, endeavored to ruin Mr. Swinton's Character. The Vice Chancellor replied, That such strong Expressions were only *matter of Form*, as in the Case of Indictments, in which Words were used of much stronger Signification, literally accepted, than what was really true: and then he repeated several Forms of Law of that kind. Mr. Baker answered, That as *meer matter of Form* he would sign it, but not otherwise" (30). Urged to accept the phrasing of the document as mere rhetorical convention, Baker assents with a declaration that his signature affirms only the figural or formal sense of the document's language—he insists, that is, on his autonomous subjectivity by attempting to frame the context for, and thus to control the significance of, the words to which he must put his name as if they came from himself.

When Swinton puts the document into circulation, however, Baker can no longer contextualize the words that Swinton has put in his mouth. As he protests to the Vice Chancellor, "the World, not knowing the conditions on which he signed it, would take the Words in their literal Sense, and conclude him the vilest and most abandoned Wretch in Nature" (31). Baker finds himself, as this last phrase makes clear, in the sodomite's position, subject to the condemnation he attempted to call down upon Rev. Swinton; his effort to expose Swinton's "crime against nature" effects the representation of his own character as unnatural, and he recognizes too late the alienability of characters, of signifiers, from any signifying intention. The "Faithful Narrative," written to reveal how unjustly Baker's character has been imposed upon by Swinton, suggests that this alienability is both implicit in, and a figure for, the crime of sodomy itself: that Baker, in effect, has been screwed.

This figuralization of the sodomitical tongue suggests that modern homophobia became entrenched in eighteenth-century England by tapping into bourgeois anxiety about authority and autonomy at a time, as Felicity Nussbaum notes, of "increasing belief that the key to real character [was] the construction of interiority."[15] The threat to that interiority, to the autonomy of a self in control of its signifiers and thus able to use them legitimately as objects of exchange, informs the text's reading of sodomy as an attempt to appropriate the subject's body and to make it speak with a foreign tongue. Four years before the publication of this pamphlet, Alexander Pope invoked the specter of sodomy in strikingly similar terms, mocking Sporus for subjecting his body to penetration by focusing on the ease with which others were able to manipulate his tongue: "in florid impotence he speaks/And, as the prompter breathes, the pupet squeaks."[16] Not speaking here but spoken through, the male body is transformed into an object whose value no longer derives from the autonomy that bespeaks its subjectivity and hence its economic agency; instead that body testifies to the alienability of its selfhood in defiance of Locke's assertion that "every man has a 'property' in his own 'person' which nobody has any right to but himself."[17] In the context of a still emerging and therefore anxiously defended ideology of middle-class social authority, sodomy takes shape as a menace to the bourgeois body's capacity to maintain, control, and articulate the signifying intentions of a self conceived as the property the bourgeois gentleman inalienably possesses *in* himself. The disenfranchisement of the tongue at stake in the eighteenth-century topos of male-male kissing as an "inlet to the detestable Sin of Sodomy" allows sodomy to figure the evacuation of interiority and, therefore, a threat to the health not only of the middle class *as* a body but also to the health of the middle-class body itself. In this context the anonymous author of *Hell Upon Earth* could write in 1729 of one Tolson "whose Constitution was so depraved and ruined that he could contain nothing within him, and who was not ashamed to confess, that he received that Debility by . . . the vile Practice of Buggery."[18] This man who can contain nothing within himself literalizes the sodomitical threat to an emergent bourgeois identity predicated precisely on self-containment, and anticipates the effeminate figure of a man whose nearness to what the nineteenth century would come to designate as inversion is represented by his inversion of the trajectory of middle-class capitalism in *Satan's Harvest Home*: an inversion that condemns him literally, or at least physiologically, to "dwindle into nothing." Given the interlocking concepts of social, economic, and physical health in the middle-class ideology then being shaped, it is small wonder that for a gentleman like William French, as depicted in the "Faithful Narrative," the disappropriation of his property in himself is not only unspeakable but constitutes so profound a threat to the foundational logic of his subjectivity that it causes him to be taken physically ill. After the Warden's sodomitical attempt, we are told, to the surprise of his acquaintances, French suffers a fit of nausea and vomits, as if to expel a poisonous or unassimilable substance from his body, or as if to cast out, to project, some foreign matter from his mouth. This visceral response to sodomy, translating its menace to the psychic construction of the middle-class body into somatic symptoms, marks a significant moment in the history of modern homophobia. For the crime against nature, once the sign of a disturbance in the moral or theological realm, now has the literal capacity to make the bourgeois gentleman *sick* precisely to the extent that sodomy dispossesses him of interiority and achieves symbolic representation, as our culture continues to put it, as a practice that is shoved down his throat. Though dominant culture may focus on its conceptual association with anality, the positional reversals condensed in the Western construction of sodomitical relations already allowed sodomy, in mid-eighteenth-century England, to signify an assault upon the logic of discourse, a crisis in social articulation, and thus a practice whose most radically disorienting effects were those that came, as it were, in one's mouth.

7

CAPITOL OFFENSES

Sodomy in the Seat of American Government

To designate Washington, D.C. as the capital of the United States is to figure the nation as a body with the federal district as its head. But given the tropology of everyday life, it is possible to identify that geographical space by means of a figure that invokes metonymically a less exalted part of the anatomy; it is not uncommon, after all, to refer to Washington as the seat of our government. This should not be taken to suggest that the territory often figured as "inside the beltway" can therefore, in any simple way, be mapped onto those parts of the body sometimes defined as "below the belt," nor should it be taken to imply, more crudely, that because the capital is the seat of the government, the government, necessarily or by definition, can be said to have its head up its ass. But the dangerously collapsible distance between those two defining features—features not so much of the body as they are of the body's politics, and, potentially, by extension, of the body politic itself—are what I want to consider here in relation to the discourse of sodomy.

Peter Stallybrass and Allon White, in their provocative study, *The Politics and Poetics of Transgression*, importantly remind us that "one cannot analyse the psychic domain without examining the processes of transcoding between the body, topography, and the social formation";[1] and while they do not directly address the place of sodomy in this symbolic economy, they suggestively note that through the nineteenth century, "whilst the 'low' of the bourgeois body becomes unmentionable, we hear an ever increasing garrulity about the *city's* 'low'—the slum, the rag-picker, the prostitute, the sewer—the 'dirt' which is 'down there.' In other words, the axis of the body is transcoded through the axis of the city, and whilst the bodily low is 'forgotten,' the city's low becomes a site of obsessive preoccupation."[2] In the discourse of the mass media throughout the 1980s, however, the locus of this social garrulity was decisively displaced, and the problems of the cities and their inhabitants were "forgotten," for the most part, while virtually every aspect of the bourgeois body was seized upon as a site of intense preoccupation. From Nautilus equipment and Soloflex machines to Jimmy Carter's hemorrhoids and Ronald Reagan's intestinal polyps, from the public discussions of herpes lesions and the modes of HIV transmission to the battle for women's reproductive freedom and the rights of gay men and lesbians to legal expression of their sexuality, the bourgeois body arguably became the most embattled and contested territory in the political rhetoric of the eighties; and as the federal war against the cities—a war of contemptuous indifference when not a war of outright and active hostility—ran its course throughout the decade, it is telling that some of our most heated domestic policy debates should have centered so insistently on defining the bourgeois "right to privacy." Most saliently for the purposes of this essay, after all, it was by denying that the "right to privacy . . . extends to homosexual sodomy" that the U.S. Supreme Court arrived at its controversial decision in *Bowers v. Hardwick.*

In the aftermath of that decision, for those of us in America near the end of a century, approaching the end of a millennium, sodomy remains the legal designation for a variety of intimate behaviors subject to legislative prohibition by the state. But the affective resonance, and therefore the power, of sodomy as a trope in American culture extends beyond the category of erotic activities subject to prosecution. For sodomy—and following the Supreme Court we might choose to specify, "homosexual sodomy"—occupies a potent position in our national imaginary; it conjures, and nowhere more so than in the rhetoric of contemporary politics, a fantasy that trenches on the cultural limits of representation itself, whether that representation refers to practices primarily aesthetic or political. D. A. Miller, for instance, elaborating on the work of Foucault, has noted that sodomy "is probably the least specific practice in the whole history of sexuality,"[3] and one might take this suggestion even further by adding that while sodomy cannot be reduced to any specific or essential practice, it has been viewed historically, at least in the West, as constitutively destructive of essence. In this way it has proven to be infinitely adaptable as a figure for the disruption or destabilization of any foundational logic.

This means that the concept of "homosexual" sodomy operates for our culture as a powerful shorthand through which to evoke what Stallybrass and White identify as "the topic of hierarchy inversion, of 'world upside down.'"[4] Consider for instance two normative examples chosen from discussions that took place in the Capitol during 1989. Deploying the rhetoric of logical reversal that seems, if not to *be*, then to be inextricable *from*, the homophobic interpretation of sodomy, Congressman William Dannemeyer alleged that homosexuals working for the "undeniably conservative administrations" of the eighties literalized the dictum that "politics makes strange bedfellows," and this, he suggests, explains why, in his words, "our national AIDS policy has been *turned upside down*" (emphasis mine);[5] invoking a similar tropology of what could, correctly, be called "inversion," Robert Dornan, in the course of a Congressional debate over an amendment to exempt religiously affiliated educational institutions from compliance with those sections of D.C.'s human rights laws that offer some protection to lesbians and gay men, denied that gays have any legitimate claim to civil rights protection, declaring: "I am amazed that we would come to a day . . . that we would equate the Afro-American heritage, the Jewish-American heritage, the Irish-American heritage, or gender, women, with sodomy. This is a crazy day in the House. It is Alice in Wonderland."[6] The reversal—or worse, the deconstruction—of rationality figured here by "Alice in Wonderland" mirrors the reversal of front and back, proper and improper, socially productive and narcissistically wasteful, that renders sodomy a practice essentially inimical to essence: inimical, that is, to the logic of being, the logic of identity, and thus to the logic of logic itself. Given this loaded tropological freighting of "sodomy" in America, we can hardly be surprised that Congressman Ron Dellums, whose eloquent defense of the federal district's human rights law immediately preceded Congressman Dornan's remarks, should have interrupted Dornan's speech to insist: "I stood in the well of this House to argue for the right of people to choose and for freedom. I was not talking about sodomy."[7] The legitimacy of the right to choose, even when that right is being defended in the specific context of the right to choose sexual relations that are legally defined as sodomy, must be protected from contamination by the taint of sodomy itself. Even where sodomy constitutes the subject of discussion, it remains a subject in favor of which no subject can properly talk. This exchange between Dornan and Dellums exposes the coercive logic of sodomy's figural construction as the antithesis of logical discourse and demonstrates just how inextricable it is from the cultural fantasmatics through which the body and the body politic are conceived.

Perhaps, then, it makes a certain sense that the summer of 1989, which began with a Congressional uproar over art, homoeroticism, and the propriety of public endowments for photographs like those of Robert Mapplethorpe—"one of which," as Senator Alan Simpson observed with "repugnance" during debate on the Senate floor, "disclosed a whip sticking out of a leering man's anus"[8]—perhaps it makes a certain sense that such a summer should end with Congressman Barney Frank acknowledging his involvement with Stephen Gobie, whom he met by responding to a personal ad that promised "a great time" by referring to Mr. Gobie's "hot bottom" and "large endowment."[9] Whatever slippage in meaning the emphasis on the size of an endowment has suffered in the interval between these two much publicized controversies, both speak to the representative place of sodomy in the contemporary political landscape: a place that always, as Senator Simpson suggests, must, at bottom, "disclose . . . [the] anus" and that threatens, in so doing, to become the site of other dangerous disclosures concerning the resistance of desire to regulation or limitation. Such disclosures make sodomy a powerful and powerfully disturbing emblem of dis-closure, an emblem of the end opened up so that anus and mouth become implicated in one another, as Congressman Dannemeyer unwittingly demonstrated when he declared in the pages of the *Congressional Record* that "Historically, [the] bowels [of homosexuals] have been full of the bulk of enteric diseases in America. Syphilis, gonorrhea, and hepatitis B have been the mainstays of their viral menu."[10] Confounding the distinction between coming in and going out, between consumption and expulsion, between the public and the private, and thereby transgressing the definitional boundaries that underwrite social identities, sodomy figures in the political imaginary precisely as a *public* and not a *private* concern—a circumstance emphatically brought home to us, as it were, by the fact that Michael Hardwick, though arrested by a policeman who observed him committing sodomy in the anticipated privacy of his home, was never brought to trial despite the Attorney General's successful claim that the state of Georgia had a legitimate interest in criminalizing his private behavior. The crucial question informing the discourse of homosexual sodomy in America, then, is not so much what individuals, or individual bodies, can be permitted to do in private, but what those bodies can *publicly be represented* as being permitted to do in private: it is a question, in other words, of whether or not sodomy is susceptible to representation.

One way of trying to get a purchase on this question is to consider Barney Frank's much ridiculed admission that his involvement with Stephen Gobie constituted an error in personal judgment, an admission in the course of which Frank made a literary "error" of another order altogether. "Thinking I was Henry Higgins," Frank declared of his relationship with Gobie, "and trying to turn him into Pygmalion was the biggest mistake I've made."[11] Although the *Washington Post*, not trusting its readers to recognize the allusion, explained that Frank "liken[ed] himself to the fabled English linguistic scientist in George Bernard Shaw's 'Pygmalion' who attempts to transform a cockney waif into a member of English society,"[12] neither it nor the *New York Times* nor the authors of the cover story in *Newsweek* noted that Frank's identification of himself with Henry Higgins would seem to require that Gobie be identified with the "cockney waif," with Eliza Doolittle, and thus, in the Ovidian myth, with Galatea rather than with Pygmalion. Gobie, however, quite clearly understood that hers was the role in which he was being cast: "This is not the case of the poor waif who is being sheltered,"[13] he subsequently told an interviewer. And to demonstrate as much he added of his erotic involvement with Congressman Frank: "This was the first time he felt good in a relationship. Here's a guy who didn't have a social life until he was 45."[14] Ironically, if not surprisingly, Gobie—by implying that it was he who brought the Congressman, like Galatea, to life—implicitly redefined himself as the very Pygmalion into whom Frank "mistakenly" admitted it had been a mistake to try to turn him. The apparent irreducibility of error in the public depiction of this relationship (for which a law professor at George Washington University urged that Frank be charged with sodomy) testifies to the difficulty of representing gay sexuality within the mythologies of heterosexual culture; at the same time, though, it allegorizes the "error" that figures sodomy itself—an error that consists of reversing such psycho-socially elaborated positions as subject and object, active and passive, spectator and spectacle: positions whose distance from one another yields the difference without which any representation would be impossible, and whose collapse produces the undecidable positioning figured by Gobie's advertisement of a "hot bottom" *and* a "large endowment." The potential allegorization of sodomitical "error" in Congressman Frank's remark makes it impossible to determine if his statement constitutes a misrepresentation after all: whether it enacts, that is, a simple mistake in literary allusion, or whether it should be seen, instead, as a revisionary representation of the "error" without which his relationship with Gobie could not have been articulated, as an accurate representation, therefore, of the culturally "improper" substitution of "sameness"—or what at first might appear to be sameness—for socially compulsory, heterosexual "difference."

But Henry Higgins and Pygmalion, of course, do not amount to "the same." Though Shaw's title implies their metaphoric relation, that metaphor measures distance as surely as identification. Indeed, among the many differences that can be made to signify in the movement from one to the other are differences between modern and ancient, between English and Greek, and between a version of the professorate and a version of the artist. More interesting to me, however, is the fact that Frank's identification with Higgins reads sexuality in terms of social stratification and the promiscuity of class encounters experienced in modern urban culture, while Gobie's implicit identification with Pygmalion focuses instead on sexuality as the activation of dormant, but *intrinsic*, desires. Seen in this light, the distance between Frank as Higgins and Gobie as Pygmalion epitomizes the distance between "public" and "private" in the tropology of sodomy and it brings us back to the question of sodomy's availability to representation.

The erotic economy of homosexual relations continues to be traced for our culture in the enduring equation of homosexuality with *male* homosexuality, of male homosexuality with sodomy, and of sodomy with anal intercourse, and, in particular, with the so-called "passive" or receptive position in anal intercourse—an equation that the eighties reinforced through the telling cliché of anal penetration as the "most efficient" mode of HIV transmission and the attendant identification of HIV infection with the condition of gay men as such. Anality, invoking as it does for us the "lowest" of the body's functions, should not be ignored as an aspect of the drama in which Henry Higgins figures. Shaw's play effects what Stallybrass and White call the "transcod[ing] of the body through the axis of the city" by evoking Eliza Doolittle as so thoroughly embodying her urban milieu that Henry Higgins characterizes her as "a thing out of the squashed cabbage leaves of Covent Garden";[15] and as if to demonstrate the symbolic economy linking the city's "low" to the body's "lower" functions, Higgins exclaims appreciatively, "she's so deliciously low—so horribly dirty."[16] That the lowness of class identified here by Eliza's urban dirt gestures toward the unspeakable dirt of "forgotten" bodily functions, may explain why Higgins—whose "inveterate old-bachelordom" derives, as Shaw tells us, from an idealization of his mother—refers to Eliza, with more than a hint of anal erotic displacement, as a "draggletailed guttersnipe,"[17] effectively repositioning *Pygmalion*'s sociological discourse of the gutter in exemplary relation to the anatomical discourse of the "tail."

This last suggestion will not, of course, immediately call forth the Henry Higgins that most Americans know and love, the Henry Higgins familiar, that is, from Lerner and Loewe's *My Fair Lady*, a theatrical text that finds its title—and gestures toward its conventional heterosexual framing—by substituting for Shaw's allusion to Pygmalion an allusion to the Galatea elided in Barney Frank's remark. In the musical, as in Shaw's play, the narrative hinges on the misrepresentation of a working-class flower girl as an habitué of aristocratic society, but the effacement of a serious discussion of class turns the musical version into a typically uplifting Broadway tale of innate or private virtue (the inner "truth" of Eliza's identity that makes her worthy of romantic love) triumphant over every impediment of class or social constraint. Indeed the scornful snickers that greeted Frank's comparison of himself to Henry Higgins responded not only to the musical's refusal to imagine Professor Higgins engaged in illicit relations with Eliza Doolittle (let alone with Colonel Pickering), but also to the musical's suggestion that Higgins's act of pedagogical "transformation," unlike Representative Frank's, made visible a truth that was always implicit but unrecognized in his pupil. Higgins, that is, undertook to misrepresent the external or socially-determined class standing of someone the audience was made to perceive as possessing that moral or spiritual value, that dispositional generosity we democratically describe as "real class," whereas Frank, in the eyes of the American public, undertook to misrepresent the *moral* standing, the social redeemability, of someone of whose intrinsic worthlessness his sexual activities, especially insofar as they involved the would-be agent of his uplift, offered such *prima facie* evidence that the *Washington Post* could describe him as "the unspeakable Mr. Gobie" and characterize him with reference to what it did not scruple to call his "loathsome pastimes."[18] The carnivalesque masquerade through which Higgins deliberately misrepresented Eliza revealed that beneath layers of surface dirt was an innately delicate sensibility; but the dismissal of Frank's identification with Higgins as a deluded misrepresentation of *himself* bespoke the pervasive homophobic belief that what was truly dirty—dirty, as it were, in the most fundamental way—was fraudulently being represented here as something it was not.

Similar beliefs figured prominently in the Congressional debate conducted earlier that summer over the funding of the Mapplethorpe exhibit—a debate in which much rhetorical energy was directed toward denouncing the hoax allegedly being perpetrated upon the American taxpayer by those Senator Helms and his allies represented as "the self-appointed experts" of "the so-called arts community." Speaking for members of Congress on the left and the right alike,[19] an article from the *Washington Times* read into the *Congressional Record* by Senator Grassley of Iowa proclaimed that "art has become a con game practiced only by professors, weirdos and fools."[20] Thus the funding controversy centered importantly on the opposition between the discursive practices associated with electoral politics on the one hand and academic culture on the other, and academic culture was warned to "get back in touch with the American people, our values,"[21] after having been condemned for promoting what might be described as a "sodomitical reading practice." For sodomitical reading, as a reversal of the commonsensical logic of relationality, as a "con game" that calls into question the self-evidence of value judgments and conceptual distinctions, dares to parade the seat in the capital by misrepresenting the anus as art—misrepresenting it, that is, as a redeemable focus of intellectual curiosity and attention. The sodomitical upending of dominant values and the repudiation of "middle-brow" taste—which defines the perversion of the academy, or at least of the humanities, from the highly politicized vantage point of a conservative social order—must be repudiated for trying to pass off as valuable that which must be understood as intrinsically implicated in the waste or filth of which a culture must be purged to be recognizable *as* a culture. The denaturalizing inversions that would characterize such a "sodomitical reading practice" explicitly become the target when Senator Helms proclaims: "The avant garde in the art world mock art that is beautiful and uplifting—even as they exalt so-called art which is shocking and depraved";[22] or when Senator Warren Rudman of New Hampshire, denying intellectuals any representative status in the politics of representation, insists: "I must say to the arts community in my State that has written to me, please do not write me any more letters defending that trash.

It is trash. Do not call it art. If it is art, it is art to people with twisted minds."[23] This "twisted" or sodomitical mode of analysis that enables the academy and the "arts community" to "mock" the values of the middle class by (mis)interpreting trash as art—or that enables Barney Frank to (mis)represent an "unspeakable" man like Stephen Gobie by comparing him, implicitly, to a woman like Eliza Doolittle (that is, to Audrey Hepburn or even Julie Andrews)—attempts to find a public space in which to represent activities that dominant discourse insists can never be *represented* at all but only *reenacted* since what passes for their public representation actually *reproduces* the disturbance of logic proscribed in the acts themselves. To speak or represent the "unspeakable," therefore, can only be registered as an assault upon the logic that naturalizes discourse itself by presupposing the foundational presence of "meaning" as *logos* or "truth."

It is largely in opposition to the possibility of such a practice of sodomitical reading that the Supreme Court exerted its interpretive authority in the case of *Bowers v. Hardwick*, a case in which much of the majority's decision attended to the question of how a legitimate reading should be pursued and how the Court can "assure itself and the public that announcing rights not readily available in the Constitution's text involves much more than the imposition of the Justice's own choice of values."[24] Such an "imposition" of ungrounded values, such a practice that inverts the logic of analysis by subordinating authorial intention or the "self-evident" language of the text to critical license or desire, distinguishes, after all, what I've designated as sodomitical reading, and the majority refused to authorize any representations of the Constitution that would perform such perverse impositions upon the textual body of the founding fathers. Perhaps that accounts for the subliminal insistence of the figurative language with which the Court, in a discussion of homosexual sodomy, disclaims the "authority to discover new *fundamental* rights *imbedded* in the Due Process Clause" (emphasis mine).[25] This figurative language evocative of the body seems to find full-scale elaboration when Justice White observes: "The Court is most *vulnerable* and comes nearest to *illegitimacy* when it deals with judge-made constitutional law having little or no cognizable roots in the language or design of the Constitution. . . . There should be, therefore, great *resistance* to expand the substantive reach of the Due Process Clause of the Fifth and Fourteenth amendments. . . . The claimed right *pressed on us* today falls far short of overcoming this *resistance*" (emphasis mine).[26] The anxious-making tactility of the rights that the Court experiences as being "pressed" upon it can be seen as materializing a latent fantasy of sexual imposition. The Court thus enacts its "resistance" to being pressed where it feels most "vulnerable," where the rights in question, explicitly, are what are deemed most "fundamental." In the context of this anxiously defensive resistance to the pressure of those who are urging the

Court to accede to "homosexual sodomy," the Court insists on preserving, instead, the integrity of its legitimacy by refusing to read the Constitution sodomitically and dis-covering "new *fundamental* rights." The fundamental right that the Court here defends is the right of the fundament to resist what is discomfitingly "pressed" upon it. Significantly, despite the pervasive stereotype that gives heterosexuals an excuse to imagine gay men as "passive" participants in sodomitical encounters, the dominant construction of "militant," which is to say, public and political, homosexuality, recurrently invokes the image of a hyper-masculine, aggressive sexual violence, most notably in the endlessly reiterated trope of gay people "shoving their homosexuality down the public's throat." The anxiety expressed in this contradictory interpenetration of active and passive positions returns us to the dismantling of positional logic effected by homosexual sodomy in the national imaginary—a dismantling whereby the public representation of so-called "passive" sodomitical practices has the effect of seeming actively to sodomize heterosexual men, to press upon or against them at the point of their greatest vulnerability and thus to threaten a loss of the inviolability that assures their legitimacy *as* men. Thus the political and legal discourse of sodomy must repudiate the "sodomitical reading practice" it ascribes to the academy, to Barney Frank, or to the attorneys representing Michael Hardwick, lest heterosexual male subjects be stripped of their privileged authority as readers and suffer themselves instead, to be seen, in Hilton Kramer's words about the male bodies on display in the Mapplethorpe exhibit, as "nothing but sexual—which is to say, homosexual—objects,"[27] objects, that is, always dangerously subject to the pressure that exposes the vulnerability of openings necessarily repressed or "forgotten" in the public discourse of what is fundamental. The logic of the "politics" predicated upon heterosexuality demands, therefore, that representation be grounded in a stable differentiation between the front and the back, the proper and the improper, the fundamental and the fundament. But if the Court supposes that the right to sodomy can be anything *but* fundamental, it may be because it intuits too well—and with a certain demotic literality—that "the law," as Mr. Bumble the beadle puts it in *Oliver Twist*, "is a ass."[28]

8

THROWING UP/GOING DOWN

Bushusuru; or, the Fall of the West

If the narrative contexts available to account for the presence, let alone the activity, of one man's head in another man's lap seem to offer us only the binary alternatives of prurience or sentimentality—the alternatives, as one might put it, of giving head or giving succor—the ideological lenses that polarize these ways of coloring such a scene may blind us to the process whereby the insistence on one can filter out the effects and operations of the other. Thus in January of 1992 when audiences in Japan and America watched with horror and fascination as their televisions repeatedly presented them with images of President Bush throwing up on Prime Minister Miyazawa before collapsing into his lap, the machinery of the news media on both sides of the Pacific was obliged to construct a context in which to construe this unusual relation of ministerial lap to presidential head. The on-scene reporter for the *New York Times*, after noting, for example, that videotape of this episode "was repeatedly shown on television both here in Japan and in the United States," went on to observe immediately thereafter that "the President's host, Prime Minister Kiichi Miyazawa, cradled his head for some minutes until Mr. Bush was strong enough to get up on his own."[1] The verb of choice, "to cradle," which secures the necessary relation of sentimentality in defining the affect proper to this disturbing interaction, appeared as well in the translation of an article from Tokyo's *Nihon Keizai Shimbun*—a translation that extended the reach of this verb by invoking a related figure from its tropological penumbra: "The tape of Miyazawa cradling Bush's head after the president collapsed at a state banquet in Japan was shown over and over again on American television, and the sight was etched into American people's minds. The scene was pregnant with symbolism of America's current need for help from Japan."[2]

Figure 1. *AP/Wide World Photos*

The notorious promiscuity of figurative language may account for the reversal of cause and effect as the spectacle of one man cradling another impregnates the scene itself, but when the pastoralizing resonance of "cradling" starts to vibrate to the frequency of impregnation, the prurience of the spectatorial investment in this representation of two men and a cradling acquires an added charge from its pointedly heterosexual mediation. Indeed, to the extent that this scene must be registered as "pregnant with symbolism" in Japan and the West, the register of the symbolic has to labor, as it were, and to labor all the more manfully, to evacuate the unregenerate physicality of the body that the insistently regenerative trope of pregnancy might otherwise push to the fore. We are not meant, that is, to conceive of a body when we read the phrase "pregnant with symbolism," since the point, after all, of characterizing the scene as pregnant with symbolism in the first place, is to interpose between our gaze and the physicality of the body the very screen that enables us to register the body as symbolic. As the logic of trope in the deployment of the phrase replaces the emptied-out belly of a man with its allusion, made ghostly by convention, to the swollen belly of a woman, so the fullness of meaning with which the symbolic reading interprets this scene as "pregnant," must similarly displace the material substance of the president's emptied-out stomach; and if the circuit of figural exchange here requires that the commerce of the symbolic be routed through the substitution of one body for another, it is obviously not without meaning for the symbolic order of meaning itself that this substitution exchanges the embarrassment of two male bodies situated in painfully discomfiting intimacy with each other for the signifier—"pregnant"—that gestures not only toward an intimacy between bodies of different sexes, but also toward the redemption of heterosexual intimacy from the taint of the merely prurient, which is to say, from the taint of the material body as such, through its invocation of the spiritualizing work of reproduction. Pregnancy itself here, in other words, names the sentimentalization of prurience that can be seen to allegorize the birth of the symbolic out of a real that is thereby both evacuated and made visible at once.

If the real can be understood as that excess of the thing that refuses assimilation or containment within the network of the signifier, if it is, as Lacan describes it, "beyond the . . . insistence of the signs,"[3] my reading, it goes without saying, can offer no access to the real of this scene; it can only repeat in a different way the gesture that empties it out. For to read this scene at all is necessarily to read it as "pregnant with symbolism," even if that reading insists on defining the event as "a simple case of the flu"[4] and imbuing it, in so doing, with the symbolic meaning that constitutes the particular discursive prerogative of contemporary medical science. Any reading or representation of Bush's vomiting and subsequent physical collapse will inevitably reenact the projective evacuation of the unassimilability of the real, an evacuation that doubles or allegorizes Bush's own disgorging or evacuation of some unassimilable material substance. But while reading, to the extent that it translates the real into something apprehensible, must perceive it as "pregnant with symbolism," my own reading wants to attend to the relation between the occlusion of the real by the symbolic and the occlusion—though occlusion precisely of what remains, perhaps, to be seen—performed by defining through figures of heterosexual productivity the inherence of meaning in this particular scene whose centerpiece, literally occluded or cut from the videotapes shown to the public, is the intimate transfer of bodily fluids from one man to another.

To provide a framework within which to allow us to think about this scene, I want to turn to a passage from Lacan that will have the effect of bringing us back to the representations of Bush's collapse. "When diplomats are addressing one another," Lacan writes, "they are supposed to represent something whose signification, while constantly changing, is, beyond their own persons, France, Britain, etc. In the very exchange of views, each must record only what the other transmits in his function as signifier, he must not take into account what the other is, *qua* presence, as a man who is likable to a greater or lesser degree. Interpersonal psychology is an impurity in this exchange."[5] This passage can be read as glossing Lacan's meditations on the subject's constitutive subjection to his status as a signifier, as an instance of the fading of being into meaning on which the symbolic depends. The real, in this context, is the excess for which the signifier cannot account, evoked here, in language that borders, but only borders, on the positivistic, as "what the other is, *qua* presence." What the other "is" and "presence" are not identical in this phrase; it is only "*qua*" presence that what the other "is" can in any way be known. For Lacan as for Wallace Stevens, we might say, "is" is only made available to us as "as" in the symbolic order. The displacement of being by meaning, therefore, that produces the split between the diplomat and the man likable to a greater or lesser degree produces an analogous split between the man who is likable and the real of what he "is." To the extent that this passage can allegorize the relation of the signifier, in this case the diplomat, to the real, or "what is, *qua* presence," within the workings of a symbolic economy, it is striking that the threat to this economy, "the impurity in this exchange," finds representation through a disturbance effected in the system of diplomatic interaction by taking into account the affection, or even the desire, that translates a diplomat into a man who cannot ignore the fact that he finds another man "likable to a greater or lesser degree." This is not to say that same-sex desire is somehow, in itself, the real, or that same-sex desire is unrepresentable within the network of the signifier, but rather that a symbolic order that rests on the regime of heterosexuality figuratively aligns the "impurity" that threatens to interrupt the production of meaning with the latency in the body—and the male body in particular—of an excess that threatens to expose as illusory the symbolic reality of the subject. The real, in other words, itself unrepresentable within the order of the signifier, is allegorized and displaced fantasmatically into a condition of latency in the body of the male. The anxiety produced by that latency must be answered by the technology of representation working to reinsert the body into the dominant matrix of heterosexual signification—the matrix that generates the symbolic by inscribing the body with the social meaning that renders it intelligible. The effect is a compulsory hystericization of the male body within the symbolic order in an effort to make it conform to the signifying imperatives that constitute the subject—a normative hystericization within a heterosexual order of meaning that achieves a spectacular embodiment in the person of George Bush.

In returning from Lacanian theory to the spectacle of George Bush's collapse in Japan (which produced a neologism among the Japanese: *bushusuru*, "to throw up, to do a Bush"), I want to align the threat to the symbolic, the impurity that disrupts the diplomatic exchange, with the occulted moment of impurity cast out of the videotapes as publicly released: the impurity, to be less oblique, of seeing President Bush in the process of throwing up, in the process, that is, of casting out impurity as he lapses into, or better yet, is appropriated by, the unconscious, and enacts in his body a lapsus, so to speak, by going down in the prime minister's lap. Watching the videotape responsible as much for producing as for chronicling this scene, we can recognize the moment of rupture where, for reasons of "taste," of course, what can be seen (that is, what can be shown) is only the absence in the videotape where there is something that *cannot* be seen. That gap in the symbolic construction of this episode commemorates, and paradoxically makes visible, the moment of impurity that is stigmatized for bearing the figural burden of the body's implication in a presymbolic materiality. Drawn down into the condition of unreadable matter, the body, as if gravitationally falling away from its standing in relation to the subject, is allowed to point only metonymically in the videotape toward the repudiated impurity of the real through its framing as the object whose deathly bulk would seem, on the face of it, to topple the fiction that it could possibly submit to being cradled. The unwieldiness, the heft of the body that the president's men and Prime Minister Miyazawa so strenuously struggle to support, testifies to the fact that a president, no less than a king, is also a thing. And yet the iconographic force of these images in the sequence as edited and shown, the force that made these tapes so compelling for East and West alike, consists in the apparent redemption of the body from the fatal pull of the real by its figural resurrection into meaning through the very machinery of representation. By this I mean to call attention to the visual citation, in the videotapes and in the photograph that was printed in magazines and newspapers around the world, that construes in the relationship of Bush and Miyazawa the lineaments of a secular pietà—a citation that prepares the way in the videotape for the quick cut to President Bush shown back on his feet again, attempting to reassert, however sheepishly, authority over his body and the spectrum of its meanings.

Now the subliminal iconography of the pietà comports with the heterosexual elaborations of this scene through figurations of pregnancy and cradling; indeed, it reasserts the emergence of the subject as the cultural work of the symbolic family. But the figural surround that would insert this moment into narrative structures that are predicated on a reading of narrative itself as an articulation of the law of heterosexuality, can only, once outed, make clear the necessity of containing or managing acts of physical intimacy between or among the bodies of men that threaten, however fantasmatic the threat, an obtrusion of the real. The fascination for me of this incident, then, which is nothing in itself, lies precisely in the way it automatically provokes the energies of containment that are central to the dominant representational regime that micromanages perception from moment to moment in everyday life. Without any need to posit a consciousness alert to the possibility that the president's nausea and subsequent collapse into the prime minister's lap might draw on the time-honored heterosexual fantasy of a gay male sexuality being shoved down its gagging throat; without any need, that is, to imagine a mobilized awareness in relation to this scene of how the scene itself reverses that fantasy's protestation that the notion of a man going down must "naturally," as if somatically, precipitate the violence of throwing up, reverses it to allow for the recognition instead that throwing up might provide—through illness or in fantasy—an excuse for a scene of going down; without any need to propose, in sum, that same-sex desire was at any moment visible to anyone in the representational construction of this scene, we can see that the framing nonetheless works precisely, and all the more precisely for working automatically, to assure the invisibility of the spectacle of male-male intimacy or desire that was never at any point considered by any consciousness as having been there to be seen at all.

It is not, therefore, remarked upon, or properly speaking remarkable, that the embarrassment of a scene that improperly foregrounds the bodily relations of two men must be organized into a narrative that celebrates the redemptive presence of a woman. "Saved by the Grace of Barbara Bush," a headline in the *New York Times* declared, and an article in the *Times* of London observed: "While America groaned yesterday at the humiliating end to George Bush's attempt to play the tough trade enforcer in Japan, the country drew some consolation from the extraordinary performance by his wife, Barbara. . . . In a few brief words, delivered amid uncertainty over her husband's true condition, she managed to counter the damaging images of presidential frailty and shore up the notion of his authority."[6] What, one might disingenuously ask, is a wife for, after all, if not to shore up the authority of the heterosexual symbolic, the Name-of-the-Father, by rescuing it from the humiliating eruption of that excess resistant to containment in the organizing narratives that cradle us all as subjects?

Let us notice, then, in this regard, that in the videotape documenting the president's collapse, a collapse that immediately preceded his scheduled delivery of a ceremonial toast, we never hear the president's voice. Even after his recovery we only see him gesture in dumb show, as if the embarrassment of the body in figural proximity to the unincorporable, unarticulated matter or stuff of the real deprived him of voice in the symbolic, disallowed him access to language. Once the president, or the president's body, however, is safely removed from our sight, we are given in his place both the image and voice of Barbara Bush instead, who, as the *Times* of London put it, "after her limp husband had staggered out of the room . . . managed to crack a joke"—a joke, as we might have anticipated, immediately represented as "loaded with symbolism."[7] The joke in question was Mrs. Bush's diagnosis of her husband's unprecedented nausea and fainting spell as responses to his unaccustomed loss that afternoon to the emperor and crown prince of Japan in what was billed as a friendly game of tennis. The symbolic force to which the reporter refers would lie in the willful reconstruction through the joke of her husband's body as athletic and his manly resolve as unyieldingly firm. But rather than suggest that this joke is symbolic, might we not say that the implicit narrative through which this whole incident gains representation has, like the symbolic order itself, the structure of a joke insofar as its operation produces meaning out of nonsense, making what is extraneous, what is materially in excess of signification, signify? So viewed, the joke lies not so much in what Barbara Bush has to say as it does in the representational necessity of producing her in the place from which she can say it.

The substitution, that is, of her body for the evacuated body of her husband, performing that social economy that the *Times* of London defined as "face-saving," serves to associate her face with his and thus to affirm the narrative logic that configures heterosexuality with the presence and the reproduction of meaning. Yet by offering her face in place of his, such representations also make evident that face here necessarily serves as a figure, a substitution of one thing for another, and that if diplomacy, like the symbolic, insists that one face can stand for another, effacing the impurity of the body's specificity as a relation to the real, that insistence doubles the process whereby the signifier "face" itself can misname through synecdochic totalization the body conscripted into the order of social meaning and regulation. That the face of Barbara Bush should be where the face of George Bush was, may reappropriate George Bush's body, then, for the heterosexual order of meaning, but it surely signals, at the same time, a more disruptive possibility as well. It reinforces what I referred to earlier as the normative hystericization of the male body obliged to represent on and *as* itself the "natural" authority of a symbolic system designed to occlude its own status as a historically-specific, and hence neither natural nor inescapable, machinery of representation. Barbara Bush, as the other face of George in the renderings of this episode, unveils, we might say, the extent to which George is just another face; standing in for her husband she exposes her husband as already a stand-in himself, as one whose frenetic stagings of his body attempt to obey, however unsuccessfully, the injunction to represent the discipline of masculinity as neither a discipline nor a process requiring the energies of representation at all. The joke, if you will, of Barbara Bush's enshrinement as the savior of her husband's face, then, is that in the process of substituting her face for his she gives his face away, calls attention to the fact that he has no face, that he is, instead, as this incident seems to underscore all too vividly, only a mouth in desperate pursuit of a face to call its own.

That the embarrassment in Japan could so readily assume its status as a defining image for both the Bush presidency and the nation he represented testifies to its peculiar capacity to instantiate the anxious orality that Bush publicly enacts in his efforts to make his body perform the symbolic work of masculinity. Can it be, after all, mere coincidence that Bush's vomiting in Japan seems an overly literal repetition of the single most memorable utterance of his presidential career, the phrase with which he will always be associated in the nation's memory: "read my lips"? That phrase, which uncannily ironizes not only the nausea, but also the dumb show that the videotape records, would register authority by suggesting that the meaning of any statement that passes those lips matters less than the fact of its enunciation by a body in control of its meanings. Crucially, though, that phrase, which speaks volumes about Bush's desire to represent himself as the embodied voice of the symbolic Other, is only, of course, an appropriation of the voice and body of someone else—of Clint Eastwood, who, like Ronald Reagan, possesses what Bush as a public figure so thoroughly lacks: the ability to embody, without visible effort, the natural assurance of phallic authority in the national imaginary. Bush, by contrast, makes even his acts of relaxation seem laborious insofar as they reveal his ghastly determination to mean what he cannot be, to incorporate into his own the masculine body as signifier of symbolic authority—a signifier beneath which his own body, like the surfeit of the real, is only able to slide by making a disconcertingly eroticized spectacle of itself and its desire. That incorporative fantasy, persistently paraded in the anxious efforts to keep it concealed, identifies Bush, in the national imaginary, with homophobically abjected drives toward oral and anal gratification. Famous for what the *New York Times* called his "well-known problems with syntax,"[8] skewered by Ann Richards, in a celebrated quip, as having been "born with a silver foot in his mouth," Bush, even before he said "read my lips," and long before he threw up in Japan, had been defined in large part by the inappropriate things that both went into and came out of his mouth. And this too figures, though figures to no one, to no consciousness that ever discerned it, in the energies of representation deployed to contain the embarrassing contiguity of the president's mouth and the prime minister's lap. Consider after all, in relation to this highly fraught axis of mouth and lap, the terms with which George Bush characterized his prepresidential niche in the consciousness of his country: "take the word 'Quayle' and insert the word 'Bush' wherever it appears, and that's the crap I took for eight years. Wimp. Sycophant. Lap dog. Poop. Lightweight. Boob. Squirrel. Asshole."[9] It requires no finely tuned ear to detect the hysteria informing this catalogue of the ways the Bush body fails in its efforts to register as adequately masculine—and fails, indeed, through the very excess of its desire so to be registered. The *Times* of London thus put it just right in remarking on Bush's inability "to play the tough trade enforcer with Japan," for Bush's gaping mouth becomes the emblem of heterosexual masculinity's impossible desire to perform an identification with, and an appropriation of, the symbolic male body that is never its own without making visible the inscription of that process in the register of desire.

In order to conclude these remarks on the representational economies engaged in the symbolic construction of the scene of the president's collapse, it remains to consider the particular inflection produced when the quondam "lap dog," become the leader of the Western world, winds up going down with his face in the lap of the prime minister of a particular country: Japan. To the extent, after all, that this scene recapitulates the president's own impossible desire to occupy the place of the Other, the name by which the Other goes in this scene is, precisely, Japan. If, therefore, the management of this scene must control the explosive excess of meanings that it registers in terms of the body, and if such efforts to control that excess are entangled with larger questions of representation in the symbolic order, the framings of this scene cannot fail to record some trace of the racial fantasies that inform the social relations of the body and the accounts of its desires. In this context the difference between the Western enactment of the male body's normative hysteria within a heterosexual symbolic order and the Western fantasmatic of the Japanese body could hardly be more pronounced. In the racial imaginary of white America and much of Western Europe as well, Japanese bodies are construed as interchangeable, as constituted less by their individuality than by their participation in a social mass. While this, historically, has contributed to the Western ascription of passivity and effeminacy to the Japanese male, following upon the triumphant expansion of Japan's postwar economy, the Japanese body increasingly appears in the racial imagination of the West as indistinguishable from the high-tech machinery that has provided the engine for economic success. Fantasized as mechanistic, efficient, and barely differentiable from the robotics with which it finds itself metonymically associated, the Japanese body becomes the token of a regulated economy of desire and it acquires thereby the capacity to figure the smooth, uninterrupted workings of the machinery of the symbolic: the unproblematic disappearance of the subject beneath the signifier without any disturbing excess of bodily specificity, without any insistent inscription of bodily desire. Japan, in this context, becomes the fantasmatic site of the very mechanics of representation, a veritable empire of signs, and thus it becomes, both literally and figuratively, the camera through which the West, in this scene of embarrassment, is required to see itself. As such it changes places with the West in the active/passive binarism, acquiring, in the fantasmatics of cultural identity, the cachet of aggressive potency that has decisively shaped the self-image of an America that construes itself now, homophobically, as "getting screwed" by Japan—a construction that expresses its desire to take in, to incorporate, the authority of a symbolic economy that "Japan" has come to name. "Japan," then, figures the place of the gaze from which the symbolic looks at us, the place that we, like Bush, try to occupy by returning repeatedly to the scene of this fall as if by properly taking it in we might somehow cast out what disturbs us about it and redeem it through a symbolic reading that not only would make it a fortunate fall, but also, in the commerce of the symbolic, would cancel the deficit in our trade with Japan.

Postscript: As if to confirm the logic of hysterical orality that this essay perceives in the unspoken erotics (representable only as "disgust"[10]) informing President Bush's experience of throwing up and going down while visiting Japan, the *New York Times* printed, three months after this essay was originally delivered, the following account of an anecdote that Bush included in a campaign speech warning America against supporting Bill Clinton, his Democratic opponent in the 1992 presidential race: "The story," as the reporter for the *Times* described it, "ended up painting Mr. Bush as a gladiator, buried up to his neck in sand, and Mr. Clinton as the lion attacking him. 'As he did the gladiator reached up and took a very ferocious bite in a very sensitive place in the lion's anatomy,' Mr. Bush said."[11] To this spectacularly self-revealing anecdote there is little a critic need add: only, perhaps, that when viewed in the context of his ill-fated trip to Japan, it makes vivid that where Bush and the complex relations entangling the male body are concerned, what the Western symbolic insists on casting out is the representation or expression of desire for what it insists, at the same time, that the subject must incorporate or take in; and thus, as Bush's disarmingly graphic self-portrait from the campaign trail suggests, his "barf" is not only not worse than, but also not different from, his bite.

9

TEAROOMS AND SYMPATHY

OR, The Epistemology of the Water Closet

On October 16, 1964, a correspondent for the *Times* of London made the following observation about the intertwining of sexuality and nationalistic ideology in the United States: "In the post war political primer for beginners perversion is synonymous with treason. A surviving McCarthyism is that homosexuality and other sexual aberrations are both dangerous to the national security and rife in Washington."[1] These remarks were prompted by the disclosure, less than three weeks before America's presidential election, that Walter Jenkins, Lyndon Johnson's chief of staff, had been arrested with another man (identified, ominously, as "Hungarian-born") and charged with performing "indecent gestures" in a basement restroom of the Y.M.C.A. two blocks from Jenkins's office in the White House. This arrest, which Laud Humphreys would later characterize as "perhaps the most famous tearoom arrest in America,"[2] precipitated the furor of a political scandal, one that some thought capable of swaying the election, when it was learned that Jenkins had not only been arrested in the very same men's room five years earlier—leaving him with a police record on which had been marked, "disorderly conduct (pervert)"—but also that this prior arrest had escaped detection by both the White House and the F.B.I. Jenkins, therefore, had had access to a variety of classified materials, including documents submitted to the National Security Council, and he had been granted the top-secret "Q" clearance from the Atomic Energy Commission.

The paranoid logic that echoed throughout the clamor provoked by these revelations found its normative expression in a column written by Arthur Krock for the *New York Times*. After sympathizing with Jenkins and his family, and asserting with self-satisfied smugness that "sympathy in such circumstances is a foremost trait of the American people," Krock proceeded to admonish his readers: "But it would be irresponsible if the American people felt no anxiety over the fact . . . that a Government official to whom the most secret operations of national security were accessible . . . is among those unfortunates who are most readily subject to the blackmail by which security secrets are often obtained by enemy agents."[3] For this reason—and because, as the editor of the *New York Times* observed, "sexual perversion," like alcoholism and drug addiction, "is increasingly understood as an emotional illness"—America's paper of record, the public voice of "liberal" sentiment, editorialized in support of the anti-gay policies that by then had affected the federal government's hiring practices for over a decade: "there can be no place on the White House staff or in the upper echelons of government," the *Times* declared, "for a person of markedly deviant behavior."[4]

For several days the Jenkins affair earned front-page attention in America's newspapers before being dislodged by events that seemed more immediately to threaten the nation's well-being: events such as the overthrow of Khrushchev in Russia and China's first explosion of a nuclear device. Aspects of the Jenkins case resurfaced in news reports during the weeks leading up to the election, but the political ramifications of the scandal were contained within ten days of the initial revelations. As soon as the story broke (and it did so despite efforts by Clark Clifford and Abe Fortas to persuade Washington editors to suppress it) Jenkins resigned from his position as special assistant to the president; said to be suffering from "high blood pressure and nervous exhaustion,"[5] he entered George Washington University Hospital where his room was kept under twenty-four-hour security surveillance. On October 14, the day Jenkins resigned, President Johnson ordered the F.B.I. to "make an immediate and comprehensive inquiry"[6] into the affair. The document generated by that investigation, released on October 22 and consisting of some 100 pages of text under the chillingly broad and all-encompassing title "Report on Walter Wilson Jenkins,"[7] reassuringly offered its official conclusion that Jenkins at no time had "compromised the security or interests of the United States."[8]

In the process, however, the report inadvertently offered tantalizing insights into the discursive contexts within which it was possible in 1964 to conceptualize both homosexual activity and the susceptibility to participation in such activity of men not homosexually identified, or not so identified in public: Jenkins himself, after all, had been married for some nineteen years at the time of the scandal and was the father of six children. According to Victor Lasky, President Johnson personally insisted that the final report "state that Jenkins was overly tired, that he was a good family man and a hard worker, and that he was not 'biologically' a homosexual."[9] As a result, even though the incident in 1964 involved Jenkins's arrest for a second time in a men's room that *Time* magazine would describe as "a notorious hangout for deviates,"[10] and even though Jenkins acknowledged to the F.B.I. that he had had "limited association with some individuals who are alleged to be, or who admittedly are, sex deviates,"[11] and even though he admitted his participation in "the indecent acts for which he was arrested in 1959 and 1964," and even though he severely qualified his denial of participation in other homosexual encounters by saying that "he did not recall any further indecent acts" and that "if he had been involved in any such acts he would have been under the influence of alcohol and in a state of fatigue and would not remember them,"[12] despite all of this it was possible for the F.B.I. to reinforce the rationale for Jenkins's sexual behavior as publicly established by the White House: Jenkins had been suffering from high blood pressure, nervous tension, and physical exhaustion as a result of being severely overworked.[13] As Lady Bird Johnson expressed this notion in one of the earliest official responses to the scandal: "My heart is aching for someone who has reached the endpoint of exhaustion in dedicated service to his country."[14]

Though I will return to this framing, in every way *political*, of the interpretive context within which, according to the White House and the F.B.I., Walter Jenkins's homosexual encounters were properly to be construed, my interest here extends beyond the specific events that followed the public revelation of his arrest. I want in this essay to consider three apparently heterogeneous pieces of information, each related in some way, however metonymic, to the Jenkins affair, and then see what sort of analysis they permit of the interpenetration of nationalism and sexuality, or rather, of nationalism and the *figurations* of sexuality—and, in particular, the figurations of *homosexuality*—in dominant cultural expression at that historical moment in America. For insofar as it marked a turning point in the formulation of nationalistic ideology in the United States—insofar, that is, as it signaled the end of what Michael Rogin has called the "cold war consensus"[15] and initiated the period of national redefinition provoked by the emergence of a significant middle-class culture of opposition that would crystallize around the incipient anti-war movement—1964 represents a critical moment in which to examine the shifting ideological frameworks within which homosexuality could be read in relation to American national identity.

I would begin, then, by calling attention to the fact that Jenkins was apprehended in 1964 by two members of the District of Columbia vice squad who had placed the restroom of Washington's G-Street "Y" under surveillance on the evening of October 7 by concealing themselves behind the padlocked door of a shower room no longer in use. *Time* magazine explained the mechanics of the policemen's stake-out in the following terms: "They . . . stationed themselves at two peepholes in the door that gave them a view of the washroom and enabled them to peep over the toilet partitions. (There are two peepholes in this and several other washrooms in the area because two corroborating officers are required in such cases.)"[16] Let me place a second item beside this description of the State's operations in the public men's rooms of our nation's capital: this one a statement made six months earlier, in May of 1964, by Senator Barry Goldwater as he set his political sights on the White House. Responding to national anxiety about America's technological prowess—an anxiety that had dominated our forays into space since the Soviet triumph with the Sputnik satellite in 1957—Goldwater, implicitly acknowledging the connection between space exploration and the military development of missile and weapons technology, declared with characteristic immoderation: "I don't want to hit the moon. I want to lob one into the men's room of the Kremlin and make sure I hit it."[17] Finally, I would adduce one further item for consideration as a cultural text: the words with which Lyndon Johnson, in a televised comment, expressed his reaction to the discovery that his oldest and closest advisor and friend had been arrested for engaging in homosexual activities in the restroom of the Y.M.C.A.: "I was as shocked," he said, "as if someone had told me my wife had murdered her daughter."[18]

In order to sketch some relationship among these fragments of the historical record, I want to consider one other event that took place in 1964; for *Life* magazine, in June of that year, entered thousands of middle-class homes across the country with a photo-essay offering a spectacular view of what it called the "secret world" of "Homosexuality in America."[19] In thus breaking new ground for a family-oriented, mass-circulation American periodical—and in the process establishing the journalistic conditions that would later allow *Time* to present so explicit and sensational an account of the Jenkins affair—the editors of *Life* felt compelled to provide some contextualizing remarks that would justify their devotion of so much attention to what they identified as a "sad and often sordid world" (66). The terms in which they framed that justification, presenting it in a sort of exculpatory preface to the two essays on homosexuality that followed, are worth considering here:

> Today, especially in big cities, homosexuals are discarding their furtive ways and openly admitting, even flaunting, their deviation. Homosexuals have their own drinking places, their special assignation streets, even their own organizations. And for every obvious homosexual, there are probably nine nearly impossible to detect. This social disorder, which society tries to suppress, has forced itself into the public eye because it does present a problem—and parents especially are concerned. The myth and misconception with which homosexuality has so long been clothed must be cleared away, not to condone it but to cope with it. (66)

The prurience with which the accompanying photographs produce the spectacle of the gay male body for consumption by an audience presumed to be straight finds its warrant here in the editors' claim that nine out of ten homosexuals are "nearly impossible to detect." *Life*, therefore, undertakes to expose the gay male body as social "problem" by exposing the problem of seeing or recognizing the gay male body itself: a purpose tellingly figured in the editors' insistence upon "clear[ing] away" the obfuscating garb with which homosexuality has, in their words, "so long been clothed."[20] Whatever else this fantasy of an unclothed homosexuality may bespeak, it establishes a sociological justification for the journalistic depiction of gay men, and in the process it draws attention to the physicality of their bodies, in terms of which the notion of a "homosexual difference" continues to be construed; for even that ninety percent of homosexuals whose sexuality is not immediately "obvious" are only, the preface informs us, "nearly" impossible to detect.[21] As the magazine later tells its readers, with the goal of making them *better* readers of homosexuality and homosexual signs: "Often the only signs are a very subtle tendency to over-meticulous grooming, plus the failure to cast the ordinary man's admiring glance at every pretty girl who walks by" (77). Thus a falseness in relation to the body, a disparity between the "truth" of gender as articulated by anatomy and the ways in which that gender is represented by the individual, can serve to assist the heterosexual in the recognition of the gay body and to effect the cultural reification of "the homosexual" itself. That is, as a "secret" or unarticulated condition that demands journalistic scrutiny and exposure, homosexuality falls from the outset of the article under the aegis of inauthenticity and of a difference all the more subversive because simultaneously threatening ("parents especially are concerned") and potentially unidentifiable.

That the ability of most homosexuals to "pass" produces an extraordinary degree of interpretive anxiety for heterosexuals—and especially for heterosexual men—becomes clear in the first of the two essays in *Life* when its author, Paul Welch, recounts how one gay executive enacts his "bitterness . . . toward the 'straight' public." Tellingly, the article contextualizes the executive's remarks by announcing in advance that he "has been under a psychiatrist's care":

> I have to make believe all day long. If we're out for lunch, I go through the same complimenting and flirting routine with girls that you "straight" fellows do. I have to be constantly on my guard not to say or do something that will make them suspect I'm "gay."
>
> At night I have to get out and forget it. I don't like to go to "gay" bars night after night; but I'll tell you what I do like to do. I like to go to "straight" bars, find some guy with a good-looking girl and take her away from him. I couldn't be less interested in the girl, but it's a way of getting even. (74)

Here, condensed into the narrative space of a single anecdote attributed only to an anonymous gay man, the article unfolds its reading of homosexuality as a threat not merely to the moral and spiritual well-being of those who are gay, but more importantly, to the happiness of "innocent" heterosexual men and women as well. Trailing his familiar cloak of psychological maladaption and misogyny, the male homosexual, according to the cultural stereotype that this story puts into play, vengefully makes use of his ability to "pass" in order to frustrate the happy ending of a heterosexual romance. A dangerous spy in the house of love, he is seen as "perverse" not merely in the orientation of his sexuality, but also in the fact that he takes less pleasure in the pursuit of his own desires ("I don't like to go to 'gay' bars night after night") than he does in sabotaging heterosexual couples in the process of pursuing theirs.

The anecdote thus reinforces the more widespread interpretation of how homosexuality threatens the security of heterosexual unions—an interpretation according to which a married man, a man like Walter Jenkins, for example, betrays his spouse through a series of anonymous homosexual encounters. Such a scenario appears at the outset of Welch's article when he evokes the following as a representative vignette of homosexual life: "By Chicago's Bughouse Square, a small park near the city's fashionable Gold Coast on the North Side, a suburban husband drives his car slowly down the street, searching for a 'contact' with one of the homosexuals who drift around the square. A sergeant on Chicago's vice squad explains: 'These guys tell their wives they're just going to the corner for the evening paper. Why, they even come down here in their slippers!'"(68). The coziness of suburban domestic ritual, figurally evoked through the culturally freighted images of newspaper and slippers, loses its ideological coherence as an index of intimacy and familiarity through the revelation of the husband's attraction to the homosexual "drift[ers]" who frequent the park. The very stability of family life, the solidity rooted in such material acquisitions as the house in the suburbs—the historical signifier of the actualization of the "American dream"—is called into question in the context of this anecdote by the disruptive and aimless circulation of men who "drift around the square" while waiting for what is dismissively portrayed as an impersonal and transient "contact." As in the subsequent account of the gay executive, moreover, this male-authored narrative protectively displaces its own anxious concern that gay male sexuality threatens to effeminize heterosexual males, as it "effeminizes" the unfortunate man in the bar who suffers the woman who has attracted his attention, that is, his desire, to be lured away from him by, of all things, a gay man. Here, though, the gay male works his wiles more directly to lure away the man most presumed to be straight, the family man with a wife at home who has every reason and right to expect that her husband, and the slippers she gave him, no doubt, for his birthday (or, more poignantly, for Father's Day), will return from their quest for the evening paper without having slipped from the straight and narrow path of conjugal fidelity—let alone heterosexual identity.[22]

If the article in this way displays an anxiety about the dangers that can result from the cultural invisibility enjoyed by homosexuals, it also reproduces the culture's inconsistent assumptions about the identification and recognition of gay men. The preface to the article insists, after all, that the vast majority of homosexuals are "nearly impossible to detect," and the article itself seeks to reinforce that point by remarking of a group of "tough-looking" men gathered on a block just west of Times Square that "few of the passers-by recognize them as male hustlers." But the captions to the photographs that illustrate the essay—and that necessarily attempt to capture the elusive "homosexual difference" in visual terms—indicate a textual imperative to reassert the recognizability of homosexual men by focusing on the markers or "signs" by which homosexuality can be discerned. The pictures, therefore, present images like the one of a tailor's mannequin draped in a flamboyant scarf and capped by an extravagant hat while the caption explains to the uninitiate that "this New York Greenwich Village store which caters to homosexuals is filled with the colorful, off-beat, attention-calling clothes that the 'gay' world favors" (68). Just opposite this, the magazine offers a full-page photograph representing two couples—one gay, one straight —passing each other on the street; this picture emblematizes, as the caption makes clear, the essay's insistence on the presentation of the gay male body as public spectacle: "Two fluffy-sweatered young men stroll in New York City, ignoring the stare of a 'straight' couple. Flagrant homosexuals are unabashed by reactions of shock, perplexity, disgust" (68).

Such readings of gay men as identifiably different thus coexist in the essay with avowals of the disturbing invisibility that homosexuals generally rely upon, and the tension of contradiction between these competing assertions produces a space for the discursive enterprise that I have designated as homographesis. For the article posits homosexuality as a legible phenomenon while simultaneously acknowledging the frequency with which it manages to escape detection; it constructs male homosexuality in terms of what the "public eye" can recognize even as it situates it in an ontological shuttle between perceptual sameness and difference. One contemporary strategy for representing this double aspect of "homosexual difference" appears in *The Sixth Man* (1961), Jess Stearn's sensationalistic, and therefore best-selling, account of homosexual life in America. In a passage that recapitulates the same astonishment with which Proust's narrator in *Cities of the Plain* witnesses what he describes as the "transformation of M. de Charlus," Stearn identifies the metamorphic duplicity not only of gay men but also of their bodies:

> They have a different face for different occasions. In conversation with each other, they often undergo a subtle change. I have seen men who appeared to be normal suddenly smile roguishly, soften their voices, and simper as they

> greeted homosexual friends. . . . Many times I saw these changes occur after I had gained a homosexual's confidence and he could safely risk my disapproval. Once as I watched a luncheon companion become an effeminate caricature of himself, he apologized. "It is hard to always remember that one is a man."

As in the case of M. de Charlus, the visibility of homosexuality in this account registers the emergence of an "effeminate caricature" or distortion of male identity, and yet, as Stearn goes on to note, "effeminate features or mannerisms . . . do not necessarily signify homosexuality."[23]

This rhetorical gesture whereby homosexuality becomes discernible in cognitive relation to effeminacy even as the necessity of that association is itself put into question, finds its anticipated place in the discussion of homosexuality in *Life*, which simultaneously published a companion piece to its exposé of America's "gay world" in which it explored "scientific" perspectives on the etiology of homosexual orientation. Ernest Havemann (can this *not* be a pseudonym?), the author of the article (titled, with a smarmy combination of pathos and hostility, "Why?"), may evoke the "loneliness" of homosexual life by comparing the lot of a middle-aged gay man to that of an "aging party girl in the other kind of society" (76), but he sets out nonetheless to correct "the mistaken notion, still held by many people, that all homosexuals have effeminate, 'swishy' manners and would like nothing better, if only they could get away with it, than to dress like women, pluck their eyebrows and use lipstick." Virtually echoing Jess Stearn, he follows this full-bodied, vividly imagined description of a commonly held but "mistaken notion" with the rather flat assertion, "in actual fact, there are many effeminate men who are not homosexual at all" (77).

The recurrence of this topos, the necessary return to this moment of "scientific" disavowal in which male homosexuality and effeminacy are denied the essential connection that the author has already laboriously, even tendentiously, delineated, pinpoints the homographic imperative to resolve the vertiginous confusion of sameness and difference by reading the gay male body in relation to the (ostensibly) determinate, (ostensibly) visible difference between the sexes. Male homosexuality, in other words, must be conceptualized in terms of femaleness not only because the governing heterosexual mythology interprets gay men as definitionally wanting to *be*, or to be *like*, women, but also because the heterosexual must insist that the gay man *is*, in fact, like a woman to the extent that his "difference" can be discerned on his body, subjecting him to discrimination in more ways than one. In consequence, where the ideological contours within which homosexuality can be conceptualized remain those of inauthenticity, dissimulation, and disguise, even the most emphatically "masculine" aspects of male homosexuality are susceptible to interpretation in terms of a displaced or occluded effeminacy.

In his piece in *Life*, for instance, Paul Welch quotes the owner of a leather bar in San Francisco, cannily putting into this gay man's mouth the article's first explicitly misogynistic and effeminophobic pronouncements: "We throw out anybody who is too swishy. If one is going to be homosexual, why have anything to do with women of either sex?" As the article goes on, however, to describe the customers who haunt these "so-called S & M bars" (68), it implicitly extends the phobic repudiation of "women of either sex" to include the brawny specimens who dress themselves up in leather and chains. "The effort of these homosexuals to appear manly is obsessive," the author writes, reinforcing the suggestion of misrepresentation implicit in the word "appear" by recourse to the language of clinical diagnosis in the pathologizing term, "obsessive." Such an exposure of the "masculinity" of gay men as merely parodic or self-deceiving—as a gesture whose logic implicitly substantiates the "truth" or self-identity of heterosexual maleness—finds an echo, conveniently enough, in the words of the man who owns the bar. "Those screaming faggots," he says, referring to effeminate homosexual men, are "afraid to come here because everything looks tough. But we're probably the most genteel bar in town" (70). Underscoring the notion that "looks" can be deceptive, the acknowledged gentility of this merely seamy-seeming establishment situates even the most assertively "masculine" version of gay male life reassuringly, for heterosexual culture, in the register of effeminacy. Seen properly, through the dominant cultural optic, the self-representations of gay men, however "butch," thus reveal an essential internal element of effeminacy-as-difference that makes it possible for the educated eye to recognize them as "visibly" gay.

Through all of this *Life* engages in the ideological labor of constructing homosexuality as a problem or social concern that cannot be disentangled from the historical process by which "homosexuals become more visible to the public" (74). Insofar as the magazine participates in this process by making the "secret world" of homosexuality visible to its (presumptively heterosexual) readership, it does so in order to foster an internalization of the repressive supervisory mechanisms of the State—an internalization that it seeks to effect by reproducing in its readers the magazine's own interest in learning to recognize those denizens of the gay world who are "nearly impossible to detect." In conjuring homosexuality as an often invisible yet potentially omnipresent concern, the magazine evokes the Cold War equation of homosexuality with Communist infiltration and subversion of the State—an equation made explicit by the words with which Ernest Havemann's article begins: "Do the homosexuals, like the Communists, intend to bury us?" (76).

Now it is significant that when Guy George Gabrielson, the Republican National Chair, helped to popularize this equation in 1950 by warning that homosexuals in the government's employ were "perhaps as dangerous as actual Communists"—and the word "actual" in this phrase is worth noting—he also explained the public's relative ignorance about the full extent of this "problem" by pointing to the moral constraints that prevented the mass media from examining the issue: "The country would be more aroused over this tragic angle of the situation," he wrote, "if it were not for the difficulties of the newspapers and radio commentators in adequately presenting the facts, while respecting the decency of their American audiences."[24] Such a statement makes clear that textual representation, especially in the journalistic media that help shape popular opinion, has gotten enmeshed in the Cold War rhetoric that conflated homosexuality with Communism. The very possibility of a public, nonmedical discourse of homosexuality now depends on the political interests that such a discourse can be made to serve. Far from disallowing, therefore, the open discussion of homosexuality, remarks such as Gabrielson's *encouraged* public consideration of it as an "issue" insofar as such consideration could efficiently promote a homophobic—and thus, metonymically, anti-Communist—agenda sufficient to "arouse," to use his own word, the unwary American public. The result, of course, was that Senator McCarthy's campaign against subversives in the American government had the effect of focusing public attention on the unrecognized pervasiveness of homosexuality as the enemy within.[25]

Less constrained in 1964 by the representational "difficulties" to which Gabrielson alluded (less constrained, in part, because Gabrielson, McCarthy, and other politicians had made homosexuality a topic of national concern), the media were able to flesh out or give body to the abstract Cold War rhetoric of homosexuality as a threat to the State by resituating it within the framework of concern about the definitional barriers between the public and the privately domestic—a concern that had served implicitly to support the ideological construction of American nationalism at the end of the forties and throughout the fifties. For the backward-looking ideology of domesticity that governed the American national consciousness in the wake of World War II sought not only to achieve such regressive social policies as the return of white middle-class women to the unpaid labor of heterosexual homemaking, but also to establish the fictive cohesiveness of a suburban national-cultural identity. Even as American cities expanded, the white middle-class imaginary was enthralled by the consumerist fantasy of the "American Dream": the bourgeois family safely ensconced in a home that was detached and privately owned. This national self-image can be viewed as a reaction against the political realities of a postwar world in which American power could no longer detach itself from military involvement in international affairs, a world in which the atomic bomb and the pirated missile technologies of the Nazis—technologies simultaneously undergoing development by East and West alike—made American isolationism strategically impossible and therefore all the more powerful as a spur to ideological formation.

As the development of weapons technology—a phrase that is already perhaps a redundancy—deprived America of the geopolitical privilege of its distance from powerful enemies, the idealization of domestic security, for both the nuclear family and the nuclear state, became an overriding national concern. Yet that ideal of a private domestic preserve could only be articulated through an insistence upon the need for new technologies of social control. Refinements in techniques of interrogation, surveillance, and security examination marked the dependence of the white bourgeois family's expectation of a privileged domestic space upon the state's girding up of that notion even—or especially—by ceaselessly violating the domain of domestic privacy itself. Such violations, however, gained considerable acceptance as necessary tools in the effort to expose the activities of subversives who were widely depicted as abusing (which is to say, using) their constitutional liberties in order to bring the United States under foreign domination. Thus the postwar machinery of American nationalism operated by enshrining and mass-producing the archaic bourgeois fantasy of a self-regulating familial sanctuary at a time when the idea of the domestic was embroiled in an anxious and unstable relation to the manifold social imperatives of the State.

If the reactionary aftermath of World War II saw a massive intensification of political efforts to demonize homosexual behavior (which had, of course, gained new visibility in the armed services during the war), those efforts promoted the popular perception of gay sexuality as an alien presence, an unnatural because un-American practice, resulting from the entanglement with foreign countries—and foreign nationals—during the War.[26] And as the importance of international and domestic surveillance became a central preoccupation of postwar America, so the campaigns against gays by local police departments, spurred by the national political identification of homosexuality with domestic subversion, made use of new modes of subterfuge and dissimulation, including the surveillance of public restrooms that would lead to the arrest of Walter Jenkins in 1964.

Now in the twentieth-century American social landscape, the institutional men's room constitutes a site at which the zones of public and private cross with a distinctive psychic charge. That charge carries, of course, at a much stronger voltage, the tension of ambivalence that the bathroom as such is sufficient to evoke. In May of 1964, for example—the same month that Senator Goldwater declared his interest in making a preemptive strike against the men's room of the Kremlin—*Life* published an article in which it noted with satisfaction that "Americans already have nearly 50 million bathrooms, more than the rest of the world put together. Now they are demanding even more —and are demanding that they be bigger and fancier."[27] Yet if this metonymic index of American cleanliness—itself, proverbially, a metonym of godliness—suggests an investment of national pride in the proliferation of its bathrooms, the opening sentence of the article sounds a note potentially more ominous: "Bedecked, bejeweled and splashed with color, the bathroom is blossoming with a flair unapproached since the fall of the Roman Empire." Thus caught between its honorific associations with industrial progress and hygienic purity, and its more pejorative associations with weakness, luxury, and a decadent indulgence of the perverse, the American bathroom in 1964 constituted an unacknowledged ideological battleground in the endless—because endlessly anxious—campaign to shore up "masculinity" by policing the borders at which sexual difference is definitionally produced, the borders at which inside and outside, same and different, self and other are the psychic stakes at risk.

That risk, for heterosexual men, is never more intense than when the bathroom in question is a public or institutional facility. Already set aside as a liminal zone in which internal poisons are cast out and disavowed, the institutional men's room typically emblematizes the ambiguity of its positioning between the public and the private through its spatial juxtaposition of public urinals and the relatively greater privacy of individual stalls. Indeed, the effort to provide a space of privacy interior to the men's room itself, a space that would still be subject to some degree of public regulation and control, had encouraged by 1964 the increasing popularity of the coin-operated toilet stall within the public washroom. It was in the anticipated privacy of just such a stall that Walter Jenkins would be spied upon by representatives of the D.C. police department as he engaged in illegal sexual acts with a Hungarian-born veteran of the U.S. army.

The transformation of Walter Jenkins from retiring and camera-shy chief of staff to a man whose sexual behavior was subject to the most sensationalized public depiction, however, was accomplished less by the police than by the social policing carried out by the press. For when Jenkins chose, on the night of his arrest, to forfeit his $50 bond, he waived his right to trial (without a confession of guilt) and, as far as the law was concerned, thus brought the matter to a close. Only when the news of his arrest was leaked to the Republican National Committee, and then leaked again by the RNC to members of the press, did Jenkins become the central figure in what many called Johnson's Profumo scandal[28]—and only then because the media coverage reenacted on an enormously magnified scale the regulatory surveillance that the vice squad detectives carried out from behind the shower room door.

Yet the scandal that led editors to pontificate about its dark implications for American security produced a strikingly different response among the American public at large. *Time* commented on the "nationwide wave of ribald jokes" while *Newsweek* referred to the widespread outpouring of "sick jokes and leering sloganeering." Johnson's reelection motto—"All the way with LBJ"—was parodically rewritten as "Either way with LBJ";[29] and wags insisted that Johnson was determined to stand "behind" Jenkins to the bitter end. Like the media's unsavory fascination with the case—*Time*, for instance, even offered its readers the measurements of the "notorious" restroom, describing it as a "9-ft. by 11-ft. spot reeking of disinfectant and stale cigars"—these jokes symptomatize a more pervasive cultural fascination that can help to illuminate Senator Goldwater's remark ("I want to lob one into the men's room of the Kremlin") with its implied symbolic connection that defines the "men's room" no less than "the Kremlin" as the source of his anxiety.

The public staging of the men's room in Goldwater's flamboyantly militaristic comment, as in the surveillance operations of the vice squad and the journalistic narratives of the Jenkins affair, must be understood in relation to the heightened social concern about the indeterminacy or invisibility of "homosexual difference" in postwar America. Consider, for example, the language with which *Time* contextualized, in 1959, the social invisibility enjoyed by the majority of gay men who were studied for a book on sexuality by Dr. Edmund Bergler: "Despite all the washroom jokes, most of Dr. Bergler's homosexuals look and act perfectly masculine." The washroom here serves as the distinctive site of a universally recognizable heterosexual mythologizing (no specification of these "jokes" is required since the audience can be counted on to know them) that defensively seeks to establish a sign by which the specificity of "homosexual difference" might be determined—a sign that would establish such a difference as explicitly as the sign on the washroom door would insist on the certainty of difference between the sexes.

That latter sign, of course, figures crucially in a celebrated diagram employed by Lacan: a diagram in which what he designates as "the laws of urinary segregation" produce the signifiers "Ladies" and "Gentlemen" in order to articulate difference between what are otherwise identical doors. It is not insignificant that Lacan should elaborate a fable from this diagram in which "Ladies" and "Gentlemen," differentiated as the paradigmatic embodiments of binary difference itself, become, through the misrecognitions of a boy and a girl sitting opposite each other on a train, "two countries" that are subject to "the unbridled power of ideological warfare," even though, as Lacan assures us, "they are actually one country."[30] Nor is it insignificant that the arbitrary construction and reification of a binary anatomical difference "comes to *figure* sexual difference," as Jacqueline Rose observes, so that, as she goes on to note, "the phallus thus indicates the reduction of difference to an instance of visible perception."[31] For I want to suggest that the men's room, whose signifier in this fable enshrines the phallus as the token not only of difference, but also of difference as *determinate*, difference as perceptually knowable, is the site of a particular heterosexual anxiety about the potential inscriptions of homosexual desire and about the possibility of knowing or recognizing whatever might constitute "homosexual difference."

This can be intuited more readily when the restroom is considered, not, as it is by Lacan, in terms of "urinary segregation"—a context that establishes the phallus from the outset as the token of anatomical difference—but as the site of a loosening of sphincter control, evoking, therefore, an older eroticism, undifferentiated by gender, because anterior to the genital tyranny that raises the phallus to its privileged position. Precisely because the phallus marks the putative stability of the divide between "Ladies" and "Gentlemen," because it articulates the concept of sexual difference in terms of "visible perception," the "urinary" function in the institutional men's room customarily takes place within view of others—as if to indicate its status as an act of definitional display; but the private enclosure of the toilet stall signals the potential anxiety at issue in the West when the men's room becomes the locus not of urinary but of intestinal relief. For the satisfaction that such relief affords abuts dangerously on homophobically abjectified desires, and because that satisfaction marks an opening onto difference that would challenge the phallic supremacy and coherence of the signifier on the men's room door, it must be isolated and kept in view at once lest its erotic potential come out.[32] The Freudian pleasure or comfort stationed in that movement of the bowel overlaps too extensively with the Kristevan abjection that recoils from such evidence of the body's inescapable implication in its death; and the disquieting conjunction of these contexts informs, with predictably volatile and destructive results, the ways in which dominant American culture could interpret the "meaning" of male-male sexual activities in 1964.

Consequently, in the representations of the Jenkins case and in Senator Goldwater's remark, the historical framing of the men's room as a focus for straight men's sexual anxieties condenses a variety of phobic responses to the interimplication of sphincteral relaxation and the popular notion of gay male sexuality as a yielding to weakness or a loss of control—a notion invoked in the Jenkins affair when James Reston, in the pages of the *New York Times*, defined Jenkins's behavior as "personal weakness."[33] In fact, in a novel that first appeared on the *New York Times*' best-seller list the week of Walter Jenkins's arrest, the title character of Saul Bellow's *Herzog* watches as a young man is brought before a magistrate to answer charges stemming from his pursuit of sexual gratification in the vast men's room beneath Grand Central Station. Herzog, whose analyses of American history led him earlier to complain of the "*invasion of the private sphere (including the sexual) by techniques of exploitation and domination*"[34] (emphasis in original), decries the young man's prosecution in terms that reassert the heterosexual identification of the men's room with the experience of epistemological crisis and the anxiety of lost control: "You don't destroy a man's career because he yielded to an impulse in that ponderous stinking cavern below Grand Central, in the cloaca of the city, where no mind can be sure of stability" (227).[35] The threat to stability—that is, to the security of (heterosexual male) identity and (heterosexual male) authority over the signifiers of difference—portended by the men's room itself, gains figural reinforcement from its contiguity to the image of the "cloaca," a term that refers not only to a sewer or water-closet, but also, as the *Random House Dictionary* phrases it, to "the common cavity into which the intestinal, urinary, and generative canals open in birds, reptiles, amphibians, many fishes, and certain mammals." The "stinking cavern" below Grand Central Station recapitulates the anatomical "cavity" denoted by the "cloaca," and together these mutually displacing spatial and anatomical tropes suggest the anxiety of an internal space of difference within the body, an overdetermined opening or invagination within the male, of which the activity of defecation may serve as an uncanny reminder. Indeed, it is worth recalling in this context the words of Kristeva: "It is thus not lack of cleanliness or health that causes abjection but what disturbs identity, system, order. What does not respect borders, positions, rules."[36]

It should come as no surprise, therefore, that in the sex-segregated environment of the institutional men's room the act of defecation remains, in most circumstances, discreetly closeted. For a host of reasons—including childhood fantasies of phallic detachability that are provoked by expulsion of the faeces; the fantasmatic interchangeability in the unconscious, as Freud puts it, of "the concepts *faeces*, . . . *baby*, and *penis*";[37] and a psychic ambivalence "memorialize[d]" in the anus, as Eve Kosofsky Sedgwick writes, as the site of a struggle "over private excitations, adopted controls, the uses of shame, and the rhythms of productivity"[38]—the heightened awareness in the men's room of the presence and the erotic potential of this space of difference within threatens to vitiate the assurance of those identities that the signifiers "Ladies" and "Gentlemen" would affirm. And by threatening the stability of the boundary between those two heavily defended "countries," the disturbing psychic associations activated in the arena of the public men's room allow for the figurative conflation of a (perceived) threat to the integrity of the nation's (male) bodies and a (perceived) threat to the integrity of the body of the nation, especially when that nation, like America after the War, finds its borders for the first time subject to penetration by the missile technology of its foes.

In a sense, then, the arrest of Walter Jenkins participates in what Herman Rapaport has called, in another context, the "false arrest" of "the sliding that occurs between signified and signified, door one and two" in Lacan's schematic representation of the restroom doors.[39] For Jenkins, like thousands of other men—not all of them gay or gay-identified—booked on similar charges before and after, could be viewed by his contemporaries in one of three ways: a) as a homosexual whose identity *as* a homosexual reinforced the binarism of "Ladies" and "Gentlemen" precisely by standing outside that binarism as the "mistake" within the system itself; or b) as the victim of some illness, physical or emotional, whose transgressive behavior did not symptomatize his (homosexual) identity but rather bespoke an exceptional *falling away* from his true (heterosexual) identity;[40] or c) as a threat to the interpretive certainty invested in the phallus as the privileged signifier of the "identity" on which patriarchal epistemology definitionally depends. That is to say, insofar as male homosexuality continued to signify as a condition indissociable from the category of gender, the only alternative to defining Jenkins as, essentially, "a homosexual," or to explaining his behavior in terms of some sort of illness or mental breakdown, was to posit a category-subverting alterity within the conceptual framework of masculinity itself. But it was, after all, to secure the integrity of that always embattled framework that the surveillance of public restrooms was undertaken in the first place, and that same defensive imperative determined the strategic responses to the Jenkins affair as orchestrated by President Johnson and the members of his staff.

In seeking, however, to circumscribe the scandal by defining it outside the context of homosexuality as such—by insisting, for instance, as Victor Lasky reports President Johnson to have done, that Jenkins was not, as he put it, "biologically" a homosexual—the White House entered into the unavoidable contradictions that structure the discourse on homosexuality in America. Thus the image of Jenkins it disseminated was that of a family man victimized by the extraordinary demands that were placed on his energy, time, and attention by his sense of civic duty. As one former insider, adhering to this official line, subsequently observed: "Whatever the nature of Jenkins's difficulty, he was obviously no simple or habitual homosexual. He was a man who for years had been destroying himself in the service of Lyndon Johnson, ten to sixteen hours a day, six or seven days a week, and finally something had snapped."[41] *Newsweek*, in its presentation of this reading of the affair, quoted from the F.B.I. report in which a colleague asserted that Jenkins "would walk 'on his hands and knees on broken glass to avoid giving President Johnson any problem,'"[42] while *Time* cited a "friend of Jenkins's" who declared, "There were two great devotions in his life: L.B.J. and his own family."[43] These testimonials, of course, endeavor rhetorically to "protect" Jenkins from any assumption that his acknowledged participation in male-male sexual acts should be interpreted as an index of "homosexuality." By presenting him as a man whose difficulties sprang from an excess of those celebrated American virtues of industriousness and loyalty, they dissociate him from a homosexuality conceived in terms of indolence, luxury, and the lack—or worse, the repudiation—of generative productivity. Those same testimonials, however, produce retroactively a more general question about the "meaning" of such excess and "devotion." They produce, that is, an epistemological doubt about the legibility of homosexuality that generates the homographic imperative to reconstruct experience after the fact in order to discern the inscriptions (understood to have been present all along) that convey a "meaning"—homosexuality—that could have been read from the outset.

Such productions of "homosexual difference" as an unrecognized but retroactively *recognizable* "meaning" imprint themselves even on the accounts of Jenkins's breakdown that are offered in order to "defend" him against charges of homosexual orientation. Max Frankel, for instance, in the front-page story with which the *New York Times* reported the Jenkins affair, produced a typically bifurcated portrait of the President's chief of staff by combining an interest in the representation of the (potentially) homosexual body with a nod toward the official explanation that over-exertion caused Jenkins's sexual misconduct: "A man of compact build, a slightly florid face, with heavy, graying hair, Mr. Jenkins has been described as a 'nervous type.' But he was also known for extremely hard work on behalf of the President."[44] The syntax of the first sentence implies a logical relationship between the reporter's attention to the particulars of Jenkins's appearance and the subsequent, unattributed characterization of the politician as a "nervous type." Whether the morphology described here confirms or confounds the conventional stereotypes of the gay physique, the fact that that morphology is subject to analysis, that it is understood as somehow telling with regard to the arrest that is being reported, indicates the need to read into it retroactively the sexual connotations already implicit in that characterological epithet, a "nervous type," that identifies, unambiguously, the "type" that most often makes straight men nervous. The specifics of his bodily representation, therefore, matter less than does the fact that such representation has now become appropriate for Jenkins's body, since such representation effeminizes by subjecting the male body to visual interrogation. And it is axiomatic in the social context within which this representation occurs that a masculinity subject to questioning is no masculinity at all.

Against this "homosexualizing" reading, however, the second sentence offers the "heterosexualizing" assertion of Jenkins's reputation for "extremely hard work." The felt contradiction between these two ideological contexts for interpreting Jenkins's activities accounts for the unexpected conjunction, "but," by which the sentences are joined. The distinction that this conjunction would insist upon, however, very quickly comes undone. For the logic that seeks to exempt Jenkins from the "taint" of homosexuality by translating his ontological status as a "nervous type" into the circumstantial condition of nervous exhaustion precipitated by too much work, gets tangled in the nexus of cultural associations whereby exhaustion is itself perceived as inherently effeminizing. "Hard work" can only account for an emotional breakdown, after all, insofar as the worker in question is already a "nervous type" to begin with—insofar, that is, as he can be categorized in terms of an effeminizing typology that defines an essential condition always subject, within its historical context, to a reading that would articulate its "meaning" as homosexuality. So powerful is the force field of that signification that even Lyndon Johnson, who aggressively denied that his closest advisor might "be" homosexual, engaged in a heavily freighted act of cross-gender figuration when he remarked that the discovery of Jenkins's arrest was as shocking to him "as if someone had told me my wife had murdered her daughter."

Because of the grandiosity with which this statement expresses the depth of anxiety informing the heterosexual reaction to the Jenkins affair, I want to consider a few of the overlapping ideological assumptions at work in this tellingly extravagant metaphor. For the president's remark, like the salacious joke that reinterpreted his campaign slogan as "Either way with LBJ," metonymically displaces the cognitive instability or epistemological uncertainty of homosexuality in order to produce a miniature model of the "conspiracy theory" central to homophobic paranoia. The joke, of course, implicates President Johnson himself in the sexual activities of his advisor by construing as suspect the bond of "devotion" that was so frequently celebrated after Jenkins's resignation. Coming less than a month after the Warren Commission released its controversial report to an audience that remained overwhelmingly unpersuaded, and coming, as well, in the midst of a campaign in which Senator Goldwater repeatedly challenged Johnson's integrity by associating him with moral failure and financial irregularity, the Jenkins scandal, perhaps inevitably, was read as a metonym for corruption at the highest levels of political power. The questions and uncertainty that had hovered over Johnson since his sudden ascent to the presidency the year before—questions that occasionally centered, as in the off-Broadway play, *MacBird*, on paranoid speculation about his involvement in Kennedy's death—could find expression in the charge of some essential ambiguity or insidious duplicity that the popular jokes implicitly leveled by suggesting that Johnson might go "either way," or that if he stood "behind" his advisor it was because they were linked, conspiratorially, in the commission of illicit deeds.

But if the metonymic "contagion" of epistemological doubt evoked by the discussion of homosexuality led some members of the public to question their ability to know or trust the president, the president's more lurid figure of speech articulates a response to homosexual activity in terms that question his own ability to know or trust his wife. The news, that is, of an unanticipated "crime" committed by one of his intimates finds displaced expression through his rhetorical conjuring of a different crime imagined as having been committed by someone presumed to be a different sort of intimate. The prohibited scene of desire between men must be represented through a scenario of violence between women, and the "shock" that responds to the "foreignness" of the homosexual activity in the men's room is translated into a betrayal interior to the structure of heterosexual domesticity. Johnson thus images his advisor's arrest as a violation of trust, and a threat to the possibility of cognitive security, by dwelling on its exposure of an unrecognized quality that calls into question the intimate knowledge and familiarity on which his relationship with Walter Jenkins was based. By emphasizing the defamiliarization effected by such a sudden revelation, the president's comment implicitly diverges from the official explanation that Jenkins had strayed from the straight, if not the narrow, as a result of too much work; instead, it positions the shock of the affair in the disclosure of what should have been known in advance. The shock, therefore, derives as much from the president's having to receive from someone else ("as if someone had told me") such information about his friend (a friend close enough to be represented in the simile by Johnson's wife), as it does from the specific nature of the information he receives. In his framing of the shock, then, as in the cross-gender elaboration through which he positions Jenkins's behavior in relation to effeminacy, the president implicitly endorses the "homosexualizing" interpretation of his advisor's actions. As if to reinforce that interpretation, moreover, the logic at work in the mobilization of this figure locates homosexuality in a conceptual space contiguous with, and impinged upon by, an anxiety-producing image of the power that women wield as mothers.

This bespeaks not merely the popular assumption of the interchangeability of same-sex desire and the disturbance of traditional gender distinctions and roles, but also the psychological truism of the period that male homosexuality both constituted, and resulted from, an inappropriate identification between the mother and her son. The president's metaphor invokes the contradictory reasoning whereby gay men were assumed, derisively, to be overly fond of and close to their mothers, even as they were assumed, projectively, to hate all women—"especially," as the editors of the Catholic journal, *America*, wrote in 1962, "the woman who is a mother."[45] Tellingly, those who charged gay men with denigrating women and "especially" mothers, did not scruple to read homosexuality as a "problem" for which mother herself should be blamed. It was, after all, the too loving mother that heterosexual culture loved to hate, the smothering mother who destroyed her son through overprotection or overindulgence. Just four months before the Jenkins affair, Ernest Havemann, borrowing heavily from the work of Irving Bieber, summarized these notions in his article for *Life*: "On the one hand, the homosexual's mother kept him utterly dependent on her, unable to make his own decisions. On the other, she pampered him, catered to his every whim and smothered him with affection" (78). As the language of this passage suggests, the mother stands accused here of effeminizing her son, of preventing his "natural" development into heterosexual manhood and thus, effectively, of consigning him to a life of nongenerative sexuality. The abjection of male homosexuality, therefore, carries the burden of an archaic patriarchal anxiety about the mother's relation to power;

as Kristeva puts it: "The abject confronts us . . . with our earliest attempts to release the hold of *maternal* entity even before ex-isting outside of her, thanks to the autonomy of language. It is a violent, clumsy breaking away, with the constant risk of falling back under the sway of a power as securing as it is stifling."[46] If the security of that power allows homosexual relations to be figured in terms of indulgence and weakness—in stark contrast to the masculinizing rigor and renunciation involved in the break from maternal control—the "stifling" that the mother allegedly effects provokes a "violent" disavowal that gets displaced and reenacted in the phobic response to male homosexuality. Hence the logic by which Johnson's comment can substitutively imagine homosexual eros through a figure of projective maternal violence; hence too its phobic evocation of the slippage from "wife," a position of subordination within the dynamics of heterosexual marriage, to mother, a position of power within the mother-child dyad.[47]

The same social pressures, of course, that conspired to "blame" the mother for male homosexuality produced the Cold War discourse of "momism" that implicated mothers in narratives of subversion through the weakening of masculine resolve against the insidious threat of Communism. In his compelling and well-documented analysis of Cold War cinema in America, Michael Rogin demonstrates how films of the fifties and early sixties "identif[y] Communism with secret, maternal influence. . . . The films suggest that the menace of alien invasion lay not so much in the power of a foreign state as in the obliteration of paternal inheritance."[48] Brilliantly exposing the contradictory implications of domestic ideology, Rogin shows how the American security state adopted the very mechanisms of illicit power that it anxiously identified with its enemies: "Men comprise the state, to be sure; but they use the techniques of motherhood and Communism—intrusion, surveillance, and secret domination" (21). These techniques, as Rogin demonstrates, were then turned against motherhood and Communism both so as to prevent the disappropriation of American masculinity. It is within this context that I want to suggest that by representing male homosexuality through the figure of a mother who murders her child, and who therefore participates in the destruction of (patriarchal) familial continuity, Johnson's comment not only restages the cultural abjection of the mother, but also recapitulates the anxiety invoked when *Life* magazine inquired if "the homosexuals, like the Communists, intend to bury us." It figurally positions homosexual behavior in the context of "the obliteration of paternal inheritance" and signals an interpretation of male-male desire not only through the filter of sentimental self-pity writ large in the melodrama of (domestic) betrayal that the president so vividly imagines, but also in a specific relation to history that equally informs Senator Goldwater's remark and the staging of the men's room in the Jenkins affair.

For when homosexuality enters the field of vision in each of these fragments of the social text it occasions a powerful disruption of that field by virtue of its uncontrollably figuralizing effects; and that disruption of the field of vision is precisely what homosexuality comes to represent: so radical a rupture of the linguistic and epistemic orders that it figures futurity imperiled, it figures history as apocalypse, by gesturing toward the precariousness of familial and national survival. If momism is the theory, then homosexuality is the practice, for it is seen as enacting the destabilization of borders, the subversion of masculine identity from within, that momism promotes. Such a reading of male homosexuality, of course, is not unique to America in the early sixties; indeed, it reactivates an anxiety about male-male sexual interaction that is older than Voltaire's expression of concern in his discussion of "Socratic Love." My point, however, is that the historical pressure upon the postwar American national self-image found displaced articulation in the phobic positioning of homosexual activity as the proximate cause of perceived danger to the nation at a time of unprecedented concern about the possibility of national—and global—destruction. Revising late nineteenth-century arguments about racial degeneration and bringing them to bear upon mid-twentieth-century social and political conflicts, historically deployed readings envisioning male homosexuality in terms of the abjection associated with the men's room could complain of the threat homosexuality posed to the continuity of civilization itself. Norman Mailer, in an essay from 1961, offers one virulent formulation of this idea: "As a civilization dies, it loses its biology. The homosexual, alienated from the biological chain, becomes its center."[49] Mailer clarifies the phobic logic that underlies this statement in an essay titled "Truth and Being: Nothing and Time," published in 1962 and reprinted (ironically?) in *The Presidential Papers* as part of a section titled "On Waste": " . . . if excrement is the enforced marriage of Tragic Beauty and Filth, why then did God desert it, and leave our hole to the Devil, unless it is because God has hegemony over us only as we create each other. God owns the creation, but the Devil has power over all we waste—how natural for him to lay siege where the body ends and weak tragic air begins."[50] Heterosexuality alone possesses the divine attribute of creativity here; homosexual activity, by contrast, leads only to waste, as Mailer insisted in an interview in 1962: "I think one of the reasons that homosexuals go through such agony when they're around 40 or 50 is that their lives have nothing to do with procreation. . . . They've used up their being."[51]

The erotic behavior proscriptively associated with the men's room as the scene of the voiding of waste thus gets entangled in the national imaginary with a fantasy of cultural and historical vastation. But the surveillance by which the law expresses the state's "need" to see homosexuality, like the sensationalism involved as that "need" is compulsively reenacted by the popular media, reveals an ill-suppressed *desire* to see, to recognize, to expose the alterity of homosexuality. That desire bespeaks a narcissistic anxiety about the definition of (sexual) identity that can only be stabilized and protected by a process of elimination or casting out. It betokens, that is, the fundamental imperative to anal sadistic behavior that organizes the heterosexual order's definition of masculinity itself—that generates our dominant understanding of masculinity through the anal sadistic projection or casting out that inheres in homophobia. Little wonder, then, that Senator Goldwater should aim his missiles at the Kremlin and the men's room both, for in the process he makes visible the aggressive anality of a culture compelled to repudiate the homosexuality it projectively identifies with the very anality it thus itself enacts. That abjectifying—and therefore effeminizing—anality is a condition that homophobic masculinity repudiates by construing it as the distinguishing hallmark of a recognizable category of homosexual person. As the cultural texts brought together here suggest, though, that reification of homosexuality is inherently unstable, its markings always subject to doubt and the anxiety of retroactive interpretation. Homosexuality, therefore, remains subject to figuration as that which threatens the catastrophic undoing of history, national and familial both, by opening an epistemological gap, a space or void, in maleness itself—a gap in which, in the end, as it were, there is nothing to be seen, and no assurance, therefore, that the visual display of masculinity's phallic ensign can suffice as evidence of the heterosexuality for which "masculinity" has become a trope. For the public insistence on the visible organ in the open space of the urinal can never dispel the magnetizing pull of the dangers that are seated in that unseen space, that cavity concealed by the toilet stall door that leads, as Lacan's fabulation would have it, toward another "country" whose agents are always already operating within—always already operating even, or even *especially*, within the men's room itself, in which, for heterosexual men, it is never sufficient for one to be in order to be, with any certainty or security, a "man."

All of the representations of gay male sexuality considered in this essay are deeply informed by the dread of that space in which the historically and culturally inflected concerns about the opening within the male body are themselves opened onto a fear of abjection that is intimately bound up with questions of visibility and the place of the visual in the symbolic determination of sexual difference. It seems fitting, therefore, to conclude this essay with a discussion of what it, like the texts it examines, has *not* been able to see. Rehearsing the events leading to Walter Jenkins's arrest, *Time* magazine reported: "On that night the cops spotted Jenkins in a pay toilet with Andy Choka, 60, a Hungarian-born veteran of the U.S. Army who lives in Washington's Soldiers' Home. Jenkins's back partly obscured the detectives' view, but they figured they had seen enough to arrest the two men for a misdemeanor, if not for a more serious morals rap."[52] What the detectives could not see, and what *Time*, of course, could not, in any case, discuss, is whatever sexual relation actually transpired between the two men. As Henry Gemmill wrote at the time in the pages of the *Wall Street Journal*, the charge inscribed beside Jenkins's name in the police blotter, "disorderly (indecent gestures)," "could cover any one of about a dozen different acts . . . rang[ing] from the seemingly trivial—'reaching over and touching a person's leg'—to the unprintable."[53] Though "unprintable" functions as a trope for that which, if known, could not *properly* be mentioned, the specific acts for which Jenkins was charged *are*, in fact, unprintable since they took place outside the detectives', or the culture's, field of vision. The policemen's sightline may have been blocked by the position of Jenkins's back, but that blockage betokens a larger blind spot in the law's view of homosexuality: its inability to see it as anything but the obverse, the backside, of the "natural" self-evidence that phallic visibility would assure. Gay male sexuality, in other words, can always only be perceived from behind by a law that is destined to find its angle of vision recurrently "obscured" by a "back." To name, therefore, what could not be seen would constitute a mystified reenactment of that blindness on another level. Even to name it, for instance, as pleasure, would be to sentimentalize its opacity, its resistance to cultural "meaning," by appropriating it for the order of recognizability and "truth." Let it remain, instead, the unseen and the unsaid: not as a token of its mystery or as a gesture toward its ultimate ineffability, but rather as a figure for the demonization of that which refuses the symbolic law of binary differentiation, that which finds expression in the abjectified scene of homosexual desire.

against gay sexual representation?

Part IV

Ocular Proof

10

SEEING THINGS

Representation, the Scene of Surveillance, and the Spectacle of Gay Male Sex

In 1810 an angry London mob attacked a group of men who were being taken to the pillory after having been convicted of assault with the intent to commit sodomy in the back room of a Vere Street pub. As Louis Crompton observes in *Byron and Greek Love*, the journalistic reports detailing the violence wreaked by the thousands who participated in this scene prompted Louis Simond, a French visitor to England, to make the following notation in the journal he kept: "We have just read in all the newspapers a full and disgusting account of the public and cruel punishment on the pillory of certain wretches convicted of vile indecencies. I can think of nothing more dangerous, offensive, and unwise, than the brutality and unrestrained publicity of such infliction. The imagination itself is sullied by the exposition of enormities, that ought never to be supposed to exist."[1]

These comments repudiate the virulence of the mob, but only by suggesting that such scenes of brutality make evident the brutalizing effects on the populace of any public discourse on sexual relations between men—effects that cannot be avoided even when such discourse is generated to make possible the prosecution of "wretches" who commit "vile indecencies." The horrifying spectacle of the riotous mob pelting the manacled convicts with, as one contemporary account reported, "mud, dead cats, rotten eggs, potatoes, and buckets filled with blood, offal, and dung,"[2] does not argue against the criminalizing of sodomitical relations, in the passage from Simond, but functions, instead, as a displaced repetition of the interdicted sexual act: it figures forth, in other words, the infectious indecency of sodomy itself by reading the atrocities committed by the crowd as yet another effect of the "indecencies" that brought those "wretches" to the pillory in the first place. Such a sentiment was by no means unusual, of course; homosexuality, or more precisely, the bias toward sodomitical relations, already had assumed, by the time Simond wrote, its extraordinarily potent, though phobically charged, relation to the signifying conventions of the West. It had already come to be construed, that is, as a behavior marked by a transgressive force reproduced, not merely designated, by naming or discussing it. For it constituted, more than an assault upon the flesh, an assault upon the logic of social discourse, an assault so extreme that not only one's morals but also one's "imagination" itself could be sullied by the "exposition of enormities, that ought never to be supposed to exist."

It is worth pausing to consider the significance attached to this scandal of supposition in which horror and violent denial seem indissociable from the representation of homosexuality. What wound, after all, can the scene of sodomy inflict to make its staging, if only in the space of the imagination, so dangerous to effect, and what within that scene has such power to implicate—and, by implicating, to sully—that such a scene, or even the possibility of such a scene, ought properly to be disavowed? Framed in these terms this scandal of supposition may begin to take shape in relation to the process whereby psychoanalysis accounts for the constitution of masculine subjectivity: a process that centers on the crisis of representation through which the subject gains a "knowledge" of sexual difference. The sexual supposition that Simond would disallow may suggest, then, not only the undecidable question of presence or absence that inheres in fetishistic supposition or belief, but also the male subject's normative interpretations or narrative accounts of sexual difference: the suppositions with which he enters the symbolic order by internalizing the "law" of castration and achieving a retroactive understanding of what Freud defines as "the primal scene." I want to examine that scene and its framing in *From the History of an Infantile Neurosis*—Freud's analysis of the Wolf Man, as his patient has subsequently come to be known—both because that case engages explicitly the question of sexual supposition and because it does so by exploring the vicissitudes of the representation of a sodomitical encounter.

Let me be clear about my purpose at the outset, however: I aim neither to privilege nor to repudiate the psychoanalytic paradigm; rather, I hope to read its relation to the inscriptions of sodomy in the primal scene as a response to the sodomitical implications of the scene of psychoanalysis itself. For that reason, along with Freud's account of the primal scene as one in which the supposition of homosexuality is embedded, I want to examine, if only briefly, passages from a number of other texts that suppose scenes of sodomy between men: passages from John Cleland's *Memoirs of a Woman of Pleasure*, Tobias

Smollett's *Adventures of Peregrine Pickle*, and Jacques Derrida's *The Post Card*. In each case a presumptively heterosexual spectator, positioned to remain unobserved, witnesses a sexual encounter between men that occasions narrative and tropological effects that are discernible in Freud's case history as well; but rather than construing the Freudian text as a master-discourse with the power to illuminate the more explicitly literary passages, or, alternatively, using the literary passages to deconstruct the project of psychoanalysis, I want to observe how in each of these texts homosexuality comes to signify as a distinctively literary or rhetorical operation in its own right. Though read differently at different historical moments, the inscription of homosexuality within a sodomitical scene proves scandalous for each of these different texts not because it occupies a position *outside* the rules governing social discourse, but precisely because it operates from *within* those rules to suggest the instability of positioning that is sexuality itself.

Perhaps it is appropriate to try to make clear the direction from which I want to come at these issues by noting that the problem I want to address is the problem, in part, of how one comes at a problem: from what direction, that is, one approaches it and in what position one chooses to engage it. Freud's metapsychological theories, after all, repeatedly articulate a structural return to a trauma occasioned by an earlier event that has no existence *as a scene of trauma* until it is (re)presented—or (re)produced—*as* a trauma in the movement of return itself. His theories, in this way, define a psychic experience in which the most crucial and constitutive dramas of human life are those that can never be viewed head on, those that can never be taken in frontally, but only approached from behind. As Mary Ann Doane perceptively notes, "The psychical layer Freud designated perception-consciousness is frequently deceived, caught from behind by unconscious forces which evade its gaze."[3]

Not for nothing, therefore, in his analytic (re)construction of the Wolf Man's primal scene, does Freud propose that the sexual encounter observed (or fantasized) by the Wolf Man in his infancy involved his parents in what Freud conceives as an act of coitus *a tergo*; for along with the numerous other ways in which this interpretation serves Freud's purpose, such a posture allegorizes both the retroactive understanding whereby the primal scene will generate its various effects, and the practice of psychoanalysis itself insofar as it too approaches experience from behind through the analyst's efforts to reproduce the distinctive logic of the unconscious.[4] Psychoanalysis, in other words, not only theorizes *about*, but also bases its practice on, the (re)construction or reinterpretation of earlier experiences in ways that evoke the disordered chronology characteristic of deferred action; and as a result of what Laplanche and Pontalis describe as the "unevenness of its temporal development," human sexuality constitutes the major arena in which the psychic effects of deferred action, or *Nachträglichkeit*, come into play.[5] With this theory psychoanalysis refuses any unidirectional understanding of the temporality of psychic development; instead, it questions the logic of the chronological and the determinate relationship of cause and effect. If temporal revisions and inversions, then, mark the production of psychoanalytic narrative, the very articulation of psychoanalytic logic can be construed in terms of metalepsis, a rhetorical term that denotes the substitution of cause for effect or effect for cause, a substitution that disturbs the relationship of early and late, or before and behind.[6] And nowhere is this metaleptic structure—a structure I propose to discuss as "(be)hindsight" in order to figure its complicitous involvement in the sodomitical encounter—more evident than in Freud's theorization of the Wolf Man's primal scene.

Perhaps it is not irrelevant, then, to remind ourselves that the Wolf Man, in his earliest expression of psychoanalytic transference, believed that Freud himself desired to "use [him] from behind."[7] At the time that he made this comment, of course, the Wolf Man did not have access to what Freud would "uncover" as his primal scene—a scene in which, according to Freud, the Wolf Man observed at first hand what being used from behind entailed. Indeed, in Freud's formulation of it, the primal scene itself can never be recollected or brought forward into consciousness but only, at best, pieced together or produced retroactively through analysis: "scenes, like this one in my present patient's case, which date from an early period and exhibit a similar content, and which further lay claim to such an extraordinary significance for the history of the case, are as a rule not reproduced as recollections, but have to be divined—constructed—gradually and laboriously from an aggregate of indications" (51).[8] Thus the supposition or construction of the primal scene is the effect of the analyst's interpretation of symptoms that subsequently will be determined to have been, themselves, effects of that constructed scene; this disarticulation of temporal logic in what I have chosen to call "(be)hindsight" exemplifies the metaleptic structure of the psychoanalytic hypothesis, especially when the trope of metalepsis is considered, as Marguerite Waller has aptly phrased it, as a "rhetorical moebius loop."[9]

Now what distinguishes the moebius loop, of course, is the impossibility of distinguishing its front from its back, a condition that has, as I have already implied, an immediate sexual resonance; but that indistinguishability bespeaks as well a crisis of certainty, a destabilizing of the foundational logic on which knowledge as such depends. Thus if *From the History of an Infantile Neurosis*, in its elaboration of the primal scene, enacts a psychoanalytic method as metaleptic, as subversive of positional logic, as the moebius loop, the self-questioning hesitancy with which Freud responds to his own positing of that scene betrays the effects of the moebius loop's epistemological disruptions; for no other case history testifies so powerfully to the psychoanalyst's inability to decide just where he wants to position himself with regard to his own enabling theoretical insights. As Nicholas Abraham and Maria Torok observe in discussing Freud's analysis of the Wolf Man: "Polemical in its explicit purpose, it also reflects another debate, that of the author with himself. Throughout this stirring account and within the meanderings of the theoretical discussion, attentive readers will sense a doubt—it is Freud's doubt regarding his own statements."[10] Indeed, throughout the case history of the Wolf Man the insistence of such doubt reflects Freud's deep anxiety that the primal scene that takes center stage in his analysis may prove to be only an illicit supposition of something that ought never to be supposed to exist.

Certainly the audacity of the scene Freud calls forth might justify such an anxiety: that the parents of a one-and-half-year-old boy—a boy who was suffering at the time from malaria—would engage in sexual relations three times while the child rested in the same room—let alone that those relations would feature penetration from behind—and that all of this would take place around five o'clock on a summer afternoon, represents, within its discursive context, so sensational an erotic vision that Freud must initially defend his construction by flatly denying that there is anything sensational in this scenario at all: "On the contrary," he writes, "such an event would, I think, be something entirely commonplace and *banal*" (38). Later, however, in an addition to the manuscript, when he undertakes to reconsider the primal scene's "reality," Freud proposes that the child may have witnessed "not copulation between his parents but copulation between animals, which he then displaced on to his parents" (57). Freud goes on to acknowledge that with this supposition "the demands on our credulity are reduced. We need no longer suppose that the parents copulated in the presence of their child (a very young one it is true)—which was a disagreeable idea for many of us" (58). That Freud designates here as straining credulity what he first described as banal, that he now presents as a "disagreeable idea" what he first called "entirely commonplace," bespeaks the ambivalence of his position and the extent of what Abraham and Torok describe as his "doubt regarding his own statements."

Now Freud himself offered a provocative insight into the nature of such doubt and the etiology of such ambivalence in a letter written in another context to Lou Andreas-Salomé. "Your derivation of the phenomenon of doubt," he tells her, "is too intellectual, too rational. The tendency to doubt arises not from any occasion for doubt, but is the continuation of the powerful ambivalent tendencies in the pre-genital phase, which from then on become attached to every pair of opposites."[11] In this Freudian genealogy, the doubt that attaches to such binary oppositions as cause and effect, or before and behind, represents the carrying forward of an ambivalence associated with the oral and anal stages of libidinal organization, stages in which, as Freud puts it, "it is . . . a question of *external* and *internal*. What is unreal, merely a presentation and subjective, is only internal; what is real is also there *outside*."[12] This description appears in Freud's essay on negation, or *Verneinung*, the psychic defense he employs in denying that the erotic spectacle he initially proposed as essential to the primal scene exceeds in any way the merely commonplace and banal. Freud's subsequent ambivalence, his expression of doubt about the status of the scene as either internal or external, imagined or real, bears the traces, therefore, of a pre-genital survival according to his own analysis; and since the mobilization of that doubt seeks to expel or cast out an anxiety about the ontological condition of the most, as it were, *fundamental* theoretical construct at work in his reading of the Wolf Man, it carries more specifically the psychic trace of anal-erotic organization.[13]

It is all the more significant, therefore, that anal-erotic fixation and the tendency toward doubt that it is said to produce figure centrally in the Wolf Man's neurosis as Freud construes it in this case history. After all, Freud attempts to account not only for the Wolf Man's predilection for heterosexual relations in which he penetrates his partner from behind, but also for his inability to move his bowel without the benefit of an enema administered by his male attendant. Freud attributes to this anal fixation, moreover, the skepticism with which the Wolf Man resisted his spiritual indoctrination into Christian piety. Freud sees in this questioning of orthodox belief the Wolf Man's desire to perpetuate his infantile erotic attachment to his father in the face of the overwhelming uncertainties and doubts occasioned by the dream of the wolves that Freud interprets as signaling the analysand's deferred recognition of the "meaning" of the primal scene. These doubts find expression, tellingly enough, in the Wolf Man's need to determine whether or not Christ "had a behind" (63) and consequently experienced the necessity of defecation. "We catch a glimpse," Freud goes on to declare, "of [the Wolf Man's] repressed homosexual attitude in his doubting whether Christ could have a behind, for these ruminations can have had no other meaning but the question whether he himself could be used by his father like a woman—like his mother in the primal scene" (64); his doubt, that is, expresses an anxiety about his own desire to be used from behind—a desire whose fulfillment seems now necessarily to subject him to the law of castration. But we only "catch a glimpse" of this structure by coming at the primal scene itself through "(be)hindsight," and Freud's interrogation within this case history of his belief in the theoretical insights he produces by approaching the scene from this direction takes shape at once as a resistance to, and an unwitting reinscription of, the disorienting confusion between outside and inside, real and imagined, analyst and analysand in the articulation of the primal scene. Freud, to put it another way, tries to distance his method from the anal erotism he identifies as characteristic of the Wolf Man by casting doubt upon the coitus *a tergo* that Freud himself had initially proposed in approaching the primal scene through analytic "(be)hindsight"; but that very doubt, however tendentiously it seeks to differentiate Freud's eros from his patient's, only reenacts the doubt or skepticism that Freud has already described as an index of the Wolf Man's anal erotism. Freud's ambivalence about the vision of penetration from behind generates, in consequence, a certain defensiveness about the status of his own analytic hypothesis—a defensiveness that may tell us a great deal about the danger recurrently posed by the representation of the sodomitical scene.

For Freud reveals himself at his most self-protective when he responds, in a section of *From the History of an Infantile Neurosis* set aside for just this purpose, to suggestions that what he labels as primal scenes are not "real occurrences" with a historical basis in the experience of the infant, but only "products of the imagination, which find their instigation in mature life" and thus constitute nothing more than fantasies that "owe their origin to a regressive tendency" (49). While acknowledging that such a "regressive tendency . . . [is] regularly confirmed by analysis" (53), and even going so far as to take credit for having been the one to identify such tendencies in the first place,[14] Freud denies that the theory of psychoanalysis demands that the primal scene be read as a retroactive fantasy. Defending his belief in the reality of such scenes, he argues instead that the early outbreak of the Wolf Man's obsessional neurosis demonstrably "limits the regressive part of the causation" and "brings into full view the portion of it which operates in a forward direction" (55).

What Freud, I would argue, feels called upon to limit in relation to the primal scene is a recognition of the metaleptic structure that marks psychoanalysis as a coming from behind; he cannot allow the primal scene that he still views at this point as real and central to the development of the Wolf Man's neurosis to be interpreted as merely a *fantasmatic* effect of the effects it is alleged to have produced. He needs, instead, to affirm the possibility of its operation in a "forward direction"—an operation that Freud hopes to "bring into full view" in the context of a case that will, if successful, "give a clear picture of this position of things" (55). Freud's defense of his theory of the primal scene thus depends upon his ability to "bring into full view" a "clear picture" of the "forward direction" of the effects produced by the primal scene: a scene that, as Freud has already shown, can only be constructed metaleptically, put together *a posteriori*, through the "aggregate indications" of those effects themselves. To complicate further the "clear picture" Freud would offer, the "forward direction" of the scene's effects must be viewed in the context of an erotic scene whose thematic content explicitly focuses on the question of what can or cannot be viewed, and on the specific positions that the actors must assume in order for the observer to be able to view specific "things" without obstruction; it is a scene, therefore, that permits a "clear" view only when the act of intercourse at its center does not take place in a "forward direction" but occurs, instead, from behind. Only thus, after all, is it possible for the spectator to gain visual access to what later will register as the signifying presence of the father's penis in relation to what at that point will be construed as the problematical absence of the mother's, an absence that will be attributed, metaleptically, to the mother's submission to the father's desire.

Freud performs in this passage an elaborate dance of forward and backward, before and behind—not a fox-trot, but a Freudian Wolf-trot perhaps; and the rigorous confusion that informs this attempt to present a "clear picture of [the] position of things," expresses his concern that the supposition of this scene, with its spectacular representation of penetration from behind, may color the relation of the analyst—or even of psychoanalysis itself—to the man who puts himself in the analyst's hands when he lies down on the analyst's couch. For the primal scene, as Freud reconstructs the perspective of the infant he imagines to observe it,[15] activates the pre-genital supposition "that sexual intercourse takes place at the anus" (78). Thus the primal scene, in the first instance, is always perceived as sodomitical, and it specifically takes shape as a sodomitical scene between sexually undifferentiated partners, both of whom, fantasmatically, are believed to possess the phallus. In a sense, then, the primal scene as Freud unpacks it presupposes the imaginative priority of a sort of proto-homosexuality, and it designates male heterosexuality, by contrast, as a later narcissistic compromise that only painfully and with difficulty represses its identification with the so-called "passive" position in that scene so as to protect the narcissistically invested penis from the fate that is assumed to have befallen the penis of the mother.[16] Insofar as the participants in the primal scene are as yet undifferentiated sexually to the infant who observes them—both, that is, in the logic of Freudian theory, are seen as phallic—it is small wonder that he has no difficulty identifying pleasurably with each of their positions; but insofar as that scene, once the law of castration imposes its binary reading of sex, must thereafter bear traces of sodomitical fantasy and homosexual desire, it is small wonder that Freud has great difficulty indeed in allowing himself or his psychoanalytic practice to be implicated in the scene at all. The "(be)hindsight" of psychoanalysis produces a correspondence too close for comfort.

One pragmatic reason for such discomfort becomes apparent when Freud responds to the charge that the primal scene is not just a retroactive fantasy, but a fantasy whose origin must be attributed to the analyst rather than to the analysand. He ventriloquizes this line of reasoning as follows: "what is argued now is evidently that they are phantasies not of the patient but of the analyst himself, who forces them upon the person under analysis on account of some complexes of his own" (52). The supposition or imagining of the sodomitical scene so destabilizes the division between real and imagined, external and internal, patient and analyst, that the psychoanalyst's imagining of the scene itself can be read as a figural enactment, a displaced *performance*, of that scene: for the analyst is now subject to representation as one who "forces" himself surreptitiously "upon the person under analysis," imposing himself, like the unconscious, in a way that evades the patient's gaze. He is accused, that is, at bottom, of wanting to "use [his patient] from behind" not only by the Wolf Man in his early imaginary or transferential relation to the analyst, but also by real, external critics of psychoanalysis as he practices it.

This charge, which was leveled against Freud by such contemporaries as Jung and Adler, has received more recent, and more persuasive, formulation in an essay by Stanley Fish. "Freud reserves to himself," Fish argues, " . . . the pleasure of total mastery. It is a pleasure that is intensely erotic, . . . affording the multiple satisfactions of domination, penetration, and engulfment."[17] Though Fish identifies, correctly in my view, Freud's implication in the primal scene's coitus *a tergo*, neither pleasure nor mastery seems adequate as a description of his response to that implication. Rather, the fancy rhetorical footwork he performs in an effort to keep the forward and backward directions of psychoanalytic operations and sexual encounters from corresponding too exactly suggests the precariousness of his relation to a scene that cannot be viewed without wounding the straight-identified spectator who is positioned to observe it. After all, as Freud himself understands, no possible response can dissuade his accusers from reading the primal scene as a fantasy that reveals the *analyst's* psychological "complexes," his *own* "perverse" desires. "On the one side," he notes with resignation, "there will be a charge of subtle self-deception, and on the other of obtuseness of judgment; it will be impossible to arrive at a decision" (53).

If the supposition of the primal scene calls forth this radical indeterminacy that always threatens to put the analyst in the position of the patient, that same indeterminacy more famously informs Freud's final remark on the ontological status of the primal scene itself: "I intend on this occasion," he declares, in a passage added after he had finished the manuscript of his text, "to close the discussion of the primal scene with a *non liquet*" (60), that is, with a legal determination that the evidence is insufficient. But the Latin phrase thus appropriated by the law means literally "it is not clear," and this denial of clarity thus marks a return of the optical metaphor always at issue in the thematics of the primal scene. By affirming a lack of clarity in the perspective from which he attempts to view or "catch a glimpse" of that theoretically indispensable scene, Freud situates himself unresolvedly before the very *psychoanalytic* scene in which the *Wolf Man's* primal scene was metaleptically constructed. His acknowledgment, in other words, of a conceptual opacity within the scene of psychoanalysis, an opacity that betokens a node of resistance internal to the *theorization* of the primal scene, reenacts the resistance of the Wolf Man, after his "recognition" of castration, to his pleasurable spectatorial involvement in the primal scene as "originally"—which is to say, fantasmatically—construed. In each case, a sexual theory undergoes revisionary rearticulation in order to protect the theorist from implication in the spectacle as initially envisioned.

Thus the Wolf Man's sexual theory, as Freud argues, at the moment he "witnessed" the primal scene, centered on his identification with the pleasure derived from (what he took to be) the penetration of the anus, a "penetration" that should be read as describing simultaneously the act of penetrating and the act of being penetrated. This double identification allowed him imaginatively to inhabit the positions of both his mother and his father in the spectacle of coitus *a tergo*;[18] but that theoretical positioning was psychically rewritten with the dream that insisted on castration as the price of gratifying what Freud defines as the patient's "homosexual enthusiasm" (78). The law of castration, by insisting on the subject's interpellation as male or female, mandates the loss or repression of specific identifications in order to achieve the singularity of a "properly" sexed and gendered identity. The fluid identifications made possible by the infant's perception of the primal scene must give way to the fixity of the law that will now keep an eye on the little man himself. Thus the dream that marks (and/or effects) the Wolf Man's understanding of castration crucially features a redistribution of spectatorial positions as well, so that the child who viewed the primal scene (and in the process experienced the pleasure of multiple erotic identifications) dreams that he himself has now become the *object* of observation (and consequently experiences the paranoid fear that he must suffer for his earlier experience of spectatorial satisfaction). Similarly, the psychoanalyst whose theory of sexual development makes the primal scene visible within the theater of analysis in order to "give a clear picture" of how psychological trauma can sneak up from behind, belatedly redefines as a "disagreeable idea" the coitus *a tergo* that he first described as "entirely commonplace and *banal*." The theorist who sought to produce a "clear picture" produces, in other words, in response to the criticism of analysts who would turn his own methods against him and make him the object of their professional gaze, a theory in which the anxious-making spectacle, the "picture" that is the primal scene, must not be made *too* clear; for as the analytic scene and the primal scene uncontrollably collapse into one another, Freud can only conclude with a *non liquet*, declaring his inability to specify with any clarity the meaning of either one.

This inability bespeaks the destabilization of definitional barriers and the undoing of the logic of positionality effected by the sodomitical spectacle; it thus makes possible the identification of Freud with the infant who identifies with both participants in the erotics of the primal scene. It puts the Freud, that is, who fails to resolve the theoretical status of the primal scene in the position he imagines the infant to occupy *within* that scene itself, a position from which real and imagined, inside and outside, active and passive are so deeply and inextricably interwoven that he simultaneously identifies with positions that only later come to be differentiated as mutually exclusive (op)positions. This disorientation of positionality is bound up with the danger historically associated in Euro-American culture with the spectacle or representation of the sodomitical scene between men, and this can be demonstrated by attending to the ways in which the logic of spatio-temporal positioning insistently marks our culture's framing of homosexual relations.

I mean by this something more than the fact that we are accustomed to using a metaphorics of "in" or "out" to measure an aspect of lesbian and gay political identity; I mean something that can be approximated more closely by noting that modern masculinist heterosexual culture conceptualizes lesbian and gay male sexuality in terms of a phallocentric positional logic, insistently (and dismissively) articulating lesbianism as a form of extended, non-productive foreplay and gay male sexual relations as a form of extended, non-productive behind-play. The scene of sodomy comes to figure, therefore, both a spatial disturbance in the logic of positions and a temporal disturbance in the logic essential to narrative development. In "Jenny Cromwell's Complaint Against Sodomy" (1692), the complainant, for example, looks back to a time "When Britains did encounter face to face/And thought a back stroke trecherous and base"; but that lost time of "homely joys," was, as Jenny Cromwell tells us, before the "Reformation/Turned all things Arsy-versy in the nation."[19] As this poem suggests, the practice of sodomy is construed as exemplifying a logic of reversal with widespread and uncontrollable implications—implications that reenact a "sodomitical" disturbance of temporal (and therefore narrative) positionality that threatens to reduce the play of history to the finality of an endgame.

Such disarticulations of positional logic find concise expression in a passage from John Cleland's *Memoirs of a Woman of Pleasure*, a novel in which Fanny Hill, that memorable woman of pleasure herself, celebrates all manner of erotic experience with the single and noteworthy exception of male-male sexual relations. Forced unexpectedly to amuse herself in a roadside "publick-house," Fanny discovers a "paper patch" concealing an opening in the moveable partition that divides her room from the one adjoining it. Piercing the patch with a needle, she manages to spy upon "two young sparks romping . . . in frolic, and innocent play."[20] Before long, however, their play turns amorous, and Fanny is able to discover, as she knowingly puts it, "what they were" (158); for theirs, in Fanny's significant phrase, is a "project of preposterous pleasure" (157). I focus on this phrase in particular because it signally condenses the disturbance of positionality that is located in and effected by the sodomitical scene; sodomy, that is, gets figured as the literalization of the "preposterous" precisely insofar as it is interpreted as the practice of giving precedence to the posterior and thus as confounding the stability or determinacy of linguistic or erotic positioning. Not surprisingly, this defiance of the order of meaning articulated through relations like before and behind—a defiance like that inherent in the very structure of the moebius loop—dominates Fanny's interest in the sexual spectacle played out before her, especially when she focuses on the erection sported by the young man being penetrated from the rear. "His red-topt ivory toy, that stood perfectly stiff," she scientifically notes, "shewed, that if he was like his mother behind, he was like his father before" (158).

The figural logic at work in this sentence must not pass unremarked, for the categories defined as "like his mother" and "like his father" bear a crucial conceptual weight. If Fanny's magnetized attention to the young man's "red-topt ivory toy" seems to specify exactly what she means in describing him as "like his father before," there remains, nonetheless, an element of opacity when she likens him to "his mother behind." Consider, for instance, that the syntax here allows as a perfectly proper interpretation that the young man who, when seen from before, is like his father *when seen from before*, is simultaneously, when seen from behind, like his mother *when seen from behind*; the sentence, that is, could be construed to assert that where his penis represents a phallic endowment comparable in kind to that of his father, his buttocks represent a posterior endowment comparable in kind to that of his mother. But the sentence, as most readers of Cleland intuit, seems to signify something else instead: that the man who, from the front, is like his father from the front, is also, from the back, like his mother *from the front*. The sodomite, therefore, like the moebius loop, represents and enacts a troubling resistance to the binary logic of before and behind, constituting himself as a single-sided surface whose front and back are never completely distinguishable as such.

In order to bring fully into focus, however, the meaning of this metaphoric equation of the young man's anus and the mother's vagina, it is useful to remember that before and behind do not just identify spatial positions, they gesture toward temporal relations as well. Psychoanalysis, of course, posits the law of castration as decisively effecting the temporal logic whereby what was perceived as phallic "before" becomes feminine "behind." Indeed, as Freud writes with specific reference to the Wolf Man's pathogenic dream of the wolves, the erotism associated with the posterior or the "behind" has, for men, a deep-seated relation to their emergent understanding of female sexuality in the wake of the castration complex:

> We have been driven to assume that during the process of the dream he understood that women are castrated, that instead of a male organ they have a wound which serves for sexual intercourse, and that castration is the necessary condition of femininity; we have been driven to assume that the threat of this loss induced him to repress his feminine attitude toward men, and that he awoke

> from his homosexual enthusiasm in anxiety. Now how can this comprehension of sexual intercourse, this recognition of the vagina, be brought into harmony with the selection of the bowel for the purpose of identification with women? Are not the intestinal symptoms based on what is probably an older notion, and one which in any case completely contradicts the dread of castration—the notion, namely, that sexual intercourse takes place at the anus? (78)

Obedient to the law of castration—the law that plays out the fort/da logic of presence and absence so that "before" and "behind" can elaborate a sequencing of loss into a coherent narrative that offers itself as the basis for the binary organization of all logic and all thought[21]—the male here must repudiate the pleasures of the anus because their fulfillment allegedly presupposes, and inflicts, the loss or "wound" that serves as the very definition of the female's castration. Thus the male who is terrorized into heterosexuality through his internalization of this determining narrative must embrace with all his narcissistic energy the phantom of a hierarchically inflected binarism always to be defended zealously. His anus, in turn, will be phobically charged as the site at which he traumatically confronts the possibility of becoming "like his mother," while the female genitalia will always be informed by their signifying relation to the anal erotism he has been made to disavow—a relation underscored by the Wolf Man's reference to the vagina as the female's "front bottom" (25).[22]

The scandal of the sodomitical scene, therefore, as Cleland has Fanny describe it, derives from its repudiation of the binary logic implicit in male heterosexualization and from its all too *visible* dismissal of the threat on which the terroristic empire of male heterosexuality has so effectively been erected. For the sodomite, after all, to be "like his mother behind" and *still* to be "like his father before," is apparently to validate the sexual theories and the libidinal cathexes of the infant as he observes the primal scene. Playing out the possibility of multiple, non-exclusive erotic identifications and positionings, the spectacle of sodomy would seem to confirm precisely those infantile sexual speculations that the male, coerced by the bogy of castration, is expected to have put behind him. It threatens to bring out of the closet, that is, the realization that the narcissistic compromise productive of male heterosexuality, the sacrifice of "homosexual enthusiasm" to defend against the prospect of castration, might not have been necessary at all. Indeed, the sodomitical spectacle, when viewed from this perspective, cannot fail to implicate the heterosexual male who is situated to observe it since it constitutes an affront to the primary narrative that orients his theory of sexuality. From such a vantage point the sodomitical scene must generate a response that can be interpreted as the negative counterpart, one might even say the *inversion*, of fetishism and the fetishistic over-estimation of the object: for if the problem engaged in the fetish is that of affirming a belief in presence over and against the knowledge of loss, the problem produced by the scene of gay sodomy is that of affirming a belief in loss over and against the knowledge of presence. In order to uphold the law of castration, the gay man must be cut off from the social prerogatives associated with maleness, signified by the penis, precisely because the vision of male-male sodomy shows that the penis has *not* been cut off as castration should demand. Its presence in the order of anatomy must be transformed into an absence in the order of culture, thus complying with the logic of the signifying processes that derive from the articulation of sexual difference through the agency of castration. The sodomitical scene, in consequence, must be overwritten with a code, one essentially legislative, that effects a psychic translation of "to have" into "to have not."

The disappropriation of "proper" relationship in the episode from Cleland's novel extends, therefore, beyond the two men subjected to Fanny's surveillance until it encompasses Fanny herself as an observer of that scene. In this context it is useful to bear in mind Nancy K. Miller's suggestion that Fanny must be viewed as "a male 'I' in female drag."[23] While this is true throughout the novel, the sodomitical encounter calls forth a particularly insistent emphasis on the reversal of gender roles and expectations and the concomitant destabilization of binary logic both for Fanny as an observer of the spectacle and for the young men more actively involved. Fanny's very spectatorial position, for example, confers upon her the power to see without becoming an object of scrutiny herself—a power culturally coded as the prerogative of the heterosexual male—and it places her in the position that the Freudian scenario associates with the analyst or the unconscious: a position from which she can come upon the sodomitical spectacle from behind. And just as she gains access to this spectacle by appropriating a male-coded place in the erotics of vision, she achieves that position by figuratively enacting the male role in a heterosexual script: by piercing, with the bodkin or needle she carries, the "paper patch" on the wall, and revealing a hole or "flaw" (157) in the partition that allows intercourse between the two rooms. Moreover, as one last instance of sodomy's capacity to implicate those who would envision or observe it, when Fanny indignantly determines to "raise the house" upon the "miscreants" whose "preposterous pleasure" has shown that they have no idea which end is up, she catches her foot unexpectedly on some "nail or ruggedness in the floor," which "fl[ings] [her] on [her] face with such violence, that [she] f[alls] senseless to the ground" (159). Lying unconscious—face down, bottom up—on this suddenly unreliable ground, Fanny embodies the instability of positioning that radiates out from the sodomitical scene and demonstrates that it was not without reason, after all, that Cleland named her Fanny.

A similar dissemination of reversals could be traced in the sodomitical episode recounted by Smollett in *The Adventures of Peregrine Pickle.* When Peregrine's companion, Pallet, observes an Italian count making amorous overtures to a sleeping German baron, he is "scandalized" by "such expressions of tenderness," and, becoming "conscious of his own attractions, [and] alarmed for his person" he flees the room and "put[s] himself under the protection" of the novel's eponymous hero, explaining to Peregrine the particulars of the "indecency" he has so distressingly observed.[24]

> Peregrine, who entertained a just detestation for all such abominable practices, was incensed at this information; and stepping to the door of the dining-room where the two strangers were left together, saw with his own eyes enough to convince him, that Pallet's complaint was not without foundation, and that the baron was not averse to the addresses of the count. Our young gentleman's indignation had well nigh prompted him to rush in, and take immediate vengeance on the offenders but, considering that such a precipitate step might be attended with troublesome consequences for himself, he resisted the impulse of his wrath, and tasked his invention with some method of inflicting upon them a disgrace suited to the grossness of their ideas. (242)

Despite his indignation at the "grossness" of this sodomitical vision, Peregrine dares not intervene for fear of "troublesome consequences to himself" — for fear, in other words, that any intervention, even if only to enact his revenge on the practitioners of vice, will lead to his being implicated in the "grossness" of the scene. But the very fact of his being prevented from intervening as his "indignation" demands identifies his implication in the positional disturbances this spectacle effects; it demonstrates, that is, how his sexual authority has been challenged by a sight that imposes upon the male a disturbing "conscious[ness] of his own attractions" and thus an awareness of his susceptibility to being taken as a potential sexual object rather than as an active sexual subject. Peregrine's implication in the sodomitical scene's disruption of gender-coded oppositions, however, is only reinforced by the strategy he adopts in order to vent his "wrath." Wary of taking action himself, he arranges for his landlady, described as "a dame of remarkable vivacity," to step into the next room in the belief that she is carrying a message to its occupants.

> The lady very graciously undertook the office, and entering the apartment, was so much offended and enraged at the mutual endearments of the two lovers, that instead of delivering the message with which she had been entrusted, she set the trumpet of reproach to her mouth, and seizing the baron's cane, which she found by the side-table, belaboured them both with such eagerness of animosity, that they found themselves obliged to make a very disorderly retreat, and were actually driven down stairs, in a most disgraceful condition, by this exasperated virago . . . (243)

If Peregrine, after witnessing the spectacle of male-male eros, is effectively unmanned by his inability to take action, the landlady becomes all the more martial and virile as she sounds the trumpet of battle, wields the baron's cane, and forces the two male lovers to make a "disorderly retreat." And as if to signal that the landlady's transformation into an animated "virago"—literally, her transformation into the simulacrum of a man—has not put an end to the logical disturbances produced by the sodomitical scene, Peregrine and Pallet celebrate the punishment of the amorous "offenders" by attending a masquerade that night, with Pallet in full female drag.

In each of these passages the effects produced by the scene of sodomy between men expose the impossibility of establishing the distance necessary to secure an "uncontaminated" spectatorial relation to such a scene. The spectatorial position is destabilized, however, not because the scene is so alien or remote, but precisely because the vision of male-male sodomy looks uncannily familiar: as familiar, that is, as the primal scene that in Freudian theory only belatedly undergoes its normative heterosexualization. Since gay male sexual relations thus threaten to disseminate what might be described as a generalized sodomitical effect—threaten, that is, to effect a contagious disturbance of positional logic—it should come as no surprise that the sodomitical passages in both these eighteenth-century texts should have been expurgated immediately after their initial publication. Like Freud or Fanny or Peregrine, after all, the straight-identified reader has too much to lose in such an encounter with or representation of the sodomitical scene.

Just what is at risk for such a reader may be illuminated from a different historical direction by catching a glimpse of one last spectator glimpsing a scene of sodomy between men. In the section of *The Post Card* titled "Envois," Jacques Derrida, producing what he suggests may be a "satire of epistolary literature"[25]—a satire, that is, of a genre that includes *The Memoirs of a Woman of Pleasure*—focuses much of his attention on a medieval drawing of Plato and Socrates that he claims to have noticed on a post card in the gift shop at Oxford's Bodleian Library. Tellingly, his espial of the post card took place, as Derrida recounts it, while he himself was being spied on and made a participant in a scene; for at the moment when his eye first fell upon the image of the two philosophers in the drawing, he had the sense that his companions, Jonathan Culler and Cynthia Chase, whom he imagines as having anticipated and arranged for this discovery, were, as he writes, "observing me obliquely, watching me look. As if they were spying on me in order to finish the effects of a spectacle they had staged (they were just married more or less)" (16). It is thus as a third party in the company of newlyweds who have staged a "spectacle" before him—a spectacle in which he finds himself both conscripted and implicated—that Derrida encounters an image that represents philosophy's primal scene; perhaps it is not coincidental, then, that he reads the image on the post card as a graphic depiction of penetration from behind. "I see *Plato* getting an erection in *Socrates*' back," he writes, "and see the insane hubris of his prick, an interminable, disproportionate erection . . . slowly sliding, still warm, under Socrates' right leg" (18). For Derrida, as for Cleland and Smollett and Freud, this scene plays out a vertiginous reversibility of positions, specifically of the spatio-temporal positions on which Western philosophy rests: "Socrates, the one who writes—seated, bent over, a scribe or docile copyist, Plato's secretary, no? He is in front of Plato, no, Plato is *behind* him" (9).

This reversal of priority between Socrates and Plato extends its metaleptic reach across the whole of Western history so that Derrida can insist not only that "S. is P., Socrates is Plato, his father and his son, therefore the father of his father, his own grandfather and his own grandson" (47), but also, as the references to grandfather and grandson suggest through their evocation of *Beyond the Pleasure Principle*, that Freud too has a part to play in this unorthodox genealogy, this narrative of a temporality articulated otherwise: "as-I-show-in-my-book it is then Plato who is the inheritor, for Freud. Who pulls the same trick somewhat, on Plato that Plato pulls on Socrates. This is what I call a catastrophe" (28). Catastrophe, "an overturning and inversion of relations" (22), as Derrida describes it, the condition of being "Arsy-versy" as in "Jenny Cromwell's Complaint," names for Derrida the deconstructive logic not only of the primal scene, but also of writing and philosophy as they are construed in the Western tradition: "S. does not see P. who sees S., but only (and here is the truth of philosophy) only *from the back*. There is only the *back*, seen from the back, in what is written, such is the final word. Everything is played out in *retro* and *a tergo*" (48). Thus for Derrida, as for Western philosophy more generally, the sodomitical spectacle constitutes the primal scene of writing;[26] philosophy—and psychoanalysis as an offshoot of philosophy—ceaselessly articulates itself by turning its back on its origin, only to turn back, through that very gesture, to the origin it seeks to deny.

This means, as I see it, something more than what Stanley Cavell, for instance, apparently intends when he writes, in an essay titled (by coincidence?) "Postscript (1989)": "I am from time to time haunted—I rather take it for granted that this is quite generally true of male heterosexual philosophers—by the origin of philosophy (in ancient Greece) in an environment of homosexual intimacy."[27] What haunts *Derrida* is not just (whatever "just" in this case might mean) the homophobic, homosocial, homoerotic, and homosexual relations that endlessly circulate within—and as—"the philosophical tradition"; at issue for him is the irreducibility of both sodomy and writing to a binary logic predicated on the determinacy of presence or absence—a binary logic that Derrida defines as intrinsic to "phallogocentrism [which] is articulated on the basis of a determined situation (let us give this word all its imports) in which the phallus *is* the mother's desire to the extent that she does not have it."[28]

Casting doubt on the analytico-philosophical "system of the symbolic, of castration, of the signifier, of the truth" ("Le facteur," 444), Derrida engages a structure of rigorously *in*determinate situations (and I give that word all its imports) that Freud, in a sentence cited earlier in part and offered now in its entirety, might gloss in the following way: "The tendency to doubt arises not from any occasion for doubt, but is the continuation of the powerful ambivalent tendencies in the pre-genital phase, which from then on become attached to every pair of opposites that dresent [sic] themselves." If the logic of paired opposites generated through castration's insistence on sexual difference supplants a pre-genital ambivalence—which is to say, an overdetermined multiplicity of identifications—that makes such distinctions as inside or outside, imagined or real, problematic, it is important to note that it is only by adopting the perspective of castration that castration can be seen as the "opposite" of pre-genital ambivalence. Castration, that is, represents itself as the *knowledge* of antithetical positioning that fixes or defines identity, and it fittingly defines itself, therefore, in opposition to what it constructs as the indeterminacy of the primal scene; it does so, moreover, by constituting itself as the very *principle* of paired opposites, as the truth of "truth" as the either-or determination of (phallic) presence or absence.

Yet in the passage cited above from Freud's letter to Lou Andreas-Salomé, the word made indeterminate through a "typographical" error in the English translation as published—and published, it may be worth noting, in association with the Institute of Psycho-Analysis—is, significantly, the word "present" itself. The "present" has thus been absented from this translation of the Freudian text through a Derridean "catastrophe," a sodomitical inversion or overthrow; "erroneously" positioned with its bottom up, the "p" has effected a sudden multiplication of its identity, has come out of the closet of typography in the disturbing drag of a "d."[29] In the context of *The Post Card*'s argument it is difficult to resist the opportunity to speculate on the "meaning" or force of this transformation; if "S. is P." according to Derrida, surely it is proper to meditate on this dislocation of "p" by "d": *P*lato, *p*hilosophy, *p*hallogocentrism, and *p*sychoanalysis *d*isarticulated by *D*errida and *d*econstruction? The fortifications of the *p*resent shown not to be a "fort" after all but a "*d*a"? In this translation of letters circulated between Freud and Lou Andreas-Salomé, letters that often anticipate the correspondence incorporated into Derrida's "Envois,"[30] the word "present" cannot present itself; it is defeated or deferred by a letter. Thus writing, performing a sodomitical reversal, gestures toward the persistence of a "pre-genital" indeterminacy that the law of castration would deny through institutionalized categories of present and not present. The *différance* of the *p*resent, figured by the "p" with its bottom up, allegorizes the insistence of the *b*ehind (another inversion: "p" as "b"?) in the very act of making present. Thus both philosophy and psychoanalysis insist on coming back to the back, returning to the behind that is always at the forefront of the "dresent": "Before all else it is a question of turning one's back," as Derrida observes, "[o]f turning the back of the post card (what is *Socrates'* back when he turns his back to *Plato*—a very amorous position, don't forget—? this is also the back of the post card: as we remarked one day, it is equally legitimate to name it recto or verso). . . . To turn one's back is the analytic position, no?" (178).

Such reversals, inversions, or conflations of (putative op)positions recur throughout Derrida's writing and mark the organization of his text; hence the "Envois," which designates a concluding passage in poetry or prose, is situated, perversely, at the beginning of *The Post Card*, a text in which Derrida has written, "I owe it to you to have discovered homosexuality" (53). What this means, of course, has everything to do with the figuration of sodomy in terms of the (il)logic that structures the moebius loop, the (il)logic that dislocates such spatio-temporal "situations" as "pre" and "post," or before and behind. For sodomy and writing insist on the (il)logical possibility that what is behind can also, and properly, come before: "In the beginning," as Derrida phrases it, "in principle, was the post" (29). If we can say of such an observation that it is, to be precise, "preposterous," we can add that what makes it "preposterous" also makes it precisely—and "in principle"—sodomitical.

Perhaps, too, we can understand better, in relation to this principle of the preposterous, why Louis Simond might have feared the imagination's susceptibility to being "sullied by the exposition of enormities, that ought never to be supposed to exist." The (il)logic by which exposition exposes its implication in such enormities, the (il)logic by which narrative produces the "crime" that it apparently only reports, the (il)logic of metalepsis that locates the cause as the effect of its effects, is, after all, an (il)logic that refutes the possibility of defining clear identities or establishing the security of fixed positions. It discovers, instead, within the either-or logic that Freud enshrined as the law of castration, the scandalous presence of another logic, the sodomitical (il)logic of the primal scene that comes always both before and behind it. Thus for Cleland and Smollett, Simond and Derrida, as for countless others who intervene more oppressively in the politics of discursive practices, the spectacle or the representation of the scene of sodomy between men is a threat to the epistemological security of the observer—whether a heterosexual male himself or merely heterosexual-male-identified—for whom the vision of the sodomitical encounter refutes the determinacy of positional distinctions, compelling him to confront his too clear implication in a spectacle that, from the perspective of castration, can only be *seen* as a "catastrophe."

11

IMAGINING THE HOMOSEXUAL

Laura and the Other Face of Gender

> ... in the analysis of film as a textual system ... cinema as an apparatus tries to close itself off as a system of representation, but constantly comes up against a vanishing point of the system where it fails to integrate itself and then has to refuse that moment of difference or trouble by trying to run away from it or by binding it back into the logic and perfection of the film system itself.
>
> And in Lacanian psychoanalysis there has been a similar and related emphasis, through the concept of the "*pas tout*," that is, the "not all" of any system of representation, the idea that there is no such system, however elaborated or elevated it may be, in which there is not some point of impossibility, its other face which it endlessly seeks to refuse—what could be called the vanishing point of its attempt to construct itself as a system.
>
> —*Jacqueline Rose*[1]

I. Perhaps no literary critic in America insisted more powerfully than did Paul de Man on the necessary *aporia* or, as Jacqueline Rose phrases it in the lines cited above, the "point of impossibility," produced by any "system of representation" in "its attempt to construct itself as a system." To offer one instance, not randomly chosen, to underscore this point, I would recall the argument of "Wordsworth and the Victorians," an essay in which de Man claims that Wordsworth's poetry, contrary to initial appearances, is not unproblematically accessible to "phenomenological and existential modes of thought."[2] Indeed, there are aspects of the poet's work, he asserts, that "refuse to fit within the uncompromising order of Wordsworth's philosophy of the experience of consciousness" (88). Examining the inconclusive results of critical attempts to establish the valence of key terms in Wordsworth's poetry by referring them to a coherent model of tropology, de Man finds only "the tension of a conflict that can no longer be reduced to existential or psychological causes" (92). That tension inheres instead, he finds, in the figure-making properties of the linguistic system itself.

De Man unfolds this argument through a reading of the ways in which Wordsworth deploys, in various texts, the figure of "face." "Face," in this analysis, comes to signify the capacity of language to posit—and thus conceptually to produce—totalized, coherent entities that it then misrepresents itself as merely having recognized or perceived. But if the verbal positing of a "face," for de Man, enacts a totalizing principle that generates "*meaning*" through the organization of what otherwise remain unmarked particularities, it also generates "a process of endless differentiation" that points toward its "*function* as the relentless undoer of its own claims" (92). This leads de Man to conclude his essay on a cautionary note, acknowledging the impulse of critical readers to defend against the undoing of linguistic reference or representation that is effected by the element of positing or performance essential to the linguistic act: "It would be naive to *believe* that we could ever face Wordsworth, a poet of sheer language, outright. But it would be more naive still to think we can take shelter from what he *knew* by means of the very evasions which this *knowledge* renders impossible" (92, emphasis mine). The point of impossibility identified in these sentences frames the alternatives of knowledge and belief in terms of a choice between two options, each of which is untenable: to face or to evade the painful "knowledge" that simultaneously produces and threatens to undo the intelligibility of language as representation.

If this last sentence seems to echo the psychoanalytic narrative that accounts for the male subject's traumatic entry into the "knowledge" of sexual difference, it is significant that in the course of his essay on Wordsworth de Man himself touches, however obliquely, on a scene crucial to the psychoanalytic drama: not the moment of cataclysmic entry into the symbolic, but its prototype, the catachresis of the imaginary when (what retrospectively will be construed to have been) bits and pieces are, as by fiat, transformed into wholes. Reading the "Blessed Babe" passage from Book II of the 1805 *Prelude*, de Man discusses Wordsworth's evocation of "the Babe,/Nurs'd in his Mother's arms," and writes: "What is later called a 'mute dialogue with my Mother's heart' begins here in the exchange of a gaze, a meeting of 'eyes.' But this encounter is not a recognition, a shared awareness of common humanity. It occurs as an active verbal deed, a *claim* of 'manifest kindred' which is not given in the nature of things" (91). The point that de Man goes on to make about this primal spectatorial "encounter" centers on the figural activity—the "claim" or "deed" that is not merely a perception—that permits both the reading of the mother's face *as a face* and the assertion of resemblance in the infant's claim of "manifest kindred" with it. Only that claim makes it possible for the child to effect its own coherence through the positing of its similarity to the object (the total form of the mother's face that is elaborated from the particular of her eye) that is now, through an act of figural reading, identified as cohesive and unitary (and that will serve thereafter as the model for all future acts of totalization):

> Without having to evoke the technical vocabulary of associationist psychology which is here used, it is clear that what is being described is the possibility of inscribing the eye, which is nothing by itself, into a larger, total entity, the "same object" which, in the internal logic of the text, can only be the face, the face as the combination of parts which the mind, working like a synecdochical trope, can lay claim to—thus opening the way to a process of totalization which, in the span of a few lines, can grow to encompass everything, "*All* objects through *all* intercourse of sense." Language originates with the ability of the eye to establish the contour, the borderline, the surface which allows things to exist in the identity of the kinship of their distinction from other things. (91)

"The identity of the kinship of their distinction": this difficult phrase condenses the rhetorical activity that de Man reads as determining all subsequent access to the cognitive markers of sameness and difference, and hence to the subject-shaping logic that differentiates between self and other.

In Wordsworth's account of the child's initial positing of bodily coherence, de Man discerns a *méconnaissance* within the order of language. Rather, that is, than psychologize the critical moment of the infant's gaze—as Lacan does, for instance, in "The Mirror Stage"—de Man points toward the primacy of a verbal act, a positing through language, that produces the figures, neither "natural" nor referential, that subsequently demand to be construed in terms of referentiality. As Cynthia Chase notes in an important analysis of de Man's interpretation of the figure of face, "prior to any perception—prior to the perception of nature, prior to the seeing of the mother's face—is the '*claim* of "manifest kindred,"' 'the starting, catachrestic *decree* of signification.'"[3] For de Man, therefore, this "exchange of a gaze" derives its value not from the way in which it introduces the child to subjectivity, but from the way in which it serves as the catachrestic entry into the signifying system that makes possible the very logic of perception. Neil Hertz, in "Lurid Figures," an incisive reading of "Wordsworth and the Victorians," summarizes de Man's argument as follows: "The child hangs at the mother's breast, the child depends on her, its sense of having a face depends upon her having a face: but it is not that 'dependency' that is being repeatedly invoked in these sentences. It is rather the logical dependence of perception and cognition on figurative language—on the figure of an outlined surface, a field or a face—that is stressed, and stressed at the expense of a more conventional intersubjective reading of the passage."[4]

Rhetoric, figuration, and the catachrestic willfulness of linguistic decree or positing thus inhere for de Man in the process of perception, in the activity of the gaze that asserts the tropological "claim" of kinship or resemblance and thereby generates "meaning." "'Face' then," as de Man insists, " . . . designates the dependence of any perception or 'eye' on the totalizing power of language" (91); and it is in this light that Cynthia Chase, unfolding de Man's gesture toward the punning relation between "figure" and the French "*figure*," can observe: "Face is not the natural given of the human person. It is given in the mode of discourse, given by an act of language. What is given by this act is figure. Figure is no less than our very face."[5] Such a rhetorization of the gaze implicates visual perception in a figuralizing—and therefore necessarily disfiguring—discourse,[6] a discourse that requires that the bounded surface figured as "face" be conceptualized as a coherent referential entity even as it renders such reference impossible since the totalized entity is only produced through the positional power of language. This placement of the gaze in a linguistic context—a context that articulates a "point of impossibility" outside the strict terms of the psychoanalytic theory so often invoked in the analysis of film—suggests a way of reconsidering the cinema as a system of representation. Making use of de Man's insight into the dependence of perceptual logic on the "verbal deed" implicit in the infant's face-making gaze, we can not only rethink what may be at stake in the insistent framing of faces in the classical film, but also examine how narrative cinema's obsessive preoccupation with faces, and the totalizing function of the gaze, figures (or gives face to) and thus disfigures (or effaces) the apparatus of cinematic inscription—an apparatus that, by means of those processes, attempts, as Rose puts it, "to close itself off as a system of representation." We can investigate, that is, the relationship that obtains between psychoanalytic and rhetorical paradigms as they attempt to read the cinema's vested interest in scopic "knowledge" and the mechanisms that produce it.

That relationship, as feminist film theorists such as Tania Modleski, Laura Mulvey, Teresa de Lauretis, Mary Ann Doane, Jacqueline Rose, and Kaja Silverman have reminded us, must always engage the way sexual difference signally informs the positioning of the gendered subject between knowledge and belief. Indeed, even in de Man's reading of the figural logic that underlies the process of face-making, the mark of sexual difference can be discerned in the particular encounter on which he focuses. For despite his efforts to distance himself from the psychoanalytic or specifically Lacanian drama acted out during the "encounter" of mother and child, de Man only resituates the specularity, the subject-making positing of identity through identification, that figures centrally in Lacan's imagination of the imaginary.[7] As Hertz demonstrates, de Man displaces the pathos implicit in the psychoanalytic scenario of subjectivity-in-formation onto figural identifications with, and designations of, the operations of language. Language or rhetoric operates as a mirror in which the displaced referent of the human "face" persistently returns. Hertz refers to these moments as inscriptions of the "pathos of uncertain agency," a pathos that evokes the presence of a desiring subject of language or action at the very moment when de Man is attempting to confront the disarticulating gap of "the difference between language as meaning and language as performance."[8] And Hertz concludes his essay by noting that for de Man, "the elective embodiment of the pathos of uncertain agency is the specular structure, one that locates the subject in a vacillating relation to the flawed or dismembered or disfigured (but invariably gendered) object of its attention."[9]

In the following pages I will consider, if only in a preliminary fashion, the implications for the cinema of such a rhetorically inflected reading of the gaze and of the gaze's relation to specular structure, face-making, and disfiguration. I want, in particular, to explore what happens when the politics of sexuality is articulated from within the conceptual space that is shared by de Man's and Lacan's accounts of the specularity informing the linguistic operation that posits the figure of the human(izing) face. Instead of conducting that consideration here in terms of gender alone, however, I want to build upon feminist theory to tease out the implications of these various issues in terms of the effect produced in and on the classical Hollywood cinema by the attempt to elicit the image of a different sort of sexual difference—the difference embodied by the figure associated in the popular mind with specularity or narcissism and in psychoanalytic discourse with the lure of the imaginary as manifest in that figure's identification with the mother. I refer, of course, to the male homosexual, whose inscription within cinema's field of vision puts into play with an emphatic spin the relations theorized by Lacan and de Man.

After all, as I suggested in Chapter One, "the homosexual" enters historical view *as a "homosexual"* only through a rhetorical operation that essentializes as a metaphoric designation, a totalized identity, what had been understood before this tropological shift as a contingent aspect of self. The "homosexual," that is, acquires a "face" only through the rhetorical redistribution of "meanings" at a specific moment in the history of the West. Thus if, as Lauren Berlant has suggested, for "post-Lacanian, post-structuralist feminists . . . woman is undefinable and unwritable,"[10] the homosexual as such can be said, by contrast, always already to be written, always already to be inscribed within the logic of a rhetoric that figures or gives face to him as a figure for the (un)decidability of sameness and difference, and thus, one might say, for the (un)decidability of figuration itself. By bracketing the negative prefix here I mean to indicate the ideological pressure exerted to contain or make sense of the homosexual by denying the anxious-making challenge to cognitive certainty that homosexuality as such can seem to pose. For as made available to representation within the Western field of discourse, the homosexual at once contests and secures the agencies through which sexual meaning is produced: precisely to the extent that the homosexual, in other words, disturbs the epistemological security afforded by the logic of sameness and difference *as these are grounded in perception*, the dominant culture demands that homosexuality be read back into—be construed, that is, as readable within—the system of visualization so that this apparent epistemological threat can mobilize ever more sophisticated forms of surveillance, enabling ever sharper discriminations of difference within figures that appear to be the same.

But even so recuperated, the homosexual as figure—especially as a figure for the figurality of identity—brings an element of disturbance into the representational system that can be interpreted simultaneously as an excess and a lack.[11] It is hardly surprising that this formula should reproduce the terms through which female sexuality becomes legible in the patriarchal social text, for sexual orientation in Western culture is persistently posited through its often contradictory assimilation to the discursive categories associated with differences historically and culturally elaborated to distinguish between the sexes. Those differences, of course, are anchored in—are alleged, that is, to be guaranteed by—the visual register that looms so large, according to psychoanalytic theory, in the formation of the sexual subject; but as Jacqueline Rose quite properly notes, despite the frequent conflation in film criticism of "the concept of the imaginary" and the "question of perception,"[12] the visual register of difference between the sexes "has absolutely no meaning outside a structure of sexual difference (the point at which boys and girls must define themselves *as* different) within which socially and historically the male term is already privileged" (218). Perception alone, as Rose makes clear, does not determine the meaning of the visual—nor prescribe the subject's responses to it—within the psychoanalytic scene of sexual differentiation that serves so often as an ur-scene in theoretical investigations of the cinema: as Rose suggests, "the aspect of the concept of disavowal which is most problematic within psychoanalytic theory itself and, not coincidentally, which has been most strongly objected to by feminism (the sight of castration, nothing to be seen as having nothing, Irigaray's '*rien à voir équivaut à n'avoir rien*'), the concentration on the visual as *simply* perceptual, is the very aspect that [Christian] Metz imports into the theory of the spectator's relation to the screen."[13] Given the construction of homosexuality as a rhetorical problematization of sexual identity and of sameness and difference as concepts unproblematically or "naturally" accessible to perception, a lesbian or gay male perspective on the cinema is far more likely to recognize the ideological insistence on "sexual difference," and far less likely, therefore, to construe "the visual as *simply* perceptual"; indeed, the oppressive force of those socio-historical structures that seek to mandate such a reading of perception constitutes a central object of analysis and resistance in any gay theory.

Against this reduction of vision to perception in the theory Rose associates with critics like Metz, and against the privileging (as the cinematic primal scene) of the scopic encounter that effects the male subject's entry into sexual difference according to psychoanalytic theory, I would propose for consideration another scene as paradigmatic of a certain relation to, and operation of, the cinema. That scene, which presents with a powerful charge the determining ideology within which perception is culturally permitted to occur, can be reconstructed from, or discovered in, a variety of different sources. The following is only one account as it appeared in a pre-Stonewall gay rights periodical from 1964:

> Two British psychiatrists are using the Pavlovian conditioned reflex theory to change homosexual orientations. The patient, who has evidenced interests in marrying and raising a family, was placed in a darkened room and a photograph of an attractive male was flashed upon the screen. The patient was given eight seconds to change the picture and, if he failed to do so, the physicians gave him an electrical shock strong enough to be considered "extremely unpleasant." The shock continued until the patient removed the picture.
>
> By this method, the doctors hoped to stop the "habit" of gazing at, or thinking about, male partners. This is comparable to what has been called "aversion therapy."[14]

What we have here constitutes a negative version of the face-making moment in the Wordsworthian text as analyzed by de Man. In this instance, the complex positings of coherence, identification, and meaning as inflected by desire are interrupted by a machinery of disfiguration that undertakes to rewrite the rhetorical structure of the figures produced by the eye. This disciplinary effort to redirect the gaze, with its "sophisticated" technological intervention in the circuitry of vision and perception, employs a cinematic *mise en scène* but only in order to allow for the projection of unmoving photographic images: the movement or kinesis at issue in this theater is located, instead, in the spectator and his manipulation of those images. But if this model does not give the "patient" a version of cinematic narrative, its operation can sum up nonetheless a signal aspect of the ideological function of narrative within the Hollywood cinema. This is not to say that the cinema enjoys so naked and coercive an influence on its viewers, nor that the ideological system of the Hollywood film is as stark and coherent as the system depicted here may seem to be. Rather, this attempt to reorient vision articulates the problem of cinema itself as a question of a) the positional power of the gaze as it is implicated in the play of desire, and b) the mechanisms by which that power can be directed or controlled.

Whatever larger theoretical affordances this paradigm may provide, it remains crucially specific in its representation of an assault on a gaze that is gay. That this should be so responds to the fact that homosexuality, as constructed in the modern West, occupies a distinctive relation to questions of the gaze and of visual perception—a relation that derives from its historical elaboration from within the pre-existing conceptual framework of male-female sexual difference. But the difference of gay difference from the difference between the sexes lies in the force of its interrogation of the identity or sameness of difference itself, its difference from and resistance to the logic of *perceptual* difference that reassuringly must embody for the dominant culture those differences determinative of "essence." In this context certain observations on the trope of "race" by Henry Louis Gates, Jr. can assist in the conceptualization of "homosexual difference" as well: "The biological criteria used to determine 'difference' in sex simply do not hold when applied to 'race.' Yet we carelessly use language in such a way as to *will* this sense of *natural* difference into our formulations."[15] To apply this phrasing to "homosexual difference" (without, in the process, acceding to its suggestion that "'difference' in sex" is not already the product of ideological naturalization), I would insert the word "strategically" where "carelessly" appears, for "the homosexual" as a distinctive type has been—and continues to be—constructed with extraordinary care in order to (mis)represent him as a body discernible through its "*natural* difference."

Indeed, though it is largely according to the template of male-female difference that the psychological qualities of "the homosexual" have been posited within our culture, it is on the model of racial difference that "homosexuality" as a category of personhood has been conceived. The conceptual overlaying of these two different models finds a useful condensation in the description of M. de Charlus offered by the narrator of *Cities of the Plain* shortly after his "recognition" of Charlus as a homosexual: "He belonged to that race of beings, less paradoxical than they appear, whose ideal is manly precisely because their temperament is feminine, and who in ordinary life resemble men in appearance only."[16] If for Proust the homosexual has "been invested, by a persecution similar to that of Israel, with the physical and moral characteristics of a race,"[17] it is important to bear in mind that the "physical . . . characteristics" that subsequently serve to identify the specificity of the homosexual are as fully tropological as are those of "race" itself and even less readily susceptible to discrimination than dominant white culture would like to believe are the inscriptions of "racial" differences in—or as—what Anthony Appiah has called "the visible morphological characteristics of skin, hair, and bone, by which we are inclined to assign people to the broadest racial categories."[18] A vast cultural project of bringing the homosexual into the realm of representation, therefore, and especially into the realm of visually recognizable representation, must be mounted strategically in order to circumscribe the dangerously indeterminate borders of "homosexual difference."

At the same time that homosexuality, however, is being constructed in terms of its (problematic) availability to visual recognition—a central aspect of the project of homographesis as I discussed it earlier—the homosexual is defined in a decisive relation to the power of the gaze. "Perhaps the most salient index to male homosexuality, socially speaking," D. A. Miller keenly observes, "consists precisely in how a man looks at other men";[19] for in what amounts to a virtual case study in the operation of "upward displacement," the gaze comes to carry the very force of gay sexuality itself.[20] It is, of course, on the basis of this displacement that the technology of homophobia, as in the psychiatric "treatment" described above, is permitted to engage in the psychological torture designed to short-circuit the gay male gaze. This association of the male homosexual with the aggressive deployment of vision, on the one hand (i.e., in his "'habit' of gazing at . . . male partners"), and with his passive susceptibility to visualization or perceptual recognition on the other (i.e., as the object of the cultural enterprise that seeks to render the gay body legible) makes the cinema a particularly important institution within which to consider the function and effect of gay inscription or homographesis. Indeed, a project worth pursuing, although I will not be pursuing that project here, would be to analyze the virtually simultaneous emergence of the medical and legal discourses of homosexuality as such and the emergence of cinema as a technology with a significant cultural force. In the absence of a full-scale investigation of that topic I will make no claims about the meaning of that historical coincidence, but even without such an investigation it is possible to insist upon the connection in the modern West between (primarily male) homosexuality and the cinema as an institution—a connection so seemingly inescapable that Stanley Cavell felt it necessary to justify the seriousness of his critical responses to American film by cautioning that "anyone who thinks such responses are 'camp' either is camping himself or else grew up in a different world from mine."[21]

This connection, of course, can be ascribed to a variety of factors—social, historical, and economic—that have led to the association of homosexuality (or proto-homosexuality) with theatricality, masquerade, and other marginalized or transgressive social practices.[22] But it also owes much to the fact that both cinema and homosexuality question, and by doing so effectively transform, the culturally determined meanings and relations of looking and being looked at, arousing, for a social order that distributes unequally the authority of subject status and the access to political power, an always potentially paranoid anxiety about the reversibility of those activities, especially insofar as they put into play an erotics of the gaze that the dominant order remains eager in each case to control. Surely it is noteworthy in this regard that the

Production Code enforced in Hollywood from 1930 to 1961 prohibited the representation of "sex perversion" even when it was a central aspect of the novels or plays—themselves most often widely and unproblematically available—from which a film was subsequently made. That prohibition reflected a belief, still punishingly current as recent American controversies about funding for the arts make clear, that homosexuality occupies so coercive a relationship to the agencies of visualization that merely to see its representations renders one somehow "vulnerable" to it, or, as I suggested in Chapter Ten, implicates one in its distinctive (il)logic; yet the cinema, like other cultural institutions in the first half of the twentieth century, felt compelled at the same time to find a face, or to be more exact, to *posit* a face, for homosexuality so as to localize and contain it. Narrative cinema in America, that is, seems, on an institutional level, to have needed to invent specifically visual terms through which to represent the homosexual (and particularly the homosexual man), however mediated or veiled such representations had to be, in order to shore up the integrity of those very sexual categories that the *explicit* depiction of homosexuality as such was thought to subvert.

Vito Russo, in *The Celluloid Closet*, traces the history of those representations, discussing the many Hollywood films that imag(in)ed homosexuality, more or less obliquely, in ways that nominally complied with the Production Code's stringent regulations. I am less interested in rehearsing that history here than I am in reading its effects on a text that faces up to the ideological pressures that impinge on the cinematic process of constructing a "face" to figure "the homosexual." For that reason I will confine my critical gaze almost exclusively to Otto Preminger's *Laura* (1944), a film that expends much of its representational energy to interrogate the salience of homosexual difference to the cinematic system of representation and that does so by exploring the relations of face and face-making to figuration and disfiguration both. At the histrionic center of *Laura*, of course, lies Clifton Webb's career-making performance as Waldo Lydecker, a "deadly sissy" in the words of Vito Russo;[23] I do not intend, however, to analyze *Laura* merely to define as homosexual an eros that the film itself does not—and given the terms of the Production Code *could* not—identify explicitly as such. I want, rather, to consider how the representation of Lydecker as offered by a film that engages self-consciously the questions of spectatorship, embodiment, and visualization, acts out a calculated sexual ambiguity that interprets gay male sexuality as a trope for ambiguity as such, especially insofar as that ambiguity informs the male body and its susceptibility to representation.

Now in modern American culture such ambiguity is anything *but* ambiguous: nothing is more decidedly and punitively "known" than the "meaning" of sexual "ambiguity."[24] And this fact is telling on a number of counts; it bespeaks, at once, the demarcation and policing of cognitive and sexual boundaries that are always mutually determining, the insistence upon stable and universally applicable categories of erotic desire, and the social imperative to recognize what are alleged to be tell-tale signs of difference. Ambiguity as such, then, is not permitted innocently or non-tropologically to enter the modern discourse of male sexual orientation since it occupies a virtually tautological relation to the construction of male homosexuality. It undergoes translation immediately into "that which is other than heterosexual," delusively reinforcing the governing fiction of heterosexuality: that it is inherently and naturally self-evident in its presence to itself. Ambiguity and homosexuality, in consequence, trope endlessly upon each other, nowhere more so than in Production Code Hollywood where the former could be acknowledged but not autonomously conceptualized and the latter could be conceptualized but not directly acknowledged. The genre of *film noir* itself, in fact, works to unfold the possibilities of this complex figural relationship by reading *male* sexuality as the true Freudian "dark continent"—one shadowed by an ambiguity it can never successfully dispel, but only, at best, temporarily *project* by positing a face that could embody, and, by embodying, efface it. That projection, and the thematization of that projection, constitutes the project of *Laura*, however much the film may attempt to misrecognize such an image of itself.

II. Manny Farber, writing in the *New Republic* on October 30, 1944, dismissed *Laura* as a "boring" murder film whose plot he summarized as follows: "Four days after the murder its supposedly murdered woman, Laura, shows up unmarked, and the New York police, the murderer and the plain-American-guy detective . . . discover that some other woman's face was shot off by mistake. Meanwhile the detective has fallen in love with Laura from her picture, and this drives the murderer, who is a former lover and hates to see anybody else handle her, to try shooting her face off again."[25] *Time* offered a contrasting evaluation of the film in a review that appeared the same day, praising it as a "highly polished and debonair whodunit with only one inelegant smudge on its gleaming surface. In swank settings that cry out for a pinch of poison or at least a dainty derringer, the victim is obliged for purposes of plot to have her pretty face blown off by a double-barreled shotgun fired at close range."[26] The prominence given in both these accounts to the question of the face recalls the visual signifier with which the film identifies itself, the signifier it uses as the background image for its opening and closing titles: I refer, of course, to the portrait of Laura that Reynold Humphries, in his reading of Fritz Lang's *The Woman in the Window* (1944), describes as "the most famous portrait in the classic Hollywood cinema."[27]

That portrait becomes the film's central signifier of the cinematic concern with the visual *as* signifier. A comparison, for instance, of Preminger's *Laura* with the novel by Vera Caspary on which the screenplay was based demonstrates that the film transforms the portrait into a signifier not only of Laura Hunt (or of Laura Hunt as the valorized object of masculine desire), but also of the distinctively cinematic status of this representation of Laura Hunt. By gesturing toward the cinematic imperative to visualize, to show (the truth of) things, the film's insistence upon the portrait stands in figural relation to cinema itself. Indeed, as if it were allegorizing across the body of the woman its distinctive properties as an aesthetic medium, Preminger's film, in its most celebrated twist, effects the resurrection, the kinetic, and thus the cinematic (re)animation of the still image that is Laura's portrait, figuring in the process its own technical ability to give (the appearance of) motion to the static image within the frame. The film seeks, in this way, to situate Laura not only as the visual cynosure *in* the film, but as the visual cynosure *of film itself*: to establish her body as the site at which the cinema declares itself in relation to the spectatorial gaze that is figured repeatedly, within the film, through the activity of staring at her portrait.

In this the film seems virtually designed to reinforce Laura Mulvey's oft-cited argument that women, in the visual economy of patriarchy, "can be said to connote *to-be-looked-at-ness*."[28] Yet for all the high glamor with which it focuses attention on Gene Tierney's cool beauty as Laura, the film's discourse of the body and of the body's susceptibility to visual representation interrogates more urgently the connotation of the male body—in particular, but not exclusively, for other men—of *not*-to-be-looked-at-ness. The emphasis, that is, on the image of Laura, on Laura as the embodiment of a female sexuality defined as the privileged object of the spectatorial and cinematic gaze, functions, in effect, as a screen for the film's less obvious desire to bring into focus both the male body and the problem of bringing the male body into focus. Indeed, the most crucially spectacularized body, the body the film investigates most insistently, whether in formal attire or complete undress, belongs not to Laura but to Waldo Lydecker as played by Clifton Webb. Contemporary reviewers of the film may not have conceptualized that fact in the terms I would use, but their critical attention was magnetized less by the mystery of Laura than by the "personality" embodied both by Waldo and by Webb.

Hailing "the sudden and startling arrival" of two "signal personalities," Bosley Crowther, writing in the *New York Times* the week after the New York openings of both *Laura* and *To Have and Have Not*, linked Clifton Webb with Lauren Bacall as actors who unexpectedly "burst upon the screen with all the dazzle of a nimble magician's bouquets." The pairing of these apparently dissimilar actors has, of course, a suggestiveness that Crowther chooses to ignore; it bespeaks at least a subliminal recognition that in Webb's case, as in Lauren Bacall's, that "dazzle" refers to a sexual meaningfulness that the cinema registers or reads off of certain bodies that it identifies, or forces the audience to identify, specifically *as bodies.* Thus Crowther characterizes Waldo as a "creature of silky elegance whose caustic wit and cold refinements display him as a super-selfish man" and he describes him in ways that make clear to the reader that Waldo himself, for Crowther, incarnates "the atmosphere of *Laura*, which reeks of refined decadence." He further notes that Clifton Webb, like Waldo, is "polished, urbane, and briskly trenchant" and that "his vivid appearance as a person assures him of a groove in audience minds."[29] Just what that particular groove might be was illuminated by Manny Farber, who aligned his own critical attentiveness to Webb's embodiment of Waldo with the interest displayed by the film itself in the depiction of this character: "the best part of the picture," he wrote, "is its description of a Brahmin columnist, named Waldo Lydecker, played with great pleasure by Clifton Webb, whose snobbishness and fastidiousness are about the only facts studied in any detail; his perfumed literary style of talking expresses a lot of auntyish effeminacy and his values get across with some force."[30] That his "values get across with some force" rearticulates Crowther's claim that Webb has earned himself a "groove" in the movie-goer's mind, an achievement that has much to do with Webb's "vivid appearance as a person," which is to say, more precisely, with the vivid appearance *of* his person, an appearance that Farber knowingly reads in terms of "auntyish effeminacy."

Farber, however, to be exact, doesn't use this phrase to characterize the person or body of Waldo or Webb; the homosexual quality denoted by "auntyish effeminacy" resonates for him, instead, in the "perfumed literary style of talking" that Webb's character affects. The body, through which and on which the meaningfulness of such effeminacy must be read, undergoes a displacement here that is matched by the sensory displacements at work in the synaesthetic image of perfumed speech that Farber offers in its place. To be more specific, as the perfume imagined to emanate from the anointed body of the male speaker metonymically signifies the artificial style of one who would anoint his body with perfume—and we know what such a "one" must "be"—so that style in this instance refers back to and obliquely evokes the body that is otherwise elided. "Perfumed" as it is, after all, that body reeks of self-representation as an avowedly *erotic* body, a self-representation that registers, by virtue of the need so to represent itself, as the antithesis of what our culture is willing to acknowledge, in a man, as *being* erotic, and therefore it proscribes such a body for *appealing* to the erotic. Defensively elided, that body undergoes a figural reinscription in the place of extravagance and misrepresentation that is interpreted as "style" or "literariness." So conceived, the (figurally elided) body of the perfumed and "auntyish" littérateur gets associated in the American cultural imaginary with the class privilege of a vanished aristocracy, the anachronistic invocation and demonization of which bespeaks its continued conceptual efficacy *only* as the locus of a phobically inflected relation to the body—a relation wherein the body is indulged and disavowed at once, emphatically "worn" or inhabited, but inhabited with a distance that renders such embodiment ironic, which is, after all, perhaps merely a way of glossing the notion of "decadence." In Farber's formulation Waldo's body, then, may be figured as a body that talks, but it does so only by denaturalizing speech, by becoming a body, in other words, that talks *as if it were written* and thereby constitutes the embodiment of artifice or "literary style." The literary resonance of Waldo's occupation as columnist, author, and radio personality serves to thematize this textual or linguistic order within which his body, his "appearance as a person," acquires the force of its social "meaning."

Our first sight of Waldo, appropriately, establishes his relationship to visualization: naked in the bath, exposed to our gaze in all his physicality or bodiliness, he sits at his typewriter generating the texts that function simultaneously: a) to compensate for his homophobically suspect (because scrawny and underdeveloped) body; b) to represent that body's underdevelopment as a mark of its inherent textuality; and c) to account for or explain that underdevelopment by virtue of the body's involvement in the sedentary labor of literary production. This textualization, as I suggested above, refers the "meaning" of this body, though anatomically male, to an interpretive framework that draws on the culturally produced differences "between" the sexes. But the female body as construed within that framework does not compel a similar process that results in its elision or figural inscription in (or even *as*) "the literary." Within the logic of patriarchy, after all, the difference from a phallic norm that defines the radical "value" of femaleness works to assure the identity, the sameness to himself, the adequacy to authority of the male. If the reassurance produced by the male's difference from this hypostatized version of difference itself coexists with a deeper anxiety about what the female body "means," that anxiety records the extent to which the female constitutes for him, as a psychological subject governed by the law of castration, the image of what he most fears, narcissistically, to *become*; but the gay male body activates for him, as a psychological *and* a socio-historical subject, a more immediate anxiety by questioning the certainty with which he knows what he already *is*.

Thus homosexuality, though from a certain perspective it seems merely to reposition it, shatters the closed system of gender binarism and the generous, though by no means absolute, security of male privilege within such a system (however variously that privilege is inflected by differences of class, ethnicity, or race and the reconfiguring force of transactions across the categories through which those various distinctions are conceived). Homosexuality, then, unforgivably, has the effect of compelling heterosexual masculinity to engage in the self-subverting labor of reading and interpreting *itself*, knowing full well that the more susceptible to interpretation it acknowledges itself to be, and the farther it gets from its "original" condition as a state of "natural" self-evidence, the more aggressively it must insist on its absolute indisputability, thereby compromising itself still more by fueling suspicion that the very insistence of its claim to be indisputable testifies to a state of being always more than potentially in dispute. Gay male sexuality, in other words, textualizes male sexuality across the board, opening its every enactment to interpretation as an act, and condemning its signifiers to the prospect of a ceaseless interrogation by forcing the recognition, first and foremost, that they are always *only* signifiers. Faced with gay men as the uncannily familiar and (therefore) intolerable mirror image of its own male-gendered face, heterosexual masculinity under patriarchy demands that the gay male body be interpreted, instead, as the other face of gender: that the textuality to which "homosexual difference" would seem to have doomed male sexuality as such be contained through a sort of conceptual quarantine and projected exclusively onto an ideologically produced and ideologically negated gay male body—a body whose meaningfulness consequently can be read not as a difference *within* the contingent *signifiers* of maleness, but rather as a difference *from* the essential *signified* of maleness. Rather than being construed, therefore, as one possible *type* of man, the gay man must be conceptualized as being no man at all.

It should come as no surprise, therefore, that the original script for *Laura* identified Waldo's apartment as "exquisite . . . too exquisite for a man,"[31] that from the first, in other words, this elegant embodiment of "auntyish effeminacy" was positioned outside the boundaries that constitute "man" as a category of gender. What *might* come as a surprise, however, is that the casting of Clifton Webb, for whose performance in *Laura* Bosley Crowther declared him "an actor who fits like a fine suede glove," encountered resistance that found expression, tellingly, in terms that lead back to the vexed relationship between representation and the gay male body. Otto Preminger, who suggested that Webb should play Waldo after seeing him on stage in *Blithe Spirit*, describes in his autobiography the initial response he received from the studio czar: "Zanuck was negative when I suggested Webb. The head of the casting department, Rufus LeMaire, who was present, took his cue from the boss's attitude and said that he had seen a test Webb made for MGM. He said the man was impossible. 'He doesn't walk, he flies,' implying that he was effeminate."[32] At the risk of belaboring the obvious, I want to pause for a moment to examine the tropological imperative that Preminger both interprets and enacts when he offers his reader a translation of LeMaire's comment as "implying" that Webb was "effeminate."

The force of LeMaire's remark, after all, is not simply that Webb was "effeminate" but that he was an effeminate *gay man.* Indeed, the figuration of gay male effeminacy in terms of "flying" rather than walking, participates in a distinctive category of tropes for male homosexuality that includes "being six feet off the ground," "being light in one's loafers," and "flitting like a fairy." In each case homosexuality as a presumed ontology produces its legibility in and on the body: produces it, more exactly, in terms of a *contradiction* in the body's relation to itself. As construed through these various figures, that is, the gay male body seems to enact a certain resistance to its own embodiment, to turn against itself as if refusing the substance, the weightiness, the gravity of bodiliness as such. This self-contradiction is conceived as effecting a denaturalization of the gay male body, translating every move into a spectacle, every gesture into a representation or a performance of that gesture. So simple a task as walking, from this intensely phobic perspective, becomes, when performed by the effeminate gay man, "prancing," or "flitting," or "flying." In this way the gay male body gets conceptualized as an error in, or a theatrical problematization of, embodiment *tout court*, thus underscoring the heterosexual (male) imperative to read male bodies homographically by constructing fantasmatic visual indices to mark gay sexual difference. According to the calculus of LeMaire's tropology as understood by Preminger, then, the man who "flies" because his body betrays its perverse relation to the bodily is a gay man whose body must be referred to the supposed ontology of the female; and since such "effeminacy" in an anatomical male, under our heterosexual dispensation, constitutes a perverse relation to the male body's ideologically invested self-identity, "effeminate" can serve as an adequate shorthand for "effeminate gay man" precisely insofar as effeminacy externalizes and projects into the zero-sum economy of a heterosexually inflected gender binarism a difference that otherwise must be acknowledged as internal and specific to the condition of maleness.

I have taken the time to unpack these figures that might seem to inhabit a cognitive space outside the film itself because they define the perceptual logic through which the film's visualization of Waldo takes place: a logic in which the distinction between the film's outside (here, the signifying status of Webb's body) and its inside (the signifying status of Waldo's) collapses, engendering epistemological confusion precisely where the question of homosexual inscription demands to be addressed. Foster Hirsch alludes to such a collapse when he observes that "whether consciously or not, Webb gives the character homosexual overtones";[33] Otto Friedrich exemplifies it when he notes that after completing his work on the film, "Clifton Webb, whose ill-suppressed hysteria was essential to the malevolent fascination of *Laura*, suffered a nervous breakdown";[34] and Leslie Halliwell virtually performs it when he claims that "although the role of Waldo turned Clifton Webb into the most unlikely star of the forties, it was essentially unsuitable for him because it flaunted his homosexuality rather than covered it."[35] Whether Webb's homosexuality brings out Waldo's or Waldo's brings out Webb's matters less than does the logic by which homosexuality, representation, and the male body are constellated in each of these critical responses to the film. For where homosexuality is read off the body as a textualization of maleness, as a figural representation of it, the very act of acting the part of a gay man, the act of embodying or representing a man whose body must be read for the signs of its difference from an "authentic," non-textual maleness, subjects the actor who does so to a scrutiny that effectively textualizes *his* body, thus positioning him in the role associated with homosexuality itself.[36] And for an actor construed as gay to undertake the performance of such a part can only increase the disciplinary vigilance of the spectator socialized to look for the "signs" by which the body of the gay actor betrays itself—betrays, that is, the "truth" of its sexuality—in ways that must be imagined as beyond the actor's conscious artistic control.

Insofar as the heterosexual social order demands that the gay male body be recognized and disavowed, that project confers an enormous political and psychological power upon those authorized to enforce it; for *any* male body, examined for visible "signs" of homosexuality, will immediately display them. Too pretty or too unattractive, too muscular or too underdeveloped, too masculine or too feminine, the body, once subjected to the necessity of interpretation, becomes suddenly unnatural, its every feature questionable, its very mode theatrical; and in a culture committed to the ideological construction of maleness as the antithesis of representation, the body so exposed in its representational force, exposed, indeed, in its representational desire, is always susceptible to being read as the spectacularized body of the gay man. Thus Lacan can observe that "in the human being, virile display itself appears as feminine"[37] because the display of the male body *as display*, the inscription of the male body in the realm of representation, registers (in our socio-historical moment) as intrinsically effeminizing, invoking the explanatory sufficiency that "homosexuality" affords. In a culture that naturalizes maleness and situates femaleness in the place of representation, thus justifying a social and economic structure based on the circulation of women as representational commodities, male homosexuality appears in the aspect of a destabilizing *mis*representation; by putting the male "goods," as Irigaray would have it, on display and into the marketplace, the gay body seems to perform a self-commodification that threatens to infect not only the male body but also the male body politic. In consequence, the textualized body that the regime of patriarchal heterosexuality compels us to recognize as "gay" enters the public imagination as a body that "flaunts" or advertises its difference, demanding the attention that straight society so eagerly (if "disgustedly") accords it and activating the force of heterosexual repugnance by the alleged coerciveness, that is, the openness, with which it displays its commodification and negotiability in the sexual marketplace.

This commodification of the gay male body may seem to have taken us far

Figure 1.

from *Laura*, but it is at just this point that I want to come back to the specificity of the film. I find it significant, after all, that four of its central characters—Laura, Waldo, Shelby Carpenter, and Diane Redfern—are associated in one way or another with the activities of a New York advertising firm, and that Laura and Waldo first meet when she requests his endorsement for a product, the "Flow-Rite" pen, and permission to feature both his image and his signature in an advertising campaign she has privately drawn up so as to further her career (Figure 1). I also find it significant that the two characters destined to be shot to death in the film—Waldo and Diane Redfern, a model —are the two characters who allow their images to be circulated in commercial advertisements, commodifying themselves for a Madison Avenue firm whose name, "Bullitt and Company," is surely not, in this context, to be ignored. Submitting oneself or one's body to public representation has fatal consequences here; the film indicts it as a form of promiscuity comparable to that overtly thematized in the erotic encounter that culminates in the murder of Diane. *Laura* thus enacts a phobic response to the circulation of bodily displays, not despite but *because of* its own cinematic involvement in such representational acts. Indeed, I would argue that this film, on every level, attempts to split off and demonize such internal differences as it finds intolerable—whether in its own representational system, its narrative trajectory, or its characters' psychologies—by enacting the mechanism of paranoiac projection that stands in a determining relation to the structures of classical Hollywood cinema even as it stands in a determining relation to the phobic imag(in)ing of homosexuality.

This splitting and projection can be seen, in the first place, in the film's stigmatization of representational practices uncannily similar to those of cinema itself. The display, circulation, and fetishization of bodies is no less central to narrative cinema, after all, than it is to the business of advertising; indeed, as Jennifer Wicke importantly reminds us, "film and photography originate in commercial, advertised enterprise. . . . [P]hotography's first and primary use was to document business sites and commercial development to convince financial speculators of the 'reality' of various properties."[38] The commodification of actors in the star system, the publicity industry generated out of the need to promote films and their associated consumer goods, the cinematic technology that offers the audience the "reality" of bodily images, all of these bespeak the indissociable interimplication of cinema and advertising. *Laura*, however, strategically endeavors to reinforce the aesthetic integrity of the former by impugning the ethics of representation operative in the latter, generating a tendentious differentiation so as to occlude and defend its own commerce in bodies, especially insofar as male bodies are central to the commerce it conducts.

A similarly willful construction of difference in the service of disavowal marks the film's most famous narrative conceit: the return of the "murdered" Laura mid-film—a return that the film, as Kristin Thompson shows persuasively, suggests may be only a dream.[39] This division or mutation within the film denotes, in a sense, a refusal to accede to (what appeared to be) its original narrative logic: the murder of Laura to be followed by the discovery and apprehension of her killer. With Laura's return or resurrection it is as if the film needed to efface the face it had thus far constructed for itself by reconfiguring the face of the woman whose face was allegedly destroyed; or as if, to carry this one step further, it needed to posit a new face to figure its own representational enterprise, and Laura, returning *as that face*, casts out or effaces another face that had threatened to occupy its figural position: the face of Waldo Lydecker, whose initial voice-over narration *of* the film, and whose narration of the flashbacks *within* the film, establishes his as the presiding consciousness through which the film, to that point, has unfolded.

The displacement of Waldo by the return of Laura gestures toward the level at which the film performs its discipline of ideological differentiation in the structural relationships it elaborates among and between its various characters. If Waldo and Diane Redfern, for instance, are linked to the extent that they occupy a similarly reprobated space of self-commodification, the film also reads Diane Redfern (and, as I argue, Waldo too) as Laura's other and double at once. Found dead in Laura's apartment, clad (only) in Laura's robe after having been interrupted in the midst of an assignation with Shelby Carpenter, Laura's fiancé, Diane Redfern is posited in terms of her identity with, and as, (a discredited version of) Laura herself, an identity that gets articulated in the plot's dependence on the misrecognition of her body as Laura's own—an ironic misrecognition given that her "transgression" centers precisely on the public circulation of (images of) her body. Diane Redfern, one might say, effectively dies *for* and *in the place of* Laura; and as her violently repudiated promiscuity redeems Laura's own potentially promiscuous involvements with Jacoby, Shelby, and the many other men who kept Waldo in a constant state of jealousy, so the disavowed public circulation of Diane's image redeems the more "private," domestically situated representation of Laura in the portrait to which the camera repeatedly returns—returns as if seeking to put its own reproduction and circulation of Laura's image under the ensign of painting as a culturally legitimated representational practice.

This is not to say that between Laura and Diane the film posits a difference without a distinction; such a distinction is constructed and defined in the film as that between a "dame" and a "lady." Yet though registered through markers that designate class, this distinction does not mark a *difference* of class. Laura and Diane are both women who work; neither claims economic privilege by birthright. The film's effort to specify their difference through the evocation of contrasting social orders testifies to its investment in a middle-class fantasy of upward mobility, *within the middle class*, through personal refinement and material acquisition,[40] but it also masks an ideologically motivated attempt to demarcate categorical distinctions within the category of female sexuality: distinctions the film articulates in terms of having or not having a face. Diane Redfern, whose face suffers literal effacement by a blast from a shotgun fired at close range, and whose naked body, the film wants us believe, cannot be distinguished from Laura's even by those who knew Laura the best, embodies the film's hysterical vision of the promiscuous, undifferentiated force of female sexual embodiment itself. One might go so far as to say that the misrecognition suffered by Diane's body plays out *Laura*'s brutal version of the brutally reductive misogynistic topos that insists that all women are alike in the dark or with a bag over their heads. So reduced by the narrative to a figure for the female body as body alone, Diane Redfern enacts the role that the film articulates as that of a "dame."

An exchange between Waldo and the detective, Mark McPherson, pinpoints the meaning of this term at a key moment. As the camera first enters Laura's apartment, following Waldo, Mark, and Shelby Carpenter in their examination of the site at which the body, still thought to be Laura's, was found the day before, Mark mentions that the police, as part of their routine, took photographs of the mutilated corpse. Waldo's protest—"McPherson, tell me, why did they have to photograph her in that horrible condition?"—draws a generically hard-boiled, dismissive, and masculinist response: "When a dame gets killed," Mark answers, "she doesn't worry about how she looks." This rejoinder defines the "dame" in terms of her availability to the male's appropriative gaze, reading her as the essence of a female sexuality viewed as narcissistic and self-objectifying at once, but it also interprets Waldo's question as an index of his own "effeminate" privileging of surface appearance over moral depth, his own narcissistic concern, that is, with the body as an object of representation.

But it is in response to a specific *technology* of representation, photography, that Waldo has voiced his concern; for photography acquires the status here of a graphically factual, de-idealizing medium, one whose documentation of such unpleasant "truths" as that of the model's mutilation serves to counter the illusory images dispersed, for instance, by the advertising industry. Still over-esteeming the image as commodity, Waldo, through his question, insists upon defining a possible *limit* of representation, and in the process gestures toward agencies of censorship that govern what one can (bear to) see—agencies of censorship at work, of course, explicitly in the Hollywood Production Code as well as in the psychic mechanisms that place the determination of what the male subject can (bear to) see, according to psychoanalytic theory, under the aegis of castration. Here the image of the woman deprived of her face, and deprived thereby of the specificity of her identity, evokes the fantasmatic masculinist image of femaleness itself as mutilation, an image that the film locates outside—but *just* outside—its visual field, and that it employs as the irreducible referent of its figural construction of woman as "dame." Thus the photographic "truth" of mutilation that exposes the ontology of the "dame" constitutes the unbearable image to which the portrait of Laura, as fetishistic refutation of that image, necessarily refers.

Appropriately, therefore, the portrait appears in the film's scenographic space at just this moment. After briefly acknowledging Waldo's exasperation at Mark's response to his question about the police photos—"Will you stop calling her a 'dame'!"—the film cuts to a shot of Laura's living room with her portrait centered over the fireplace. "Look around," Waldo continues, "Is this the home of a 'dame'?" Then, turning toward the portrait, calling it to Mark's attention, he adduces it as evidence to counterbalance the (elided) photographic representations of (what is still thought to be) Laura's mutilation, her facelessness as a "dame": "Look at *her*." When Mark turns to face the portrait, to gaze at Laura's image while the image seems to gaze back at him, the camera follows suit with a cut to the portrait as it appeared while the opening credits unrolled; but now, for the first time, the camera presents it without the obstruction of intervening titles or script. This first close look at the portrait of Laura may follow the line of Mark's wary gaze, but it is produced by Waldo's solicitation of that gaze, by Waldo's active *direction* of it toward an image on which Mark and the camera both pause. With his imperative—"look at *her*"—Waldo voices the demand that Mark recognize Laura, that he acknowledge the face that distinguishes her from a "dame," by replacing the photographic images that offer the "truth" of mutilation, the "truth" as such for the police, with the painterly image that expresses a countervailing "truth" for the artist or aesthete. But this moment during which Waldo orchestrates successfully the direction of the spectatorial gaze so that his and Mark's and the camera's all meet at the site of Laura's portrait, constitutes a sort of seduction, laying the groundwork for Waldo and Mark to establish what Eve Kosofsky Sedgwick's work has enabled us to read as a dangerously intensified homosocial—and, as such, always potentially homophobic—connection between men that plays itself out in a triangulated structure across the body of the woman.

In this context it is worth noting that the solicitation of Mark's gaze echoes an earlier moment in the film when Waldo attempted to exert a similar mastery over the detective's angle of vision. The moment I have in mind takes place near the beginning, when Mark first visits Waldo's apartment. Having been questioned already by the detective, and dressing to join him as he interrogates others who might shed some light on Laura's death, Waldo asks Mark, rather coyly, "Do you *really* suspect me?" The detective answers tersely—"Yes"—and turns away while Waldo, examining his image in a mirror, finishes arranging his tie. At this point, as Mark is shown focusing his attention, for the first—but not the last—time, on a toy he carries, a small box he manipulates in an exercise of dexterity that attempts to align ball bearings with the shallow indentations on which they can be brought to rest, Waldo calls out, "McPherson, if you know anything about faces look at mine. How singularly innocent I look this morning. Have you ever seen such candid eyes?" But even before Waldo has finished extending this invitation for Mark to study him, Mark and the camera emphatically refuse it, as if to avoid being compromised by aligning theirs with Waldo's too obviously self-admiring gaze or by being compelled to meet that gaze at the site of his bodily reflection. The film, instead, cuts suddenly to a close-up of the toy, which, as we now discover, bears an inscription—the single word, "Baseball"—and shows a scene of players on a baseball field, the bases of which are the indentations on which the ball bearings must be brought to rest.

The over-protestation, at just this moment, evident in the film's deliberate attention to this heavy-handed signifier of heterosexual masculinity (and its childishly macho values), demands to be read in relation to the opening scene in its entirety, a scene that deserves—and would certainly reward—more thorough consideration than I can offer here. The film's obtrusive and exaggerated interest in Mark's toy—of which Waldo inquires with contempt, "Something you confiscated in a raid on a kindergarten?"—responds, after all, to the elegant sequence at the outset of the film in which the camera glides slowly across Waldo's apartment, observing the precious objects that give it the look—and the lifeless atmosphere—of a museum. Even before we first meet him, these objects define the man who owns them in terms of an aesthetic sensibility that renders suspect, in the ideological context of Hollywood cinema in 1944, both his politics and his sexuality. That the camera focuses, at the initial fade-in, on an "Oriental" statue, and after showing us Waldo's delicate glassware and his apartment's antique furnishings, pans across a wall on which "Oriental" masks are included in a display, serves to condense the sexual and political subversiveness that this *mise en scène* defines: it frames our reading of Waldo, that is, by invoking the vicious anti-Asian racism of American culture during the war with Japan alongside (and in a mutually defining relationship with) the predisposition to view any rarefied or aesthetic interests on the part of a man as betokening either a lovable and sexually latent eccentricity (consider, for example, Gary Cooper in the first half of Howard Hawks's *Ball of Fire* [1941]) or a "decadent" and potentially virulent sexual "irregularity" (consider Humphrey Bogart's impersonation of a gay man who collects rare books in Hawks's *The Big Sleep* [1946]). The insert shot of Mark's toy *in place of* the solicited examination of Waldo's face thus defends against the threat such a gaze might pose to the institution of heterosexual masculinity, an institution figured here (perhaps not wholly unironically) as distinctively American—as American as baseball itself.[41] Indeed, as if asserting the majoritarian ideology that push-pin is better than Plato, the shot of this cheap, diverting toy establishes Mark's heterosexual credentials to the extent that his concentration on it serves to dissociate him from the elitist bric-a-brac of Waldo's "too exquisite" milieu. The film's cut to this particular shot, then, must be viewed as a deliberate *substitution*, a meaningful refusal of the complicity that acceding to a look at Waldo's reflection might imply, precisely because that look could too easily be, or be mistaken for, or even become, a look of love.

In this way the film's phobic response to Waldo's appeal to the detective's attention depends upon the anxious cultural identification of male homosexuality with the male-male gaze as I considered it above. The full force of this phobic response, however, only becomes apparent through its differential repetition when Waldo solicits Mark's gaze once again, directing it toward the portrait of Laura in the scene already discussed, a direction with which Mark and the film are both quite willing to comply. If the visual logic worked out in the film's differing responses to these analogous moments puts Mark's toy and Laura's image in equivalent positions as signifiers of male heterosexual identity (and perhaps less obviously locates those signifiers *away from the heterosexual male body itself*), the parallelism also places Waldo and Laura in equivalent positions as objects that seek out or impose upon the heterosexual male gaze. The film, in other words, reads Waldo, like Diane, as a reprobated, intolerable image of the Laura that it systematically idealizes. Such an idealization aligns the film with the logic of "painting" over the logic of "photography," and thus has a meaningfulness for the film's self-allegorization of its representational system that I will consider more fully later; for now, however, it is important to note that the film depicts Waldo and Laura as doubles of one another in numerous ways.

The matching clocks in their respective apartments, and the film's emphasis on the fact that the clocks are identical through the part their sameness plays in the resolution of the plot, serve as the most obvious visual tokens of the way in which Waldo and Laura themselves are constructed as antithetical inflections of a single shared identity. Both, after all, are ambitious and intelligent; both earn their livings by using the mass media to manipulate the emotions of the public; and both find themselves involved in ambiguously eroticized relationships in which each plays the part of economic sponsor to a person whose romantic affections turn out to be directed toward someone else. Laura's relationship with Shelby Carpenter, that is, parallels Waldo's relationship with Laura herself, and in each case Galatea's interest in Pygmalion leaves something to be desired. The film, needless to say, focuses greater attention on Waldo's importance to Laura's career than on Laura's importance to Shelby's. In part this articulates the wariness or distance with which the film engages the sexual inversion and reversal that it everywhere discovers;[42] but it signifies, too, the film's thematic concentration on Waldo's investment not only in making Laura into one more aesthetic object for his collection, but also in making her over as the idealized image of himself.

Consider that in transforming her he focuses on every aspect of her physical, intellectual, social, and professional representation of herself until he produces her as the exquisitely perfect embodiment of his own exquisitely perfect taste: until she becomes, in a sense, the embodiment of his own narcissistically cathected bodily ego. His act of recreating her thus gives *him* a different body: a body masculinized insofar as she covers it with the protective mantle of heterosexuality,[43] but feminized insofar as the bodily image she gives him turns out to be her own. "He gives her class and she gives him sex," as Katharine Hepburn famously quipped of Fred Astaire and Ginger Rogers; but in terms of the relationship between Waldo and Laura, the sex that she gives him is less sexual than sexed: she inscribes the taste and the "sophistication" that are the manifestations of his "class" in the register of the femaleness toward which his effeminacy can only gesture. Hers, one might say, is the "perfumed" body in which the "auntyish effeminacy" expressed in his "perfumed literary style of talking" finds its "proper," heterosexual referent.

Figure 2.

Figure 3.

FIGURE 4.

The film thus positions Waldo as the other face of female sexuality, the intolerable, monstrous image closeted in the straight man's imagination of femaleness itself: an image that poses the psycho-sexual question—"What's the difference?"—time and again, because the answers are never sufficient, or never persuasive, or never make sense.

At one significant moment the film directly *envisions* the figural relationship it produces by this schematic positioning of Waldo and this interpretation of his investment in Laura. Following the montage showing Laura's ascent, guided by Waldo at every stage, to power and success in the advertising world, the film discovers Waldo and Laura in the domestic space of his apartment where, as he tells us, they were accustomed to spending Tuesday and Friday nights together. "I read my articles to her," he recalls as the film shows him holding the draft of an essay while he sits beside Laura, who is perched just above him, puffing on a cigarette and staring into space as she listens to his latest piece of work. The camera moves in slowly, dropping Waldo from the frame, and capturing Laura's unfocused gaze in a glamorous, contour-lighted close-up that renders her perfectly smooth and unblemished: "The way she listened," Waldo comments in voice-over, "was more eloquent than speech." Although Waldo refers to the way she listens, that activity can only be represented imagistically through the synaesthetic substitution of the way she looks; and while that last phrase may shuttle strategically between alternative identifications of Laura as "active" subject and "passive" object of the gaze, the camera's artful and loving composition of her almost inhumanly flawless image defines her unreadable, objectless look as the object that Waldo and the camera both conjure as the focus for the spectator's own.

If the way she listens as she looks into space proves "more eloquent than speech," though, it is the eloquence of Waldo's writing to which that eloquent look responds. Her physical presence, synecdochically adduced through the close-up of her face, embodies, that is, the aesthetic quality of Waldo's sensibility. She is, which is to say, she *incarnates*, his literary eloquence, giving it a body that he desires to own, not merely in terms of objectification, but in terms, more exactly, of *identification*: she provides his sensibility with the body that the film reads him as wanting to own *as his own*. And at just this point, as if to emphasize the film's prophylactic positioning of him as the difference in and of female embodiment and sexuality, the three-quarters profile shot of Laura dissolves into a head-on close-up of him, momentarily allowing the shadow of her image to cut diagonally across the framing of his, constructing him—*as if revealing him*—as a monstrous, composite creature whose "true" identity is literally, if fleetingly, written across his face (Figures 2–4).

To read this visual imprinting of the "meaning" of Waldo's relationship with Laura as a figure of either androgyny or hermaphroditism would be to miss the point; the image, rather, articulates a condition that cannot be named as it cannot be faced: it constitutes, that is, the face of what the film can only give face to as facelessness itself. This visualization, in other words, responds to the need to identify the sexual difference intended by the intimations of Waldo's "ambiguity" as a difference that is *visually marked* and marked specifically *upon his body*. So inscribed, of course, and made graphic, that difference or "ambiguity" ceases to be ambiguous; it acquires a face that defines it and hygienically articulates it away from the maleness of the heterosexual male. With its merely momentary conjuring of this image the film, however, acknowledges its ability to envision this uncloseted face of difference only in the context of an anxious awareness that such difference, for the most part, remains faceless—as faceless as it is to Laura herself or to the logic of her involvement with Waldo as the Production Code permits it to be portrayed. Thus the composite image appears only as a transitional or even fantasmatic effect, a ghost image in the camera's passage from Laura's face to Waldo's. Though it can be isolated, of course, and examined in a photographic still, the film allows this image to appear only as, and in the process of, a *movement*; like Zeno's arrow, its meaning and its presence at any moment can only be located in the differential relation it draws out between the temporal and spatial coordinates it traverses.[44]

This phantom image reads Waldo, then, as Laura's *différance*; and even though it seeks to unmask within his image the "presence" of a determinate face of difference (homographically unpacking the "meaning" of the film's attentiveness to his body and thereby resecuring the epistemological privilege of male heterosexuality), at the same time it necessarily admits the pervasive facelessness of this difference, the lack of any visual specificity that would instantly and invariably confess it. If this "outing" of Waldo's other face, then, confirms what the film has already signaled the savvy spectator to suspect—and even to *know* insofar as suspicion, in the realm of sexuality, is itself a form of knowledge—it also suggests that suspicion is the *only* way of knowing or discerning that face, that the fact of our ability to catch a glimpse of it here bespeaks the possibility that we might *not* have done so had we not been prepared to identify what otherwise has the ability to "pass." Implying as it does the need for a defensive and preemptive paranoia, this logic interprets Waldo's "difference" as a facelessness that the film must give face to if only to register it thereby *as* facelessness; and the image that gives face to, or figures, this facelessness precisely by its ghostly disfiguration of Waldo's face, must, in consequence, both be seen and not seen within the film at once: it must be present but its presence must be limited to the cinematic movement of the dissolve wherein its "accidental" or merely "technical" presence marks it with the trace of its own absence.

The representational system of the film thus insists on its technological ability to posit the (fantasmatic) face of Waldo's facelessness, but it cannot see, it cannot (bear to) look at, that facelessness itself—any more than it could (bear to) look at the effacement of Diane Redfern's face.[45] In each instance facelessness is made to signify with reference to castration, and, consequently, as a threat to the logic of bodily integrity and totalized identity; each instance poses a challenge, therefore, to the "naturalness" of an identity that the image of Laura—especially as rendered in her portrait—undertakes to establish for the film, to establish, that is, in allegorical relation to the representational closure or self-identity of the filmic system itself. Laura's portrait, after all, functions as more than a fetish that substitutes for what has been lost; it makes possible, through the very intensity of the film's commitment to its idealization, the narrative enactment of the fetishist's constitutive fantasy as truth: the actual return of what was missing and thus the denial that it had been, or could indeed *be*, lost. Laura's reappearance (Figure 5), following—and even following from—the pivotal scene in which Mark falls asleep in her apartment after an evening spent drinking and staring at her portrait, performs for the film a disavowal of such loss, hence an assertion of bodily integrity and a confirmation of identity that rescues Mark—and with Mark, the film—from the nascent "perversion" that Waldo recognizes in the detective's obsessive fixation on Laura and Laura's portrait: "You'd better

FIGURE 5.

watch out, McPherson," he warns Mark earlier that evening, "or you'll end up in a psychiatric ward. I don't think they've ever had a patient who fell in love with a corpse."

This displacement of erotic "perversion"—in the particularly lurid garb of a fetishism that Waldo interprets as necrophilial desire—onto the character that Manny Farber described as "the plain-American-guy detective" responds to the film's ascription of an infectiously destabilizing or disorienting force to the facelessness of Waldo's unspecified sexual "difference." In Chapter Ten, I considered how disturbances of spatio-temporal positional logic were represented in a variety of texts as resulting from the sight of sodomitical relations between men; here, however, the *inability to see*, or, more exactly, the inability to see with certainty, the face of male (homo)sexual difference—an inability that allows such difference to be read, if only tropologically, as "sexual ambiguity"—renders ambiguous, and thus disorients or denaturalizes, heterosexual male identity. As Ken Worthy, writing in 1965 in a book titled *The Homosexual Generation*, put the matter bluntly: "With evidence of the stepped-up activities of homosexuals all around us, it is only natural that one will sometimes stop and think, 'My God—am *I* a latent homosexual?'"[46] Worthy notes in this regard that Dr. Karl Menninger and Dr. George S. Sprague drew up a list of questions, "the answers to which can reveal just how strong is the homosexual urge in any individual" (110). As an instance of the paranoia-inducing, identity-questioning, textualization of male sexuality that results from the potential indistinguishability, the facelessness, of gay men, Worthy's annotated list of possible positions men may take with regard to homosexual desire deserves citation in full:

> 1. I want a man homosexually. (Here is recognition and acceptance of the homosexual instinct without deviation)
> 2. I want a man, but not homosexually. (A partial admission of homosexuality)
> 3. I want a man, but on a guarded basis. (Partial suppression)
> 4. I don't want a man homosexually. (Simple denial and repudiation)
> 5. I want a man, but pretend he is a woman. (A sparing of guilt over recognition of one's homosexuality)
> 6. He and I have similar, heterosexual interests. (A disguised interest is shown in the object's sexuality. A familiar pattern with the man's man type of man who prefers the company of men to that of women under any circumstances)
> 7. I want many women. (The Don Juan who seeks by overcompensation to avoid self-discovery of homosexuality)
> 8. A man wants me homosexually. (A familiar projection onto another of one's own homosexuality)
> 9. Others think I am homosexual, but I am not. (Partial recognition, projected onto others so that he can defend himself against himself) (110–111)

What such a list reveals, of course, is that given the fact of a cultural mandate to "read" homosexuality in the face of its all-pervasive facelessness (and such an assertion of its facelessness constitutes, of course, the paranoid obverse of the effort to define the visual and even bodily markers that can be construed as figuring its face), male heterosexuality effectively subverts the possibility of any stable, uncompromised ground on which *it itself* might stand. "Wherever homosexuality exists," Worthy maintains, "the rights of others are threatened" (67), and those rights are threatened because the very existence of this faceless homosexuality denaturalizes heterosexuality and makes necessary the project of "reading"—so as to authenticate—*its own face.*

For Mark McPherson this means that his contact with the ambiguity figured by Waldo has the subversive effect of threatening to reconfigure *him.* His refusal to share Waldo's self-admiring gaze in the mirror, the resolute and emphatic attention he devotes to the toy baseball game instead, may define his phobic "normalcy" in relation to the homosexual erotics culturally construed as informing the male-male gaze, but it also locates an anxiety, a node of tension or potential threat, against which the "normalizing" baseball game is mobilized as a defense. After all, when an exasperated Waldo later angrily demands, "Will you stop playing with that infernal puzzle? It's getting on my nerves," Mark coolly sizes him up and replies, "I know, but it keeps me calm." The toy that keeps him calm by allowing him to displace and work out his tensions invariably testifies, at the same time, to the *presence* of tensions that the film unpacks as erotic. From the detective's first encounter with Waldo, where the camera frames Mark in pointed close-up, sneering as he watches Waldo rising from his bath; to his subsequent refusal to inspect Waldo's face when Waldo invites him to do so; to his evening at Montagnino's, where he dines with Waldo at the very table that Waldo and Laura were accustomed to share, Mark finds himself gradually drawn into the orbit of Waldo's "ambiguity" and implicated in the disorientation that it represents and produces in the film. Indeed, during the dinner with Waldo at Montagnino's—a dinner whose semiotic framing carries all the connotations of romance (musicians playing Laura's theme, wine, dim lights, a table for two)—the detective finds himself, literally, occupying Laura's place; and it is, significantly, at just this point that the film calls forth the dissolve that discloses what I suggested above must be interpreted as the figure or face of Waldo's facelessness.

While not wanting to suggest that that facelessness propels Mark away from heterosexuality, I do want to argue that it provokes a disturbance in the fixity of his sexual identity that brings him closer to the "ambiguity" that Waldo represents within the film. The extent of that disturbance becomes evident in the sequence that leads up to Laura's return. Entering her apartment alone at night, Mark stares at her portrait and turns brusquely away, loosening his tie to signal his undoing of the "uniform" he wears throughout the film. In fact, when he takes off his jacket (the only time we see him do so) before sitting down at Laura's desk, he reveals, as it were, his private, internal, or psychological self. So revealed, he no longer attends to his professional business of detection; instead, exhibiting signs of tension, he wanders into Laura's bedroom where he begins fetishistically to make contact with objects that bear the trace of her lost presence: a delicate, translucent handkerchief that he lifts gingerly out of her drawer (a handkerchief like the one draped elegantly over her shoulder in the portrait), the perfume whose scent he inhales before hurriedly returning the stopper to the bottle, and the clothes he stares at longingly when he looks inside her closet—clothes he moves forward to touch or examine before quickly and visibly resisting that impulse and shutting the closet door.

Critics have viewed the undeniably "neurotic" or fetishistic aspect of this sequence as an indication of the intensity of Mark's (heterosexual) romantic desire for Laura. I would suggest, however, that this desire, at the same time, triangulates his relationship with Waldo, thus identifying his interest in

Laura with Waldo's and implying that, like Waldo's, his desire to *have* Laura may mask a desire to *be* Laura, and so to have the things she has, things that she (a working woman as Mark himself is a working man) acquired only through Waldo's good offices, only through his guidance as an older, wealthy, and sophisticated sponsor. The point is not that Mark, as a psychological entity, is represented in the film as harboring an unconscious erotic attraction to Waldo; rather, the indeterminacy of Waldo's difference disseminates an ambiguity that overtakes even, or even *especially*, Mark as the "plain-American-guy detective." Waldo, who shows up at Laura's apartment after Mark has withdrawn from her bedroom and proceeded to pour himself the first of many drinks from her bar, initiates an exchange with the detective that brings out the force of that ambiguity:

> Waldo: I happened to see the lights on. Have you sublet this apartment? You're here often enough to pay rent.
> Mark: Any objections?
> Waldo: Yes. I object to you prying into Laura's letters, especially those from me.
> Mark: Why? Yours are the best in the bunch.
> Waldo: Thanks, but I didn't write them to *you*. Haven't you any sense of privacy?
> Mark: [Taking the toy baseball game out of his coat pocket] Murder victims have no claim to privacy.
> Waldo: Have detectives who buy portraits of murder victims a claim to privacy? Lancaster Corey told me you've already put in a bid for it.
> Mark: [Concentrating on the toy] That's none of your business.
> Waldo: McPherson, does it ever strike you that you're acting very strangely? It's a wonder that you don't come here like a suitor with roses and a box of candy. Drugstore candy, of course. Have you ever dreamed of Laura as your wife, by your side at the policeman's ball, or in the bleachers? Or listening to the heroic story of how you got a silver shinbone from a gunbattle with a gangster? I see you have.

Interpreting Mark's obsession with Laura as an extreme version of a common heterosexual social script, Waldo nonetheless notes in Mark's actions a potential subversion of that script. It is Mark who now reads the private and implicitly "romantic" letters that Waldo intended for Laura's eyes alone ("I didn't write them to *you*"), just as Mark now inhabits her apartment, handles her belongings, helps himself to drinks from her bar. If his nightly visits to Laura's apartment define him, that is, on the one hand, as hyperbolically heterosexual, acting out a romantic passion more powerful than the shadow of death itself, they define him, on the other hand, as neurotically engaged in a "perverse," because non-productive, sexuality that takes Laura less as its object than as its idealized self-image, a sexuality that looks for satisfaction by installing Mark in Laura's place.[47]

FIGURE 6.

Perhaps this explains why Mark so emphatically must shut the closet door; for Laura's closet, in such a context, can too easily turn into his. Nor is it insignificant that that door should be mirrored, and that when he shuts it Mark looks, for the only time in the film, at his own reflected image, engaging in a specular recognition that *Laura* otherwise permits only women—and, of course, Waldo—to perform. As this moment of self-investigation is atypical, so too is what it reveals. Seeing his disturbed—and hence disturbing—reflection, Mark passes his hand across his eyes, as if to deny or efface what the mirror already has disclosed (Figure 6): a face that is unfamiliar, an image that conflicts with the coherent identity by which he knows himself. What he sees, in short, is the image of his own disfiguration, not necessarily because he "is" or is "becoming" a "homosexual," but because the heterosexual fetishization of Laura, cast in the distinctive light of *film noir*, begins to look uncannily similar to the gay-inflected "ambiguity" that Waldo represents and that the film construes as his desire to *be* or to *be embodied in* the body of Laura. From the intolerable image of his disfigured face Mark turns his attention to Laura's portrait, substituting a heterosexually coded gaze for the specular encounter with his own unnatural representation in the closet mirror; but that portrait can no longer sustain the burden of assuring his heterosexual identity. The "meaning" of that gaze, its rhetorical positioning, has been thrown into crisis insofar as it can offer only a *figural staging* of Mark's heterosexuality at a point in the film when figure itself has been colored through its association with the disfiguring force of Waldo's "ambiguous"—and thus effectively *non*-heterosexual—sexuality.

To put all this another way, Waldo, whom the film defines in terms of his aggressive sophistication and irony, embodies the destabilizing force of irony within the film itself. The facelessness of his difference, as given face within the film, dismantles the cognitive borders by which identities are fixed and reconfigures the meaningfulness of the signifiers that we assume, in the first place, to mean, and whose meanings we assume, in the second place, that we are able to discern. "Irony comes into being when self-consciousness loses its control over itself," Paul de Man asserted in an interview. "For me, at least, the way I think of it now, irony is not a figure of self-consciousness. It's a break, an interruption, a disruption. It is a moment of loss of control, and not just for the author but for the reader as well."[48] As the film's locus of indeterminacy, as the site at which the assumption of meaning confronts the disfiguring force of figuration, Waldo—which is to say, Waldo's "literary style" as a displacement of his body—disseminates such a loss of control by proposing the "sophisticated" possibility not only that meaning is not natural, not literal, and therefore not something that can be taken with assurance at face value, but also that meaning itself may be only the fictional face with which we dissimulate the contingency, the randomness, or the facelessness of experience.

This is not to say that the film is merely staging a textual allegory of the operation of language; it is not, in other words, as if the body's materiality (and the socio-cultural contexts that allow us to conceptualize its materiality) were simply ancillary to the film's unfolding of some trans-historical deconstructive insight into the structural contradictions at work in any representational system as such. For if irony here can be said to find filmic representation in the body of Waldo, it is only because Waldo's body—as a male body subjected to textualization, and thus to heightened homophobic scrutiny—already has been socially constructed as a privileged site of irony. His effect both on and in the film is to suggest that the symbolic (hetero)sexual order established by the reading of sexual differentiation through the polarizing narrative of the castration complex imposes a (not necessarily necessary) fiction of sexual identity. That fiction reenacts the contradictory temporality of the Lacanian mirror stage, a temporality in which totalized identity is posited by a decree that phobically disavows the definitional incoherence of the bits and pieces imagined as having preceded the constitution of the subject, precisely because the subject anxiously anticipates the possibility of succumbing to such an incoherence once again.[49] The sexual identity so structured is endlessly paranoid in its need to assert the inevitability and security of its narcissistic totalization, and thus the subject actively refuses—

indeed, aggressively attempts to efface—whatever would ironize its claim to an identity *intrinsic to and coextensive with the fact of its existence.* Such ironization, after all, exerts a profoundly disintegrative energy that challenges the constructs through which the subject (and the subject's world) takes on a human face—a face that is only perceptible now as marked by sexual difference; the irony associated here with Waldo reads such constructs, that is, as *mere* constructs, performative positings within a psycho-sexuality that operates both *like* and *as* a linguistic system. Seen as threatening to reduce the symbolic structure of (hetero)sexuality to the chaos that is the imaginary's imagination of what it was but is no longer, what it emerged from to become itself, the irony located in and disseminated by the gay male body deconstructs the heterosexual subject's myth of a self-evident, non-textual heterosexuality to the extent that such irony operates upon the psycho-sexual system with the force that deconstruction ascribes to the operation of language itself: its effects, in other words, as seen from the perspective of the heterosexual subject, are disturbingly anti-foundational and, as de Man remarks of the linguistic system, "totally indifferent in relation to the human."[50]

Language's indifference to the human, its mechanistic unfolding of linguistic events that have no meaning except as effects of a system whose systematicity is itself perhaps only another willful totalization, thus finds its figural counterpart and achieves its thematic enactment in the film's depiction of Waldo and of Waldo's impact on the fiction of a necessary or natural heterosexuality. I said earlier that the film inscribes Waldo in the realm of textuality, interpreting him, as Manny Farber put it, in terms of his "perfumed literary style," his "sophisticated" deployment of language, and thus deliberately recalling the style and the stylishness associated with Oscar Wilde (to whom Waldo's name and characterization surely owe a debt).[51] And just as Wilde's own "scented"[52] sophistication provoked reviewers of *The Picture of Dorian Gray* to protest that his novel, if "undeniably clever," showed a "lack of true humanity"[53]—which we can translate as acknowledging Wilde's own depiction of the "human" face as mere figure, his own disfiguration or denaturalization of its lineaments—so the film reads Waldo's cleverness and his command of literary fluency in relation to an inhumanly mechanistic quality that it visualizes in his bodily stiffness—his tendency to sharp, staccato movements—and that it thematizes in his killing of Diane Redfern and his subsequent attempt on Laura's life. In its "sophisticated" deployment of language, his high-brow literary and aesthetic style—the morally bankrupt worldliness that lets him play with words and lives indifferently, demonstrating his willingness to empty both of meaning with equal ease—thus signifies here as irony in de Man's sense of "a break, an interruption, a disruption" of the "control" that a naturalized identity assures, whether that identity consists of a "reliable" heterosexual identity or the "reliable" identity of language and the phenomenal world to which it refers. It would not, then, be an exaggeration to say that, as rendered in *Laura*, sophistication kills; nor, I think, would it be an exaggeration to add that it kills precisely to the degree that it threatens to ironize the "authenticity" of heterosexual male identity by producing a "sophisticated"—and therefore, given the film's ideology, a "gay"—interpretation of language, and psycho-sexuality, as figure-making systems. The sophistication articulated, in this context, as the severing of language from its "natural" reference through the play of figuration, is definitionally, then, a false sophistication, the empty posturing of those defined as inauthentic in themselves; and false sophistication, for nearly a century, has been to the homophobic designation of gay men what "cosmopolitanism" has been to the anti-Semitic designation of the Jews: the label by which they are stigmatized as posing a threat to the natural order through their embodiment of an urbanity that counter-intuitively calls the natural into question.

Thus when Mark's involvement in the sophisticated world that Waldo made accessible to Laura (and that he has begun, to some extent, to make accessible to Mark) produces the disfiguration that Mark observes in the closet mirror, he turns his gaze to Laura's portrait in an effort to reassert his "natural" heterosexual identity; but that fetishistic gaze, as *figure* or *substitution*, can no longer guarantee it. The integrity of his heterosexuality, and the integrity of the film insofar as its representational system is invested in Mark's heterosexuality, depends upon a repudiation of the irony that language as figuration necessarily elaborates, an irony that the film gives face to, that it personifies, in Waldo; the film must elicit a counter-force to the disruptions produced by figure that will have the effect of seeming to embody *literality itself.* It is out of this need that the detective, having drunk himself to sleep before Laura's portrait, awakens to find himself confronted with a Laura literally come to life and come to life as the face of the "truth" or "presence" of the literal. Her resurrection makes possible the re-erection of his heterosexual authority by affirming the redemptive naturalness of their attraction to one another. Though such a reading greatly condenses the narrative trajectory of the film's second half, the chiastic pattern that the narrative unfolds can be seen in Mark's reclaiming of Laura from the emptiness of aesthetic representation that the film positions Waldo and his literary style to represent. Where Waldo, that is, sought to refashion Laura as a cultured and "knowing" sophisticate, Mark must return her to her "proper" sphere as a plain-speaking, domesticated wife.[54] Laura and Mark, accordingly, can be said to "rescue" one another: she rescues him from the sexual ambiguity provoked by his encounter with Waldo, and he rescues her from the "death" that her relationship with Waldo both requires and entails: a "death" that consists of her construction as the image of Waldo's unnatural (because denaturalizing) "sophistication" and hence her removal from the "productive" sphere of "natural" familial responsibility.

Laura's return, however, is able to affirm the sexual and epistemological security of heterosexual masculinity only by effecting a noticeable rupture in the text of the film itself. As I mentioned earlier, the very endeavor by which the film seeks to *assure* its own coherence mandates a splitting and demonization that *sunders* its narrative coherence. In her "neoformalist" analysis of the film, Kristin Thompson makes clear that Laura's reappearance is framed to imply that the scene of her return may be only a wish-fulfilling dream—that it may constitute an eruption of unconscious desire (on the part of both the film and the detective) that is never recontextualized by a return to the "reality" upon which it would have obtruded. "The apparent dream which begins about midway through *Laura* is the film's structural center," she writes. "It is also so ambiguous and misleading as to be potentially disruptive to the narrative."[55] Thompson persuasively argues that despite the "relatively transgressive" (192) nature of this structural device, *Laura*, like the classical cinema in general, is able successfully to "weave these devices through the texture of the film's dominant" (194); but what interests me more in this transgressive disturbance of narrative continuity is that the film, in its effort to adduce an ideologically privileged and heterosexually identified literality, finds itself condemned to enact the play of Wildean or Waldo-ean paradox; for it can only shore up its integrity through this act of structural violation and it can only call forth its image of the literal in a sequence that the film positions ambiguously, and suggests may be counter-realistic.

That this violation and ambiguity can nonetheless generate the *sense* of logical coherence and resolution underscores the film's mobilization of larger cultural structures—socio-historical and psychological both—that enable and (as in the case of castration) demand a disavowal of indeterminacy in order to affirm heterosexuality as natural and therefore as naturally conclusive.[56] Indeed, the film's very capacity to ignore, deny, or contain the violence through which it achieves its heterosexual resolution links this operation of *Laura*'s narrative to the psychiatric experiment (discussed earlier in this essay) in which electrical shocks were administered to gay men to induce them to repudiate and displace the images of attractive males projected before them. The structural mutation of *Laura* itself performs just such a switch, supplanting the dangerously attractive body of wit and sophistication that Waldo, as the face of irony, presents in the film's first half with the reconfigured face of Laura, adduced as the literal thing itself to which Waldo's "auntyish effeminacy" and sexual (mis)representation can only tropologically—and thus, as the film would have it, defectively—refer. The wish fulfilled by Laura's (re)appearance, then, is less a wish for Laura herself than a wish for an unquestioned and unquestionable heterosexual male identity that Laura's literality is intended to assure; her non-ironic literality, however, ironically enough, can only figure the text's own need to refuse the indeterminacy of figure that Waldo figures in the film. The narrative disruption that accompanies the switch from his face to hers, therefore, enacts on the level of structure a violence that is ultimately directed against him and that finds its thematic fulfillment when Waldo is killed at the film's conclusion.

I have said that the film performs a switch, substituting Laura's face for Waldo's, in the scene of Laura's return, the scene in which material that may emerge from the unconscious erupts into and commandeers the narrative. It may not be irrelevant, then, that *Laura* thematizes a strikingly similar textual displacement in its opening scene. During his initial interview with Waldo, Mark asks him about an article he published some years before:

> Mark: Two years ago, in your October 17th column, you started out to write a book review. But at the bottom of the column you switched over to the Harrington murder case.
> Waldo: Are the processes of the creative mind now under the jurisdiction of the police?
> Mark: You said that Harrington was rubbed out with a shotgun loaded with buckshot—the way Laura Hunt was murdered night before last.
> Waldo: Did I?
> Mark: Yes. But he was really killed with a sash weight.
> Waldo: How ordinary. My version was obviously superior. I never bother with details, you know.

Waldo's text, like the narrative of *Laura*, interrupts itself, "switche[s] over" to introduce a story that reflects the pressure of more immediate psychic needs; and this disturbance finds justification here in Waldo's appeal to the freedom and sovereignty enjoyed by the "creative mind." In the aftermath of work by such writers as Michel Foucault and D. A. Miller, of course, and given the recent reprehensible example of Senator Jesse Helms, we know full well that the "creative mind" is always under "the jurisdiction of the police" and that the purpose of such policing is to protect the constitutive boundaries of the face by which a social order figures itself to itself; one might say that this policing bespeaks the extent to which the symbolic order is mobilized to defend an imaginary self-image against those forces that are seen as threatening to unmask it as always *only* imaginary. Such forces, to which the social order desires to remain unconscious, erupt in Waldo's column as he "unconsciously" declares his own subversive desire to "rub out" or efface the face of "truth" as it is socially construed. In place of an "ordinary" attention to facts, which he sees as so many humdrum "details," Waldo proposes a "superior," that is, a more "sophisticated" or aestheticized version of the literal events in the Harrington murder case—an imaginative version that explicitly thematizes the very process of effacement involved in his "literary" rendering or revision of the "truth."

Waldo's switch, then, as the film permits us to read it, attempts to disfigure the "natural" order, the order of "truth" itself, while the violence through which the film, by contrast, switches its narrative logic undertakes, like the psychiatric experiment, to restore that "natural" order and to secure it through a displacement—however disruptive it may be—of Waldo's unnaturally attractive image by the more "properly" attractive image of Laura as the face of the natural itself. In restoring the "natural" through the "unnatural" disturbance of narrative logic and coherence, however, in supplanting the figural by the production of Laura as a figure for the literal, and in disavowing ambiguity by a sequence "so ambiguous and misleading as to be potentially disruptive," the film seems to find itself trapped in the destabilizing force field of an irony that requires us to read its own representational system in terms of the disfiguration it attributes to the facelessness that Waldo, as the personification of gay-inflected irony, both embodies and disseminates. There is a sense, in other words, in which the film that has labored to demonize the gay man as the face of an intolerably ironizing facelessness, must nonetheless recognize that the gay man's facelessness is ultimately its own: that the camera can succeed in disavowing the irony induced by the gaze of—and the gaze at—the gay man only by confronting its own implication in a systematic figuralization of the body that is figured (and disfigured) by (and in) the "gaze" of the camera itself. That acknowledgment, as I see it, occurs in the concluding sequence of the film as the camera offers one last look at Waldo in the context of disfiguration, and in the process figures its own relation to the visual production of "meaning."

III. *Laura* ends with the failure of Waldo's second attempt to murder the woman he describes as "the best part of [him]self." Aiming his shotgun at Laura, he tells her that Mark will "find us together . . . as we always have been, as we always should be, as we always will be," but the sound of the police breaking in just then momentarily distracts him. Laura, seizing her opportunity, pushes Waldo and his weapon aside, seeking safety in Mark's protective arms. Waldo fires wildly, striking the clock that has represented his union with Laura, as a bullet from a policeman's pistol hits him squarely in the chest. The camera frames him as he crumples forward, Laura's portrait visible behind him, and then, as if cued by his words, "Goodbye, Laura," it pans to her in medium close-up standing in front of Mark. With a look that expresses distress, relief, and resignation at once, Laura moves offscreen toward Waldo and then, after a moment's pause during which he follows her only with his glance, Mark follows her physically out of the frame, toward Waldo. But the camera does not move with him. Instead, as the dying Waldo whispers his valediction to Laura, "Goodbye, my love," the camera maintains its former framing, focusing now on the shattered clock that became visible when Laura and Mark moved offscreen. As the camera tracks in for a closer view of this broken piece of machinery, the music of Laura's theme rises once more, and then the screen goes dark. There is nothing left but for the film to announce its conclusion with a parting shot of Laura's portrait, written over the face of which appears the apparently extra-diegetic inscription of the title card: "The End."

It would not, I think, be inaccurate to suggest that the effect and significance of both these final images is to put an end to the face, or that the image of the clock, no less than that of the portrait, demands to be read in such terms. Kristin Thompson observes that the "final tracking movement," which insists that the viewer attend to the clock,

> is the only overt authorial commentary in the film. Here a symbolic interpretation of the shattered clock seems called for. In one sense, the main object that suggested Laura's constricting links with Lydecker has now been destroyed and she is free of him. In another sense, Lydecker has tried to kill the one woman he loved and ends by shattering the emblem of their strictly intellectual relationship. The clock also parallels and stands in for the murder of Diane Redfern; there have been several references to how the shotgun blast mutilated her beyond recognition, and clearly the film could not present a literal representation of her corpse.[57]

Implicit—but *only* implicit—in these comments, especially those that read the image of the clock in relation to the violence of Diane Redfern's destruction, is the fact that the film concludes with the vision of a shattered or mutilated face; for the "authorial commentary" to which Thompson refers centers less on the "shattered clock" than it does, to be exact, on the shattered *face* of the clock. As a figure, then, of disfiguration, this image evokes not only the elided sight of Diane Redfern's effacement, but also the ultimate effacement of Waldo as performed by the film itself; it stands in metonymically, that is, for the man whose last words are heard offscreen as the camera focuses on the timepiece.[58] In this way the film's purgation or effacement of Waldo's disfiguring facelessness finds its textual inscription in the visual field through the figure of a disfigured face—a face that both is and is not a face, precisely to the extent that that "face" is a figure.

To speak of the "face" of a clock, after all, is not only to engage a rhetorical figure, it is also to invoke a classic and self-allegorizing *example* of that figure. As Paul de Man argues, "*prosopon-poiein* means to *give* a face and therefore implies that the original face can be missing or nonexistent. The trope which coins a name for a still unnamed entity, which gives face to the faceless is, of course, catachresis. That a catachresis can be a prosopopeia, in the etymological sense of 'giving face,' is clear from such ordinary instances as the *face* of a mountain," or, as we might add in this context, the face of a clock. If catachresis as such produces a face insofar as it names what is otherwise nameless, the particular catachresis that operates by mis-naming the area of the clock's dial precisely *as* its "face" allegorizes the operation of catachresis itself; indeed, by reading this use of "face" as a figure, it gestures toward the figurality of any "face"—gestures, that is, toward the dependence of all language, and hence all cognition, on what de Man has called "the starting, catachrestic decree of signification."[59] That "decree," of course, is the "active verbal deed" that the de Man of "Wordsworth and the Victorians" locates in the passage from *The Prelude* where Wordsworth's "Blessed Babe" "[c]laims manifest kindred" with his mother through a totalization that generates her face as the primal face of face itself, as the catachrestic positing of perceptual meaningfulness through an initial act of figuration. De Man's analysis suggests not only that the face, far from being literal or "natural," is always a necessarily "figural" construction, but also that catachresis, though traditionally construed as aberrant or abusive, as the very trope of "mis-naming," is actually the fundamental principle of language and thus of naming itself. I want to propose that the negotiation between what gets construed as aberrant and what gets construed as "natural" in this reading of catachresis and the positing of "face," is implicated in, and bears crucially upon, the logic through which homosexuality takes cognitive shape in the modern West and, moreover, that the conclusion of *Laura* speaks precisely to this constellation of sexual and rhetorical issues. In order to understand the relation between the final catachresis of the mutilated face in *Laura* and the film's framing of Waldo as a "faceless" (which is to say, as a sexually ambiguous) man, and thus as a man who is constitutively subject to being interpreted as homosexual, I want to remain with de Man's essay for a moment and consider how sexual issues obtrude upon its discussion of catachresis, however rigorously de Man may try to keep those issues at bay.

In unfolding an allegory of language from the "Blessed Babe" passage in *The Prelude*, de Man makes every effort to resist a psycho-sexual or thematic interpretation of the specular encounter of mother and child. Indeed, the point of the essay is that criticism of Wordsworth's poetry has suffered from persistent efforts to "domesticate it by giving it at least a recognizable content" (86). De Man's analysis, by contrast, proposes to do away with the comforting moral, philosophical, or phenomenological face by which that poetry has been (mis)recognized historically, and toward that end he examines Wordsworth's handling of the figure of face itself in order to demonstrate how his poetry deconstructs the "naturalness" of "face" by reading it in relation to what de Man describes as "the totalizing power of language" (91). Though de Man's essay, therefore, may explicitly raise the question of what he calls "the sexual taboo" (84), by which he refers to critical discussions of Wordsworth's relationship with Annette Vallon and more recent considerations of the poet's potentially incestuous fantasies concerning his sister and/or his daughter, it characterizes the critical transgression of this taboo as continuous with, and not as a deviation from, the "nineteenth-century standards with which Wordsworth is to be understood and evaluated" (84–85). Yet however much de Man may refuse the "moral and religious" (85) questions that underlie the thematic focus on such topics as the "sexual taboo," his essay returns in its own figural constructions to the very site of such erotic speculations. The passage below, for instance, follows immediately after de Man's assertion that critical discussion of the "sexual taboo" has failed to assist in the larger project of identifying and illuminating what he describes as "a certain enigmatic aspect of Wordsworth" (84):

> The place where the truly puzzling element in Wordsworth makes its presence felt can be located by ways of the somewhat irrelevant but insistent question which has shaped Wordsworth criticism for generations: is he a poet or a philosopher—or, somewhat less naively put, what is it in his work that forces upon us, for reasons that philosophy itself may not be able to master, this question of the compatibility between philosophy and poetry? Common sense tells us that poetry and philosophy are modes of discourse that should be kept distinct: to couple such power of seduction with such authority is to tempt fate itself. Hence the urge to protect, as the most pressing of moral imperatives, this borderline between both modes of discourse. (85)

Neil Hertz, carefully elaborating the implications of de Man's own figurative language, notes "that there is a whiff of the oedipal triangle in that image of the dangers readers face when confronting poetry's 'power of seduction' coupled with the 'authority' of philosophy: the danger that prompts the urge to reestablish clear demarcating lines would seem to be the threatened collapse of that triangle into a more archaic structure, at once cognitively unsettling and menacing to the integrity of the preoedipal subject."[60] I will return to Hertz's invocation of oedipal collapse and the threat of "a more archaic structure," but I want to pause for a moment on the phrase with which de Man locates the source of this danger: "to couple such power of seduction with such authority," he writes, "is to tempt fate itself."

Within the context of the sexist and heterosexist logic that determines the cultural associations and connotative valences of language, the "power of seduction" here registers as female while the concept of "authority" retains its historically privileged relation to the male. The "coupl[ing]" of these attributes, therefore, seems to posit their union in the heterosexual terms that would generate Hertz's "oedipal triangle." But according to the logic that de Man reads without necessarily endorsing, the coupling at issue here is dangerous because it is *counter*-intuitive; in fact, as de Man makes clear, "common sense" insists that these two "modes of discourse . . . should be kept distinct" precisely insofar as this coupling does *not* invoke a union that is neatly heterosexual, a union that works to reinforce the clearly drawn lines of sexual differentiation, but invokes instead a union that erases or effaces sexual difference as known by "common sense," a union that produces an epistemological ambiguity such as that informing the cultural construction of homosexuality. The coupling at issue here, that is, takes place *within* not *between*; it is a coupling like that made visible in *Laura* through the momentary superimposition of Laura's face on Waldo's in the heavily loaded context of his dinner with Mark at Montagnino's—a superimposition that gives face to the destabilizing facelessness of a homosexuality whose "danger" resides precisely in its ability to couple Waldo's authority with Laura's power of seduction, and thereby to produce such consequences (for the heterosexual male) as those presented to the viewer in the spectacle of Mark's disappropriation of identity.

In this way *Laura* enacts what Hertz calls the "threatened collapse of [the oedipal] triangle into a more archaic structure," a structure, to be exact, of erotic identification older than the law of sexual difference elaborated out of castration. The "collapse" that is both embodied in and disseminated by Waldo, the "collapse" broadly associated in modern Western culture with male homosexuality itself, can be construed as the collapse of heterosexual masculinity (which is to say, in societal terms, masculinity as such) back into the "archaic structure" of an all-encompassing—indeed, a primal—identification with the fantasmatic phallic mother. Seen from such a perspective, heterosexual masculinity takes shape as an imaginary totalization that is, like the Lacanian ego, structurally paranoid insofar as it articulates itself out of and against the abyssal facelessness of its own "original" participation in the undifferentiated libidinal experience of preoedipal sexuality—a preoedipal sexuality that is, in retrospect, decisively associated with the mother. Expressions of gay male sexual desire thus tend to signify within this context as a form of "failure" or "weakness"[61] to the extent that they register as a falling *away* from the always endangered "integrity" of maleness as culturally construed, and thus as a falling *back* into that dreaded but seductive, maternally identified preoedipal eros from which, on the one hand, heterosexual masculinity is imagined to have emerged, and against which, as an absolute alterity, it needs, on the other hand, to define itself. At least in part, then, this need to repudiate the instability of preoedipal erotic positioning may explain why the coupling of seduction with authority produces, in de Man's formulation, a more dangerously potent—and hence unacceptable—female-coded capacity for seduction; to effect such a coupling, after all, is "to tempt fate," as de Man announces, an act of temptation that reinforces and repositions the original "power of seduction."[62]

As contextualized in de Man's essay, of course, the "power of seduction" designates a specific property of poetry while "authority" pertains to the discourse of philosophy as it is hypostatized in our culture; but the relation in his essay between these two modes of discourse keeps coming back to the question of the body.[63] So when de Man calls attention to "face" as "another key word in the corpus of *The Prelude*" (89), or when he argues that "words such as 'face' can be said to embody" (92) an incompatibility between their meaning and their function, the body of writing and the writing of the body remain locked in what we might, for strategic reasons, choose to call an embrace—an embrace like that wherein "the Babe" is seen to be "nurs'd in his Mother's arms." For in this light the passage from Wordsworth on which de Man focuses his attention seems relevant as much for its "recognizable content" as for its meta-figural meditations on the (seductive and authoritative) attributes of language. This is the burden of Hertz's persuasive reading of de Man, and I would call particular attention to the following passage from Hertz's discussion:

> In privileged texts like the "Blessed Babe" lines in *The Prelude*, or in phrases like that describing the merging of poetry and philosophy into a daunting combination of seduction and authority, [de Man] would seem to be attending to narcissistic or "borderline" structures of the sort Julia Kristeva has recently explored, structures that play out the earliest exchanges between infant and mother. Hence the pathos of the familial, when it appears in de Man's writing, is often concerned with the maternal. (88)

More specifically, as Hertz proceeds to show, de Man's musings on the maternal call forth "a fantasmatic subject, ambivalently active and passive, guilty and innocent, murderous and/or bereft" (89), who haunts even his vision of the deconstructive relation between linguistic positing and linguistic meaning: "How are we to reconcile the *meaning* of face, with its promise of sense and of filial preservation," de Man wonders, "with its *function* as the relentless undoer of its own claims?"[64] Speaking to the "surfacing" in this question of a pathos suppressed in de Man's reading of the "Blessed Babe" passage, Hertz observes that such a pathos "returns here as another specular pairing, mother and child, but equivocally charged. It can be read as an attempt to align 'meaning' with the mother's preserving (read: sheltering) tenderness, 'function' with the child's aggressive (read: both positing and undoing) 'claims.' But the ambiguity of 'filial preservation'—the child could be taken as either the beneficiary or the agent of that saving act of sense making—keeps the sentence from stabilizing itself in any clear-cut fashion" (99).

Now the model for such a stabilization that depends upon a logic of the "clear-cut" might be found in the project of castration, the project, that is, of the sexual narrative through which the fiction of castration effects the self-constitution of the (heterosexual) male. The "ambiguity" condensed in the deployment of de Man's phrase, "filial preservation," by contrast, speaks to the uncertainty or instability of positioning against which the "clear-cut" either/or logic of castration is produced in the first place. It speaks, in other words, to the indeterminacy that precedes male oedipalization, and hence to the inextricability of the preoedipal infant's identity and libidinal desires from those of the fantasmatic mother who embodies for him the coupling of seduction and authority. The logic of castration thus unfolds as a catachrestic mechanism for the "saving act of sense making" whereby "filial preservation" ceases to be ambiguous (or, as we might prefer to say, faceless) and registers, instead, as a decisive act of filial *self*-preservation, an act through which the child becomes the agent of his own disentanglement from the embrace of the mother, and thus of his disentanglement from the identity of the mother, through a rhetorical claim in which he willfully produces the face of (heterosexual) maleness as a symbolic—that is, as a culturally negotiable and therefore "authentic"—structure, rather than as an imaginary or specular construct like those that will be associated subsequently with the mother and, by extension, with femaleness itself. Considered in this light, heterosexual masculinity can be viewed as a *prosopon-poiein* in the de Manian sense of a willful "giving" of face, one predicated on, but directed against, the initial catachrestic face-making gesture wherein, according to de Man's reading of Wordsworth, the infant "[c]laims manifest kindred" with its figural totalization of the mother's face. Or to put this last point another way, the heterosexual male face as elaborated out of the narrative of castration—and posited therefore as a "clear-cut," positive presence in relation to which the female becomes the clearly "cut" or negative counterpart—functions to refuse or efface the recognition that the act of face-making whereby it differentiates its own face from the mother's must always, despite its own best efforts, refer nonetheless to the mother's as the very template or paradigm of face; it serves to deny that identity and totalization always come back to the mother, always wear her face, as it were, making the face of heterosexual maleness at best but a catachresis of the initial catachrestic act whereby the mother's face took shape. One could rewrite more narrowly, therefore, de Man's question about the deconstructive implications of the meaning and function of the figure of face by asking "how are we to reconcile the *meaning* of [the heterosexual male's assertion of a determinate, authentic, and hence a non-figural] face, with its promise of sense [that can be founded on the determinacy of "clear-cut" oppositions] and [thus with its promise of] filial [self-]preservation [in its struggle against subsumption within the mother's seductive authority], with its *function* as the relentless undoer of its own claims [insofar as this "face" is only a figure for the totality of a self whose "self"-identity derives from its identification with the totalization of the mother's face as produced through catachresis]?" The unbearable implication for heterosexual masculinity of so denaturalizing a reading of face is that maleness as such finally *has* no face, *can have* no face, that is not a mere figural repositioning of the preoedipal mother's always already figurally constructed face.

If the face of male heterosexuality thus engendered by means of the castration complex must constitutively misrecognize its status as a mask, as an inessential fiction, in order to disavow its indeterminacy or facelessness, if it must posit itself through the denial that its own self-identity is a catachrestic decree attempting to obscure its identification with the (m)other who always stands in the place of identity itself, this constitutively defensive masculinity can be expected to project the intolerable image of the faceless, specularly fixated, and mother-identified male onto a specific category of person against whom it then can define and defend itself. To say this, however, is to say that such facelessness must first be given face to *as facelessness* in order to preserve the integrity and bounded totality of the straight male face; hence the gay man must not only be posited, but must be construed simultaneously as *lacking* a distinctive face and as being *susceptible to recognition*, to visual determination, despite this lack. This double imperative propels the enterprise I have defined as homographesis, and it articulates the gay male body in constitutive relation to writing or inscription as a mark of the differential relation whereby that culturally constructed body is linked to the specularity and indeterminacy of a maternally identified preoedipal eroticism. The gay male body, in other words, must be *marked and indeterminate at once*; consequently, it is imagined to be marked *as* indeterminate with the result that indeterminacy effectively ceases to *be* indeterminate and becomes, instead, the gay male body's determinate mark.

If it is possible for us to read this critical moment in the imagination of heterosexual masculinity—a moment in every way *determining*—as a reenactment of the very specularity it so phobically undertakes to project, this projection nonetheless attempts to position heterosexual masculinity outside the differential economy associated with what we might see as a generalized writing: outside, that is, the endless displacements and self-contradictory identifications that the empire of castration defines as—or better, *decrees to be*—its absolute other in a gesture that mirrors, but reverses and undoes, the decree whereby the boundedness or fixity of identity was initially linked to the mother through the catachresis of her face. Because the compelling seductiveness of her authority as the figure of identity, however, problematized the integrity of any identity in relation to hers, castration turns the catachresis of face-making (as the clear-cut determination of boundaries in the service of totalization) against the mother whose face and body first acquired conceptual coherence by means of that very rhetorical figure, thereby generating the concept of conceptual coherence as figured by face. In order to affirm castration's catachrestic "decree of signification," however, heterosexual maleness must forget, deny, or efface its catachrestic structure, investing itself, instead, with the naturalness, the inevitability, the authority of origin and identity that castration as a cultural narrative works to define and secure.[65] Read, then, as the embodiment of the heterosexual male's repudiated indeterminacy of erotic positioning and thus of his uncertain identity, read, in other words, as the projection of (male hetero)sexuality's literariness or figurality, the gay man is both *necessary* to confirm the "integrity" of the face of male heterosexuality and *intolerable* insofar as his presence is a reminder of the fictionality of that face. It is, in other words, precisely as a threat to the authenticity or literality of the heterosexual male face—the face that he is made culturally visible in order to guarantee—that the gay man, like Waldo in *Laura*, must be produced so as to undergo effacement himself.

I want to conclude by unfolding some of the specific implications this has for systems of representation, and I want to do so by looking once more at the invocation of Waldo through the catachrestic image of the clock's shattered face. If this image collapses cause and effect, if one of the many ways it gestures toward Waldo is by reference to his mutilation of Diane Redfern's face, it is crucial to note that this figuration of Waldo serves, simultaneously, as a figure for the machinery of the cinema itself. When the camera tracks in as if magnetized by the sight of this disarticulated face, as if enthralled by the clock to the exclusion of the death scene being enacted just offscreen, it approaches, in a sense, its own specular image, a displaced vision of the enabling facelessness of the camera as synecdoche for the materiality, the mechanical "body" of cinematic representation. As Roland Barthes suggestively observes, "at first photographic implements were related to techniques of cabinetmaking and the machinery of precision: cameras, in short, were clocks for seeing."[66] *Laura* underscores this connection through its visual configuration of the clock's broken face; in close-up the lens-like dial of the timepiece now opens onto the internal workings of the clock that spill out in a profusion of what looks uncannily like strips of celluloid film (Figure 7).

The clock that figures the camera, however, figures Waldo as well; we can say, therefore, that with this image the film *recognizes* Waldo, recognizes that its own elided mechanisms of visual representation come back to the problematic of face and facelessness that Waldo himself embodies. Indeed, if the film, as I suggested earlier, resurrects Laura so it can efface Waldo by positing hers as the face with which it substitutively figures its own representational practice, its persistent thematization of splitting and projection suggests that the viewer must take into account the anxiogenic identity of, or continuity between, Waldo and the filmic system that compels the film to disavow him. Like Waldo, after all, the camera, at least in the classic Hollywood cinema, is a machine for "shooting" faces. And just as the film disavows its continuity with Waldo, so the photographic medium that underpins the production of

FIGURE 7.

the cinematic shot undergoes systematic misrecognition and disavowal in *Laura*; for the film ideologically aligns itself with painting over and against the appropriative violence it identifies with photography, a medium that it interprets in terms of a de-idealizing mutilation. Ironically, while Waldo expresses the film's opposition to photography through his objections to the photographs of (what he believes to have been) Laura's disfiguration, he himself, as the author of that disfiguration, is positioned as the *agent* of "photography," where "photography" emerges specifically as a form of *writing*. He functions, in other words, as the mechanism by which the aesthetic image is disfigured by being deprived of a "natural" face. And if, as Roland Barthes has written, "photography is essentially (a contradiction in terms) only contingency,"[67] then photography is another form of the irony or facelessness that Waldo's literariness, his figurality, and his homosexuality always already connote. The photographic shot can be said, therefore, to disfigure or denaturalize the face precisely to the extent that it inscribes it in the realm of contingency or figuration.

Laura, however, distancing itself from the merely photographic, envisions the idealized portrait as its imaginary double. In part this self-presentation responds to the anxious aesthetic politics of film as a cultural practice in America. Identifying itself with the painting, the film seeks to appropriate the cachet of "art" for a medium conceived as popular entertainment.[68] The film, however, limits the brow-level of the "art" to which it aspires. If it hopes to exert the appeal of the portrait, it wants, nonetheless, to distinguish itself from the elitist aesthetic embraced by Waldo and depicted as sterile sophistication. The film, in fact, is sophisticated enough to play off the portrait, as the externalized figure of its own imaginary aesthetic face, against Waldo's more insistent and ostentatious aesthetic sophistication; the portrait, after all, exercises its fascination on the detective, not on the aesthete. Waldo, in fact, observes that Jacoby, the painter of the portrait, "was in love with [Laura] when he painted it, but he never captured her vibrance, her warmth." Indeed, in the column that he recalls having written to undermine Laura's attraction to Jacoby, Waldo "demolished [Jacoby's] affectations, exposed his camouflaged imitations of better painters." The film identifies itself, then, as a medium that achieves the individuality, the uniqueness, of "art"—as opposed to photography, which remains contingent in its mechanical reproducibility—while emphasizing that the art to which it aspires is aimed directly at the middle class, or at those who cathect the (homophobically) circumscribed "sophistication" that a certain version of the middle class can represent.[69]

In large part the film's repudiation of photography and its self-(mis)-identification derive from its perception of photography as the ghost that haunts the cinematic machine: photography, as the enabling but repressed technology at the origin of the moving picture, calls forth the stasis and fixity of death while cinema insists on its fidelity to life by bestowing motion, vitality, animation on the photographic still.[70] Where the photograph testifies always to absence, the classic Hollywood cinema strives for the illusion of fullness and presence, which mandates, above all, the strategic effacement of the cinematographic apparatus through which that illusion is produced. One could follow, then, the logic of *Laura*'s identification of Waldo with photography by noting his ideological positioning, as a gay man, outside the domestic siting of heterosexuality as a reproductive, or animating, institution. Thus her association with Waldo keeps Laura from marriage and the (pro)creation of a family since Waldo perceives every man who might offer her marriage as a threat, resorting to murderous disfiguration when he thinks that Laura's wedding to Shelby Carpenter is inevitable. I prefer, however, to read the film's reading of Waldo in relation to photography, and therefore in disturbing relation to the cinematic medium itself, in terms of the self-implicating irony that Waldo embodies both *in* and *for* the film.

Like the camera in the economy of classic narrative cinema, Waldo's homosexuality is the unacknowledged lens, the structurally determining but repressed machinery, that makes possible the representational system of male heterosexuality. And like the camera to which we must catachrestically give face so as to efface more effectively its status as machine (reenacting thereby what de Man defines as the paradigm of linguistic positing by producing the camera's "subjectivity" as a totalization of the rhetorical fiction that permits us to construe it in the first place as an "eye"), so the homosexuality that Waldo embodies must be given face to as the embodiment of an otherwise faceless machinery, a machinery as disturbing, destabilizing, and invisible as irony within the fictive "transparency" of discourse. By producing the face of the facelessness against which it constructs its own identity, heterosexual masculinity can deny, on behalf of its own alleged authenticity, the merely mechanistic status of sexuality as such. The gay male body, in other words, thus finds itself installed in the place of the representational apparatus within a regime of naturalism: the place of non-closure, the point of impossibility, the system's "other face," to which Jacqueline Rose refers in the epigraph with which this essay began. When the camera closes in on the clock's shattered face in the final moments of *Laura*, therefore, it acknowledges a displaced reflection of itself that marks its own non-identity, thus signaling a final reflection upon the disfiguring force of figuration with which Waldo, as the figure of figurality, has been identified throughout the film. Approaching the clock as its non-identical twin, as the projection of its own machinery, the camera is condemned to frame even this close-up image of the shattering of face *as a face*, for as Gilles Deleuze observes in his taxonomy of cinematic images, "as for the face itself, we will not say that the close-up deals with it or subjects it to some kind of treatment: there is no close-up *of* the face, the face is in itself close-up, the close-up is by itself face."[71] The face that this culminating close-up presents, then, is the non-"face" of cinema's apparatus, a non-"face" that must remain as visibly invisible as the non-"face" of gay male sexuality. Both, after all, have the capacity to expose the "natural" face as a figure, and the wounding force of that disfiguration is what the institution of heterosexual masculinity as such is constitutively unable to face: for to face such a notion is to lose its own face and to acknowledge that heterosexual masculinity, like its cinema, is a machinery of projection that endlessly seeks to integrate itself in a clear-cut system of definitions by violently casting out specularity in a resolutely specular gesture that is helpless to do more than endlessly enact the impossibility of ever defining its own impossible identity.

Notes

Preface

1. Quoted in Andrew Rosenthal, "Quayle Attacks a 'Cultural Elite' in Speech Invoking Moral Values," *New York Times*, June 10, 1992, p. 1; "Deconstruction Derby," *New York Native*, June 15, 1992, p. 14. The *Native* appears on newsstands prior to the publication date.

1. Homographesis

This essay is a significantly revised version of a lecture presented at a conference, "Lesbian/Gay Studies '87: Definitions and Explorations," sponsored by the Center for Lesbian and Gay Studies at Yale and by the Whitney Humanities Center. I would like to thank all those who helped organize the conference for making possible a valuable and impressive exchange of ideas; in particular I would like to thank Professor Ralph Hexter for inviting me to participate in it.

1. "The Supreme Court Opinion: Michael J. Bowers, Attorney General of Georgia, Petition v. Michael Hardwick and John and Mary Doe, Respondents," *New York Native*, July 14, 1986, 13.

2. Sir William Blackstone, *Commentaries on the Laws of England*, ed. James DeWitt Andrews, vol. 2 (Chicago: 1899), 4:1377.

3. Sir Leon Radzinowicz, *A History of the English Criminal Law*, vol. 4, *Grappling for Control* (London: Stevens and Sons, 1968), 316.

4. John Cleland, *Memoirs of a Woman of Pleasure*, ed. Peter Sabor (New York: Oxford University Press, 1985), 159.

5. Cited in Jeffrey Weeks, "The Construction of Homosexuality," *Sex, Politics and Society: The Regulation of Sexuality Since 1800* (New York: Longman, 1981), 111.

6. Oscar Wilde and Others, *Teleny*, ed. John McRae (London: GMP, 1986), 134.

7. Cited in Weeks, "The Construction of Homosexuality," 100.

8. Marcel Proust, *Remembrance of Things Past*, vol. 2, *Cities of the Plain*, trans. C. K. Scott Moncrieff and Terence Kilmartin (New York: Random House, 1981), 636. The original reads, "sur la surface unie de l'individu pareil aux autres sont venus apparaître, tracés en une encre jusque-là invisible, les caractères qui composent le mot cher aux anciens Grecs." *A la recherche du temps perdu*, vol. 2 (Paris: Pléiade, 1954), 613–614.

9. James Baldwin, *Another Country* (New York: Dell, 1988), 170.

10. Alan Bray, *Homosexuality in Renaissance England* (London: GMP, 1982), 92. Randolph Trumbach, following the lead of Mary McIntosh, has also come to a similar conclusion: "I would now agree with Mary McIntosh that a profound shift occurred in the conceptualization

and practice of male homosexual behavior in the late seventeenth and early eighteenth centuries. It was a shift caused by the reorganization of gender identity that was occurring as part of the emergence of a modern Western culture" ("Sodomitical Subcultures, Sodomitical Roles, and the Gender Revolution of the Eighteenth Century: The Recent Historiography," *'Tis Nature's Fault: Unauthorized Sexual Behavior During the Enlightenment*, ed. Robert Maccubbin [New York: Cambridge University Press, 1988], 118).

11. Eve Kosofsky Sedgwick, "The Epistemology of the Closet (I)," *Raritan*, 7:4 (Spring 1988): 55. This essay has been revised and reprinted in Sedgwick's *Epistemology of the Closet* (Berkeley and Los Angeles: University of California Press, 1990). For an earlier working out of this argument, see her ground-breaking study *Between Men: English Literature and Male Homosocial Desire* (New York: Columbia University Press, 1985).

12. Eve Kosofsky Sedgwick, "Comments on Swann," *Berkshire Review*, 21 (1986): 107.

13. Michel Foucault, *The History of Sexuality*, vol. 1, *An Introduction*, trans. Robert Hurley (New York: Vintage, 1980), 43.

14. Cf. Jacques Lacan, "Sexuality in the Defiles of the Signifier," *The Four Fundamental Concepts of Psychoanalysis*, ed. Jacques-Alain Miller, trans. Alan Sheridan (New York: Norton, 1981), pp. 149–160, esp. p. 154.

15. Cited in Jane Gallop, *Reading Lacan* (Ithaca: Cornell University Press, 1985), 124. We can reinterpret Lacan's words to suggest that metaphor imposes meaning upon a prior metonymic relationship that can only be *recognized* as meaningful by virtue of its being read as metaphorical. This pattern, of course, will recall the process of deferred or retroactive meaning that Freud sees as crucially operative in the constitution of sexuality itself. Jean Laplanche articulates the intimate connection between sexuality and deferred meaning as follows: "*Why sexuality?* Freud's answer is that sexuality alone is available for that action in two phases which is also an action 'after the event.' It is there and there alone that we find that complex and endlessly repeated interplay—midst a temporal succession of missed occasions—of 'too early' and 'too late'" (Jean Laplanche, *Life and Death in Psychoanalysis*, trans. Jeffrey Mehlman [Baltimore: The Johns Hopkins University Press, 1976], 43). What follows in this essay will, I hope, give retroactive significance to this notion of retroactive meaning. Note for now Lacan's formulation: "The legibility of sex in the interpretation of the unconscious mechanisms is always retroactive" (Jacques Lacan, "The Partial Drive and Its Circuit," *The Four Fundamental Concepts of Psychoanalysis*, 176).

16. Arno Karlen, *Sexuality and Homosexuality: A New View* (New York: Norton, 1971), 185.

17. This essay focuses exclusively on issues of male homosexuality not because the issues of lesbian inscription are not of interest or do not warrant attention, but because the issues involved are, in my opinion, very differently constituted. Although lesbianism, when it finally achieves a public articulation, comes to be read in terms of male homosexuality, that reading is itself a masculinist appropriation of a relationship with a distinct history and sociology. While lesbians and gay men often have been, and for the most part remain, allies in struggling for their civil rights, the fact of their common participation in same-sex relationships should not obscure the differences of experience that result from the differences in their social positioning within a culture that divides human beings into separate categories of male and female.

18. Marie-Rose Logan, "Graphesis . . . ," *Graphesis: Perspectives in Literature and Philosophy, Yale French Studies*, 52 (1975): 12.

19. See Jacques Derrida's discussion of writing in "Ellipsis": "As soon as a sign emerges, it begins by repeating itself. Without this, it would not be a sign, would not be what it is, that is to say, the non-self-identity which regularly refers to the same. That is to say, to another sign,

which itself will be born of having been divided. The grapheme, repeating itself in this fashion, thus has neither natural site nor natural center" ("Ellipsis," *Writing and Difference*, trans. Alan Bass [Chicago: University of Chicago Press, 1978], 297).

20. See Randolph Trumbach, "London's Sodomites: Homosexual Behavior and Western Culture in the Eighteenth Century," *Journal of Social History*, 11:1 (Fall 1977): 1–33.

21. See Trumbach, "Sodomitical Subcultures," esp. 117. See also the description by Ned Ward (1709) of the behavior of homosexual men gathered together in the molly houses: "They fancy themselves women, . . . affecting to speak, walk, tattle, curtsy, cry, scold and mimick all manner of effeminacy" (cited in Trumbach, "London's Sodomites," 12–13). Cleland, in *Memoirs of a Woman of Pleasure*, has Mrs. Cole remark of sodomites that "they were scarce less execrable than ridiculous in their monstrous inconsistency, of loathing and contemning women, and all at the same time, apeing their manners, airs, lisp, skuttle, and, in general, all their little modes of affectation, which become them at least better, than they do these unsex'd male-misses" (160). This insistence on monstrosity, inconsistency, and parodic substitution should recall the traditional arguments against writing that Derrida traces in *On Grammatology*: "The inversion of the natural relationships would thus have engendered the perverse cult of the letter-image: sin of idolatry, 'superstition of the letter' Saussure says in the *Anagrams* where he has difficulty in proving the existence of a 'phoneme anterior to all writing.' The perversion of artifice engenders monsters. Writing, like all artificial languages one would wish to fix and remove from the living history of natural language, participates in the monstrosity" (Jacques Derrida, *Of Grammatology*, trans. Gayatri Chakravorty Spivak [Baltimore: The Johns Hopkins University Press, 1976], 38).

22. Trumbach, "Sodomitical Subcultures," 119.

23. Trumbach, "Sodomitical Subcultures," 118.

24. See, for instance, Paul de Man's observation that "the inference of identity and totality . . . is constitutive of metaphor." In "Semiology and Rhetoric," *Allegories of Reading: Figural Language in Rousseau, Nietzsche, Rilke, and Proust* (New Haven: Yale University Press, 1979), 14.

25. Oscar Wilde, *The Picture of Dorian Gray* (New York: Oxford University Press, 1987), 18. All subsequent citations will be to this edition and will be indicated in the text.

26. Ed Cohen, "Writing Gone Wilde: Homoerotic Desire in the Closet of Representation," *PMLA*, 102 (October 1987): 808.

27. Cohen, "Writing Gone Wilde," 806.

28. Cohen, "Writing Gone Wilde," 808.

29. At this point one might want to think about Freud's discussions of the development of the ego—especially as they are reformulated by Jean Laplanche in *Life and Death in Psychoanalysis*. As Laplanche implies, the ego is an organization that reads its own metonymic relation to the living organism in metaphorical terms so that it comes to name not only the part, but the whole, through that act of misrecognition.

30. *The Three Trials of Oscar Wilde*, ed. H. Montgomery Hyde (New York: University Books, 1956), 131.

31. *The Three Trials*, 132. It is worth noting that the difference metaphorically appropriated as identity by Dorian when he "recognizes" himself in the painting is informed by that of the artist, Hallward, whose own sexual identity is inscribed in the work of art. *Dorian Gray*, in this respect, articulates the circulation of homosexual desire in relation to the notion of "influence." Significantly, that notion also played an important role in Wilde's trials. Denying that the passage cited earlier in the text suggests "unnatural vice," Wilde declared that it "describes Dorian as a man of very corrupt influence, though there is no statement as to the

nature of the influence." Moments later, denying that a man could ever corrupt a youth, Wilde asserted, "I do not think one person influences another" (132). But when Wilde himself was put on trial, Alfred Wood testified against him, insisting that Wilde and he "went up to a bedroom where [they] had hock and selzer. Here an act of the grossest indecency occurred. Mr. Wilde used his influence to induce me to consent" (202).

32. Proust, *Cities of the Plain*, 635. The original reads: "Dès le début de cette scène, une révolution, pour mes yeux dessillés, s'était opérée en M. de Charlus, aussi complète, aussi immédiate que s'il avait été touché par une baguette magique. Jusque-là, parce que je n'avais pas compris, je n'avais pas vu" (613).

33. Proust, *Cities of the Plain*, 637. The original reads: "En M. de Charlus un autre être avait beau s'accoupler, qui le différenciait des autres hommes, comme dans le centaure le cheval, cet être avait beau faire corps avec le baron, je ne l'avais jamais aperçu. Maintenant l'abstrait s'était matérialisé, l'être enfin compris avait aussitôt perdu son pouvoir de rester invisible, et la transmutation de M. de Charlus en une personne nouvelle était si complète que non seulement les contrastes de son visage, de sa voix, mais rétrospectivement les hauts et les bas eux-mêmes de ses relations avec moi, tout ce qui avait paru jusque-là incohérent à mon esprit, devenait intelligible, se montrait évident, comme une phrase, n'offrant aucun sens tant qu'elle reste décomposée en lettres disposées au hasard, exprime, si les caractères se trouvent replacés dans l'ordre qu'il faut, une pensée que l'on ne pourra plus oublier" (614).

34. De Man, "Semiology and Rhetoric," 5.

35. De Man, "Semiology and Rhetoric," 5.

36. Barbara Johnson, *A World of Difference* (Baltimore: The Johns Hopkins University Press, 1987), 12.

37. Gallop, *Reading Lacan*, 132.

38. For a fuller analysis of this issue, see Chapter Five, "The Mirror and the Tank: 'AIDS,' Subjectivity, and the Rhetoric of Activism."

2. Redeeming the Phallus

This essay is a revised and expanded version of a lecture originally presented at a conference on "Pedagogy and Politics" sponsored in 1988 by the Center for Lesbian and Gay Studies at Yale. I would like to thank Wayne Koestenbaum for inviting me to participate on the panel discussing "Gay/Lesbian Literary Theory."

1. Llewelyn Powys, "The Thirteenth Way," *Dial*, July 1924; reprinted in *Wallace Stevens: The Critical Heritage*, ed. Charles Doyle (Boston: Routledge and Kegan Paul, 1985), 64.

2. Raymond Larsson, "The Beau as Poet," *Commonweal*, April 6, 1932; reprinted in *Wallace Stevens: The Critical Heritage*, 94.

3. *Letters of Wallace Stevens*, ed. Holly Stevens (New York: Knopf, 1977), 287.

4. William Empson, *Listener*, March 26, 1953; reprinted in *Wallace Stevens: The Critical Heritage*, 377.

5. Frank Lentricchia, "Frank Lentricchia," in Imre Salusinszky, *Criticism in Society* (New York: Methuen, 1987), 183.

6. In the final chapter of her pioneering study, *Between Men*, Eve Kosofsky Sedgwick discusses the fate of publicly identifiable representations of gayness in England and America in the aftermath of the Wilde trials; she notes that "the durable stereotype that came to prevail has been close to Symonds only as Symonds resembled Wilde: a connoisseur, an interpreter of aristocratic culture to the middle class, a socialist insofar as socialism would simply expand

the venue of leisure, privilege, and high culture" (*Between Men: English Literature and Male Homosocial Desire* [New York: Columbia University Press, 1985], 217).

7. Offering a revision of Toril Moi's critique of feminist essentialism, Lentricchia asserts that "patriarchal oppression also consists of imposing certain social standards of masculinity on all biological men, in order precisely to make us believe that the chosen standards for masculinity are *natural.*" Or, as he rephrases this a few sentences later: "the ancient social process called 'patriarchy' consists also in the oppression of patriarchs" ("Patriarchy Against Itself—The Young Manhood of Wallace Stevens," *Critical Inquiry*, 13 [1987]: 774. All future references to this essay will be given parenthetically in the text).

8. Donald Pease, "Patriarchy, Lentricchia, and Male Feminization," *Critical Inquiry*, 14 (1988): 379.

9. Pease, "Patriarchy," 379.

10. This is immediately striking at the outset of Lentricchia's essay when, quoting from *The Hite Report on Male Sexuality*, he notes the anger of men's responses when asked "How would you feel if something about you were described as feminine or womanly" (742). Surveying the comments (e.g., "Enraged. Insulted. Never mind what women are really like—I know what he's saying: he's saying I should be submissive to him"), Lentricchia concludes that "our relations with women are problematic, those with ourselves something worse" (743). What he leaves out of consideration completely is the historically specific overlaying of the question of sexuality and the question of gender in modern Western cultures. He ignores, that is, the way in which the issue of sexuality has been ideologically constructed upon a naturalized gender binarism that not only allows but, implicitly, requires that the image of a "womanly" or "feminine" man be interpreted within the field of associations that radiate from the culturally endorsed interpretation of male homosexuality.

11. Sedgwick, *Between Men*, 88–89.

12. In *Love and Death in the American Novel* (New York: Dell Publishing, 1966) where he describes the tradition of male-male bonds, Fiedler comments tellingly on his own movement from the use of the word "homosexual" to the use of the word "homoerotic": "'Homoerotic' is a word of which I was never very fond, and which I like even less now. But I wanted it to be quite clear that I was not attributing sodomy to certain literary characters or their authors, and so I avoided when I could the even more disturbing word 'homosexual'" (349).

Gilbert and Gubar, in their response to Lentricchia ("The Man on the Dump versus the United Dames of America; or, What Does Frank Lentricchia Want?," *Critical Inquiry*, 14 [1988]: 386–406), see him as reiterating claims made not only by Fiedler, but by "Henry Nash Smith, Alfred Habegger, and Nina Baym" (390) as well. It may be significant that Habegger's book, *Gender, Fantasy, and Realism in American Literature* (New York: Columbia University Press, 1982), is filled with offensively heterosexist assumptions about normal and healthy sexual development, and Nina Baym's essay, "Melodramas of Beset Manhood: How Theories of American Fiction Exclude Women Authors" (in *The New Feminist Criticism*, ed. Elaine Showalter [New York: Pantheon, 1985]), articulates its often perceptive remarks about the fate of female authorship in American literary history side by side with expressions of unselfconscious homophobia (e.g., "One should add that, for a homosexual male, the demands of society that he link himself for life to a woman make for a particularly misogynist version of this aspect of the American myth, for the hero is propelled not by a rejected attraction but by true revulsion" [73]).

13. Luce Irigaray, "Women on the Market," *This Sex Which Is Not One*, trans. Catharine Porter with Carolyn Burke (Ithaca: Cornell University Press, 1985), 171.

14. Irigaray, "Women on the Market," 172.

15. Henry Louis Gates, Jr., "Significant Others," *Contemporary Literature*, 29 (1988): 613.

16. Gilbert and Gubar make a similar point when they link the logic of Lentricchia's essay to the processes of cultural masculinization that it anatomizes. They describe Lentricchia, like Lentricchia's Stevens, as undertaking "virilization-as-defense" ("The Man on the Dump versus the United Dames of America," 406).

17. If academic life in general, and academic work in the humanities in particular, is "feminized" by the culture at large, within the humanities a micro-sociology prevails wherein "theory" generally is seen as having the effect of "masculinizing" a field, that is, of adding substance and weightiness to it—making it less "humanistic" and more like a (respectably masculine) science. Thus the prestige of feminist theory among some male academics is enhanced, ironically, by the extent to which its theoretical purchase assimilates it to a culturally coded masculinity. And, given the inevitable recapitulation of larger cultural patterns within the academic world, critical theory that focuses on issues of economics and materiality acquires an even greater force of "masculine" association.

18. Frank Lentricchia, "Andiamo!," *Critical Inquiry*, 14 (1988): 411.

19. Cited by Gilbert and Gubar, "The Man on the Dump versus the United Dames of America," 386.

20. Lentricchia, "Andiamo!," 407.

21. Gilbert and Gubar, "The Man on the Dump versus the United Dames of America," 404. The "infamous photograph" is reprinted in Lentricchia's response. It is paired there, however, with another picture (subsequently used as the jacket photograph for *Ariel and the Police*) taken "later that same day" ("Andiamo!," 409) in which a kinder, gentler Lentricchia smiles engagingly from behind an array of candles, candlesticks, and wine bottles. If the earlier picture, in isolation, seemed to represent him, in Maureen Corrigan's words, as the "Dirty Harry of contemporary critical theory" (cited in Gilbert and Gubar, "Man on the Dump," 404), the subsequent pictures together could be seen to represent him as a sort of one-man Cagney and Lacey in their good cop/bad cop mode.

22. Lentricchia, "Andiamo!," 411.

23. Lentricchia, "Andiamo!," 412.

24. "Life on a Battleship" (1939) was first published in *Parts of a World* but excluded, at Stevens's request, from his *Collected Poems* (1954). The text from which I will be quoting appears in *Opus Posthumous*, ed. Samuel French Morse (New York: Random House, 1957), 77–81. All subsequent references will be to this edition and the line numbers will be given in parentheses.

25. Harold Bloom, *Wallace Stevens: The Poems of Our Climate* (Ithaca: Cornell University Press, 1977), 177.

26. Joseph Riddel, *The Clairvoyant Eye: The Poetry and Poetics of Wallace Stevens* (Baton Rouge: Louisiana State University Press, 1965), 160.

27. On November 5, 1936, Stevens wrote a letter to Ronald Lane Latimer in which he declared, "I don't believe in Communism; I do believe in up-to-date capitalism." Later in the same letter he goes on to insist that "Whether or not all men are enemies, all egotisms are voluntarily antipathetic" (*Letters of Wallace Stevens*, 292).

28. Sedgwick, *Between Men*, 14.

29. I have no quarrel with the usefulness of "homosociality" as a category through which to consider the range of male-male relations. Sedgwick, in *Between Men*, does an exemplary job of articulating the extent to which that category can help to disentangle the homosexual from

the homophobic. What I mean to suggest here, however, is that homosociality, as a signifier, can have the effect of insulating the category of heterosexuality from ideological scrutiny. Not that homosociality is necessarily located outside of the realm of the heterosexual, but *as a signifier* its prefix allows it to be inscribed in the realm of that which is already identified with the homosexual—that is to say, in the realm that Irigaray would read as the "hom(m)o-sexual." Yet what is at issue in my remarks is precisely the extent to which the processes in question are characteristic of that which defines itself as heterosexual. I should add that I do not intend, by this discussion, to privilege or reify the opposition homosexual/heterosexual as in any way possessing a fixed transhistorical significance or as corresponding to any "essential" binary distinction. This polarity, however, does have profound cultural power and can produce extraordinary experiential effects. For that reason, if for no other, it is imperative that the terms themselves not be jettisoned, or their utility in an identity politics slighted, before the inequality of political and discursive power that they label is redressed.

30. In this regard it is useful to consider the following meditation by Derrida: "The logic of the apotropaic: castrating oneself *already*, always already, in order to be able to castrate and repress the threat of castration, renouncing life and mastery in order to secure them; putting into play by ruse, simulacrum, and violence just what one wants to preserve; losing in advance what one wants to erect; suspending what one raises: *aufheben*" (*Glas*, trans. John P. Leavey, Jr. and Richard Rand [Lincoln: University of Nebraska Press, 1986], 46).

31. *Souvenirs and Prophecies: The Young Wallace Stevens*, ed. Holly Stevens (New York: Knopf, 1977), 82.

32. Unlike Lentricchia's narrow focus on "social engenderment" in terms of a masculine/feminine dichotomy, this perspective would restore the full force of the response, cited earlier, offered by an unidentified man in *The Hite Report on Male Sexuality* to the question of how he would feel if something about him were described as feminine or womanly. See note 10 for a fuller discussion.

33. To call this a "hom(m)o-sexuality" for which, as Irigaray puts it, "heterosexuality has been up to now just an alibi," is to suggest that the category of heterosexuality has been unjustly impugned by the mere lip service patriarchy pays it and that "true" heterosexuality constitutes the redemptive territory in which a less oppressive relation between men and women may be found. What I am trying to suggest, however, is that it is precisely the complicity of compulsory heterosexuality with patriarchal structures of power that *produces* this repetitive scenario in which homosexuality is discredited by being read as the "real meaning" of patriarchal organization while heterosexuality is redeemed and positioned once again as an ideal that offers hope for a more progressive distribution of power between the sexes.

34. Lentricchia, "Andiamo!," 410.

35. Frank Lentricchia, "Anatomy of a Jar," *South Atlantic Quarterly*, 86 (1987): 390.

36. Lentricchia's gleeful imagining of the "TestaREEa" and its "big jars" would seem designed to ward off the anxiety that finds expression in the tellingly worded paraphrase with which he dismisses Sandra Gilbert's reading of Emily Dickinson: "Dickinson, therefore, not Whitman or Stevens, has real balls" (785).

3. The Part for the (W)hole

1. James Baldwin, "Nobody Knows My Name," in *The Price of the Ticket: Collected Nonfiction 1948–1985* (New York: St. Martin's Press, 1985), 184.

2. Frantz Fanon, *Black Skin, White Masks*, trans. Charles Lam Markmann (New York: Grove Press, 1967), 222. Where the context makes clear that this work is being cited, subse-

quent page references to this edition will be noted in parentheses following the quotation in my text.

3. bell hooks (Gloria Watkins), "Reflections on Race and Sex," *Yearning: Race, Gender, and Cultural Politics* (Boston: South End Press, 1990), 58.

4. See, for instance, the quotation from Theodore Kupferman in W. J. Weatherby's *James Baldwin: Artist on Fire* (New York: Dell Publishing, 1989), 192–193.

5. D. A. Miller, "Secret Subjects, Open Secrets," *The Novel and the Police* (Berkeley: University of California Press, 1988), 195.

6. I put the word "race" in quotation marks here to indicate the culturally variable and ideologically constructed nature of the discourse surrounding it. Henry Louis Gates, Jr., in his introduction to *"Race," Writing, and Difference* and again in his epilogue, "Talkin' That Talk," lucidly and persuasively discusses the figural import of "race" in the West. (See *"Race," Writing, and Difference*, ed. Henry Louis Gates, Jr. [Chicago: University of Chicago Press, 1986].)

7. "Races: Freedom—Now," *Time*, May 17, 1963, p. 23. Where subsequent references to this essay are made clear by context, the page number will be given in the text.

8. In writing of Baldwin as gay, I do not mean to deny that he could also be represented (and, indeed, on many occasions represented himself) as a bisexual man. Rather, I want to suggest that "gay" and "bisexual" are political terms that enter into contestation with the presumption of normative heterosexuality in different ways at different times. To the extent that the category of "bisexuality" can appear to position itself between reified polar opposites of "heterosexual" and "homosexual," it has the potential to read those orientations as essences in a way that I would resist. However, to the extent that I accept the arbitrariness and psychic fluidity of sexualities, to the degree, that is, that I adopt what Eve Kosofsky Sedgwick discusses as a "universalizing" attitude toward sexual possibilities, I can embrace "bisexuality" (however much it limits itself to a binary system of sexual categorization) as the name for that psychic disposition. In our cultural context, however, the stigmatization of Baldwin's sexuality, and the descriptions in his novels of such stigmatizations, derives not from a specifically "bisexual" oppression, but from the oppressiveness of homophobia.

9. I do not, in using these terms, desire to affirm the demeaning identification of female sexuality with the figure of the "hole" or of male sexuality with the figure of the "part"; rather, I want to identify the masculinist logic that works through such reductive designations in order to explore the interrelationship of racism, sexism, and homophobia in the dominant cultural imaginary.

10. Hortense Spillers offers an indispensable caveat to any elaboration of such scenarios of white male violence against black men: "The African female subject, under these historic conditions [of slavery and the appropriation of her flesh], is not only the target of rape—in one sense, an interiorized violation of body and mind—but also the topic of specifically *externalized* acts of torture and prostration that we imagine as the peculiar province of *male* brutality and torture inflicted by other males. A female body strung from a tree limb, or bleeding from the breast on any given day of field work because an 'overseer,' standing the length of a whip, has popped her flesh open, adds a lexical and living dimension to the narratives of women of color" ("Mama's Baby, Papa's Maybe: An American Grammar Book," *Diacritics* 17:2 [Summer 1987]: 68).

11. Marlon Riggs, "Black Macho Revisited: Reflections of a SNAP! Queen," *Brother to Brother: New Writings By Black Gay Men*, ed. Essex Hemphill, conceived by Joseph Beam, project managed by Dorothy Beam (Boston: Alyson Publications, 1991), 255.

12. Homi Bhabha, to whose work I am indebted in many aspects of my reading here, offers a compatible, but differently focused account of the relation between "part" and "whole" in

his important essay, "Signs Taken for Wonders: Questions of Ambivalence and Authority under a Tree Outside Delhi, May 1817," in *"Race," Writing, and Difference.* He writes, for instance: "What radically differentiates the exercise of colonial power is the unsuitability of the Enlightenment assumption of collectivity and the eye that beholds it. For Jeremy Bentham (as Michel Perrot points out), the small group is representative of the whole society—the part is *already* the whole. Colonial authority requires modes of discrimination (cultural, racial, administrative . . .) that disallow a stable unitary assumption of collectivity. The 'part' (which must be the colonialist foreign body) must be representative of the 'whole' (conquered country), but the right of representation is based on its difference" (172).

13. James Baldwin, *Tell Me How Long the Train's Been Gone* (New York: Dell Publishing, 1969), 47.

14. Ishmael Reed, "Steven Spielberg Plays Howard Beach," *Writin' Is Fightin': Thirty-Seven Years of Boxing on Paper* (New York: Atheneum, 1990), 146.

15. Malcolm El-Hajj Malik El-Shabbazz, *The Autobiography of Malcolm X,* with the assistance of Alex Haley (New York: Ballantine Books, 1990), 201; James Baldwin, "No Name in the Street," reprinted in *The Price of the Ticket,* 549.

16. Cited in Diana Fuss, *Essentially Speaking: Feminism, Nature, and Difference* (New York: Routledge, 1989), 73.

17. Mae G. Henderson, "Toni Morrison's *Beloved*: Re-Membering the Body as Historical Text," *Comparative American Identities: Race, Sex, and Nationality in the Modern Text* (New York: Routledge, 1991), 70.

18. James Baldwin, *Just Above My Head* (New York: Dell Publishing, 1984), 91.

19. Bhabha, "Signs Taken for Wonders," 72.

20. In this context consider Cornel West's remark: "Black people rarely get free from their fear of the White gaze" (in bell hooks and Cornel West, *Breaking Bread: Insurgent Black Intellectual Life* [Boston: South End Press, 1991], 41).

21. Judith Butler, *Gender Trouble: Feminism and the Subversion of Identity* (New York: Routledge, 1990), 44.

22. hooks, "Reflections on Race and Sex," 62.

23. Frederick Douglass, *My Bondage and My Freedom,* 1855 edition (New York: Dover Publications, 1969), 51.

24. Henry Louis Gates, Jr., "Binary Oppositions in Chapter One of 'Narrative of the Life of Frederick Douglass, An American Slave,'" *Figures in Black: Words, Signs, and the "Racial" Self* (New York: Oxford University Press, 1987), 91.

25. Teresa de Lauretis, "Desire in Narrative," *Alice Doesn't: Feminism, Semiotics, Cinema* (Bloomington: Indiana University Press, 1984), 121. It should be clear, I hope, that the conditions endured by African and African-American slaves were by no means comparable to the conditions experienced by white women under patriarchy; the point, rather, is that slaves, male and female alike, were conceptualized through an optic that read them in terms of the *radical* otherness of "woman" under patriarchy—"woman" without the protective mediation of the historical institutions that (differently for different classes) gild the patriarchal cage, or perhaps, pad the patriarchal cell if we bear in mind the metaphorics of madness unpacked by Sandra Gilbert and Susan Gubar in the literature of white women authors.

26. Spillers, "Mama's Baby, Papa's Maybe," 80.

27. W. E. B. Du Bois, *The Souls of Black Folk* (Harmondsworth: Penguin, 1989), 5.

28. Houston A. Baker, Jr., "Generational Shifts and the Recent Criticism of Afro-American

Literature," *Black American Literature Forum* 15:11 (Spring 1981); reprinted in David H. Richter, ed., *The Critical Tradition: Classic Texts and Contemporary Trends* (New York: St. Martin's Press, 1989), 1345.

29. Homi Bhabha, "Of Mimicry and Man: The Ambivalence of Colonial Discourse," *October* 28 (1984): 129.

30. James Baldwin, "Everybody's Protest Novel," *Notes of a Native Son*; reprinted in *The Price of the Ticket*, 33. Eldridge Cleaver comments on this process of internalization that produces a sort of masochistic, or self-alienating, narcissism; he reads it in relation to the "cultural neurosis" of whites and he identifies the historically pathogenic effect of that "narcissism" on blacks as well as whites: "Separate-but-equal marked the last stage of the white man's flight into cultural neurosis, and the beginning of the black man's frantic striving to assert his humanity and equalize his position with the white. Blacks ventured into all fields of endeavor to which they could gain entrance. Their goal was to present in all fields a performance that would equal or surpass that of the whites. It was long axiomatic among blacks that a black had to be twice as competent as a white in any field in order to gain grudging recognition from the whites. This produced a pathological motivation in the blacks to equal or surpass the whites, and a pathological motivation in the whites to maintain a distance from the blacks" ("The White Race and Its Heroes," *Soul on Ice* [New York: Dell Publishing, 1968], 79).

31. Julia Kristeva, in a passage that will bear upon subsequent sections of this essay, notes that the drives, in the process of primal repression, "serve to correlate the 'not yet' ego with an 'object' in order to establish both of them. Such a process, while dichotomous (inside/outside, ego/not ego) and repetitive, has nevertheless something centripetal about it: it aims to settle the ego as center of a solar system of objects" (*Powers of Horror: An Essay on Abjection*, trans. Leon Roudiez [New York: Columbia University Press, 1982], 14).

32. Sigmund Freud, "On the Mechanism of Paranoia," *General Psychological Theory*, ed. Philip Rieff (New York: Collier, 1976), 30.

33. B.[utler] H.[arrison] Peterson, "Is the Negro as Morally Depraved as He is Reputed to Be?," *Twentieth Century Negro Literature; or, a Cyclopedia of Thought on the Vital Topics Relating to the American Negro*, ed. D. W. Culp (Toronto: J. L. Nichols and Co., 1902), 237; reprinted in the series, *The American Negro: His History and Literature* (New York: Arno Press and the *New York Times*, 1969).

34. This representation of male heterosexual anxiety induced by the hierarchical disposition of power in a context of intensified homosocial dependency unfolds a system of homophobic abjection that bears comparison to the similar system at work in Stevens's "Life on a Battleship," discussed in Chapter Two.

35. Note that in his analysis of a passage from Michel Cournot's *Martinique*, Fanon declares: "when one abandons oneself to the movement of its images—one is no longer aware of the Negro but only of a penis; the Negro is eclipsed. He is turned into a penis. He *is* a penis" (*Black Skin, White Masks*, 169–170).

36. Toni Morrison, *Beloved* (New York: New American Library, 1987), 107–108.

37. Baldwin, *Tell Me How Long the Train's Been Gone*, 179.

38. Fanon writes: "No anti-Semite, for example, would ever conceive of the idea of castrating a Jew. He is killed or sterilized. But the Negro is castrated. The penis, the symbol of manhood, is annihilated, which is to say that it is denied" (*Black Skin, White Masks*, 162).

39. The difference implicit in "equals" as the very signifier of sameness can be understood as the anxiogenic spur to identity formation even as it is the thread that will unravel all such identities. It thus captures in miniature the cultural project I have described as "homographesis."

40. The social and political framing of this agonistic "subject-annihilation" should be considered in relation to, but should not be subsumed too quickly within, that dispersal of selfhood that Leo Bersani identifies as characteristic of male anal receptivity in sex. See Bersani, "Is the Rectum a Grave?," *AIDS: Cultural Analysis/Cultural Activism*, ed. Douglas Crimp, *October* 43 (Winter 1987).

41. I use this term to ventriloquize the contempt with which it resonates in a homophobic culture, and to inflect it, by so doing, with some of the meaning that Baldwin, in *Just Above My Head*, implies when the narrator of that novel, Hall Montana, insists that his late brother, Arthur, though an active gay man, "was nobody's faggot" (37).

42. hooks, *Breaking Bread*, 83.

43. LeRoi Jones (Imamu Amiri Baraka), *Black Magic* (New York: Bobbs-Merrill, 1969), 112. Cited in Ron Simmons, "Some Thoughts on the Challenges Facing Black Gay Intellectuals," *Brother to Brother*, 217.

44. Cleaver, in his well-known attack on Baldwin, writes with reference to the "black homosexual": "The white man has deprived him of his masculinity, castrated him in the center of his burning skull, and when he submits to this change and takes the white man for his lover as well as Big Daddy, he focuses on 'whiteness' all the love in his pent up soul and turns the razor edge of hatred against 'blackness'" ("Notes on a Native Son," *Soul on Ice*, 103). Asante discusses homosexuality in *Afrocentricity: The Theory of Social Change* (Buffalo: Amulefi, 1980).

45. Kenneth Burke writes of synecdoche as "the figure of speech wherein the part is used for the whole, the whole for the part, the container for the thing contained, the cause for the effect, the effect for the cause, etc." (*The Philosophy of Literary Form: Studies in Symbolic Action* [Berkeley: University of California Press, 1973], 25–26).

46. James Baldwin, "Here Be Dragons," *The Price of the Ticket*, 686.

47. Not surprisingly, in this context, even "heart," the image of essence, the name for the principle of interiority that stands in the place of identity itself (what, after all, could be more one's self than the "beating of one's heart"?), serves throughout the novel as a figure for a male-male bond not limited to, but able to include, explicitly sexual relations; as Baldwin writes of Red and Peanut, members, along with Crunch and Arthur, of "The Trumpets of Zion," a gospel quartet that toured the South as part of the organized movement for black civil rights: "They did not think of Crunch and Arthur as lovers, a condition they could not, yet, really imagine, but as two cats who had something very deep going for each other: in the same way that Red was Peanut's 'heart'" (211).

48. Jacques Lacan, "The Mirror Stage as Formative of the Function of the I as Revealed in Psychoanalytic Experience," *Ecrits: A Selection*, trans. Alan Sheridan (New York: Norton, 1977), 4.

49. In "Dark Continents: Epistemologies of Racial and Sexual Difference in Psychoanalysis and Cinema" (in *Femmes Fatales: Feminism, Film Theory, Psychoanalysis* [New York: Routledge, 1991], a brilliant essay published after the bulk of this chapter was written, Mary Ann Doane usefully discusses the relations among race, sexuality, and the logic of visualization. Though her focus is primarily on the question of gender, and though she does not address the question of homosexuality, her work makes a number of points that are similar to those I make here and it should be read by anyone interested in thinking seriously about the issues that this chapter tries to address.

50. In this regard it is important to observe that the logic by which the Republicans were able, in the 1988 presidential campaign, to use "Willie Horton" in order to mobilize white anx-

iety about the (sexual) threat posed by blacks is not merely *metonymically* connected with the same party's mobilization, during the 1992 campaign, of the dominant culture's hatred of gays. Both blacks and gays are susceptible to such assaults precisely because the *visibility* of their presence is construed as an assault, in the cultural imaginary, on the symbolic order itself.

51. The extremity of this anxiety can most easily be recognized in the violence with which straight men often react to the experienced of being "cruised" by another man.

52. For a fuller discussion of heterosexual masculinity and the logic of castration, see Chapter Ten, "Seeing Things: Representation, the Scene of Surveillance, and the Spectacle of Gay Male Sex." For a powerful account of the problematic relations of identification and desire worked out in terms of female homosexuality, see Diana Fuss, "Freud's Fallen Woman: Identification, Desire, and 'A Case of Homosexuality in a Woman,'" a chapter from her forthcoming study on psychoanalysis, identity, and identification.

53. In his discussion of tropology, Hayden White notes that synecdoche "is regarded by some theorists as a form of Metonymy," but he distinguishes between them by suggesting that "Metonymy is *reductionist*, [and] Synecdoche is *integrative*" (34). Synecdoche, he suggests, permits a substitution on the basis of a part that figures the essential quality that defines the whole. See *Metahistory: The Historical Imagination in Nineteenth Century Europe* (Baltimore: The Johns Hopkins University Press, 1973), especially 31–38.

54. This is not, of course, to suggest that lesbians or gay men cannot be racist, but rather that racism as we know it intersects with the anxious stigmatization of male passivity underlying both misogyny and homophobia and shaping the socio-cultural attitudes of women and men, whether straight or gay.

55. Kimberly W. Benston, in an essay that bears some relation to my own in its attention to questions of "race" and the visual economy, discusses the reunion of Celie and Nettie at the end of *The Color Purple* in a language that provocatively broaches some of the issues I am talking about here: "Celie and Nettie, in short, no longer seek to read each other: they are each other, and in this melting they pose a radical challenge to our own liminal stance as interpreters, as negotiating judges between distanced parties. For the end of the tradition imagined in the topos of facing would be the effacement of an encounter *face-to-face*, the scene beyond the vertiginous exchanges of master-slave and oedipal positions, where the spatial and temporal predicaments of tradition are suspended, where immediacy is no longer an illusion of scopic power but the dissolution of specular relations altogether" ("Facing Tradition: Revisionary Scenes in African American Literature," *PMLA*, 105 [January 1990]: 106).

56. In a piece of critical writing to which I am greatly indebted, Barbara Johnson, commenting on an essay by Zora Neale Hurston, observes that "Difference is a misreading of sameness, but it must be represented in order to be erased. The resistance to finding out that the other is the same springs out of the reluctance to admit that the same is other." She concludes the paragraph in which these sentences appear by cogently remarking: "The difference between difference and sameness can barely be said. It is as small and as vast as the difference between 'like' and 'as'" ("Thresholds of Difference: Structures of Address in Zora Neale Hurston," *A World of Difference* [Baltimore: The Johns Hopkins University Press, 1989], 178).

57. Of course the meaningfulness of gospel music, hymns, and work songs in the African-American tradition derives in large measure from their ability to carry messages, otherwise prohibited, in a language that can "pass." When Arthur and Crunch, performing in concert with their gospel quartet in a Birmingham church, "confess" their love by means of a song in which, as in their love-making, they enter into one another— "they had never sung like this before, [Arthur's] voice in Crunch's sound, Crunch's sound filling his voice" (198)—their homographic repositioning of the devotional lyric tropes on the practice described by Freder-

ick Douglass whereby slaves "were, at times, remarkably buoyant, singing hymns" that had, as he puts it, "a double meaning," allowing them to express their anticipation of "a speedy pilgrimage toward a free state, and deliverance from all the evils and dangers of slavery" (Douglass, *My Bondage and My Freedom*, 278, 279).

58. Henry Louis Gates, Jr., "Editor's Introduction: Writing 'Race' and the Difference It Makes," *"Race," Writing, and Difference*, 13.

59. It is useful to consider, in such a context, the myth that Eldridge Cleaver constructs to account for "the roots of heterosexuality." Cleaver describes the "Unitary Self" or "Primeval Sphere" that was the "unknown ancestor of Man/Woman" as undergoing a "weird mitosis of the essence" and producing male and female hemispheres that became, through evolution, separate entities: man and woman. In the aftermath, and as a result, of that initial act of differentiation, a "Primeval Urge," as Cleaver names it, "exerts an irresistible attraction between the male and female hemispheres, ever tending to fuse them back together into a unity in which the male and female realize their true nature—the lost unity of the Primeval Sphere." The differentiation into male and female, like the articulations of identity that will attend the fracturing of imaginary unity by the Name-of-the-Father, produces a new order in which the goal is to recuperate the very unity that has been fractured. But that wholeness, paradoxically, can only be restored by the policial insistence on difference. As Cleaver puts it: "Each half of the human equation, the male and female hemispheres of the Primeval Sphere, must prepare themselves for the fusion by achieving a Unitary Sexual Image, i.e., a heterosexual identity free from the mutually exclusive, antagonistic, antipodal impediments of homosexuality." In order to return to the Unitary Self in which male and female are indistinguishable, it is necessary, according to this logic, to maintain their absolute differentiation through the achievement of a "Unitary Sexual Image." Thus heterosexuality here names the difference that makes possible the return to sameness, while homosexuality names the sameness that insures the perpetuation of difference. (See Cleaver, "The Primeval Mitosis," *Soul on Ice*, 177.)

60. Houston A. Baker, Jr., "Caliban's Triple Play," *"Race," Writing, and Difference*, 391. The page numbers of subsequent references to this essay will be noted in parentheses following the citation in my text.

61. Baker, for instance, describes Henry Louis Gates, Jr. as having "executed a signal and substantial triple play with *"Race," Writing, and Difference* by invading the territories of the Western Enlightenment and appropriating to his own *vale* the entire panoply of issues held in trust for so many years by whitemales" (395).

62. Baldwin, "Here Be Dragons," *The Price of the Ticket*, 690.

4. THE PLAGUE OF DISCOURSE

The earliest version of this essay was presented at a session on "The Literature of AIDS" at the 1987 MLA Convention. I would like to thank Michael Cadden and Elaine Showalter, the other panelists, for offering helpful suggestions. "AIDS" is placed in quotation marks throughout this essay and the essays that follow in order to resist its reduction to a singular, coherent, medical phenomenon, and to call attention, instead, to its status as the ideologically determined site at which a variety of medical, social, and political crises historically converge.

1. Lee Grove, "The Metaphor of AIDS," *Boston Globe Magazine*, February 28, 1988.

2. David Black, *The Plague Years: A Chronicle of AIDS, The Epidemic of Our Times* (New York: Simon and Schuster, 1986), 80.

3. H.D. (Hilda Doolittle), *Tribute to Freud* (Boston: D. R. Godine, 1974), 86.

4. Johns Hopkins University, Population Information Program, "Issues in World Health," *Population Reports*, Series 50, no. 14 (1986): 198.

5. Plato, "Timaeus," in *The Dialogues of Plato*, trans. Benjamin Jowett (Oxford: Oxford University Press, 1953), 3:89.

6. Jacques Derrida, "Plato's Pharmacy," in *Dissemination*, trans. Barbara Johnson (Chicago: University of Chicago Press, 1981), 101.

7. Derrida, "Plato's Pharmacy," 79.

8. Derrida, "Plato's Pharmacy," 149.

9. Cited in Black, *Plague Years*, 17–18.

10. Black, *Plague Years*, 30.

11. Frances FitzGerald, "The Castro—II," *New Yorker*, 62 (July 28, 1986): 50.

12. William H. Masters, Virginia E. Johnson, and Robert C. Kolodny, "Sex in the Age of AIDS," *Newsweek*, March 14, 1988, p. 48.

13. Derrida, "Plato's Pharmacy," 149.

14. Derrida, "Plato's Pharmacy," 153.

15. "The Constitutional Status of Sexual Orientation: Homosexuality as a Suspect Classification," *Harvard Law Review*, 98 (1985): 1294.

16. Harold Bloom, "Freud and the Sublime," in *Agon: Towards a Theory of Revisionism* (New York: Oxford University Press, 1982), 107.

17. Cited in Derrida, "Plato's Pharmacy," 152–153.

18. Johns Hopkins University, "Issues in World Health," 198.

19. Johns Hopkins University, "Issues in World Health," 198.

20. Derrida, "Plato's Pharmacy," 128.

21. Emily Dickinson, "A Word Dropped Careless on a Page," in *The Complete Poems of Emily Dickinson*, ed. Thomas H. Johnson (Boston: Little, Brown, 1960), 553.

5. The Mirror and the Tank

Earlier drafts of this essay were presented at New York University (1992) and the Center for Literary and Cultural Studies at Harvard (1992). I would like to thank Marcos Becquer, Chris Straayer, Marge Garber, and David Halperin for extending these invitations.

1. Leo Bersani, "Is the Rectum a Grave?," *AIDS: Cultural Analysis/Cultural Activism*, ed. Douglas Crimp, *October*, 43 (Winter 1987): 199. Where subsequent references to this work are contextually clear, page numbers will be given parenthetically in the text.

2. Paula Treichler, "AIDS, Homophobia, and Biomedical Discourse: An Epidemic of Signification," *AIDS: Cultural Analysis/Cultural Activism*, 32; Lee Edelman, "The Plague of Discourse: Politics, Literary Theory, and 'AIDS,'" Chapter Four in this volume.

3. Jeffrey Weeks, "Post-Modern AIDS?," *Ecstatic Antibodies: Resisting the AIDS Mythology*, ed. Tessa Boffin and Sunil Gupta (London: Rivers Oram Press, 1990), 133–141.

4. Roberta McGrath, "Dangerous Liaisons: Health, Disease, and Representation," *Ecstatic Antibodies*, 144.

5. Donna Haraway, "A Manifesto for Cyborgs," *Coming to Terms: Feminism, Theory, Politics*, ed. Elizabeth Weed (New York: Routledge, 1989), 185.

6. Robert Glück, "HTLV-3," *Personal Dispatches: Writers Confront AIDS*, ed. John Preston (New York: St. Martin's Press, 1989), 83.

7. Simon Watney, "The Spectacle of AIDS," *AIDS: Cultural Analysis/Cultural Activism*, 85.

8. Douglas Crimp and Adam Ralston, *AIDS DemoGraphics* (Seattle: Bay Press, 1990), 19. Where subsequent references to this work are contextually clear, page numbers will be given parenthetically in the text.

9. Fredric Jameson, "Postmodernism and Consumer Society," *The Anti-Aesthetic: Essays on Postmodern Culture*, ed. Hal Foster (Port Townsend, Washington: Bay Press, 1983), 114.

10. In the argument that follows it might be useful to bear in mind Mary Ann Doane's suggestion that "it is as though masculinity were required to effectively conceptualize access to activity or agency (whether illusory or not)" (8). Such a requirement derives from the cultural coincidence (which is, of course, not coincidental) of masculinity, agency, and the authority of subject status as embodiments of the principle of activity. Hence, as Teresa de Lauretis observes, "the hero, the mythical subject, is constructed as human being and as male; he is the active principle of culture, the establisher of distinction" (119). (See Mary Ann Doane, *The Desire to Desire: The Woman's Film of the 1940s* [Bloomington: Indiana University Press, 1987]; and Teresa de Lauretis, *Alice Doesn't: Feminism, Semiotics, Cinema* [Bloomington: Indiana University Press, 1984].)

11. Simon Watney, "Representing AIDS," *Ecstatic Antibodies*, 173, 174. Where subsequent references to this work are contextually clear, page numbers will be given parenthetically in the text.

12. Judith Butler, whose work has been instrumental in helping me to think about these issues, persuasively argues that the very attempt to distinguish between sex and gender furthers the ideological project of naturalizing the body and its "sex" in terms that already bear the cultural inscriptions of a "gender" that is imagined as deriving from the "naturally" sexed body in the first place. See *Gender Trouble: Feminism and the Subversion of Identity* (New York: Routledge, 1990).

13. Attributed to Jim Finnegan, this quotation is cited by Andrew Merton in "AIDS and Gay-Bashing in New Hampshire," *Boston Sunday Globe*, June 9, 1991, p. 2NH.

14. David Halperin, "The Democratic Body: Prostitution and Citizenship in Classical Athens," *One Hundred Years of Homosexuality and Other Essays on Greek Love* (New York: Routledge, 1990), 95. Where subsequent references to this work are contextually clear, page numbers will be given parenthetically in the text.

15. In a recent interview, William Burroughs offers a related, though somewhat differently inflected, reading of the biblical myth parodically figured in such accounts of "AIDS." "Another poll showed that an enormous number of people," he observed, "believe that homosexual intercourse can cause AIDS even if neither party had the virus! Now that's an immaculate conception!" ("Burroughs: On Tear Gas, Queers, *Naked Lunch*, and the Ginsberg Affair," an interview with David Ehrenstein, *Advocate*, 581 [July 16, 1991]: 43).

16. Eve Kosofsky Sedgwick, "Some Binarisms (I)," *Epistemology of the Closet* (Berkeley: University of California Press, 1990), 128.

17. "Addiction" (understood as addiction to "drugs") and gay male sexuality are joined together in the popular discourse on "AIDS" not only as practices through which the body suffers "improper" penetration, but also, and more significantly, as practices that signify the renunciation of active self-mastery and control. Hence, for instance, in an article published in Jerry Falwell's *Liberty Report* and titled "Henry Waxman: The Bodyguard of Homosexuals," the unnamed author reflects on Congressman Waxman's efforts to protect the civil liberties of HIV-positive women and men: "If it were Barney Frank or Gerry Studds taking the lead in preferring megadeaths to public disapproval of sodomy, this might be easy enough to understand. But no one has ever suggested that Waxman himself is addicted to what, in a more delicate era, was known as 'unnatural vice'" (*Liberty Report: The Newspaper of the Moral Majority* [November 1987]: 3, 19).

18. The other frequently encountered originary myth of "AIDS," of course, plays out the racist fantasy of its dissemination from an undifferentiated "Africa," as Cindy Patton notes, where monkeys and humans live side by side and sexual relations are, in the white imaginary, fundamentally "different." (See Cindy Patton, "Inventing 'African AIDS,'" *Inventing AIDS* [New York: Routledge, 1990], 77–97.) Though always widely available for activation, this fiction presents itself as a more "scientific" attempt to understand the cause of the epidemic; while frequently repeated by journalists, therefore, it does not generate the same affective charge as does the mythic primacy of male-male anal sex, largely because the (white) Western public, generally indifferent to and ignorant of the history and experiences of Africa's nations and peoples, construes "African AIDS," with its largely "heterosexual" modes of transmission, as distinct from Western "AIDS," which, however much it may be bruited to "spread" from gay men and intravenous drug users, continues to be perceived as a disease linked *in its origins* to those identities.

19. Michelangelo Signorile, "Gossip Watch: Michelangelo the Red Queen," *OutWeek*, 105 (July 3, 1991): 100.

20. Craig Owens, "The Discourse of Others: Feminists and Postmodernism," *The Anti-Aesthetic: Essays on Postmodern Culture*, 58.

21. See Chapter Eleven, "Imagining the Homosexual: *Laura* and the Other Face of Gender."

22. Jane Gallop, "Where to Begin?," *Reading Lacan* (Ithaca: Cornell University Press, 1985), 85.

23. Ovid, Book III, *The Metamorphoses*, trans. Horace Gregory (New York: New American Library, 1958), 99. All quotations from Milton in the following pages refer to the edition of *Paradise Lost* reprinted in John Milton, *Complete Poems and Major Prose*, ed. Merritt Y. Hughes (Indianapolis: Bobbs-Merrill Company, 1957).

24. In a recent essay Regina Schwartz has argued that *Paradise Lost* attributes the Fall to Adam's inability properly to accept his role as subject, choosing, instead, to remain fixated in a specular relation to Eve: "At the core of Milton's myth of the Fall is Adam's identification with Eve, an attraction that makes him fail to embrace that 'masculine autonomy' Raphael instructs him in." This would suggest that *Paradise Lost* could be read as a text that both produces and enforces the modern construction of a proto-heterosexuality conceived as that which works against the fall back into a state of psychic non-differentiation that figures, from the point of view of the subject, the Fall into mortality itself. (Regina Schwartz, "Rethinking Voyeurism and Patriarchy: The Case of *Paradise Lost*," *Representations*, 34 [Spring 1991], 99.)

25. Mary Nyquist, "Gynesis, Genesis, Exegesis, and the Formation of Milton's Eve," *Cannibals, Witches, and Divorce: Estranging the Renaissance*, Selected Papers from the English Institute, 1985, ed. Marjorie Garber (Baltimore: The Johns Hopkins University Press, 1987), 196.

26. Michael Warner, "Homo-Narcissism; or, Heterosexuality," *Engendering Men: The Question of Male Feminist Criticism*, ed. Joseph A. Boone and Michael Cadden (New York: Routledge, 1990), 202.

27. D. A. Miller, "Anal *Rope*," *Representations*, 32 (Fall 1990), 128. Reprinted in *Inside/Out: Lesbian Theories, Gay Theories*, ed. Diana Fuss (New York: Routledge, 1991).

28. Paul Monette, *Love Alone: Eighteen Elegies for Rog* (New York: St. Martin's Press, 1988). References to poems from this volume will be given by title and line number in my text.

29. Larry Kramer, "Who Killed Vito Russo?," *OutWeek*, 86 (February 20, 1991), 26; Patrick Buchanan, *New York Post*, June 26, 1991, cited in "Media Watch: Buchanan on Essex," *New York Native*, 429 (July 8, 1991): 15.

30. Bersani, "Is the Rectum a Grave?," 222.

31. Simon Watney, *Policing Desire: Pornography, AIDS, and the Media* (Minneapolis: University of Minnesota Press, 1987), 49.

32. Watney, "Representing AIDS," 173, 189.

33. Larry Kramer, "Oh, My People," *Reports from the Holocaust: The Making of an AIDS Activist* (New York: St. Martin's Press, 1989), 191; "I Can't Believe You Want to Die," *Reports*, 163.

34. Isaac Julien and Pratibha Parmar, "In Conversation," *Ecstatic Antibodies*, 100.

35. Andreas Huyssen, "Mapping the Postmodern," *New German Critique*, 33 (Fall 1984): 44.

36. Thomas Yingling, "Sexual Preference/Cultural Reference: The Predicament of Gay Culture Studies," *American Literary History*, 3:1 (Spring 1991): 194.

37. Diana Fuss, "The Question of Identity Politics," *Essentially Speaking: Feminism, Nature, and Difference* (New York: Routledge, 1989), 106. Where subsequent references to this work are contextually clear, page numbers will be given parenthetically in the text.

38. Donn Teal, *The Gay Militants* (New York: Stein and Day, 1971), 29.

39. Cited in Jonathan Ned Katz, "The Stonewall Rebellion: Edmund White Witnesses the Revolution," *Advocate*, 527 (June 20, 1989): 40.

40. Alexander S. Chee, "A Queer Nationalism," *Out/Look*, 11 (Winter 1991): 15.

41. Allan Bérubé and Jeffrey Escoffier, "Queer/Nation," *Out/Look*, 11 (Winter 1991): 14.

42. John Weir, *The Irreversible Decline of Eddie Socket* (New York: HarperCollins, 1989), 99.

43. Alain Emmanuel Dreuilhe, *Corps à corps: journal de SIDA* (Paris: Gallimard, 1987), 23. Where subsequent references to this work are contextually clear, page numbers will be given parenthetically in the text. The parenthetical English translation, here as elsewhere throughout this chapter, is my own.

44. From the perspective of a phobic heterosexual culture, "AIDS" inscribes the gay body as text in the latest instance of what I define in Chapter One as the project of "homographesis," the disciplinary and projective fantasy that homosexuality is visibly, morphologically or semiotically, written upon the flesh so that homosexuality comes to occupy the stigmatized position of writing itself within the Western metaphysics of presence. Harking back to the work by Oscar Wilde that most strikingly puts into play, however ironically, the homographic belief in the legibility of gay sexuality as a recognizable category of difference, Dreuilhe describes the effects of "AIDS" as discerned in his reflected image: "J'ai pris dix ans en un an, les cernes sous mes yeux, malgré mes pratiques d'ermite, pourraient faire croire que je mène une vie de débauche, à moins que ce soudain changement ne soit analogue à celui de Dorian Gray" (192).

45. D.A. Miller, "Sontag's Urbanity," *October*, 49 (Summer 1989): 95.

46. Samuel R. Delaney, *The Motion of Light in Water: Sex and Science Fiction Writing in the East Village, 1957–1965* (New York: New American Library, 1988), 175.

47. Hervé Guibert, *A l'ami qui ne m'a pas sauvé la vie* (Paris: Gallimard, 1990), 242 (translation mine).

48. This does not mean, of course, that "narcissism," "passivity," or "luxury" have any essential, trans-historical relation to the individual experiences of lesbians or gay men; but it does mean that the ideological stigmatization of those categories in order to define a realm of "significant" activity representative of a "healthy" community reproduces the exclusionary logic that constitutes "homosexuality" as a demonized category within the dominant culture of Western modernism.

49. Marlon Riggs, "Black Macho Revisited: Reflections of a SNAP! Queen," *Brother to Brother: New Writings by Black Gay Men*, ed. Essex Hemphill, conceived by Joseph Beam, project managed by Dorothy Beam (Boston: Alyson Publications, 1991), 255.

6. The Sodomite's Tongue and the Bourgeois Body

A shorter version of this essay was presented in 1990 at the MLA convention in Chicago. I would like to thank Carol Flynn and David Marshall for organizing the panel in which I participated.

1. *Satan's Harvest Home*, reprinted in *Hell Upon Earth, or, The Town in an Uproar. And Satan's Harvest Home* in the series *Marriage, Sex, and the Family in Eighteenth Century England 1660–1800*, ed. Randolph Trumbach, vol. 20 (New York: Garland, 1985), 45. Subsequent page references to this text will be given in parentheses following the quotation in my text.

2. This institutionalization can be seen in the expectation of jurists, in the course of the century, that young boys would have had discussions about sodomy and sodomites among themselves. After James Hearne, a fifteen-year-old who charged Charles Bradbury with sodomy, acknowledged his friendship with a fellow apprentice, he was asked in court, "Did you never talk about mollies?" (Randolph Trumbach, "Sodomitical Assaults, Gender Roles, and Sexual Development in Eighteenth-Century London," in *The Pursuit of Sodomy: Male Homosexuality in Renaissance and Enlightenment Europe*, ed. Kent Gerard and Gert Hekma [New York: Harrington Park Press, 1989] 412).

3. Cf. G. S. Rousseau, "The Pursuit of Homosexuality in the Eighteenth Century: 'Utterly Confused Category' and/or Rich Repository?," in *'Tis Nature's Fault: Unauthorized Sexual Behavior During the Enlightenment*, ed. Robert Maccubin (Cambridge: Cambridge University Press, 1988), 132–168.

4. Fashionable, in such a context, one might note, signifies the ideological distancing of the middle class from the excesses associated with the court.

5. For a discussion of this see Randolph Trumbach, "Sodomy Transformed: Aristocratic Libertinage, Public Reputation and the Gender Revolution of the 18th Century," *Journal of Homosexuality*, 19 (1990): 109.

6. *Select Trials at the Sessions-House in the Old Bailey* (1742), vols. 1 and 2, reprinted in *Marriage, Sex, and the Family in England 1660–1800*, ed. Randolph Trumbach, vol. 21 (New York: Garland, 1985), 106.

7. *Select Trials at the Sessions-House in the Old Bailey* (1742), vols. 1 and 2, reprinted in *Marriage, Sex, and the Family in England 1660–1800*, 368.

8. *Select Trials at the Sessions-House in the Old Bailey* (1742), vols. 3 and 4, reprinted in *Marriage, Sex, and the Family in England 1660–1800*, ed. Randolph Trumbach, vol. 22 (New York: Garland, 1985), 36.

9. *Sodomy Trials: Seven Documents*, in *Marriage, Sex, and the Family in England 1660–1800*, ed. Randolph Trumbach, vol. 24 (New York: Garland, 1986), 7.

10. Reprinted in *Sodomy Trials*. Subsequent page references to this edition will be given in parentheses following the quotation in my text.

11. Although the ellipsis here testifies to the unspeakability of the male body's anal opening, it does so by putting the mark of its rupture into the text itself.

12. Sodomy, that is, could readily be discussed as a vice of the aristocracy or of the lower orders, but discursive representations of the violability of the middle-class gentleman's body too dangerously threatened the identity of that emergent figure whose ideological construc-

tion was bound up so closely with autonomy and interiority, with the principle of his inalienable economic property in himself. This economic ideology thus has a key part to play in the emergence of a widely disseminated discourse—and discipline—of homophobia.

13. The details of the Earl of Castlehaven's sodomitical assaults were popularly represented in a pamphlet about his 1631 trial that was published in England in 1699.

14. Leo Braudy, "Penetration and Impenetrability in *Clarissa*," in *Modern Essays on Eighteenth Century Literature*, ed. Leopold Damrosch, Jr. (New York: Oxford University Press, 1988), 267. One might consider, as well, that the bourgeois antipathy to sodomy may also reflect the concern that sodomy comes too close to certain aspects of bourgeois identity-formation as expressed, for instance, in Braudy's characterization of Richardson's main theme as follows: "the efforts of individuals to penetrate, control, and even destroy others, while they remain impenetrable themselves" (266).

15. Felicity Nussbaum, "Heteroclites: The Gender of Character in the Scandalous Memoirs," in *The New Eighteenth Century: Theory, Politics, English Literature*, ed. Felicity Nussbaum and Laura Brown (New York: Methuen, 1987), 149.

16. Alexander Pope, "Epistle to Dr. Arbuthnot" (317–318), *The Poems of Alexander Pope*, ed. John Butt (New Haven: Yale University Press, 1970). That the act of sodomy is construed as effecting a (symbolic) castration is implicit in this invocation of the "pupet," which, in addition to its suggestions of prostitution, is famously linked, in the eighteenth century, to the appearance of castrati. Ben Jonson's *Bartholomew Fair*, of course, includes a well-known revelation of the puppet as sexless when the puritanical Zeal-of-the-Land Busy says of puppets, "you are an abomination for the male among you puts on the apparel of the female and the female of the male." When the puppet's garment is raised, however, he observes that they "have neither male nor female among them." In this regard it is instructive as well that *The Spectator* compared an Italian Opera and a puppet show in the following terms: "by the squeak of their voices the heroes of each are eunuchs" (cited in George Speaight, *Punch and Judy: A History* [London: Studio Vista, 1970], 52).

17. John Locke, *Two Treatises of Government*, intro. W. S. Carpenter (New York: Dutton Publishing, 1975), 142.

18. *Hell Upon Earth*, in *Marriage, Sex, and the Family in England 1660–1800*, ed. Randolph Trumbach, vol. 20 (New York: Garland, 1985), 42.

7. CAPITOL OFFENSES

This essay began in 1989 as an MLA talk presented at the convention in Washington, D.C. I would like to thank Dolores Knoll who organized the session at which I delivered it.

1. Peter Stallybrass and Allon White, *The Politics and Poetics of Transgression* (Ithaca: Cornell University Press, 1986), 144.

2. Stallybrass and White, *Politics and Poetics of Transgression*, 145.

3. D. A. Miller, "Sontag's Urbanity," *October*, 49 (Summer 1989), 93.

4. Stallybrass and White, *Politics and Poetics of Transgression*, 4.

5. *Congressional Record*, June 29, 1989, H3511.

6. *Congressional Record*, October 11, 1989, H6947.

7. *Congressional Record*, October 11, 1989, H6948.

8. *Congressional Record*, September 29, 1989, S12214.

9. *Advocate*, 534 (September 26, 1989): 9.

10. *Congressional Record*, June 29, 1989, H3513.

11. "Representative Frank Tells of Link to a Male Prostitute," *New York Times*, August 26, 1989, p. 1.

12. "Rep. Frank Hired Male Prostitute as Housekeeper," *Washington Post*, August 26, 1989, p. 1.

13. "TV Movie Led to Prostitute's Disclosures," *Washington Post*, August 27, 1989, p. A6.

14. "TV Movie Led to Prostitute's Disclosures," A6.

15. George Bernard Shaw, *Pygmalion* (New York: Brentano, 1916), Act IV.

16. Shaw, *Pygmalion*, Act II.

17. Shaw, *Pygmalion*, Act II.

18. "The Gobie Story," *Washington Post*, August 30, 1989, p. A22.

19. Senator Tim Wirth of Colorado responded to the Helms amendment by dismissing the entire question of art and eros as unworthy of the Senate. "Senators in the greatest deliberative body in the world," he declared, "should not be allowing ourselves to be diverted with this kind of activity but, rather, should belly up and be serious about the defense of the Constitution of the United States" (*Congressional Record*, September 28, 1989, S12114). Seriousness here is defined in terms of the body, deliberative as it is, manfully positioning itself "belly up" and not diverting itself with considerations of sodomitical practices that carry the risk of turning that body upside down—or "bottom" up.

20. *Congressional Record*, September 28, 1989, S12131.

21. Senator Fowler, *Congressional Record*, September 28, 1989, S12130.

22. *Congressional Record*, July 26, 1989, S8808.

23. *Congressional Record*, September 28, 1989, S12121.

24. "The Supreme Court Opinion: Bowers v. Hardwick," *New York Native*, July 14, 1986, p. 12.

25. "Supreme Court Opinion," 13.

26. "Supreme Court Opinion," 13.

27. Hilton Kramer, "Is Art Above the Laws of Decency?," *New York Times*, July 2, 1989, Section II, p. 7.

28. Charles Dickens, *Oliver Twist*, Chapter 51 (New York: Signet, 1961), 463.

8. THROWING UP/GOING DOWN

This essay was delivered as a talk at a conference titled "Dissident Spectacles, Disruptive Spectators" sponsored by the Center for Literary and Cultural Studies at Harvard in 1992. I would like to thank Marge Garber, Jann Matlock, and Rebecca Walkowitz for their roles in organizing the conference.

1. Michael Wines, "Bush Collapses at State Dinner with the Japanese," *New York Times*, January 9, 1992, p. 1.

2. Yashuhiro Tase, Tamura Hideo, and Takeyuki Kumamura, "Trade Tension," translation from the *Nihon Keizai Shimbun* published in the *World Press Review* (April 1992): 11.

3. Jacques Lacan, "Tuché and Automaton," in *Ecrits: A Selection*, trans. Alan Sheridan (New York: Norton, 1977), 53–54.

4. This is the characterization offered by the White House Spokesman, Marlin Fitzwater, in the *New York Times* ("Bush Collapses at State Dinner with the Japanese," 1).

5. Jacques Lacan, "The Subject and the Other: Aphanisis," in *The Four Fundamental Concepts of Psycho-Analysis*, ed. Jacques-Alain Miller, trans. Alan Sheridan (New York: Norton, 1981), 220.

6. "Saved by the Grace of Barbara Bush," *New York Times*, January 9, 1992, p. A8; Charles Bremmer, "Charm, a Joke, and Damage Control Lesson," *Times* of London, January 9, 1992, p. 6.

7. Bremmer, "Charm, a Joke, and Damage Control Lesson," 6.

8. Lawrence K. Altman, "The Doctor's World," *New York Times*, February 18, 1992, p. C3.

9. This quotation was cited by Senator Alan Simpson and printed in *Newsweek*'s "Overheard" column on January 20, 1992, p. 13.

10. For a cogent analysis of the phenomenon of "disgust" see Joseph Litvak, "Delicacy and Disgust, Mourning and Melancholia, Privilege and Perversity: *Pride and Prejudice*," *qui parle*, 6:1 (Fall/Winter 1992), 35–51.

11. "Bush Says Rival Would 'Pull a Fast One' Over Taxes," *New York Times*, August 7, 1992, p. A14.

9. TEAROOMS AND SYMPATHY

This essay, in a much shorter form, was originally presented as a talk at the conference on "Nationalisms and Sexualities" held at Harvard University in June of 1989, co-sponsored by Harvard's Center for Literary and Cultural Studies, Amherst College, and *Genders*. I am grateful to Andrew Parker and all the other people who helped to organize this conference.

1. "President Johnson's Cause Threatened by New Scandal," *Times* of London, October 16, 1964, p.11.

2. Laud Humphreys, *Tearoom Trade: Impersonal Sex in Public Places* (Chicago: Aldine Publishing Company, 1975), 19, n. 10.

3. Arthur Krock, "The Jenkins Case," *New York Times*, October 18, 1964, Section E, p. 11.

4. Editorial, "The Jenkins Case," *New York Times*, October 18, 1964, Section E, p. 10.

5. This quotation from Dr. Charles Thompson, Jenkins's physician, is cited by *Time* magazine, October 23, 1964, p. 22. The *New York Times*, in its first story on the Jenkins case, October 15, 1964, observed that Dr. Thompson had been quoted "by The Associated Press as saying that Mr. Jenkins was suffering from 'insomnia, tensions and agitation' and that he was 'just worn out'" (31).

6. Cited in Tom Wicker, "Johnson Denies Jenkins Cover-Up; Sets F.B.I. Inquiry," *New York Times*, October 16, 1964, p. 1.

7. *Newsweek*, November 2, 1964, p. 26.

8. Cited in Tom Wicker, "Jenkins Cleared of Security Slip in F.B.I. Report," *New York Times*, October 23, 1964, p. 1.

9. Victor Lasky, *It Didn't Start with Watergate* (New York: The Dial Press, 1977), 192.

10. *Time*, October 23, 1964, p. 21.

11. Wicker, "Jenkins Cleared of Security Slip," *New York Times*, October 23, 1964, p. 1.

12. Wicker, "Jenkins Cleared of Security Slip," *New York Times*, October 23, 1964, pp. 1, 31.

13. A similar sort of reasoning was used to explain the suicide of Lord Castlereagh. As Louis Crompton observes, Castlereagh's suicide responded to his concern that he would be charged with sodomitical offenses, but "the official account given out was that overwork from his arduous duties had led to a mental breakdown in the throes of which Castlereagh had

opened his carotid artery while unattended" (Louis Crompton, *Byron and Greek Love: Homophobia in 19th-Century England* [Berkeley: University of California Press, 1985], 302).

14. *Time*, October 23, 1964, p. 22.

15. Michael Rogin describes the period "between 1943 and 1964" as "the years of the cold war consensus." During this period, as he notes, subversives, who "signified control by a sophisticated, alien order," could no longer be recognized by their racial or ethnic differences; they "melted into their surroundings." And the reactionary response to the threat perceived to be posed to dominant cultural values was twofold: "One was the rise of the national security state. The other was the production and surveillance of public opinion in the media of mass society" ("Kiss Me Deadly: Communism, Motherhood, and Cold War Movies," *Representations* 6 [1984]: 2).

16. *Time*, October 23, 1964, p. 21.

17. Cited in "President Finds G.O.P. 'Smearlash,'" *New York Times*, October 22, 1964, p. 45.

18. Cited in *Newsweek*, November 2, 1964, p. 27.

19. *Life*, June 26, 1964, pp. 66–80. Subsequent page references to this article will be given in the text.

20. As we will see, however, this desire to unclothe the subject of homosexuality, and perhaps the homosexual subject as well, enters into a complex and contradictory account of the relationship between homosexuality and an identificatory garb. The essay desires to expose the "truth" of homosexuality but it is not sure if the truth is that homosexuality clothes itself in straight "drag" so as to pass, or that such a notion is itself the misconception with which homosexuality has been "clothed" by heterosexuals.

21. One might note that in the *New York Times* article first announcing Jenkins's arrest, the mere fact of his having been charged with homosexual behavior seems to authorize an invocation of his body as spectacle, as if his body might testify as to the truth of the allegations against him.

22. In "Superman in the Supermarket," written in 1960, Norman Mailer evokes this "treachery" in terms that bear significantly on the argument of this essay; describing Los Angeles' Pershing Square, he views it as "the town plaza for all those lonely, respectable, small-town homosexuals who lead a family life, make children, and have the Philbrick psychology (How I Joined the Communist Party and Led Three Lives)" (*The Presidential Papers* [New York: G.P. Putnam's Sons, 1963], 34).

23. Jess Stearn, *The Sixth Man* (New York: McFadden Publications, Inc., 1963), 29.

24. *New York Times*, April 19, 1950, p. 25.

25. The publication of the Kinsey Report in 1948, of course, provided a context in which the concern about widespread and unrecognized homosexual behavior could be mobilized.

26. This sort of argument about the "sources" of homosexual behavior in a given society is, of course, quite common historically. Louis Crompton, in his study of Byron, cites a passage from the British anti-war newspaper, the *Morning Chronicle*, from 1810, which offers a strikingly similar analysis by ascribing the "prevalence" of homosexuality in England to "the unnecessary war in which we have been so long involved. It is not merely the favour which has been shewn to foreigners, to foreign servants, to foreign troops, but the sending of our own troops to associate with foreigners, that may truly be regarded as the source of evil" (Crompton, *Byron and Greek Love*, 167).

American fiction of the fifties suggests in a number of different ways the connection between war-time experiences and homosexual behavior. In Dennis Murphy's novel, *The Sergeant*, for instance, published in 1958, the title character's coercive expressions of his erotic interest in the private, Tom Swanson, signify in terms of the text's initial recollection of the sergeant's decoration-earning bravery during an ambush in World War II; the narrative, evoking that primal moment, lingers provocatively over his violent and intimate struggle with a German soldier and thus underscores the element of desire that first finds expression in this lethal encounter. Allen Drury's *Advise and Consent*, published the following year, similarly implies a link between homosexuality and the War by situating Senator Brigham Anderson's fateful exploration of his homosexual tendencies during a rest period in Honolulu in the midst of World War II. When this episode, which Anderson has concealed throughout his subsequent marriage, finally surfaces as his political opponents attempt to control the Senator's vote, Anderson must finally try to explain his homosexual encounter to his wife: "People go off the track sometimes, under pressures like the war" (*Advise and Consent* [Garden City, New York: Doubleday & Company, 1959], 432). More interestingly, the novel establishes a structural analogy between homosexuality and communism by pairing them as the guilty secrets that "come out" in the course of the political maneuvers prompted by the effort to confirm Robert Leffingwell as Secretary of State.

27. "Elegant Decor in Bathrooms," *Life*, May 15, 1964, p. 68.

28. In a front-page article for the *Wall Street Journal* on October 16, 1964, for instance, Henry Gemmill quotes "one prominent Republican Senator," as follows: "It seems to me there's now a direct parallel to Britain's Profumo case—except here it's boys instead of girls." The coverage of the scandal in *Newsweek*'s article on October 26, 1964 also features a photograph in which demonstrators protest at a Johnson rally in Pittsburgh by raising an enormous banner that queries, "Jenkins, LBJ's Profumo?" (32).

29. Shelley Ross, *Fall from Grace: Sex, Scandal, and Corruption in American Politics from 1702 to the Present* (New York: Ballantine Books, 1988), 213.

30. Jacques Lacan, "The Agency of the Letter in the Unconscious," *Ecrits: A Selection*, 152.

31. Jacqueline Rose, "Introduction—II," *Feminine Sexuality*, ed. Juliet Mitchell and Jacqueline Rose, trans. Jacqueline Rose (London: MacMillan Press, 1983), 42.

32. Significantly, one common response, especially in the fifties and early sixties, to the fear of homosexual activity in men's rooms, particularly in those on college campuses, was the removal of the doors from toilet stalls so as to produce a space enclosed on three sides which thereby continued to gesture toward privacy, while simultaneously functioning, as the absent fourth wall hints, as a stage upon which the actor could always be subject to surveillance.

33. James Reston, "Setback for Johnson," *New York Times*, October 15, 1964, p. 31.

34. Saul Bellow, *Herzog* (Harmondsworth, Middlesex: Penguin Books, 1988), 166.

35. Note how close this comes to the words with which Lyndon Johnson's brother described the arguments made by Fortas and Clifford as they tried to persuade the Washington press not to publicize Jenkins's arrest: "You can't condemn a man for one single moment of weakness" (Sam Houston Johnson, *My Brother Lyndon*, ed. Enrique Lopez [New York: Cowles Books, 1969], 175).

36. Julia Kristeva, *Powers of Horror: An Essay on Abjection*, trans. Leon Roudiez (New York: Columbia University Press, 1982), 4.

37. Sigmund Freud, "On Transformations of Instinct as Exemplified in Anal Erotism," *On Sexuality*, trans. James Strachey, The Pelican Freud Library, vol. 7 (Harmondsworth, Middlesex: Penguin, 1983), 296.

38. Eve Kosofsky Sedgwick, "A Poem is Being Written," *Representations*, 17 (1987): 126.

39. Herman Rapaport, "Lacan Disbarred: Translation as Ellipsis," *Diacritics* 6:4 (Winter 1976): 58.

40. Three days after Walter Jenkins resigned, the *New York Times* carried a story under the headline: "Ex-Homosexual Got U.S. Job Back." The article reports that the administrator of the Federal Aviation Agency, Najeeb H. Halaby, had ordered reinstatement of a 32-year-old employee who had been fired in 1960 when he admitted having engaged in four homosexual acts when he was 18. Mr. Halaby explained that the employee was "fully rehabilitated and competent" and "should not be scarred for life for a youthful mistake." The article substantiated this notion by then observing: "The employe [sic], now 32 years old, is married and the father of three children. The Government, in effect, conceded that he now had a normal sex life and that the homosexual incidents had been youthful indiscretions." In addition, however, the article offers two other interesting pieces of information: first, although the employee was ordered to be reinstated, the report concludes by assuring the public, "He will not actually control air traffic"; second, the article notes that despite the reinstatement, a memorandum from the White House had recently been circulated calling for more stringent security screening before hiring employees in order to avoid other cases in which such questions could arise. The memorandum, in an ironic twist that the author of the article clearly relished, turns out to have been written, of course, by none other than Walter Jenkins.

41. Eric Goldman, *The Tragedy of Lyndon Johnson* (New York: Knopf, 1969), 250–251.

42. "The Jenkins Report," *Newsweek*, November 2, 1964, p. 26.

43. "The Senior Staff Man," *Time*, October 23, 1964, p. 21.

44. Max Frankel, "President's Aide Quits on Report of Morals Case," *New York Times*, October 15, 1964, p. 1.

45. "The 'Mother' Image," *America*, May 12, 1962, p. 227. In this virulently homophobic article the editors endorse an assertion by Eric Sevareid that homosexuals exercise pernicious international control over the worlds of fashion, theater, film, and design. The implications of a conspiracy are reinforced by Sevareid's description of homosexual power imposed through "loose but effective combines." Sevareid's vehement denunciation of gay men, as quoted in the editorial, touches so many of the familiar bases in this sort of rhetorical outburst that it seems worthwhile to quote from it here: "The homosexual is usually capable of neither loving nor understanding a woman; so, in his fashions, the woman's body is merely a skeletal frame for his artistic experiments in design; in his films the woman is generally a prostitute or an overbearing clod. In the theatre, they [homosexuals] portray neither high triumph nor high tragedy, for these involve acts of will and decision. In their world there is no decision and no will; there is only a degraded helplessness against 'forces,' because being sick themselves, they must see society as the sickness" (227). The occasion for this outburst in the pages of *America* was the celebration of an "antidote," one described as "providential," to the "malevolent . . . influence of the homosexual" in "defiling the image of mother." That "antidote" was the decision of Pope John XXIII to allow the 1964 World's Fair in New York to exhibit the "Pietà" of Michelangelo. The irony of *such* an "antidote," as the language of the article would have it, can hardly fail to recall Jacques Derrida's reading of the *pharmakon* in "Plato's Pharmacy" (*Dissemination*).

46. Kristeva, *Powers of Horror*, 13.

47. It may be worth noting that the name by which Johnson's wife was known, "Lady Bird," foregrounds the distinction of sex that bears so decisively on questions of power. The fact that the mother's destructive power is unleashed upon the female child responds, of course, to the historical circumstance that Johnson had two daughters and no sons. His naming of those daughters, however, suggests his eagerness to perpetuate the paternal inheritance insofar as both daughters were given names that made their initials identical to his (and to his wife's after her marriage to him): LBJ. The murderousness of the mother in this figure might position "Lady Bird" in the role of another lady, "Lady MacBeth," in which case she, as a

tropological substitution for Walter Jenkins, would articulate male homosexuality in relation to the notion of being "unsex[ed]."

48. Rogin, "Kiss Me Deadly: Communism, Motherhood, and Cold War Movies," 9.

49. Norman Mailer, "Theatre: *The Blacks*," *The Presidential Papers*, 210.

50. Norman Mailer, "Truth and Being: Nothing and Time," *The Presidential Papers*, 275.

51. Norman Mailer, "A Note to the 6th Presidential Paper—A Rousing Club Fight: An Impossible Interview," *The Presidential Papers*, 144.

52. *Time*, October 23, 1954, p. 21.

53. *Wall Street Journal*, October 16, 1964, p. 14.

10. Seeing Things

This essay was first presented, in a much shorter form, at the 1989 conference on Lesbian and Gay Studies held at Yale University.

1. Louis Crompton, *Byron and Greek Love: Homophobia in 19th-Century England* (Berkeley: University of California Press: 1985), 169.

2. *Trying and Pilloring of the Vere Street Club* (London: J. Brown, 1810), cited in Crompton, *Byron and Greek Love*, 166.

3. Mary Ann Doane, "Veiling over Desire: Close-ups of the Woman," *Feminism and Psychoanalysis*, ed. Richard Feldstein and Judith Roof (Ithaca: Cornell University Press, 1989), 105. Similarly, Kaja Silverman, in her excellent essay "Too Early/Too Late: Subjectivity and the Primal Scene in Henry James," notes that the Freudian model of the psyche in *The Interpretation of Dreams* "rests precisely upon the possibility of forward and backward movement between the unconscious and the preconscious/conscious system" (*Novel*, 20:2/3 [Winter/Spring 1988]: 149). Silverman touches on a number of issues related to those that I am examining here. Although she uses Freud as the source of a psychic model that she then applies to James, her account of James's inscriptions of anality can itself be "turned around" upon Freud. In any case, despite its differences from mine, her project constitutes an important source for anyone working toward the possibility of re-envisioning the primal scene. See also the revised version of this essay in Silverman's *Male Subjectivity at the Margins* (New York and London: Routledge, 1992).

4. See, for instance, Freud's remark in *From the History of an Infantile Neurosis*: "Of the physician's point of view I can only declare that in a case of this kind he must behave as 'timelessly' as the unconscious itself, if he wishes to learn anything or to achieve anything," in *The Standard Edition of the Complete Psychological Works of Sigmund Freud*, ed. James Strachey (London: The Hogarth Press, 1955), 27:10. All subsequent references to this case history will be given in the text.

5. J. Laplanche and J. B. Pontalis, *The Language of Psychoanalysis*, trans. Donald Nicholson-Smith (London: The Hogarth Press, 1983), 112.

6. Though his focus is quite different from mine, Jonathan Culler provides a cogent discussion of metaleptic narrative structures, and frames them briefly in terms of Freud's analysis of the Wolf Man, in "Story and Discourse in the Analysis of Narrative," *The Pursuit of Signs: Semiotics, Literature, Deconstruction* (Ithaca: Cornell University Press, 1981), see especially 172–182.

7. Quoted in Peter Gay, *Freud: A Life for Our Time* (New York: W.W. Norton & Co., 1988), 287.

8. Freud, *From the History of an Infantile Neurosis*, 51. See also Freud's earlier assertion that

"these scenes from infancy are not represented during the treatment as recollections, they are the products of construction" (50–51).

9. Marguerite Waller, "Academic Tootsie: The Denial of Difference and the Difference It Makes," *Diacritics* 17:1 (Spring 1987): 2.

10. Nicholas Abraham and Maria Torok, *The Wolf Man's Magic Word: A Cryptonymy*, trans. Nicholas Rand (Minneapolis: University of Minnesota Press, 1986), 2.

11. Sigmund Freud, *The Letters of Sigmund Freud and Lou Andreas-Salomé*, ed. Ernst Pfeiffer, trans. William and Elaine Robson-Scott (London: The Hogarth Press and the Institute of Psychoanalysis, 1972), 77.

12. Sigmund Freud, "Negation," *The Standard Edition of the Complete Psychological Works*, vol. 19 (1961), 237.

13. Stanley Fish has persuasively read this case history as an "allegory of persuasion" (938) in his essay, "Withholding the Missing Portion: Power, Meaning and Persuasion in Freud's 'The Wolf-Man,'" *Times Literary Supplement*, August 29, 1986, pp. 935–938. He too focuses on Freud's anal-erotism, though he sees its inscription not in Freud's manifestations of uncertainty or doubt, but in his management of information, his withholding and then delivering of crucial interpretive details at strategic moments in his narrative. Fish's insights have been valuable to me in formulating my reading, though I am primarily interested in reading the discursive logic of Freud's positioning in relation to the primal scene, a logic of which Freud is not the master and which bears a determining relation to the discourse of homosexuality, while Fish undertakes to examine Freud's rhetoric as a sign precisely of his insistent mastery over the reader, however much that rhetoric may have its "sources in his deepest anxieties" (938).

14. "I was the first—a point to which none of my opponents have [*sic*] referred—to recognize both the part played by phantasies in symptom-formation and also the 'retrospective phantasying' of late impressions into childhood and their sexualization after the event," *From the History of an Infantile Neurosis*, 103, n. 1.

15. The use of the masculine pronoun here is intended to signify that my reading of the primal scene, like Freud's, focuses on an experience whose implications are emphatically affected by gender. In the case under discussion here, the gender of the subject in question is male.

16. The primal scene, to put this another way, always starts as the mobilization of libidinal energies that will be defined, after the fact, as homosexual; the scene only later becomes heterosexualized, and that heterosexualization induces the horror and anxiety that the Wolf Man experiences in his pathogenic dream.

17. Fish, "Withholding the Missing Portion," 938.

18. It should be recalled that Freud insists that the infant signals this dual libidinal identification by passing a stool and interrupting his parents' lovemaking with a scream. Reading this activity as a "sign of [the infant's] sexual excitement," Freud argues that it "is to be regarded as characteristic of his congenital sexual constitution. He at once assumed a passive attitude, and showed more inclination towards a subsequent identification with women than with men" (81).

19. "Jenny Cromwell's Complaint Against Sodomy," cited in Dennis Rubini, "Sexuality and Augustan England: Sodomy, Politics, Elite Circles and Society," *The Pursuit of Sodomy: Male Homosexuality in Renaissance and Enlightenment Europe*, ed. Kent Gerard and Gert Hekma (New York: Harrington Park Press, 1989), 381.

20. John Cleland, *Memoirs of a Woman of Pleasure*, ed. Peter Sabor (New York: Oxford University Press, 1985), 157. All subsequent references to this work will be given in the text.

21. In the psychic economy of the heterosexualized male, the *narrative* of castration, however frightening its content, achieves a fetishistic, recuperative status to the extent that its explanatory coherence domesticates the violence that it thematizes. It becomes, in effect, a primal screen to obscure the primal scene. Jacques Derrida offers a related observation in "Le facteur de la vérité": "In this sense castration-truth is the opposite of fragmentation, the very antidote for fragmentation: that which is missing from its place has in castration a fixed, central place, freed from all substitution" (*The Post Card: From Socrates to Freud and Beyond*, trans. Alan Bass [Chicago: University of Chicago Press, 1987), 441]. All subsequent references to this work will be given in the text).

22. Eve Kosofsky Sedgwick provides a powerful reading of such figurations in "A Poem is Being Written," *Representations*, 17 (1987): 110–136. In particular, she analyzes the significance of the fact that in colloquial discourse "women's *genital* receptivity is described as 'ass,' as in 'a piece of'" (129).

23. Nancy K. Miller, "'I's' in Drag: The Sex of Recollection," *The Eighteenth Century*, 22:1 (1981): 53.

24. Tobias Smollett, *The Adventures of Peregrine Pickle*, ed. James L. Clifford (New York: Oxford University Press, 1964), 242. All subsequent references to this work will be given in the text.

25. This phrase appears in the "letter" printed on the back cover of *The Post Card*.

26. Throughout *The Post Card*, and particularly in the "Envois," Derrida elaborates a theory of textual rivalry within the philosophical tradition that echoes Harold Bloom's formulations of literary revisionism and the anxiety of influence. Derrida suggests, for example, that "In compromising Socrates Plato was seeking to kill him, to eliminate him, to neutralize the debt while looking as if he were taking on the entire burden. In *Beyond* . . . , precisely on the subject of Aristophanes's discourse, Freud starts it all over, he forgets Socrates, erases the scene and indebts up to Plato" (146). This implies the need to reconsider the Bloomian scenario of Oedipal rivalry in relation to a sodomitical scene that presents a more complicated network of anxieties, identifications, and desires.

27. Stanley Cavell, "Postscript (1989): To Whom It May Concern," *Critical Inquiry*, 16 (1990): 256.

28. Jacques Derrida, "Le facteur de la vérité," *The Post Card*, 480.

29. This can be seen by paying attention to the serifs of the letters "p" and "d" in the text. It is worth adding that both Freud and Derrida provide justifications in their writings for taking errors of transcription, typing, or typesetting seriously. See, for instance, Derrida, "Du Tout," *The Post Card*, 513–515; an important discussion of typographical distortions and Freud's relation to the Wolf Man can be found in Maria Torok, "Afterword: What is Occult in Occultism? Between Sigmund Freud and Sergei Pankeiev Wolf Man," *The Wolf Man's Magic Word: A Cryptonomy*.

30. Compare for instance the recurrent anxieties about the reliability of the post in both collections. Freud writes, "Let us hope that the postal authorities will not continue to be unfavourably disposed toward us. My lost letter contained all the details that were meant for you better than I can repeat them today" (*Sigmund Freud and Lou Andreas-Salomé: Letters*, 148); Derrida writes, "Hound them at the post office. Does the search go through them? No, I will never rewrite it, that letter" ("Envois," 57). Or compare Freud's comment that "not every arrow reaches its mark" (172) with Derrida's famous assertion, "A letter can always not arrive at its destination" ("Le facteur," 444).

11. Imagining the Homosexual

A much shorter version of this essay was presented in 1991 at a conference on "Homotextualities" sponsored by the Buffalo Theory Group and the Program on Comparative Literature at the State University of New York at Buffalo. I would like to thank Andrew Hewitt for organizing this conference.

1. Jacqueline Rose, "Woman as Symptom," *Sexuality in the Field of Vision* (London: Verso, 1989), 219.

2. Paul de Man, "Wordsworth and the Victorians," *The Rhetoric of Romanticism* (New York: Columbia University Press, 1984), 86. All subsequent citations will be given in the text.

3. Cynthia Chase, "Giving a Face to a Name: De Man's Figures," *Decomposing Figures: Rhetorical Readings in the Romantic Tradition* (Baltimore: The Johns Hopkins University Press, 1986), 84.

4. Neil Hertz, "Lurid Figures," *Reading de Man Reading*, ed. Lindsay Waters and Wlad Godzich (Minneapolis: University of Minnesota Press, 1989), 98.

5. Chase, "Giving a Face," 84.

6. Cynthia Chase, in the essay cited above ("Giving a Face") offers an exemplary discussion of "disfiguration" or "defacement" in de Man's reading of the relation between language as representation and language as a positing or positional force. "Prosopopoeia, or the giving of face," she writes, "is *de*-facement, then, insofar as if face is given by an act of language it is 'only' a figure" (85).

7. Hertz locates within de Man's own writings the return of those elements of pathos, desire, and sexual differentiation from which language as a figure-making activity (and, consequently, as an agency of disfiguration or disarticulation) cannot be separated. Insisting on the "need to ask in what ways, and at what point, the rhetorical operations [de Man] is concerned to track engage questions of gender" (100), Hertz focuses on the specular structures that govern any reading of linguistic operations; for as he demonstrates in his account of de Man's own texts, the most rigorous attempt to face that which gives or produces face will yield in the process figures that uncannily mirror the subject's own face.

8. Hertz, "Lurid Figures," 100.

9. Hertz, "Lurid Figures," 102.

10. Lauren Berlant, "The Female Complaint," *Social Text*, 19/20 (Autumn 1988): 252.

11. For further elaboration of this idea, see Chapter Ten, "Seeing Things: Representation, the Scene of Surveillance, and the Spectacle of Gay Male Sex."

12. Rose, "Woman as Symptom," 217.

13. Jacqueline Rose, "The Cinematic Apparatus—Problems in Current Theory," *Sexuality in the Field of Vision*, 202.

14. "News-Abroad," *Drum: Sex in Perspective*, 4 (December 1964): 30.

15. Henry Louis Gates, Jr., "Editor's Introduction: Writing 'Race' and the Difference It Makes," *"Race," Writing, and Difference*, ed. Henry Louis Gates, Jr. (Chicago: University of Chicago Press, 1986), 5.

16. Marcel Proust, *Remembrance of Things Past*, vol. 2, *Cities of the Plain*, trans. C. K. Scott Moncrieff and Terence Kilmartin (New York: Random House, 1981), 637.

17. Proust, *Cities of the Plain*, 639.

18. Anthony Appiah, "The Uncompleted Argument: Du Bois and the Illusion of Race," *"Race," Writing and Difference*, 21.

19. D. A. Miller, "Anal *Rope,*" *Representations,* 32 (Fall 1990); reprinted in *Inside/Out: Lesbian Theories, Gay Theories*, ed. Diana Fuss (New York: Routledge, 1991).

20. From the many possible examples with which one might instantiate this connection, I will cite only one recent instance, the rap song "Whatcha Lookin' At?" (Audio Two, First Priority) in which the heterosexual male fear of being subjected to the gay gaze leads to the expression of a violently homophobic threat:

> What' matter witcha boy
> Are you gay?
> I hope that ain't the case
> 'cause gay mothers get
>   punched in the face.
> I hate faggots
> They're living in the Village
> Like meat on some maggots.

Quoted in "Gay-Baiting Lyrics," *New York Native*, August 6, 1990, p. 4.

21. Stanley Cavell, "An Autobiography of Companions," *The World Viewed: Reflections on the Ontology of Film*, Enlarged Edition (Cambridge, Mass.: Harvard University Press, 1979), 6. It should be noted that theater in general has historically appealed to a gay male audience in much the same way that cinema has. Yet while both allow for imaginative identifications—the representation of role-playing, a certain opportunity for cross-dressing, or misrepresenting the self in other ways—the cinema affords the gay male spectator an opportunity to focus on the issue of bodiliness and ways of wearing the body precisely because the image on the screen is disembodied and fragmented. It allows, that is, for the intense scrutiny of the body as such—and from close up—without fear of being seen in the guilty enterprise of looking. The screen image, then, seems incapable of looking back as the stage actor, one either hopes or fears, might.

22. For an excellent discussion of the full range of these issues see Terry Castle, *Masquerade and Civilization: The Carnivalesque in Eighteenth-Century English Culture and Fiction* (Stanford: Stanford University Press, 1986), and Joseph Litvak, *Caught in the Act: Theatricality in the Nineteenth-Century English Novel* (Berkeley: University of California Press, 1992).

23. Vito Russo, *The Celluloid Closet: Homosexuality in the Movies* (New York: Harper and Row, 1981), 94.

24. Eve Kosofsky Sedgwick has written incisively about the various uses to which the willful formula, "We Know What That Means," has been put by a homophobic culture. See *Epistemology of the Closet* (Berkeley and Los Angeles: University of California Press, 1990), 45, and 182–212.

25. Manny Farber, "Murdered Movie," *New Republic*, October 30, 1944, p. 568.

26. "The New Pictures," *Time*, October 30, 1944, p. 54.

27. Reynold Humphries, *Fritz Lang: Genre and Representation in His American Films* (Baltimore: The Johns Hopkins University Press, 1989), 115.

28. Laura Mulvey, "Visual Pleasure and Narrative Cinema," *Women and the Cinema: A Critical Anthology*, ed. Karyn Kay and Gerald Peary (New York: Dutton, 1977), 418.

29. Bosley Crowther, "A Big Hello," *New York Times*, October 22, 1944, section 2, p. 1.

30. Farber, "Murdered Movie," 568.

31. I translate these words from the French version of the filmscript published in *L'Avant Scène du Cinéma*, 211/212 (July–September 1978): 13. Vito Russo, in *The Celluloid Closet*, also refers to this remark, but he punctuates the phrase differently. See his discussion on 45–46.

32. Otto Preminger, *Preminger: An Autobiography* (Garden City, New York: Doubleday, 1977), 73.

33. Foster Hirsch, *The Dark Side of the Screen: Film Noir* (New York: Da Capo Press, 1981), 120.

34. Otto Friedrich, *City of Nets: A Portrait of Hollywood in the 1940s* (New York: Harper and Row, 1986), 184–185.

35. Leslie Halliwell, *Halliwell's Harvest* (New York: Scribners, 1986), 125.

36. Examples of this process continue to proliferate around us. One recent instance may be worth quoting because it both performs and comments on the defensive responses to this anxiety. An article discussing a television film about the life of Rock Hudson begins as follows:

> Hollywood press handouts don't usually provide information about the private lives of single actors, but a short bio on Thomas Ian Griffith states that he "resides in the San Fernando Valley with his girlfriend, actress Mary Page Keller." Griffith, a tall and still unknown 29-year-old, is playing the title role in ABC's docudrama "Rock Hudson," scheduled for Monday Jan. 8, at 9 P.M. (ET). The release is meant to tell us something, and that something is as clear as a bumper sticker: Thomas Ian Griffith isn't gay.

(Susan Littwin, "Will America be Shocked by Rock?," *TV Guide*, 37 [January 6–12, 1990], 14.) Griffith's costar, appearing as Hudson's lover in the movie, expressed a concern that makes even more apparent the inescapability of the homographic where the issue of gay embodiment is concerned: "William R. Moses, who plays Christian, talks about his fears with disarming candor. 'When they asked me to play this part, I said, "Why me? I played football"'"(15).

37. Jacques Lacan, "The Meaning of the Phallus," *Feminine Sexuality*, ed. Juliet Mitchell and Jacqueline Rose, trans. Jacqueline Rose (London: MacMillan Press, 1983), 85.

38. Jennifer Wicke, *Advertising Fictions: Literature, Advertisement, and Social Reading* (New York: Columbia University Press, 1988), 12.

39. Kristin Thompson, "Closure Within a Dream? Point of View in *Laura*," *Breaking the Glass Armor: Neoformalist Film Analysis* (Princeton: Princeton University Press, 1988), 162–194.

40. Joseph Litvak has done important work on these concepts in his readings of *The Picture of Dorian Gray* ("Class Acts: Theatricality, Vulgarity, and Aestheticism in *The Picture of Dorian Gray*," an unpublished lecture presented at the 1989 MLA Convention) and *Pride and Prejudice* ("Delicacy and Disgust, Mourning and Melancholia, Privilege and Perversity: *Pride and Prejudice*," *qui parle*, 6:1 [Fall/Winter 1992] 35–51).

41. Mark McPherson is described as the man with a "legful of lead," thus identifying him with the wounded war veteran returning to a country that has been run by those who enjoy Waldo's privileged social and economic standing. In the context of the film's desire to articulate the sexual "decadence" of Waldo's milieu, it is noteworthy that Mark's wound was suffered in a shootout that came to be known as "the Siege of Babylon."

42. Foster Hirsch summarizes a number of these elements in a breezily effective way:

> Vincent Price [Shelby Carpenter] plays a kept man, and like Webb, the actor has a prissy quality. The two of them seem like old-fashioned gay types, confirming in their bitchiness and superciliousness popular stereotyped notions of homosexual behavior. . . . Price and Webb have some sharp exchanges; their tones are well-matched, which makes them a more likely pairing than Webb with Laura, or than Price with Laura's high society friend [actually, her aunt], played by Judith Anderson. Anderson's masculine presence completes the tone

of sexual ambiguity that runs through the film. Playing a grande dame who keeps attractive young men [Hirsch engages in a bit of imaginative elaboration here], Anderson brings to the part her natural assertiveness. Her deep authoritative voice emphasizes the character's dominating qualities, and her attempted control of Price echoes Waldo's "creation" of Laura. But her interest in Laura, while remaining implicit, is more convincing than her nominal attraction to the Price character (*The Dark Side of the Screen: Film Noir*, 120).

43. It is significant, in this context, that their relationship begins when she seeks his endorsement for the "Flow-Rite" pen. Though he initially resists her overtures, claiming to write with a "goose-quill dipped in venom," he finds Laura strangely appealing and chooses to endorse the product in order to become better acquainted with her. This heterosexualization, therefore, is enabled by her gesture of presenting him with the opportunity to inscribe himself in the realm of the pen; she thus "masculinizes" him by serving as the bearer of the pen(is). As I argue below, she serves a similar function for Mark McPherson insofar as her return from the dead realizes what his fetishistic investment in her portrait can only substitutively represent: she brings (back) to him, that is, the lost object that his devotion to the painting sought to deny as ever having been lost.

44. Jonathan Culler presents an important deconstructive reading of Zeno's paradox in *On Deconstruction: Theory and Criticism After Structuralism* (Ithaca: Cornell University Press, 1983), 94–95.

45. To look at that facelessness itself would mean, in the case of Waldo, to articulate his sexual "ambiguity" without any of the markers that serve to give it a recognizable face. It would mean, that is, acknowledging a non-heterosexuality that could not be distinguished visually from heterosexuality and that allowed the (presumptively heterosexual) spectator no epistemological privilege, and thus no epistemological security.

46. Ken Worthy, *The Homosexual Generation* (New York: L.S. Publications Corp., 1965), 109.

47. Taken to its pathological extreme, this obsessive fetishization as a form of substitutive embodiment, as a displacement of the bodily ego, can transform the "plain-American-guy detective" into a figure as clearly transgressive as Norman Bates in Alfred Hitchcock's *Psycho* (1960).

48. Cited by Barbara Johnson ("Preface to the Paperback Edition," *A World of Difference* [Baltimore: The Johns Hopkins University Press, 1989], xii) from Robert Moynihan, *A Recent Imagining: Interviews with Harold Bloom, Geoffrey Hartman, J. Hillis Miller, and Paul de Man* (Hamden, Conn.: Archon, 1986), 137.

49. Jane Gallop gives a provocative reading of the temporal logic at work in the mirror stage in "Where to Begin? (*Reading Lacan* (Ithaca: Cornell University Press, 1985), 74–92.

50. Paul de Man, "'Conclusions': Walter Benjamin's 'The Task of the Translator,'" *The Resistance to Theory* (Minneapolis: University of Minnesota Press, 1986), 96.

51. That debt may be mediated through such figures as Alexander Woollcott, Noel Coward, and even Monty Woolley, but the cultural genealogy on which the representation of Waldo depends certainly leads back to Wilde himself. Vera Caspary's version of Waldo's origin is recounted by Rudy Behlmer in "The Face in the Misty Light: *Laura*," *Behind the Scenes* (New York: Samuel French, 1990), 178–179.

52. John Addington Symonds in a letter to Horatio Brown, cited in *Oscar Wilde: The Critical Heritage*, ed. Karl Beckson (New York: Barnes and Noble, 1970), 78.

53. Unsigned review from *Theatre*, June 1, 1891, cited in *Oscar Wilde: The Critical Heritage*, 81.

54. On the day after she returns from "the dead"—or Connecticut, if you prefer—when Mark brings the materials for breakfast to her apartment, he already manages to position her in the domestic role of caretaker: "My mother always listened sympathetically to my dreams of a career," she tells him, explaining her culinary skills, "and then taught me another recipe." It is worth noting, as well, that the redomestication of Laura by Mark responds to the process—already underway in 1944—of returning the largely female wartime workforce to the domestic sphere in order to make room for returning veterans.

55. Thompson, *Breaking the Glass Armor*, 171.

56. In this regard I refer the reader to my comments in Chapter Ten, "Seeing Things," on the heterosexual-fashioning (and heterosexually fashioned) narrative of castration.

57. Thompson, *Breaking the Glass Armor*, 180–181.

58. The film establishes this connection decisively at the moment Mark discovers the opening or cavity (with all its erotic implications) inside the clock in Waldo's apartment. As he hurries off to test his hunch that the murder weapon will be found concealed in the matching cavity of the clock in Laura's apartment, the camera lingers on Waldo's clock and then that image dissolves to a shot of Waldo, talking with Laura in her apartment, with her clock situated prominently in the background behind them both.

59. Paul de Man, "Hypogram and Inscription," *The Resistance to Theory*, 48.

60. Hertz, "Lurid Figures," 84–85.

61. See Chapter Nine, "Tearooms and Sympathy; or, The Epistemology of the Water Closet."

62. It is worth noticing as well in this regard that such a phobic response to the possible coupling of seduction and authority enacts the anxiety that continues to pass as the "logic" behind the exclusion of gay women and men from (uncloseted) participation in the American armed forces and that serves as a legal justification for anti-gay violence (including murder) under the guise of the "homosexual panic" defense, a defense that argues the legal propriety of extreme measures on the part of heterosexual men to "protect" their virtue, the "integrity" of their bodies, from anything that can be interpreted as a "homosexual advance."

63. In "Shelley Disfigured" de Man's interpretive inscription of Shelley's body, and his death from drowning, in the text of *The Triumph of Life* provides a sort of warrant for such a recognition of the body's persistent demands. "The final test of reading, in *The Triumph of Life*," he writes, "depends on how one reads the textuality of this event, how one disposes of Shelley's body" (*The Rhetoric of Romanticism*, 121).

64. De Man, "Wordsworth and the Victorians," 92.

65. It is an irony worth more careful commentary than this short note can provide that castration itself, in Freud's writing, though it serves as the anchor of culturally achieved sexual identities (and, indeed, as the anchor of psychoanalysis) is not itself given a unitary or stable reading in Freud's work. It is a term whose shiftiness, whose range of implications and whose over-determined psychic genealogies refute the enterprise of grounding that it is imagined to perform.

66. Roland Barthes, *Camera Lucida: Reflections on Photography*, trans. Richard Howard (New York: Hill and Wang, 1981), 15.

67. Barthes, *Camera Lucida*, 20.

68. This is especially significant among those films produced by emigré directors in America during World War II.

69. Literally scoring, as it were, the same point, the film's theme music by David Raskin, which became a popular favorite and reached number one on the Hit Parade upon its release

with lyrics by Johnny Mercer, enters the narrative proper of the film when Mark discovers a recording of it on Laura's record player. "It was one of Laura's favorites," Shelby explains, "not exactly classical, but sweet."

70. For this reason the only photograph we see in *Laura* is the image of Diane Redfern, and the stasis of the image serves as a token of her death.

71. Gilles Deleuze, "The Affection-Image: Face and Close-up," *Cinema 1: The Movement-Image*, trans. Hugh Tomlinson and Barbara Habberjam (Minneapolis: University of Minnesota Press, 1986), p. 88.

Index